BERLIN
IN THE BALANCE
1945-1949

BERLIN IN THE BALANCE 1945–1949

The Blockade The Airlift
The First Major Battle of the Cold War

THOMAS PARRISH

ADDISON-WESLEY

Reading, Massachusetts

Library of Congress Cataloging-in-Publication Data

Parrish, Thomas (Thomas D.)
   Berlin in the balance, 1945–1949 : the blockade, the airlift, the
first major battle of the Cold War / Thomas Parrish.
      p.   cm.
   Includes bibliographical references and index.
   ISBN 0-201-25832-3
   1. Berlin (Germany)—History—Blockade, 1948–1949.   2. Cold war.
3. United States—Military policy.   4. Berlin (Germany)—History—
1945–1990.   I. Title.
DD881.P27   1998
943'.1550874—dc21   97–52968
                                                                      CIP

Addison-Wesley is an imprint of Addison Wesley Longman, Inc.

Jacket design by Adrian Morgan/Red Letter Design
Text design by Dede Cummings
Set in 11-point Simoncini Garamond by Pagesetters

1 2 3 4 5 6 7 8 9-MA-0201009998
First printing, April 1998

Find us on the World Wide Web at http://www.aw.com/gb/

CONTENTS

War by Other Means

EVERYBODY BEYOND CHILDHOOD remembers the night the cold war ended, when television showed us people dancing on top of the Berlin Wall and hacking pieces out of it for grim souvenirs. For almost thirty years, the symbol of Berlin had been that ugly barrier of cinder block and barbed wire put up in 1961 by the Soviet and East German governments.

Disturbed by the flight to West Berlin of increasing thousands of discontented East Germans, Soviet Premier Nikita Khrushchev had spoken of the city as "a bone in my throat"—a problem he intended to solve. His answer, sealing off West Berlin from the Communist world around it and sealing in the people of East Germany—an answer enforced by border guards who shot to kill—produced revulsion throughout the non-Communist world. But in January 1963 Khrushchev declared himself well satisfied with the project: no longer could "subversive forces" use the border with West Berlin to "undermine the very foundations of socialism." Six months later President John F. Kennedy toured the wall and then, addressing a huge crowd, made his own declaration: "Two thousand years ago the proudest boast in the world was *Civis Romanum sum.* Today, in the world of freedom, the proudest boast is *Ich bin ein Berliner.*" More than two decades later another U.S. president, Ronald Reagan, issued a challenge to another Soviet leader: "Mr. Gorbachev, tear down this wall!" In June 1989, when a German reporter asked Mikhail Gorbachev whether the wall might actually come down someday, he received the reply, "Nothing is eternal in this world." Five months after that enigmatic answer, the wall had fallen.

At the beginning of 1989, nobody would have believed it possible. For decades people in the West had feared that a war could begin in Berlin, which sat more than a hundred miles inside East Germany, its western half an island in a Communist sea. The wall, the division of Berlin, the cold war itself all seemed almost eternal. The wall had not actually created the division of Berlin; it merely turned that division from a political and psychological into a physical reality. (Barbaric as the wall was, said a British historian, no one should have supposed that an antagonist "conventionally regarded as ruthless and materialistic would act out of character by remaining inactive when pressure was applied to a key point in his system.")

By the time the wall went up, Berlin had already been two cities, East and West, through the thirteen years since 1948. In that year Berlin saw its greatest crisis: the dreaded war seemed to be on the point of breaking out, the military planes of both sides took to the skies. The origins of the crisis trace back to the latter days of World War II in 1945, and events then move forward on many fronts—through increasing strains and conflicts between the Western Allies (the United States, Britain, and France) and the Russians over the control and future of the German nation they had combined to defeat in 1945. The story told here is really the story of the developing cold war itself, with Germany as the key and the fate of Berlin in the balance. When the Soviets attempted to starve West Berlin and drive out the Allies by a land and water blockade, the West fought back with its remarkable answer, the airlift.

So began the first battle of the cold war. Like other battles it involved politicians and generals and diplomats, but this one was fought by aircrews not with guns and bombs but with food and fuel and even roofing paper, and with weather as a constant enemy. In its own way it produced as many heroes as any conventional war.

An American reporter caught the flavor of this different kind of war. At six o'clock on a wintry evening, an air force sergeant picked him up in Frankfurt for the ride out to the airport, called Rhein-Main, through soupy weather—a thin, cold rain mixed with a thick fog. At the terminal the noise turned conversation into a shouting match, as planes—Douglas C-54 Skymasters—ignoring the weather, took off and landed in steady streams, bare minutes apart. Trucks wheeled onto loading strips, bringing coal and flour and also dehydrated potatoes and other foods of all kinds, even such remarkable (and limitedly popular) commodities as dehydrated beets.

Flight time was eight o'clock. Carrying a flight bag, the reporter trotted out to his assigned C-54: the Berlin airlift, he knew, waited for nobody. Narrow benches ran along each side of the plane, and passengers—American, British, and French officers and civilian workers—faced each other over piles of mailbags. Patches of grime and a layer of white dust on all the surfaces told you that this plane, though designed to carry people—as it was doing this night—had hauled many tons of cargo into Berlin.

As the C-54 moved away from the ramp, it seemed to the reporter that its nose was touching the tail of the plane in front, and he knew that another plane followed close behind. Looking through one of the small, dirty round windows, he could see perhaps thirty other planes loading or taking their places in the fog-shrouded line. The roar of the engines now reached its peak and the C-54 rushed down the runway, no more than two hundred yards behind the plane ahead. Airborne, it headed for Tempelhof airport in Berlin, 278 miles northeast.

Then came a change in plans. The pilots got word from Berlin that a C-54 had crash-landed at Tempelhof, turning over and exploding. Men in asbestos suits were trying to haul crew members from the wreckage; no planes would be landing at Tempelhof until the strip was cleared. The pilots would go to Gatow, the British field in Berlin, and merge with the line of York aircraft landing there. The controllers deftly fitted the C-54 into the line of landing Yorks, separated by no more than sixty seconds from the planes in front and behind. As the C-54 began its final approach, the pilot said to the reporter, "Notice those people down there? They're always there watching—day and night."

As the plane landed at Gatow and taxied, a yellow jeep like a fussy tug moved in front, and the pilot dutifully obeyed the instruction in the green neon sign on the jeep's tail: FOLLOW ME. The C-54 moved off the busy runway and onto its assigned position. If, as was normally the case, it had been stuffed with food or fuel, a big sixteen-wheel truck would have come to meet it, backing into position as the plane's side door opened. No time, not even a second, would have been wasted. In ten minutes the truck would have its load, the pilots would report to the tower that they were ready for takeoff, and they would trundle to their assigned place in line.

This remarkable, unprecedented operation—*die Luftbrücke,* the air bridge—was certainly not peace. It was war by other means, with large and long-range issues at stake for both sides, issues that found differing definitions. It was a great adventure and a great experiment, and in a remarkable way it took by surprise not only the public in the West and the Russians but the Allied political leaders and commanders, the very people who created it to defend a city that their countries had done their best to demolish only three years before.

"The Russians no longer scoff at the airlift," wrote the reporter who had flown from Rhein-Main on the foggy night. "As for the Germans, they see democracy in action in the air; and they like what they see." In the kind of prose one could still write fifty years ago, words with something of the spirit of World War II about them, the reporter added: "The kids who fly the lift, who guide the trucks, who run the control towers, are farm boys and lads from our city streets. There's a swagger to their walk, and they talk lightly of the risks they take. And if they carry a chip on their shoulders, who can blame them? For that chip is a bright thing called 'democracy.' They wear it well."

Airlift:
Corridors to Berlin

North Sea

Baltic Sea

Schleswigland

Lübeck

Fuhlsbüttel

HAMBURG

Fassberg

Celle

BRITISH

Wunstorf

ZONE

BERLIN

G E R M A N Y

SOVIET

ZONE

Wiesbaden

Rhein/Main

✈ Air corridor

• Airfield site

⋯ Zonal boundary

FRENCH

ZONE

U.S.

ZONE

N

0   25   50
Miles

PART I: THE RISING CONFLICT

CHAPTER 1

The Prize

DURING THE MORNING of May 8, 1945, three DC-3 transport aircraft carrying a number of high-ranking American, British, and French officers flew eastward across Germany. The passengers on these planes—a group including Air Chief Marshal Sir Arthur Tedder, the Allied deputy supreme commander representing General Dwight D. Eisenhower; General Carl A. Spaatz, commander of U.S. strategic air forces in Europe; and Lieutenant General Jean de Lattre de Tassigny, commander of the French First Army— were bound for Berlin. There they would join the Soviet commander, Marshal Georgi Zhukov, in signing a document ratifying Germany's unconditional surrender to the Allies.

Already, in the early hours of May 7, Allied and German representatives had signed a document of capitulation at Eisenhower's Supreme Headquarters at Reims in northeastern France. But before Ike could get to bed that morning, he had received a message informing him that the Soviets would not accept the Reims document, even though a Russian general had taken part in the ceremony. A formal ratification must take place in Berlin, which was occupied by the Red Army. Like many other Western leaders, Eisenhower held great hopes for postwar collaboration between the West and the Soviet Union, but now he went to bed with a sense of foreboding. Would the West really find it possible to work with the Soviet Union in rebuilding Europe from the devastation wreaked by six years of war?

As the DC-3s (C-47s, in army usage) droned toward Berlin, their passengers could look down on a country that had fought to the utter end against Allied soldiers, artillery, and bombers and, in doing so, appeared to have committed suicide. Even small villages showed few signs of life, with roofless farmhouses gaping at the sky, and here and there a shattered church steeple rising above the rubble. After rendezvousing with the German delegation at Stendal, west of Berlin, the Allied representatives acquired an escort of Soviet Stormovik fighters that accompanied them to Tempelhof airport, south of the center of the capital. As the C-47s neared the city, in which the fires of war burned on, they encountered clouds of bitter-smelling yellowish smoke. Streaming through a break in the overcast, the noontime sun lit up what seemed an endless stony wasteland. Long blocks of roofless houses appeared to make up a gigantic maze, their insides gutted by fires from incendiary bombs.

Battered for many months by Allied aircraft, whose attacks had destroyed the center of the city, Berlin had also faced massive artillery and rocket barrages from Red Army troops as they fought German defenders building by building—defenders, as an American correspondent observed, "who fear the Russians as no nation has ever feared a conquering army." "Each stone of the city, each meter of street is against us," wrote a Soviet reporter. "We have to take them with our blood." To another Soviet correspondent, Berlin during this week presented a horrific vision of "ruins, craters, smashed guns, tramcars riddled with holes, half-demolished trenches, heaps of spent cartridge shells, fresh graves, corpses still awaiting burial." Though the suburban area through which the Allied representatives were driven to Soviet headquarters in Karlshorst, about seven miles southeast of the city center, showed less evidence of the bombing and ground fighting, it gave Air Chief Marshal Tedder a "weird impression of being in some sort of coma."

In the spring of 1945, indeed, all of Germany lay in a psychological and economic coma. Just three years before, the Third Reich had dominated Europe as no previous power had ever done, controlling the Continent from the North Cape of Norway to Sicily and from the Bay of Biscay to the Caucasus. But now, at the end of the war, the nation had lost some four million mostly young men of its armed forces, who either had been killed or had simply disappeared; many more had been permanently disabled. Three hundred thousand civilians had died in Allied air raids. Deprived of its vigorous young manpower, the part of Germany west of the Oder River now had to take in several million people from the Sudetenland, which Hitler had stripped from Czechoslovakia in 1938 but which was now being returned. The western region also must absorb more than four million people—largely elders, women, and children—whom the Russians had driven from their homelands in the East and who had plodded westward carrying what few possessions they had. In addition, the population of Germany on the day of Allied victory included more than eight million "slave laborers," foreign civilian workers and prisoners of war brought into the country to work on farms and in factories as replacements for Germans serving in the armed forces. "There are tens of thousands of Russian and Polish and Czech and French and Yugoslav and Belgian slave laborers around here," a correspondent reported, "and they pour in every day in truckloads to the camps which the 82nd Airborne now runs. There is apparently an inexhaustible supply of human beings who were seized from their families and who lived in misery for years, with no medical care and on starvation rations, while working twelve hours a day for their German masters."

The sight of Germany prostrate in the spring of 1945 did not move Western soldiers or civilians to pity. "In Germany," wrote this same American correspondent, "when you see absolute devastation you do not grieve. We have grieved for many places in many countries but this is not one of the countries. Our soldiers say, 'They asked for it.' " Just a month before the surrender, three top American generals—Eisenhower, Omar Bradley, and George S. Patton—had visited a "horror camp," as Ike called it. In this slave-labor camp, at Ohrdruf, Eisenhower "first came face to face with indisputable evidence of Nazi brutality and ruthless disregard of every shred of decency"—rooms piled with corpses, a gallows with its noose of piano wire to produce maximum final agony for dying prisoners. Great black scabs on the bodies showed where starving prisoners had torn at the entrails of the dead for food. Although the sights and the unearthly stink made members of his party violently sick and drove some of them out of the camp, Ike, grim-faced, insisted on seeing everything, and later that same day he sent messages to Washington and London calling on the U.S. and British governments to dispatch reporters and legislators to see the horrors for themselves and report them "in a fashion that would leave no room for cynical doubt" on the part of those who might regard accounts of such atrocities as nothing more than war propaganda.

During that same week the famous CBS radio correspondent Edward R. Murrow, declaring that he was not interested in talking about "the surface of Germany," described his visit to the Buchenwald camp, near Weimar. "There surged around me an evil-smelling horde," said Murrow. A group of these men tried to lift their visitor to their shoulders, but they were too weak; many of them could not even get out of their bunks. Originally a stable for eighty horses, the building held twelve hundred men, five to a bunk. In an adjacent building Murrow saw "two rows of bodies, stacked up like cordwood. They were very thin and very white. Some of the bodies were terribly bruised, though there seemed to be little flesh to bruise." Murrow estimated that more than five hundred dead men and boys lay in the two neat piles. Those still alive in the camp included Germans and also people from other countries—doctors, a leather worker, the former mayor of Prague, a professor at the Sorbonne. These inmates judged that in March some six thousand people had died in the camp, most of them from starvation.

On April 29, little more than a week before the German surrender, troops of the U.S. Seventh Army had liberated 33,000 prisoners from Dachau, the original Nazi political concentration camp, near Munich. Some of the prisoners had been held there for twelve years; three hundred of the inmates had died of various kinds of sickness just the day before the Americans arrived, and for good measure fleeing SS guards had shot another thousand. Now, "behind the barbed wire and the electric fence," wrote an American reporter, "the skeletons sat in the sun and searched themselves for lice."

Installations like Ohrdruf, Buchenwald, and Dachau were the concentration camps in Germany itself. American and British generals and journalists had not yet seen the mass production death camps in the East.

The ratification ceremony took place at Marshal Zhukov's headquarters, established in an engineering school in suburban Karlshorst because the city itself offered no large building sufficiently intact to serve as offices. On the day before, Stalin had telephoned Zhukov expressing his disapproval of the just-signed surrender at Reims. The Soviet dictator made the point, Zhukov recalled, that "it was the Soviet people who bore the main brunt of the war, not the Allies. Therefore the Germans should sign the surrender before the Supreme Command of all the countries of the anti-Hitler coalition, and not just before the Supreme Commander of the Allied Forces." Besides, Stalin said, revealing some shaky geographical knowledge, he could not "agree to the unconditional surrender being signed in a provincial German town and not in Berlin, the center of Fascist aggression." Hence the Reims ceremony should be regarded as no more than a preliminary affair. In the same call, Stalin appointed Zhukov chief of the Soviet zone of Germany and also commander in chief of Soviet occupation forces.

Although the Western representatives had arrived at noon, expecting everything to be settled in time for a three o'clock announcement, the Russians spent the remainder of the day raising endless questions on matters of detail: Should Spaatz and de Lattre, who were not commanders in chief, be allowed to sign the document? If so, in what capacity? And just where? After all, was not even Air Chief Marshal Tedder himself a highly dubious figure? He certainly was not Eisenhower, the West's supreme commander. Where, indeed, was Eisenhower? He ought to be present. (Told of this new mission on being awakened at six o'clock that morning, Tedder's aide had asked his chief the same question; Tedder simply said, "He won't go." Since the Germans had already surrendered unconditionally, Ike seems to have regarded the "ratification" in Berlin as a primarily Soviet affair.)

A worldly, pipe-puffing officer who perfectly fitted the popular picture of an RAF commander, Tedder attributed the quibbling to the "deeply suspicious nature of the Russians" and specifically to the presence at Zhukov's elbow of the Soviet deputy foreign minister, Andrei Vyshinsky, who had won fame as the brutal state prosecutor during Joseph Stalin's Great Purge trials of the middle 1930s. Dispatched from Moscow by Stalin to serve as Zhukov's political supervisor, Vyshinsky flew in on the same day the Western delegation arrived. At one moment when Vyshinsky had left the room, the soldierly Zhukov, putting his hand on Tedder's shoulder, said earnestly, "Please believe me, I am not trying to be difficult, but we must get this right now, otherwise there will be trouble later." "We have three flags to consider," Tedder told Zhukov; "you have one." It took the debaters until midnight to reach a conclusion: Spaatz and de Lattre would sign the document, as witnesses, beneath the signatures of the principals. At that point "the Russians nearly broke up the conference by demanding the virtual right to blow up everything in Germany if the treaty was not thoroughly fulfilled." But with this rhetoric damped down, the victors were finally ready to summon the representatives of the defeated enemy to the whitewashed main hall of the building to sign the instrument of capitulation.

Perfectly turned out in his dress uniform, holding high his baton, Field Marshal Wilhelm Keitel, who had been chief of the high command of the German armed forces, led an admiral and a Luftwaffe general with accompanying staff officers into the room. Despite his commanding appearance and his haughty style, Keitel was not the Prussian tiger he seemed to be; he came from a middle-class Hanoverian family and, for his slavish devotion to Adolf Hitler, had long ago earned the nickname Lakaitel, a play on the German word for lackey. At a few minutes past midnight, allowing his monocle to drop and dangle on its cord, then reeling it in and jamming it into his right eye, Keitel marched to the head table. He removed his right glove, took up the pen, and affixed his signature to the five copies of the surrender document lying on the green cloth before him; the admiral and the air force general followed. Then, brushing aside Keitel's request for additional time to notify distant troops of the surrender, Zhukov ordered the German delegation to leave the hall. A strange figure to serve as the war's last official symbol of German militarism, "Hitler's head clerk," as Keitel had often been called, picked up his baton, his hat, and his right glove and strode out. Almost a year and a half later, on October 16, 1946, he would be hanged as a war criminal.

After the ceremony was over, Marshal Zhukov, in the standard Soviet style for great occasions, played host at a reception and banquet, with rounds of toasts proposed by the Western officers and the Soviet generals. "Much was said in the most heartfelt expressions about the desire to consolidate for ever friendly relations between the countries of the anti-Fascist coalition," Zhukov wrote later. "This was said by the Soviet Generals, by the Americans, French, and British, and all of us wanted to believe it would be that way." In one toast Tedder declared that, at a terrible cost, the military people had learned how to understand each other; those present should now hope that the politicians ("the men in gray," he called them—Vishinsky wore the standard gray Soviet political uniform) could do the same thing. Leaning over to Tedder, Zhukov responded, "He'll not let that go without a speech." He was right: Vishinsky thereupon "orated for twenty minutes on how we should cooperate against Germany." The banquet ended in the morning with singing and dancing; "the Soviet generals," said Zhukov, "were the best dancers by far."

The Germans had now surrendered twice. Though mopping-up operations would continue for a few more days, World War II in Europe had come to its end. The German defeat had been total, the capitulation unconditional. The Western Allies and the Soviet Union now held in their hands the present and future of the Reich and, in a special way, of Berlin.

Not quite three-quarters of a century earlier, on the afternoon of June 16, 1871, excited crowds had stood deep along the Berlin boulevard called Unter den Linden and squeezed themselves together in viewing stands and even on every rooftop; the Brandenburg Gate wore garlands of flowers, and everywhere flags fluttered in the breeze. Soon the blare of military brasses heralded the approach of a mass of troops with plumes and flashing spiked helmets. At the head of the column rode Wilhelm I, king of Prussia and now German emperor, who at one point halted to receive the keys to Berlin from a deputation of girls dressed in white. This splendid parade marked not only the victory of Prussia over the France of Napoleon III in the recent war but also the assumption of a new dignity for Berlin. The city, which would henceforth demand the attention of Europe, had now become an imperial capital.

In contrast to other famous cities of the Continent—London, Paris, Vienna—Berlin had no rich history as the capital or metropolis of a great state or dynasty. Like the shifting political entities for which it had served as the political center—the mark of Brandenburg, the kingdom of Prussia, Germany—Berlin had always exuded a kind of nervousness, a feeling of insecurity that no measure of power seemed to assuage. And it was not a city that inspired composers and poets: who had ever sung about Berlin, "city of my dreams"?

For many years from its founding at the beginning of the thirteenth century—its official birth year was 1237—Berlin had been universally looked on as an outpost on the far side of European civilization. Even the title of the margraves of Brandenburg (incorporating the word *mark*—borderland), who ruled Berlin and became electors of the Holy Roman Empire, conveyed the idea of border. In 1415 the emperor granted that title to Friedrich von Hohenzollern, whose family came from Swabia, in southwestern Germany. Moving quickly to take firm control of his new domain, this prince asserted his power by restricting the privileges of the established patrician families. His actions aroused such opposition that old chroniclers called it the *Berliner Unwille* (Berlin indignation). This angry reluctance, the historian Gerhard Masur commented, "would seem a prelude to the resistance to authority that marks Berlin's entire history."

By 1701 the ambitious Hohenzollerns, who dreamed of empire, had acquired a small dukedom on the Rhine and also, as a fief from the king of Poland, the duchy of Prussia, lying to the northeast of Berlin. They had thus cobbled together a new kingdom—which they endowed with the name Prussia—to go with the standing army they had pioneered. In so doing they created the basis for the later comment that whereas most countries were states with armies, Prussia was an army with a state, an army vitally needed to hold together this collection of scattered political units.

Berlin began to reflect its status as the capital of a kingdom in 1709, when Friedrich I, the first sovereign of the new monarchy, united the town with others in the area to create a royal seat more like a city. Under Friedrich's successor, Friedrich Wilhelm I, Berlin became not only a capital but a collection of soldiers' barracks, as the new "sergeant king" pursued his aim of making Prussia into a garrison state. Even so, Berlin remained a border city not only in relation to Western Europe but to the rest of Germany—an isolated provincial town of perhaps 80,000 people, with no less than ten percent of its population made up of soldiers. But though nothing grander than the capital of an upstart kingdom, Berlin experienced notable growth during the eighteenth century, and by 1800, still in the preindustrial era, it ranked as the sixth largest city in Europe, with a population of about 170,000.

Berlin's population could claim some special characteristics marking it off from the people of other cities. Because the city "had not grown up in the shadow of a cathedral," the German historian Wolfgang Haus commented, it had neither strong nor deep religious influences, and in fact in the seventeenth century it had become a refuge for victims of religious persecution in other countries. By the Edict of Potsdam in 1685, the elector had invited the Huguenots expelled from France by Louis XIV to make a new home in Brandenburg. Masters of a variety of arts and crafts, these hard-working Calvinists had quickly moved to the top of Berlin society and enriched the local culture, even inspiring among Berliners a fondness for cauliflower, artichokes, and asparagus. As the city grew in the eighteenth century, workers from across Germany and from other countries as well came to help man the textile, metalworking, and porcelain factories. Visiting Berlin in 1778, Johann Wolfgang von Goethe, the young poet and philosopher who would become Germany's greatest literary figure, responded to this mixed breed he saw—the Berliner—as *"ein verwegener Menschenschlag,"* an audacious type of human being. But its growth still had not, at least in some eyes, made Berlin a true metropolis. Even after Friedrich II (Frederick the Great), who reigned from 1740 to 1786, had almost by sleight of hand made Prussia into a true great power and had embellished his capital city with palaces, an opera house, and other great buildings in a distinctive baroque style, a Prussian minister of culture could describe Berlin as a "mere village" in which one had to search extensively just to find a wagon.

On October 27, 1806, proud Berlin experienced one of the most painful moments of its history when Napoleon I led his victorious legions through the Brandenburg Gate, thus opening a period of French domination. For a time Berlin ceased to be the capital of anything at all. In an almost immediate response, a group of scholars, winning the blessing of King Friedrich Wilhelm III, created the University of Berlin, which became the center of an intellectual flowering. Resounding with names like Humboldt, Fichte, Schelling, Schleiermacher, and Hegel, the movement aimed at national spiritual and political reform. Though these efforts at regeneration did not lead directly to the establishment of a German national state—a destiny that fate seemed determined to withhold from the Germans—all the talk and writing gave Berlin a fresh luster among German cities. Proud of their great new university, Berliners liked to boast about the eminent scholars and thinkers associated with it, a habit that only swelled their reputation for arrogance.

By the middle of the nineteenth century the population of Berlin had surpassed that of Vienna, the old imperial capital. In 1871 the city, now numbering 825,000 inhabitants, became the capital of the new German Empire crafted by Chancellor Otto von Bismarck, the "little Germany"— so called in contrast to *Grossdeutschland,* Greater Germany, because it excluded Austria. In large part because the Austrian Germans were outside it, this empire would always have an artificial, jerry-built quality. Observing that Bismarck's empire did not follow "the customary European national-democratic road to unity," Thomas Mann described it as "purely a power structure aiming towards the hegemony of Europe." During the June 1871 official celebration of the transition to empire, the newly minted emperor, Wilhelm I (who preferred what he considered his only true title, king of

Prussia), told his little grandson, "This is a day you will never forget." Seventeen years later this grandson would come to the throne as Wilhelm II, to be forever known in the world as "the Kaiser," the central figure of World War I.

In 1872, inspired by the creation of the new empire, a British writer paid the first of several lengthy visits to its capital in order to give his readers a thorough picture of "a city out of the regular highway of continental travel" but destined thenceforth to play an important part in the world. Arriving on a warm day, Henry Vizetelly discovered a city that had not yet become a true metropolis. No matter where he went, he could not escape "the rankest compound of villainous smells that ever offended nostril," at some times more offensive than at others, depending on whether "the fetid filth is in sluggish motion or stagnant at the bottom of the open and inefficiently flushed drains," which in many places were simply uncovered sewers bordering the roads on either side. The streets themselves were so poorly paved that the horses had to wear special shoes; other streets, macadamized, stayed in such poor repair that people and cattle sank ankle-deep in the mire. The sidewalks, maintained only by the proceeds of a tax on dogs, proved to be no better, with the result that everybody clumped along in heavy double-soled shoes and boots. (The dismal state of the roads and walkways even exerted an anatomical effect. If the French liked to accuse Englishwomen of having large feet, Vizetelly commented ungallantly, they ought to see the "remarkable development of the pedal extremities which characterises the Berlin belles.") Nevertheless, construction was booming, with "new quarters being laid out, new streets planned, new houses rising up everywhere," and the array of new buildings in the heart of the city made it seem as though the capital of the new empire had been entrusted to some "Prussian Haussmann" to be redone. With its nexus of canals and railways, Vizetelly decided, Berlin was acting like an "immense suction pump in the plains of Brandenburg."

By the time of Wilhelm II's accession in 1888, the German Empire was in soaring flight, experiencing the full force of industrial development and in all ways playing the role of most powerful country in Europe. Greater Berlin, now an industrial metropolis pulling in workers from all parts of the Reich, had a population of about two million; some spoke of it as the Chicago of Europe. Before the outbreak of war in 1914, the figure had risen to more than 3.7 million. This growth, accompanied by and partly caused by the centralization of authority in the city as the imperial capital, aroused hostility across the country, not least in Prussia itself—the kind of criticism, as Haus observed, that represents a common complaint against all national capitals, "which soon outgrow the characteristics they had as simple provincial centers, losing their national identity as they become cosmopolitan."

Critics said that the huge new city "had not experienced a healthy, natural growth, that it lacked historical legitimation as the capital, and that, as a frontier city and an 'East-Elbian capital,' it had no solid national tradition." Conservatives in Prussia and elsewhere held special fears of Berlin because, like many other national metropolises, it served as a natural home and refuge for radicals. Bismarck himself often had his doubts as he contemplated the political doings of some of his fellow Berliners; certainly he devoted himself to keeping the local radicalism from affecting the policies of the Prussian and imperial governments.

With heavy Victorian buildings dominating its squares and avenues, imperial Berlin, though it had its attractive features, could not lay claim to possessing beauty. "In external appearance," said Baedeker, the city "is somewhat deficient in interest; its situation is unpicturesque, and it lacks the charm of mediæval and historical edifices," but "there is no want of architectural display." The Tiergarten, a one-time hunting ground of Prussian kings that had become a great park in the center of the city, presented visitors with the remarkable spectacle of rows of marble Hohenzollerns along what was called Sieges Allee (Triumphal Avenue); as a standard part of their education, schoolchildren took field trips to the Tiergarten to study these effigies of Wilhelm II's ancestors. Created on the command of the Kaiser, these family statues evoked a rueful comment from an unfortunate artist whose studio overlooked the park: "All I can do is to wear blue goggles, but it is a life sentence."

In June 1913 came the high noon of glory for Berlin and Germany, as the people of the empire celebrated the silver anniversary of Kaiser Wilhelm II's accession to the throne. "Wondrous and eloquent are the statistical revelations of Germany's bounding growth in population, of Imperial Berlin's rise to metropolitan splendour," said a correspondent who did double duty for the *Daily Mail* of London and the *New York Times*. "The streets of Berlin were impassable," wrote the Kaiser's daughter, Princess Viktoria Luise; they were "crammed with festively dressed folk waving innumerable flags," all of them "rejoicing in twenty-five years of peace and golden economic boom." Just since the beginning of the century, the princess noted, German trade had doubled and now led the world, surpassing that of the traditional leader, Britain. As a devoted daughter, Viktoria Luise gave her father much of the credit for Germany's remarkable progress during the past quarter-century. This opinion, which would win no subsequent endorsement from any even halfway responsible historian, was nevertheless not hers alone. The *Mail* and *Times* correspondent declared that "the world at large, fascinated by his kaleidoscopic and picturesque personality, is prone to accord the Kaiser almost exclusive credit for the Fatherland's magic leap into *Weltmacht*."

In creating the empire that dominated the Continent as the fateful summer of 1914 approached, Bismarck had kept German liberalism weak and scattered. He had "broken the nation's backbone," wrote the great historian Theodor Mommsen back in the 1880s; Mommsen decried "the subjugation of the German personality, of the German mind," which he considered "a misfortune that cannot be undone." Bismarck's policies and his force of character gave Germany an imperial capital and a long period of peace and unparalleled prosperity that outlived him, but that era came to a sudden and violent end in the great cataclysm that followed the assassination of the Austrian Archduke Franz Ferdinand in Sarajevo, Bosnia, on June 28, 1914.

Like all the capitals of nations involved in World War I, Berlin swelled with new kinds of activities and with the bureaucracy this new kind of war made necessary. As food shortages and other privations made themselves felt, the city and its administration had to face what Haus called "the manifold tasks associated with maintaining the existence of a mass community in times of crisis." In so doing, "a great service was rendered by Berlin in those days, for its precedents and solutions were examples to the rest of Germany." In these crises "Berliners showed that behind the pretentiousness and brashness for which they had so often been criticized, there was a solid capacity to bear up under difficult conditions." The years 1917 and 1918 were not the last time Berliners would draw on these valuable characteristics.

As the German Empire collapsed into defeat, there came revolution and the flight of the Kaiser to Holland, the proclamation of a republic—November 9, 1918—and continuing upheaval and street violence. Because Berlin remained too turbulent to serve as the meeting place of a national assembly, the constitutional delegates gathered some 150 miles away in the town of Weimar, previously known in history as the shrine to which, a hundred years earlier, pilgrims from all over Europe had come to see and admire Goethe. Henceforth Weimar would lend its name to the new republic and to the fourteen-year era through which it would survive.

In many ways the most celebrated phase of Berlin's history, the Weimar years saw the city become a center not only of municipal planning and architectural design but of a new kind of frenetic literary and artistic culture, which existed side by side with older forms in music and the other arts. In the eyes of other Germans, "especially in aesthetics," wrote Haus, "everything that came out of the city was looked upon as 'democratic,' 'socialistic,' and 'left-wing,' and these for many of the Germans of the time were derogatory epithets." The "skeptical, rather than enthusiastic attitude of its people, their tendency to irony and negative criticism—actually, it was as often as not directed at themselves and their own city—and the cool, detached big-city atmosphere made it difficult for outsiders to muster any real affection for Berlin." However it was viewed, Berlin in the 1920s became the center of various new movements in the arts. Most generally familiar today of all the products of the time is undoubtedly the acid-toned anticapitalist piece of high cabaret theater, *Die Dreigroschenoper (The Threepenny Opera)* by Bertolt Brecht and Kurt Weill, which appeared in 1928—and one of whose songs would years later, in a remarkable cultural transmogrification, find great popularity through Louis Armstrong.

When the onset of the Great Depression put an end to the period of German recovery from World War I and made Adolf Hitler and the Nazis a formidable political force, "Red Berlin" became the prize most sought by the party leadership. After coming to power in January 1933, the Nazis were able to collect this prize, but they did it over the opposition of the Berliners themselves; even in an election for the city assembly held in March 1933, almost two months after Hitler became chancellor, the Nazis, for all the bullying influence they exerted, won only 86 seats out of 222. Characteristically, the Nazis then installed a party member as virtual dictator on behalf of the national government, and in 1936 they formalized an arrangement whereby the mayor became a state official. But the most important voice in local government belonged to the party *gauleiter* (district leader) of Berlin, better known to the world as the Reich propaganda minister, Dr. Joseph Goebbels.

Count Hermann Keyserling, a determined anti-Nazi, told a friend who had been forced to flee Germany that the regime represented "the dictatorship of the nonintellectuals" and therefore held great popularity with the lower middle class, particularly "farmers and small shopkeepers, vendors of cheese and 'sour gherkins.' " But, despite all their speeches and drums and torchlight parades, the Nazis, in the view of Wolfgang Haus, never succeeded in winning over the mass of Berliners and thus making the city their true capital; though the party indeed acquired many members in the city, the Berliner is "fundamentally averse to pompous exuberance" and, too much a cosmopolitan to take Nazi doctrines seriously, tended to view the regime as something as insubstantial as the cardboard columns that were set up to decorate Unter den Linden for all the Third Reich festivals.

With Berlin the host city of the 1936 Olympic Games, the government strove to create a favorable impression on foreign visitors. Hermann Göring, the leading Nazi next to Hitler and the head of the new air force, "behaved like a schoolboy," said Princess Viktoria Luise, "and obviously enjoyed having so many prominent international personalities there in attendance." Like the other chief totalitarian regimes of the day, those of Italy and the Soviet Union, the Nazi government favored massive and stony architecture that stood at the opposite pole from the works of Walter

Gropius, Marcel Breuer, and the other Bauhaus masters who had made Germany a world leader in design in the Weimar era. Despite this unfortunate propensity on the part of his patrons, the architect Werner March produced for the Olympics a "magnificent sport-field, with a stadium for a hundred thousand" that provided a new grace note for the city. Those outside Hitler's circle did not know, however, that March's original plan for a "glass box" had caused the Führer to threaten cancellation of the games, a decision he rescinded when a young architect for whom he had developed a liking, Albert Speer, showed him how the "steel skeleton already built could be clad in natural stone."

The public buildings put up in Berlin during the latter 1930s gave only hints at the great new capital city dreamed of by the Führer and Speer. The plans of this new Germania, as Hitler wanted to call the city, demanded the razing of much of Berlin—"nothing but an unregulated accumulation of buildings," said the Führer—and its replacement by vast avenues (one of them 400 feet wide) and buildings of megalomaniac immensity, including, as Speer later described it, "a huge meeting hall, a domed structure into which St. Peter's Cathedral would have fitted several times over. The diameter of the dome was to be eight hundred twenty-five feet." To offset this monster of a hall, Hitler planned an arch of triumph 400 feet high. In addition, since he intended for Berlin to become the permanent home of the Olympic Games (after they were duly held in Tokyo, the capital of his Japanese allies, in 1940), he looked forward to the creation of a truly suitable stadium, one that would hold 400,000 people. (Some years later, Speer decided that, at least during the winter, the great meeting hall with its 1,000–foot-high copper dome would have posed a regrettable meteorological problem. As the exhaled carbon dioxide and evaporated sweat from a massed Nazi audience rose to the roof, the mixture would have collided with a layer of cold air, with predictable results: the Führer would have found his oratorical performance rained out.)

The coming of war in 1939 saved Berlin from the bizarre fate Hitler and Speer planned for it. Yet in an uncontemplated way, American and British heavy bombers and Soviet big guns would accomplish the razing of the city contemplated by Führer and architect. In the triumphal days of 1940, after the defeat of France, Hermann Göring assured Germans that they need not fear British air attacks. "If an enemy bomber reaches the Ruhr," declared the newly minted Reichsmarschall, "my name is not Hermann Göring: you can call me Meier." Within only a few days, however, the Royal Air Force, retaliating for the first German bombing of London, had carried out an attack not on the Ruhr, in western Germany, but on Berlin itself. Given the aircraft of the day and the 1,150-mile round-trip distance they had to travel, the raid could only be a small-scale affair (just twenty-nine aircraft were able to drop their bombs), but it was clearly big enough to give Berliners the right to call Göring whatever they chose. From this limited effort by twin-engine bombers on August 25, 1940, would grow an Anglo-American around-the-clock offensive, with heavy Lancasters and B-17 Flying Fortresses, that culminated in the great air battles of 1943–45.

Before the war, air planners in all countries had presumed, and many politicians had fearfully agreed, that bombing could not only disrupt a nation's industrial production but, by creating reactions ranging from mass exhaustion to mass panic, could destroy the morale of the nation's people. Airmen prewar dreamed of a "future enemy moral collapse in which a crazed and deprived civilian population roamed the streets shooting and looting and demanding peace behind the back of their own armies." Politicians, for their part, tended to speak of their fears for their own countries; in 1932, well before the day of the long-range four-engine bomber, Stanley Baldwin, once and future British prime minister, said grimly that the citizen must realize that "there is no power on earth that can protect him from being bombed. Whatever people may tell him, the bomber will always get through. The only defence is in offence, which means that you have to kill more women and children more quickly than the enemy if you want to save yourselves." Such horrifying visions underlay much of the British and French faltering in the later 1930s before Hitler's threats.

Yet night after night from 1942 on, RAF Bomber Command battered Germany in its campaign to destroy cities and "dehouse" workers. By day the men of the U.S. Eighth Air Force, trying to fulfill the official doctrine of precision bombing, pursued their strategic targets, such as aircraft factories, synthetic-oil plants and, in two famous and costly raids, ball-bearing factories. "Hitler and his Nazi gang have sown the wind," Prime Minister Winston Churchill, a strong supporter of the bombing offensive, had said in an address to the Canadian House of Commons in December 1941. "Now let them reap the whirlwind." In November 1943 Sir Arthur Harris, the commander in chief of Bomber Command, told Churchill that "we can wreck Berlin from end to end" and so "cost Germany the war." Harris, who nursed an obsession with the German capital, then launched the series of sustained attacks that became known as the Battle of Berlin. But just as London had failed to crumble during the Luftwaffe's assault in 1940, the people of Berlin and other German cities, faced with far greater attacks from bigger bombers and often forced to move underground, doggedly stayed at their machines, and the factories themselves proved far more resilient than Allied planners and commanders had expected. In fact, the Allies later learned with some amazement, despite all the dislocations and problems brought by the raids German aircraft production actually increased in 1944.

In January 1945, with the Soviet tide rolling closer, Hitler left his longtime headquarters in East Prussia and returned to Berlin. On January 30, the twelfth anniversary of his appointment as chancellor of the Reich, he declared in a speech that Germany would not be lured into surrender and designated the faithful Goebbels "Defender of Berlin." Though Goebbels had proved remarkably resourceful in many situations and would do his best during the next three months, rushing here and there through the rubble to sustain the morale of youngsters who had been handed rifles and told to hold off the advance of Russian tanks, successful execution of this assignment lay far beyond the powers of any mortal. Even then, in the kind of surrealistic unintentional comedy peculiar to the Nazi regime, Goebbels took the time to announce a national competition for the design of a new Berlin.

Coming to the existing Berlin to try to win freedom for one of her sons clapped into prison by the Gestapo, Princess Viktoria Luise, whose fate had remained interwoven with that of the Fatherland through the century, found herself caught on the autobahn during an air raid. "I thought my last hour had come," she wrote. "Bombs detonated all around me and flames from burning cars lit the highway like flaming torches right up to the capital." Meanwhile, as the inevitable end approached, the Führer spent most of the time in his special bunker beneath the chancellery, talking in long monologues to his associates and secretaries and, ever the architectural dreamer, planning the rebuilding of Linz, his boyhood home, with Albert Speer.

In the early hours of Monday, April 16, people in eastern districts of Berlin heard the distinctive distant thunder that told the war veterans among them that a great battle had begun. With a massive artillery barrage, the Red Army, now just thirty-five miles from the city, had begun its final battle for Berlin. In the following days, after crossing the Oder and Neisse rivers, Soviet troops thrust the two prongs of a pincer movement toward Berlin. Marshal Zhukov's First Byelorussian Front (army group) advanced in a broad frontal assault while, attacking from the left, units of Marshal I. S. Konev's First Ukrainian Front wheeled northward. On April 25, as Soviet and U.S. forces were meeting at the Elbe, near Torgau, the Russian fronts completed a circle around Berlin, joining near Potsdam, southwest of the city. Slowly but irresistibly the Russians pushed into Berlin. Displaying amazing tenacity against hopeless odds, Goebbels's defenders piled over-turned streetcars and masonry from shattered buildings into barricades in depth; tanks and artillery fired on the invaders from positions inside cellars and houses. But by April 27, in fierce brick-by-brick fighting, Red Army forces had cleared about three-quarters of the city. On April 30 Hitler celebrated his fifty-sixth birthday by committing suicide in the bunker. On

May 2, as Russian soldiers toppled the Nazi eagle from the skeleton of the Reich chancellery, the Soviets completed the conquest of the enemy capital.

The royal city of Frederick the Great, the booming imperial metropolis of Bismarck and Kaiser Wilhelm II, now saw its past buried under the rubble of complete defeat. Berlin was no longer a capital; it no longer had a country—Winston Churchill's December 1941 wish had become a profoundly fulfilled prophecy. The people of Berlin faced an unknown new world. The Russians held the city as a great trophy of conquest, and the Americans, the British, and the French would soon arrive to claim their shares of this symbolic prize.

CHAPTER 2

"Frau . . . komm!"

WHAT SHOULD THEY do with Germany after victory? That question had demanded continuing attention from the Western Allies and the Soviet Union. On a visit to the Kremlin in December 1941, the British foreign secretary, Anthony Eden, had proposed the adoption of generalized statements of good intentions for postwar Europe, only to be told by Joseph Stalin: "Declarations—that's like algebra. Treaties or agreements—that's practical arithmetic. We prefer arithmetic to algebra." But the Western powers were not at this early stage ready to move from hypotheses to the specific and binding pacts—arithmetic—Stalin wanted. In a March 1943 discussion in Washington, President Roosevelt and Eden agreed that "under any circumstances, Germany must be divided into several states," so that it could not again become a dominant power; Stalin, they believed, held the same view.

Later that year, at a conference of foreign ministers held in Moscow—at which Secretary of State Cordell Hull represented the United States; Eden, Great Britain; and V. M. Molotov, the Soviet Union—the Allied powers established a supporting group, called the European Advisory Commission, to study and make recommendations concerning Germany. At this time much high-level opinion, at least in the United States, held that even though the great Allied coalition had been forced into existence by Axis attack rather than assembled on the basis of any common principles, the wasteful and tragic nature of war demanded a new approach to international conflicts—something better than the balance-of-power mechanism that Hull saw as a relic of the unhappy past; the three powers at Moscow pledged to continue their "present close collaboration and cooperation" into the period following the end of the war.

Allied opinion now shifted in the direction of keeping "Hitlerite Germany" (a favorite Russian term) intact and giving it a course in democratization, with the aim of producing, in due course, a state that would act as a respectable member of international society. This approach would require a period of occupation by the victors; perhaps the thorniest problem concerned the assignment of zones of occupation. The British drafted an agreement that the Russians accepted with pleasure, since Soviet thinking had put the line of East-West demarcation farther to the east. The Soviets now rejected the joint occupation of Hamburg or the Kiel Canal that they themselves had earlier contemplated, but they seemed to expect combined Anglo-American occupation of the western part of the country. Berlin, everybody agreed, would have a separate status from all other cities; Russian drafts, interestingly enough, called for dividing the city into East Berlin and West Berlin. At this point in the war, months before the Normandy invasion, the Western Allies were, in Stalin's terms, still in the algebra stage— they had no way of knowing where their armies would stand on the Continent at the time of German surrender. Nevertheless, they had to make decisions.

After laboring for many months, the European Advisory Commission produced various protocols and documents designating three zones of occupation in Germany and three sectors of occupation in Berlin; an agreement also provided for the establishment of an inter-Allied governing authority for the city. The USSR would have the eastern zone of Germany and the northeastern sector of Berlin; Britain, the northwestern zone of Germany and the northwestern portion of Berlin; and the United States, the southwestern zone of Germany and the southern part of Berlin. The zonal division of Germany, it was later said, gave the Russians the farms, the British the factories, and the Americans the scenery. In November 1944 a French representative joined the commission, a change that would clear the way for French participation in the occupation of Germany and Berlin.

At the Yalta Conference in the Crimea in February 1945, the Big Three—with President Franklin D. Roosevelt then representing the United States—confirmed the zonal arrangements for Germany. Stalin raised no objections to France's receiving a zone of occupation for Germany and a sector in Berlin, as long as they came from the areas allotted to the British and the Americans. The conference also accepted the European Advisory Commission's recommendation for the creation of an Allied control council to deal with matters affecting Germany as a whole; the plan called for this council to supervise the activities of the anticipated "German central administration." The council would be made up of the three (with France, four) national commanders in chief, each of whom would exercise supreme authority in his own zone. A commander in chief could be overruled only by the unanimous decision of the Allied Control Council; that is, he could be overruled only if he decided to vote against himself. The hope—and for the

West generally, the expectation—was that the victors would quickly create a national German government, so that the zonal arrangements would be only temporary affairs.

The briefest look at a map shows that these arrangements held not only the seeds but the buds and even the blooms of discord and crisis. Since the British zonal boundary ran, at its closest point, more than a hundred miles from Berlin, the city would become an island in a Soviet-occupied sea. Along with this geographical problem would come the working of the unanimity principle in the Control Council. With this principle giving each commander—and hence, each country—independence from all the others, the implications for isolated Berlin, and for the isolated Western troops that were to garrison their parts of the city, could well be ominous. In the most curious aspect of all, though the Soviets throughout the war had shown themselves tireless, finicky, and often truculent negotiators—even in discussions designed to confer benefits on them—none of the protocols and arrangements put forward by the European Advisory Commission and accepted by the heads of government made any reference whatever to methods of Western access to Berlin. Highways, railroads, air corridors would be theirs to use by right, would they not?

The diplomats of the European Advisory Commission tended to explain this omission in two separate but related ways. Earlier, Ambassador John G. Winant, the U.S. representative, had raised the issue with his superiors in Washington but had been brushed off; now he declared that the right to occupy a sector of Berlin carried with it the right of access, an opinion apparently shared by the British representative, Sir William Strang, a veteran Foreign Office official who had special experience in dealing with the Russians. (In 1939 he had been sent to Moscow by Prime Minister Neville Chamberlain on a belated, bleak, and indeed hopeless mission to seek an arrangement against Hitler with the Soviet Union.) From the point of view of the Western diplomats, asking the Soviets for free access to Berlin would be a backward step, weakening the agreement that declared the city the seat of a four-power government. To this legalistic view, the diplomats—who conducted their discussions in the triumphal stages of a long and arduous war, in an atmosphere that, if not roseate, at least produced many gleams of optimism—added the thought that, after struggling through all the negotiations that had led to the various agreements, they did not wish to introduce complications that might unravel the whole affair. To raise the issue of access in connection with the agreements, Winant said, would be likely to arouse Soviet suspicions and complicate future dealings.

Several times during 1944 General Eisenhower, looking ahead to the period after the end of the fighting, had expressed his opposition to the

contemplated establishment of separate U.S. and British military governments in Germany. Instead, Ike told his superiors, it would be far more
efficient and effective to maintain the Allied command structure for the
occupation of the western parts of Germany. The forces of the two countries
would, of course, operate in their own individual areas, as had been the case
during the war, but no line of demarcation would be drawn between those
areas. Otherwise, Eisenhower feared, British and American zone commanders would find themselves opposing each other on some questions,
leaving the door wide open for the Soviets to take sides. Although he
emerged from the war as history's most effective executor of unified command, Ike won no support for his suggestion. Each country, and the French
in their turn, wished to have its own force operating under its own command in its own zone.

At the beginning of June, SHAEF, the great Anglo-American director-
ate that had produced victory in the West and was soon to be dissolved,
moved its headquarters from Versailles to the I. G. Farben complex in
Frankfurt—a huge eight-story building with a central spine and six wings
on either side—which was to serve as U.S. headquarters in Germany. Here
Ike took on his new, double-barreled job as U.S. military governor of
Germany and commander of American forces in Europe. On June 5 the
commanders who would constitute the Allied Control Council—
Eisenhower, Field Marshal Sir Bernard Montgomery, General de Lattre,
and Marshal Zhukov—met in Berlin to declare the assumption of "supreme
authority with respect to Germany" by the governments of the four occupying powers. Discussion then turned to a question that preoccupied—
indeed obsessed—the Russians: in the last phases of the war, Eisenhower's
forces had pushed the Germans well back into Saxony, Thuringia, and
Mecklenburg—areas, with a normal population of almost nine million,
assigned to the Soviets for occupation—and the Russians wanted the Americans and the British out. Indeed, they made it obvious that they would do
no business on any issue until they had taken over all of their zone. They also
"made it plain," as President Truman later put it, that the Allies could not
move into their assigned sectors of Berlin until they had pulled back west
into the boundaries of their zones.

This issue had its complexities, which had to find resolution on the
highest levels. Winston Churchill wanted Western forces to hold on to this
prime bargaining counter until the West and the Russians had at least
settled questions relating to the occupation of Austria. Though not endorsing Churchill's view, the U.S. Joint Chiefs of Staff objected to accepting
Western withdrawal as a prerequisite for the Russians' turning over the
Western sectors of Berlin to their intended occupiers. President Truman
settled the debate by declaring that the Western powers must abide by the

existing agreement on occupation zones. Finally, over Churchill's protests, July 1 became the official date for the beginning of Allied withdrawal to the Western zones; advance British and American billeting parties could come to Berlin on the same date, with full occupation beginning when the Soviets had completed their movement west.

Making Zhukov's acquaintance for the first time at the June 5 session, Ike strongly took to his host, the most eminent of the Soviet World War II commanders. To Eisenhower's displeasure, however, the afternoon was marked by a series of vaguely explained delays, like those that had figured in the May 8 meeting and often characterized dealings with the Soviets. Ike also noted, as he told a visitor a few days later, that Zhukov would not answer any of his questions without first consulting Vyshinsky. The visitor, Harry Hopkins, who had been President Roosevelt's closest associate and was now en route home from a mission to Moscow for President Truman, told Ike that "Stalin had made it very clear that Zhukov would have very little power concerning political affairs in Germany." Despite Ike's minor annoyance, he and Zhukov quickly developed something in the nature of a friendship. Indeed, the marshal's affability to Eisenhower contrasted sharply with his frostiness toward Montgomery; perhaps Ike's 1944 vision of Soviet divisiveness toward the U.S.-British allies was already materializing. (On the other hand, no person of any nationality other than British had ever been able to develop much warmth toward the cocky and condescending Monty. Ike found him "as small inside as he was outside.")

For Eisenhower, this meeting served as the prelude to a round of foreign travel that would consume much of the next several months. Just before he left Germany, however, he played host in Frankfurt to Zhukov with a huge luncheon and troop review; the Soviet marshal played a part as well, presenting medals to Eisenhower and Montgomery. This gala occasion, wrote David Eisenhower, marked "the zenith of Allied-Soviet cordiality." Ike then departed to give a speech in London; visit Paris and Prague; appear before Congress in Washington; receive a triumphal reception in New York; visit his mother, who still lived in the family's little white frame house in Abilene; and travel with Zhukov to Moscow. His job as U.S. military governor came as a sharp anticlimax to commanding the great Allied force that had battled the Wehrmacht in a life-and-death struggle; Ike, his son John said, was "let down after the excitement of the war." Administering the occupation of Germany he found a frustrating job that yielded little glory and much criticism; his continuing absences brought to the center of the stage in Berlin an officer who would become one of the most important American figures of the entire cold war period, the U.S. deputy military governor, Lieutenant General Lucius D. Clay.

On June 29, with both General Eisenhower and Field Marshal Montgomery on home leave, General Clay and his British counterpart, Lieutenant General Sir Ronald Weeks (a business executive who had entered military service early in the war), came to Berlin for a meeting with Marshal Zhukov concerning arrangements for the American and British takeover of their occupation zones. Four days earlier, Clay had received strong instructions from the U.S. Army chief of staff, General George C. Marshall, to arrange transit rights into Berlin with the Soviets; Marshall took explicit note of the European Advisory Commission's failure to deal with the question. After taking care of a number of matters relating to the movement of forces between zones, the meeting, which Zhukov ran as chairman, turned to the Western request for access routes. The Allies wanted the right to use two superhighways (autobahns), three railroad lines, and two airlanes, not exclusively but also not with restrictions, much as highways and other transportation routes would be used anywhere else in the world. Zhukov, amiably enough, declared that these requests seemed excessive; "the necessity of protecting these roads and lanes," he declared, would pose for the Soviets "an extremely difficult administrative problem." One central rail line (Magdeburg-Berlin) and one highway, also running through Magdeburg, both for exclusive Western use, ought to be enough, said the marshal. He presented what seemed a reasonable enough argument: the movement of Soviet forces in their zone would create enough congestion without two other armies possibly using the same routes at the same times, and in any case, if the arrangement turned out to be unsatisfactory, the Allied Control Council could take a fresh look at it.

As a drama, the meeting took the shape of the Western generals proposing and Zhukov disposing. Clay and Weeks settled for Zhukov's proposal as a temporary arrangement; unfortunately, however, the two Western generals emerged from the session with no signatures, nothing on paper. But that was the way Clay wanted it. He shared Winant's and Strang's view, as he wrote a few years later, that accepting specific routes "might be interpreted as a denial of our right of access over all routes." Besides, the Allies were looking toward "establishing quadripartite government, which we hoped would develop better understanding and solve many problems." In other words, the Americans and the British expected various problems and hassles but anticipated no major clashes. As they saw it, they were working with the Russians, not against them, and they did not, Clay said, "fully realize that the requirement of unanimous consent would enable a Soviet veto in the Allied Control Council to block all our future efforts." More immediate problems preoccupied the Western officers—troop movements, refugees, acquiring and delivering food to the millions of people for whom they held responsibility. They gave no thought to any future blockade of the city.

As the Soviet armies advanced into Germany, a great fear preceded them, a single horror expressed in interchangeable words: violation . . . rape . . . *Vergewaltigung.*

As a seven-year-old boy in April 1945, Uwe von Tschammer lived with his mother and younger brother, the three of them sharing the basement of an apartment building with all of the other tenants. Family members would go upstairs to cook a meal or perhaps take a bath, but they warned each other to stay away from the windows, since the Russians were on the lookout for artillery spotters. "If they see anybody moving," an elderly man told them, "they fire direct." And so it proved. When two women took the only available stew pot, a sort of laundry tub, upstairs, they quickly drew enemy fire; neither the room they were in nor the pot survived.

At the beginning of May, word spread along the street: "The Russians are coming, the Russians are coming." The women, most of them older, responded by blackening their faces with dirt; an eighteen-year-old girl was hidden in a side area, behind potato bags. A Soviet officer in dress uniform suddenly appeared in the basement and moved through the area, flashing a light on each woman. "Some of the older women were trying to hold him back," said Uwe, "and I think that gave the young girl away. If they had just sat tight, he would have looked around and left. We heard her crying, and the officer came storming out and the old people spat at him; his uniform was disarranged. After about five minutes everybody made sure he was gone, and then two of the ladies went in the back and got the girl. I can still see her. They dragged her out, literally—she wasn't able to walk—and she was disarranged. So that was our first encounter with the Russians."

"Three of my closer friends committed suicide in the first days of the Soviet occupation," said Ingeborg Dedering, a teenager in Berlin in 1945. "Two of them were young wives who poisoned themselves after they had been mistreated in the worst way by drunken Russian soldiers. The third one, a sixteen-year-old boy, got hold of a Russian gun and shot himself after he had been forced to watch the execution of his father, who had attempted to defend his wife against the Soviets. The first Russian troops mainly consisted of soldiers between seventeen and twenty years of age. There was hardly one who was not drunk, hardly one who did not make use of his gun if he did not get what he wanted: German property and German women." Ingeborg managed to stay out of the way for days by hiding in a potato box in the basement of the house; her father would bring her a piece of bread when he could. "Occasionally the door to the completely dark room was opened, and Soviet soldiers appeared with flashlights searching for something worthwhile to be taken along. None thought the heaps of frozen potatoes on the floor or the wooden box in the corner appealing." Ingeborg, who had spent the entire war in the city, declared: "If I had a choice between the very worst that air raids could do and the entry of Russian soldiers into Berlin, I would choose bombing without a moment's hesitation."

"We were half-starved," said Karin Hueckstaedt, who was twelve in 1945, "and we had just been through a war and gotten beaten to death by the Russians in the end. But the fighting for Berlin was so fierce because they wanted to hold off the Russians long enough for the Americans to come." Having no access to the Allied higher councils, the Berliners did not know that the Red armies alone would take Berlin—and would have the city to themselves for two full months. Questioned about this period, Karin said, "I don't really want to go into it, but it was pretty gruesome." Women quickly learned to dread the sound of the only two German words many of the soldiers knew: *"Frau . . . komm!"*

In the early days a friend of Karin's mother's did some sewing for a Soviet political officer who warned her about worse trouble on the way: the regular soldiers who had taken Berlin would be removed, to be replaced by supply and other secondary troops, many of them "Mongols" and others from the far reaches of the Soviet Union. The officer said, in substance, "Look out for them. They are bad." His advice proved sound. Women followed a basic principle: "Keep your doors locked, and don't make yourself noticed. They were just . . . well, how shall I describe it? It wasn't just that they had won the war, it was just that they were so uncontrollable. Even their own officers couldn't control them. And when they got hold of any kind of alcohol—they drank anything—they were totally . . . it was like they lost their minds." To get a place in line at the bakery, mothers would frequently send their children, sometimes as early as four o'clock in the morning. Soviet soldiers stood alongside, with machine guns trained on the people in line. "Most women sent their children, because if a woman was in line, there was a good chance that some Russian soldier would take a fancy to her and pull her out of line."

"The Russians were always very keen to our fears of them," said Alice Sawadda, a notably beautiful woman who was twenty-one in 1945. "We were very relieved when the Americans and the British came to Berlin. Before that, you didn't dare to go on the street because the Russians would take you and assault you. My mother would not let me go out." Even after the Western forces arrived, she said, she was "once in a very dangerous situation—a Russian soldier took me from behind and tried to take me, but

I screamed and other people walked by, and nothing happened. This happened to many women." Before the Anglo-Americans came, she had not dared to leave the house at all. With her father killed in an air raid near the end of the war, her brother missing, her mother chronically ill, and her family home bombed out, she had no way to raise money since she had nothing to sell on the black market. As soon as she could, she got a job at the Siemens plant, eighteen kilometers from her house. "When I rode a bicycle to work, I was always anxious on my way," she said.

Another woman, Charlotte Beelitz, had a particularly strong memory of April 23, 1945, when two Russian soldiers dragged her and another woman upstairs in a building. "One went to the right with the other girl and the other into the left apartment with me," Charlotte said. She walked straight to the window, using her hand to feel whether any glass remained in it—"there was no window anymore." When the Russian closed the door, Charlotte "grabbed hold of the wooden part of the window which forms the cross and jumped straight onto the road"—thirty feet below. She was in shock for a while, she said, but soon began working again. The other woman, a girl of seventeen, was raped and needed continuing medical care. Unlike Alice Sawadda, Charlotte did not stay in the house until the Western Allies arrived. The tactic she and people she knew used was to make themselves look ugly, by smearing dirt or coal dust on their faces and swathing their heads in scarves. This method did not solve all problems: "Russian soldiers tried again and again to get to a German woman, so, for example, when citizens noticed some Russian soldiers were approaching a German woman, they took pots and pans and made a lot of noise by banging them against each other, and when other neighbors heard them, they joined in." This katzenjammer was supposed to draw the attention of Soviet officers, who, the people hoped, would put a stop to the behavior of the soldiers.

Another Berliner, Hans-Karl Behrend, who had been drafted into the Volkssturm in 1944 at fifteen, was wounded during an air raid and discharged in March 1945. In April, when the Russians arrived at the family home in Zehlendorf in southwest Berlin, the grandfather had sent the boy's mother up into the attic, which did not have stairs leading to it; the others then hid the ladder. "It was fortunate we took this precaution," Behrend said. "With other houses and other families, things were worse." Fortunately, as well, the grandfather had served in Russia in World War I and remembered some Russian words, so that one night when Russian soldiers tried to break into the house, he cried "Help, help!" and the soldiers moved on.

One night after many weeks of Soviet occupation, as her family sat inside behind their locked doors, Karin Hueckstadt watched through the window as the Russians "did their usual thing," making a fire in the middle of the street, singing, and getting drunk. But the next morning, to their amazement, "there were no Russians." The Berliners had no source of news to tell them what had happened, but after a while the residents of the building went downstairs and out into the street, wondering where the Russians had gone. Then "around the corner—I will never forget it until the day I die—came the first American jeep I ever saw. And I will never forget that it was a black sergeant that was driving it. And other Americans came after that." The people had feared that the district, called Britz, on the eastern side of Neukölln, would form part of the Soviet sector, but fortune put the boundary between sectors just east of it. "I can't describe it to you," Karin said. "When the Americans came, we could hardly believe our good luck. We were exhilarated." After a while the people felt their joy waning somewhat when they learned that the newcomers wanted one of the large buildings on the street for a headquarters, which meant that its occupants would have to find new lodgings. But that proved to be a minor point: "The Americans were always appreciated in Berlin, very much so."

Though the Russians had offered all sorts of blandishments—promises of coal and food—to induce Berliners to move to the East, they found few takers. Karin's mother offered one reason, having nothing to do with warmth and shelter. Shortly after taking the city, the Russians had opened movie theaters, which showed only Russian movies. Delighted at this chance for entertainment, Karin's mother took her daughter to see what turned out to be "from the best I could tell, about a tractor driver." During the screening a Russian female soldier stood up front and narrated—not translating the sound track but simply describing the action the members of the audience could see with their own eyes: "Here comes Ivan driving the tractor. Now Ivan gets off the tractor, and here comes Natasha and he hugs Natasha. . . ." After enduring this spectacle for a while, Karin's mother led her daughter out of the theater, saying, "If I have to live with this kind of culture for the rest of my life, I'm going to kill myself."

In July, when the U.S. Second Armored Division moved into Berlin, Hans-Karl Behrend was standing nearby when a sergeant yelled, "Well, can't you help unload the truck?" Having studied English and also, through radio, having become a fan of Glenn Miller and Tommy Dorsey, "I was happy to do this," said Behrend, "particularly to see whether an English-speaking person was able to understand my English." Not only did his work prove satisfactory, but he was invited to go through the chow line. After some NCOs had noticed the portions he was stowing away, they asked whether he would like second helpings. "They were very polite about it, but apparently they had never seen a single person devouring such an amount of food." Since his school was "out of business," as he put it, he took a job working KP for the Americans. Although there was officially no fraternization at the time, he had a friendly relationship with his employers. Then the company moved out for two days; when the men came back, the mood had changed. He and a friend who worked with him "saw at once that there was a hostility toward us. We were only given orders—there was to be no talking." Later he learned that the men had been taken to see a Nazi concentration camp.

The people of Germany and Berlin had been primed to sense the coming of the Russians as the advance of a barbarous Asiatic tide, the realization of fears that had always gripped the people of the Mark, living on the exposed flank of metropolitan Europe. In 1914 panic at the presence of Russians on East Prussian soil had caused the German high command to pull troops out of France and ship them eastward, thus throwing away the chance of victory in the West. In the latter stages of World War II, Dr. Goebbels's propagandists had attempted to stiffen Berlin's defenders by warning them of the fate awaiting their wives and children if they fell into the hands of the Russians. Certainly during the two months in 1945 in which they held absolute control over all of Berlin, the Soviets did their zealous best to even the score for the maniacal cruelty with which the SS *Einsatzgruppen* and other Nazi organizations had treated Russians during the war. One heard few echoes of Czarina Alexandra's wish to her husband in 1914 that "our troops should behave exemplarily in every sense and not rob and pillage—leave that horror to the Prussian troops." Had not Marshal Zhukov told his soldiers: "Woe to the land of the murderers. We will get our terrible revenge for everything"?

In commenting on Ingeborg Dedering's story, an editor of the time thought he ought to point out that these were "the impressions of a young girl, and that soldiers—even our own American troops—have often gone to extremes after a city has been captured." Western troops in Germany indeed engaged in a great deal of sexual activity with German women, who were "willing and, during the early period of the occupation when the proportion of females was so high in relation to German males, even eager to engage in sexual relations with American males." Incidents of rape did occur, though they were uncommon; these actions commonly took place in a context of vulgarities and black-market dealings of one kind or another—Western occupiers had few claims to sainthood. But the breadth and the texture of endless testimony from Berliners reveals something far more pervasive and persistent at work with the Red Army—and this testimony comes, of course, not only from those who survived but from those who did not have the worst experiences; those who suffered most simply will not relive the nightmare. The factual record is plain as well. In East Prussia, as the army advanced, it was common for Soviet soldiers to rape every female over the age of twelve or thirteen in a village; "the reports of women subjected to gang rapes and ghastly night rapes are far too numerous to be considered isolated incidents." A Soviet captain who tried to control a group of soldiers on the rampage found himself accused of "bourgeois humanism." A fellow young officer, Alexander Solzhenitsyn, described a looted house: "The little daughter's on the mattress, / Dead. How many have been on it / A platoon, a company perhaps?"

"The taking of Berlin was accompanied by an unrestrained explosion of sexual violence by Soviet soldiers," as one historian described it. Summing up the common experience, the mayor of one Berlin district said that "innumerable cases of rape occurred daily. A woman could not escape unless she kept in hiding." In the view of some analysts, the Russian soldiers saw themselves as retaliating for their humiliating early defeats in the war and for the Germans' arrogant racial attitudes. The Soviet soldier, who had always been told that the West was a world of deprivation, also saw with surprise and anger the luxury even of bombed and defeated Germany, as compared with his own shabby and primitive homeland: these were the high and mighty people who had needlessly brought fire and destruction to poor Russia. As a historian of the Soviet occupation summed it up, "The resulting combination of an inferiority complex, a desire for revenge, and the occupation of Germany was humiliating if not deadly for German women." These feelings of inferiority and resentment perhaps accounted for the remarkable number of instances in which soldiers raped a woman in front of her husband and then killed them both: to do its whole job and make its statement, rape had to be a public business. But these explanations do not account for the truly wild behavior of the second wave—the non-combat troops—the Tatar and other Far Eastern soldiers, hardly more Russian than German. Many observers, including the officer who had given the warning about them, seemed to regard them as Asians who would consider the sexual use of women as simply a natural reward of victory.

In any case, the behavior of Soviet soldiers in Germany did not arrive without ample historical precedents. In medieval times Russian armies customarily raped the women of a defeated foe—it was the greatest insult one could deliver to an enemy. In the Germany of the postwar years, this particular Russian insult, aside from its intrinsic horrors, would produce important political consequences.

In early July, a few days after U.S. and British forces began their belated arrival in Berlin to occupy their sectors of the city, an American reporter, surveying the scene, eavesdropped on two girls who stood on Unter den Linden, staring through an iron gate that closed off the path to a small, smashed-up limestone building. Inside the building stood a slab of black granite, the Ehrenmal, that bore an inscription honoring the Prussians who died in World War I. The wreath that had once sat atop the slab had fallen to the ground, and it and the slab itself were smeared and littered with muck and debris.

"*Ach, ja,* poor Berlin," said one of the girls. "How they beat us to pieces!" Then after a moment, carrying their rucksacks filled with wood, the girls moved on. They carried sacks for wood because Berlin had no gas, no coal, and no oil; the people had to burn wood from ruined buildings, and, said the reporter, "they have no trouble finding plenty." Most of the nearby buildings on the avenue, even if they looked reasonably intact from the outside, were only gutted shells; the fire that consumed the famous Adlon Hotel was said to have been fed by the 400,000 bottles in Herr Adlon's treasured wine cellar.

Because the Russians had forbidden the sale of tobacco in Berlin, cigarettes had become the hottest medium of exchange. A single cigarette cost as much as twenty marks—two dollars at the official rate—but a pack of Chesterfields could bring as much as ninety dollars. You could have money, however, without having a whole cigarette: "Remain solitary on a Berlin street while you smoke a cigarette, and likely as not you will soon have around you a circle of children, able-bodied men, and whiskered old men, all waiting to dive for the butt when you throw it away." Practically everybody in Berlin seemed to be engaged in the practice of *Kippensamm-lung,* or butt collecting; *Kippen* could be exchanged for goods and services just as if they were cash.

Encountering this tobacco-based economy, an American officer wondered when a cigarette was actually smoked by anybody. "Since it was a fairly fragile item," he said, "it was evident that, sooner or later, it was going to have to stop being money and start being a cigarette if its value was not to be lost completely." This officer, perhaps without realizing it, had identified what would become one of the most divisive problems of the occupation of Germany. What, indeed, would replace the cigarette?

CHAPTER 3

To the Fantasy House

IT WAS THE Berlin of *Frau . . . komm!* and *Kippensammlung* that President Harry S. Truman, Prime Minister Winston Churchill, and Premier Joseph Stalin chose as the site for the last Big Three meeting of World War II. The leaders would hold their full-scale sessions in a palace that had been the fantasy home of a prince whose world had long since vanished.

In June 1905 Kaiser Wilhelm's oldest son, Crown Prince Wilhelm, had married Duchess Cecilie of Mecklenburg-Schwerin. Though this prince was to hold titular command of one of the German armies on the Western Front in World War I, he was a frivolous young egotist with a most unmilitary swagger—hands on hips, cap at a rakish angle, tunic nipped in at the waist. Proving, perhaps, that no man can be a hero to his dentist, he not only had no idea of punctuality, said Dr. Arthur Davis, but was "such a physical coward that it was almost impossible to work on him satisfactorily." Disdainful of such civilian niceties as traffic laws, the crown prince was "the despair of the traffic policemen and the taxi-drivers and private chauffeurs," once going so fast that his car leaped the curb and crashed into a lamppost. Besides, like his father he had "an inordinate love for posing in public." He also had the bizarre and somewhat antisocial habit of greeting an acquaintance with a penetrating stare and a handshake so sudden and vigorous that it often threw the other person off balance.

Having agreed that the princely couple should have a fitting home of their own in Potsdam, the Hohenzollern pleasure-dome suburb some eighteen miles from the center of Berlin, the Kaiser ordained the creation of a palace to be christened the Cecilienhof, after his daughter-in-law. Construction began in 1913, and during the following years, while the German armies grappled in mortal struggle with the forces of Britain, France, and Russia, workmen in Potsdam spent their days putting up what proved to be the last royal palace built in Europe, a 176-room stone-wood-and-stucco *ersatz* Tudor—a German writer called it Scottish—country house. Had it been built three-quarters of a century later, the Cecilienhof would surely have found itself in Disney World. With its "mock-Elizabethan windows and stone portals that appear embarrassed by their lack of moats and drawbridges," as one writer described it, the Cecilienhof made a suitably frivolous home for a frivolous prince.

The family took up residence in 1917, the year in which German strategy—the unrestricted submarine campaign against merchant shipping—and German policy—the plan to lure the Mexicans into attacking the United States in order to win back their "lost provinces"—combined to bring the Americans into the war and thus to tip the balance against Germany. Before the end of the next year, the Kaiser had fled the country, and the crown prince, also chosing exile, had lost his fanciful new home. But after five years the Weimar government relented and allowed the prince to return to Germany and his various residences, including the Cecilienhof. At the beginning of the Nazi regime, ten years later, the crown prince posed for a photo in a Nazi uniform and told an interviewer that Hitler had "saved the Reich from Bolshevism." Soon, however, he declared his view of the Führer as "a demagogue and a little philistine," and he remained at home, more or less out of politics, through the Nazi era.

During the Weimar years, Potsdam had served as a suburban retreat for members of the Berlin film industry, and along with its many palaces—including, besides the Cecilienhof, Frederick the Great's famous Sans Souci, and the 700-foot-long New Palace (the Kaiser's favorite residence, also built by Frederick)—the town had numerous opulent private houses dating back through the preceding two centuries. In 1945, though many of its buildings showed damage from bombing, Potsdam seemed almost intact compared with devastated Berlin. Hence, when the Soviets, as masters of the area, sought a site for an inter-Allied conference, Marshal Zhukov suggested that the political officials in charge look into Potsdam and the neighboring suburb of Babelsberg, the prewar residence of "prominent government officials, generals and many other noted Fascist leaders." Practically undamaged, Babelsberg offered comfortable villas, with greenery and flowers, that could serve as residences and office quarters for the participants in the conference and their staffs. The Cecilienhof, located nearby, would provide a main conference hall and workrooms for experts and advisers.

The Potsdam area also possessed an advantage of great importance to the Soviets: it lay in their assigned zone of occupation, yet it was close to the Western sectors of Berlin. The Americans and the British declared that this time, however, they would provide for their own needs; they were willing to meet in Soviet-controlled territory, as they had at Yalta, but they would not come again as houseguests of the Russians.

In the early afternoon of Sunday, July 15, Prime Minister Winston Churchill, concluding a brief vacation in the south of France, boarded a plane at
Bordeaux to fly to Berlin. Having sought the Potsdam Conference for
"grave discussions on which the immediate future of the world depends,"
Churchill carried with him a complex of concerns. His French holiday had
followed an election campaign that ended on July 5, when British voters
went to the polls to make their choice between Churchill's Conservatives
and the Labour Party, led by Clement Attlee. Owing to the time required to
collect and count absentee ballots from soldiers, he would not know the
results for three weeks; the Conservative leaders and people in general
expected, however, a reasonably comfortable victory for the great war
leader who for almost everybody seemed in his person to symbolize the
victory. One observer who had no doubts about the identity of the winner-
to-be was Joseph Stalin, who took it for granted that since Churchill had
called the election, he would also control the outcome.

　　Apart from his personal political concerns, Churchill felt great anxiety
over the situation on the Continent. Just four days after Marshal Zhukov
and Sir Arthur Tedder had presided over the German surrender in Berlin,
the prime minister expressed his worries in a telegram to President Truman,
who had now been in office exactly one month. After remarking that he had
always worked for friendship with Russia (that is, presumably, during the
war), Churchill pointed to the Soviets' "misinterpretation of the Yalta
decisions, their attitude towards Poland, their overwhelming influence in
the Balkans . . . the difficulties they make about Vienna, the combination of
Russian power and the territories under their control or occupied, coupled
with the Communist technique in so many other countries, and above all
their power to maintain very large armies in the field for a long time."

　　Behind these explicit concerns rose Churchill's vision of a Europe with
the American armies back on their own side of the Atlantic and hence no
sizable force on the Continent to oppose the Red Army or to influence the
thinking of its masters. At Yalta FDR and Churchill had fought with Stalin
for the democratization, at least to some degree, of the puppet regime he
had established in Poland, and they had advocated the adoption of a U.S.-
drafted document called the Declaration on Liberated Europe, designed to
allay American public fears that representative democratic governments in
Eastern and Southeastern Europe were being aborted by Soviet control
before they could even begin to emerge. In this declaration the Allies
pledged themselves to help create interim governments that would be
broadly representative of all democratic elements in the populations of
liberated areas and to facilitate the holding of elections. Stalin had accepted

the declaration, but neither in Poland nor elsewhere in Eastern Europe did the Yalta agreements seem to affect actual Soviet conduct. Indeed, Stalin had seen to it that sixteen non-Communist Polish leaders were invited, under safe conduct, to a meeting at Marshal Zhukov's headquarters and then were clapped in jail for "diversionary activities." In Austria, one of the troubled areas to which Churchill pointed, the Russians had unilaterally set up a government as soon as their troops entered the country and had ordered Allied missions out of Vienna. Churchill could feel, he later wrote, "the vast manifestation of Soviet and Russian imperialism rolling forward over helpless lands."

On an immediately practical level, the American and British commanders in Germany could get little information about the nature and significance of Soviet troop movements. More generally, Churchill expressed his concern to Truman that the Western Allies did not know what was happening in all the Soviet-controlled areas. He expressed this concern in a metaphor that, though confined for the time being to top-secret correspondence, would within a year be on its way not only to becoming an identifying phrase of the cold war but to signifying a geographical reality as palpable as the English Channel or the Rhine. The Allies lacked information about activities in the Soviet areas, Churchill said, because "an *iron curtain* is drawn down upon their front" (italics supplied). In view of all the problems, the prime minister, with a note almost of desperation, declared that British and American forces should not withdraw to their assigned zones of occupation—and thereby discard their strongest bargaining counter—before the Western Allies could come to an understanding with the Soviet Union. To reach such an understanding, the leaders must have a personal meeting. So began the negotiations and preparations that led the Big Three to Potsdam in July.

Well before the conference began, however, Churchill had lost the argument about withdrawing the troops.

At 9:50 in the evening of July 6, just the eighty-fifth day since he had taken the oath of office after the shocking news of FDR's death, President Harry S. Truman boarded a special train at Washington's Union Station for the trip to Newport News, Virginia, where the heavy cruiser *Augusta* lay waiting to receive the presidential party. At seven the next morning, with the president, Secretary of State James F. Byrnes, Fleet Admiral William D. Leahy, and other officials aboard, the *Augusta* got under way, bound across the Atlantic for Antwerp. Mrs. Truman, the president noted in his diary, "wasn't happy about my going to see Mr. Russia and Mr. Great Britain—neither am

I." He had even stronger thoughts about his mission: "How I hate this trip! But I have to make it—win, lose or draw—and we must win. I'm not working for any interest but the Republic of the United States." Truman had been to Europe once before, in 1918, when he served as a Missouri National Guard artillery battery commander in France.

In the morning after that fateful April evening when he succeeded to the powers and responsibilities long held by Roosevelt, the most commanding American political figure of the century, Truman had freely spoken of his apprehensions. "If you fellows ever pray, pray for me," he said to reporters, and he declared that he felt as if "the house, the stars, and all the planets" had fallen on him. In his first visit to the White House map room, whose innocuous name gave no hint of its function as the top-secret code room, the new president had looked calm and confident as he received his first briefing, but a young officer sitting nearby saw that his legs were trembling violently. Yet early in his presidency, Truman showed signs of making a rapid adjustment to the mighty office he had inherited. Seeing him in a newsreel for the first time, a high school girl felt a sense of relief. She had been afraid for the country after FDR's death, she said years later, but the sight of "that cocky little guy striding along in his double-breasted suit and his white shoes" reassured her. "I suddenly felt," she said, "that everything was going to be all right."

Admiral Leahy, a former chief of naval operations and a properly gruff old sea dog, had served President Roosevelt during the war as chief of staff to the commander in chief. In contrast to the new president, whose sudden accession found him almost virginally inexperienced in the realms of high policy, Leahy had attended all the Allied conferences since Casablanca and knew all the secrets that passed through the White House map room; he even had the only copy of the Yalta agreement. Realizing his need for such an experienced counselor, Truman had prevailed on the admiral to stay on the job. Together with Harry Hopkins, Leahy had given Truman intensive tutoring in Allied affairs, "spending hours with him, while he dug, as though cramming for final exams, into the conference records of Casablanca, Cairo, Teheran, Quebec, and Yalta."

With Secretary of State Byrnes the president had a different kind of relationship. A devoted man of the Senate, to which he had first been elected in 1934 and in which he felt happily at home, Truman had expected to end his political career in that august club, and before the 1944 Democratic Party convention, he had agreed to make a vice-presidential nominating speech for his longtime friend Byrnes. A former senator himself, Byrnes had also served on the Supreme Court, and for most of the war, as "assistant president," he had directed the national home-front mobilization. The Democratic kingmakers had other plans for the vice presidency, however, and Roosevelt had agreed to accept Truman, their choice; in fact, he refused to let the Missouri senator beg off. "You tell him," FDR said to Bob Hannegan, the Democratic chairman, "if he wants to break up the Democratic Party in the middle of a war, that's his responsibility."

Partly by way of compensating Byrnes for his having been shunted aside, Truman had decided to make his friend secretary of state; the appointment became effective just two weeks before the departure for Potsdam. But the relationship of the two men had a fatal flaw: one was president of the United States, and the other believed, without making much of a secret of it, that *he* ought to be president—indeed, that he would have been president had he not been cheated out of the job by the incumbent. "Under such circumstances," said Charles E. Bohlen, one of the leading Foreign Service officers, "Byrnes believed that he held an independent position as Secretary of State." He would have been less than pleased had he been able to peek into Truman's diary and see himself characterized as the "able and conniving Secretary of State."

At a few minutes past ten o'clock in the morning of July 15, the *Augusta* moored to the municipal pier at Antwerp. After receiving a welcome from General Eisenhower and other high-level officers, Truman and his entourage set out in a long motorcade for the thirty-five-mile drive to the Brussels airport. Pausing briefly for a review of the honor guard, the party then departed in three four-engine C-54 transports for Berlin, and by five o'clock in the afternoon, Truman had arrived at his quarters for the Potsdam Conference, a three-story stucco house with an imperial address—2 Kaiserstrasse, the street running along the Griebnitzsee, a clear and inviting arm of the Havel River—in the area of Babelsberg called Neubabelsberg. The building, which looked "purely German," reminded the president of Union Station in Kansas City.

As they had done everywhere else in the area, the Russians had completely stripped the house—"not even a tin spoon left," the president commented—and then had replaced the furniture with an eclectic mix of pieces. In his bedroom, said Truman, "there is a birdseye maple wardrobe and an oak chest matching the two ton sideboard." The president believed, as he wrote in his memoirs, that the house had belonged to the German film czar, who supposedly had been shipped off to a labor camp in the Soviet Union. But after his book appeared, Truman received a letter from the grandson of the German publisher who had built the house in 1896. "Ten weeks before you entered this house," wrote Herr Mueller-Grote, "its tenants were living in constant fright and fear. By day and by night plundering Russian soldiers went in and out, raping my sisters before their own parents and children, beating up my old parents." Far from being away in Russia when the president arrived, said Mueller-Grote, the proprietor of the house "lived, with his wife, no more than 500 yards away, in miserable surroundings." Throughout eastern Germany, the Americans saw how the people dreaded the Russians like conquerors of old, Oriental barbarians dedicated to pillage and rape.

At eleven in the morning of the day following his arrival, President Truman received a call from a distinguished guest and his party. It was the first meeting of the new president and the man who, as the spirit of British defiance of Nazi Germany, had during the war become a great hero to Americans. Winston Churchill, eager to meet Roosevelt's successor, arrived with an entourage including not only Anthony Eden and Sir Alexander Cadogan, but his daughter Mary, a member of the forces who frequently came with him on trips. Churchill later, in an often-quoted sentence, described his initial reaction to the president; he was "impressed with his gay, precise, sparkling manner and obvious power of decision." (The British diplomat Sir William Hayter, describing Truman at Potsdam, not only had a similar reaction but used almost the same language, calling the president "perky, precise and very definite in his manner.")

In his diary entry for the day, Truman made a great effort to tell himself that he had not fallen under the spell of this titan of the twentieth century. "He gave me a lot of hooey about how great my country is," wrote the president, "and how he loved Roosevelt and how he intended to love me etc. etc." He added: "I am sure we can get along if he doesn't try to give me too much soft soap. You know soft soap is made of ash hopper lye and it burns to beat hell when it gets into the eyes. It's fine for chigger bites but not so good for rose complexions. But I haven't a rose complexion." Truman conceded that he and Churchill "had a most pleasant conversation," but defensiveness provided the keynote of his diary reflections—the boy from Missouri told himself that he was not going to be taken in by this transatlantic slicker.

At about twelve-thirty the two statesmen ended their conversation— they talked no business, Truman said; the visit had been a "courtesy call," official spokesmen told the two hundred reporters quartered in the press camp outside the restricted area—and Churchill strolled off toward his quarters at 23 Ringstrasse, about two blocks north of the "Little White House." A few minutes later an old friend of the president's, Fred Canfil, who had been a sergeant in Truman's Battery D in France in 1918 and had come along on this trip as a "pro-tem" member of the Secret Service detail, paid a call of his own. He suggested that, since Stalin's absence had delayed the start of the conference, the president make the most of the unplanned afternoon off by seeing Berlin for himself. (According to Truman, Canfil was "the most vigilant bodyguard a President ever had. While the conferences were going on, he would stand by a window with his arms folded and scowl out the window at everybody who passed in the street, as if he would eat them alive if they bothered the President of the United States.")

The president liked the plan, and at 3:40 reporters on watch saw his car drive out of the restricted area and head for the autobahn leading into Berlin. The presidential party, which included Leahy and Byrnes, made a stop almost immediately, to acknowledge the greeting of the Second Armored (Hell on Wheels) Division, the largest armored division in the world, drawn up along one side of the road. With hat off, Truman accepted the salutes and then awarded a citation to an engineer company for its achievement in having spanned the Rhine under fire. "I am only sorry," the president said, "that I didn't get a chance to participate in some phase of this war myself." The party then sped into Berlin, passing under the Brandenburg Gate, where the president drew a salute by Colonel-General Alexander Gorbatov, the Soviet commander of the city. The presidential car then proceeded past the Reichstag and stopped outside the shattered hulk of the Reich chancellery that Albert Speer had created for the Führer only six years earlier. More depressing than the sight of the ruined buildings, the president wrote, was "the deluded Hitlerian populace"—the "old men, old women, young women, children from tots to teens carrying packs, pushing carts, pulling carts, evidently ejected by the conquerors and carrying what they could of their belongings to nowhere in particular." The president saw history's continuing patterns of destruction, from Babylon and Nineveh to Carthage and Rome and now Berlin, as poor auguries for peace in the coming years.

On the walk home from the Little White House, Churchill told his daughter that he "liked the president immensely—[we] talk the same language." He went on to say he was sure he could work with Truman, Mary wrote her mother: "I nearly wept for joy and thankfulness." After lunch, Churchill, like Truman, decided to take advantage of the unexpected postponement of the first session of the conference. Just about ten minutes after Truman left the Reich chancellery, a British party including the prime minister and Eden drove up to the ruins. Unlike Truman, who had stayed in his car, Churchill spent half an hour stalking through the ruins of the chancellery, taking a close look at Hitler's office and going down into the stench of the underground bunker to see the room in which his adversary had committed suicide. "This is what would happened to us if *they* had won the war," Churchill said to an aide, biting on his cigar. "We would have been the bunker."

Upstairs, Eden pointed to a shattered room, saying, "I had dinner with Hitler right over there in 1935."

"You certainly paid for that dinner, Anthony," Churchill growled in response. As usual in exchanges with his foreign secretary, the prime minister had managed to have the last word.

On arriving in Babelsberg to perform his duties at his third Big Three conference, Colonel Charles Donnelly, a secretary of the U.S. Joint Staff Planners, found the town reminiscent of Pine Lake, a suburb of Detroit, back in his home state of Michigan, with "the same kind of relaxing atmosphere" and its inviting lake; the houses charmed him with their carved wooden gables and varnished beams set in stucco. One fact Colonel Donnelly noted immediately: "The only humans in sight were Russian soldiers; it was a ghost town, as I found out later." Donnelly and three of his colleagues were quartered in a comfortable house that had belonged to "upper-middle-class people with excellent taste"; the colonel drew what had obviously been the daughter's bedroom. Looking at the family portraits that still hung on the walls, he "had an ambivalent feeling toward this unseen family." They were citizens of a country that had embarked on a war costing many millions of lives and untold anguish and suffering and had treated the people in occupied countries with extreme harshness. Still, the family "had been evicted from their home with only two hours' notice and allowed to take only such clothing and small possessions as they could carry or drag on a small cart." The colonel wondered where they had gone and what they were living on and "how many times had the daughter been raped by Russian soldiers."

Later, driving through the center of Potsdam, Donnelly discovered what had become of some of the people who had been expelled from their homes for the convenience of the Allied delegations. Small groups of men and women, clearly middle class, dressed as if going to the office or to museums for the afternoon, were picking up rubble from the sidewalks and streets. The Soviets, it appeared, had issued a no work–no eat order that applied to everybody except small children and those too sick to perform such labor.

During his first day of work, Donnelly made another discovery. The Joint Staff Planners had been given office space in what had been a nunnery ("God knows what has become of those unfortunate women," Donnelly wrote); their bosses, the Joint Chiefs of Staff, held meetings in a house across the street. When he went to lunch on his first day, Donnelly took a shortcut from the JCS building through the rear garden to the house in which the mess was located. Just outside the back door rose a mound of earth that looked exactly like a fresh grave. When the Russians were preparing the Babelsberg area for the conference, Donnelly learned, they had given the occupants of this house their standard two hours' notice. The *Hausfrau* had complied, leaving in due time, but then came back to retrieve some precious possession or keepsake. When the Red Army soldier guarding the house refused to let her go back in, she began to argue, and the guard shot her. She was buried on the spot. The story took the edge off Donnelly's appetite.

Joseph Stalin came late to Potsdam. On meeting President Truman at noon on July 17, the generalissimo (he had conferred this new title on himself just three weeks earlier) apologized for the delay. He explained that he had been held up by talks with the Chinese. "I wanted to fly," Stalin said, "but the doctors forbade it." Some Westerners ascribed the one-day delay instead to a mild heart attack. Stalin's later biographer Dmitri Volkogonov declared, however, that the generalissimo had made his late entrance purely to enhance his importance; he liked this device well enough to use it more than once. In any case, Stalin's remark about having wanted to fly had little truth to it. In 1943, before the Big Three had settled on Tehran as the site of their first conference, Stalin had rejected all proposals for a site farther from his headquarters on the grounds that he had to stay close to home to direct the war; he had chosen not to mention that he had never flown and dreaded the experience. After making his relatively short, one and only flight to Tehran, during which he clung terrified to his armrests, Stalin had resolved never again to undergo such a threatening experience. Hence he had made the journey to Potsdam by train.

So marked a fear of assassination gripped Stalin that Lavrenty Beria, head of the secret police (then called the NKVD), mounted a major operation to get his chief to Potsdam and take care of him there. The precautions included lining the 1,200-mile route with more than 18,000 troops; eight armored trains would also patrol the track. In Potsdam a force equivalent to eight regiments would provide security. At Babelsberg, where the leaders would live during the conference, Stalin would have a fifteen-room house. And, Beria added enticingly, "stocks of game, poultry, delicacies, groceries, and drink have been laid in," and "two bakeries are at work."

After taking up residence in Babelsberg, Stalin had himself driven the few miles to the Cecilienhof, past double lines of guards all along the route. Perhaps not realizing that the crown prince's fantasy house had not been the residence of the Kaiser himself, the generalissimo declared himself unimpressed. "Hmm, nothing much. A modest palace," he declared, adding, with paradoxical loyalty, "Russian tsars built themselves something much more solid!"

At noon on Tuesday, July 17, the circle of Big Three acquaintanceship was completed when Stalin paid his call on Truman. The president noted his surprise at the generalissimo's height—only five feet five or six inches. Although the plan did not include lunch, Truman invited the generalissimo to stay; Stalin said that he couldn't. "You could if you wanted to," Truman recalled himself saying, whereupon Stalin accepted the invitation. "I told Stalin that I am no diplomat," Truman recorded, "but usually said yes & no to questions after hearing all the argument. It pleased him." Indeed, Truman found the generalissimo polite and good-humored, and the two discussed Spain, China, the Italian colonies, and the Soviet Union's participation in the war against Japan, which, Stalin promised, would come on August 15. "I can deal with Stalin," Truman concluded. "He is honest—but smart as hell."

The president of the United States had now met "Mr. Britain" and "Mr. Russia." In a few hours their first formal session would begin.

CHAPTER 4

Veils of Understanding

AT TEHRAN AND Yalta, round tables had served as centerpieces of the Big Three meetings; having neither head nor foot, they endowed no national leader with status higher than that of his peers. In accordance with this precedent, the statesmen at Potsdam came together at a big round table that had been moved into the banquet hall of the Cecilienhof, across from a large, many-paned bay window. The table had room for fifteen—five from each of the three delegations—with chairs placed in an outer ring for advisers and assistants and small tables for members of the secretariat. Usually each of the Big Three sat in the middle of his delegation, with his foreign minister and another adviser on his right and his interpreter and another adviser on his left. Besides President Truman, the American group normally included Secretary of State Byrnes, Admiral Leahy, Bohlen (then an assistant to Byrnes, who served as interpreter), and Joseph E. Davies (a former—and very friendly—ambassador to the Soviet Union) or Averell Harriman (the ambassador at the time of the conference). Churchill was flanked by Foreign Secretary Eden; the leader of the Labour Party, Clement Attlee, who, in a courteous and constructive move, had been included by Churchill in the party; Sir Alexander Cadogan, the permanent undersecretary at the Foreign Office; and Major Arthur Birse, the interpreter. Sir Archibald Clark Kerr and Sir William Strang (the British representative on the European Advisory Commission) also participated in the meetings, though in nonspeaking roles—in the plenary sessions, indeed, the heads of government themselves did almost all of the talking. Molotov; Vyshinsky; Andrei Gromyko, a rising young diplomat who served as Soviet ambassador in Washington; and V. N. Pavlov, the interpreter, normally sat with Stalin, whose one-of-a-kind generalissimo's uniform caused a British diplomat to liken him to "the Emperor of Austria in a bad musical comedy; cream jacket with gold-braided collar, blue trousers with a red stripe and one jewelled order."

The three national leaders peered across the big table at each other through veils of limited understanding, and sometimes they heard each other's words with no comprehension at all. Even the two Western representatives, though from English-speaking democracies that had created the most intimate alliance of major powers in modern history, often gave different connotations to political and economic terms and had differing perceptions of the realities that confronted them in Europe. Yet in spite of such differences, the British prime minister and the American president belonged to a common world of discourse. When, for instance, they spoke of a free election, they had no need to define the term for each other. Although Gromyko overstated the case in saying that the two Western leaders "understood each other almost intuitively"—he was building up a case for claiming Anglo-American hostility to Soviet policies and actions, and he certainly had not peeked into Truman's diary—he nevertheless had a sound point.

As events since the Yalta Conference had seemed to show, either Joseph Stalin gave different—non-Western, Communist—definitions to terms like *democracy* and *free election,* or the meanings of such words were matters of indifference to him. Stalin came to the table at Potsdam as the head of a mighty state, though the Western leaders had never, throughout the war, been able to decide exactly how great his authority was. Besides holding the leadership of a great power, the generalissimo reigned as the pope of a worldwide political movement that professed an ideology as detailed and complex as the creed of any supernaturally based religion. The practitioners of this ideology at times made use of such terms as *democracy* and even allowed ostensibly legislative bodies to play a part in government, but behind it all stood the doctrines preached by V. I. Lenin, the guiding spirit of this secular religion. "A parliamentary republic," Lenin had declared, "would be a step backwards"; indeed, said Mark Vishniak, writing a few months after Potsdam, the "dictatorship of the proletariat" called for by Leninist ideologues represented "a flat negation of bourgeois-democratic principles" and must be—as Lenin had frequently said—"won and maintained by the use of violence and unrestricted by any laws." Yet when it suited him, Lenin could boast that the Soviet Union was "a million times more democratic than any bourgeois democracy."

How strong was Stalin's own Leninist faith? The Western leaders could never be quite sure. By the mid-1930s, Soviet political thought, dominated by Stalin, had given a fresh shading to the Marxist-Leninist concept of a dictatorship of the proletariat by speaking of two deserving classes, the proletariat and the peasants, together with a third sector of society, the intelligentsia; but the notion of dictatorship lost none of its force. Andrei Vyshinsky, a legal philosopher as well as a ruthless prosecutor of alleged traitors, called the Soviet constitution drawn up in 1936 at Stalin's direction the "greatest expression of the development of proletarian democracy"; it mandated a one-party USSR controlled by "the most active and politically conscious citizens." The Western statesmen may not have kept themselves well informed about Soviet doctrinal subtleties, but leaving aside the question of one-person rule, they would have agreed with Vishniak that one-party rule could "scarcely be described as government 'by' the people, at least without doing violence to the commonsense meaning of words." Even before the Yalta Conference, President Roosevelt had commented to Harry Hopkins that the Russians didn't seem to use words the way Americans used them, and in the week FDR died, Averell Harriman had told the president in a cable from Moscow that words like *democracy* "had entirely different meanings to the Russians than to us."

Some years earlier a thoughtful Polish observer of Russian culture and society, in expressing a similar thought, had said that "this pitiful fate of a country held by an evil spell, suffering from an awful visitation for which the responsibility cannot be traced either to her sins or her follies, has made Russia as a nation so difficult to understand by Europe." The country had always had "to breathe the atmosphere of despotism; she found nothing but the arbitrary will of an obscure autocrat at the beginning and end of her organisation." And so arose "her impenetrability to whatever is true in Western thought. Western thought, when it crosses her frontier, falls under the spell of her autocracy and becomes a noxious parody of itself." For these and associated reasons, declared this writer, "the Russia of today has not the right to give her voice on a single question touching the future of humanity, because from the very inception of her being the brutal destruction of dignity, of truth, of rectitude, of all that is faithful in human nature has been made the imperative condition of her existence." Written in 1905 by Joseph Conrad, these observations of course had to do with czarist Russia, but within little more than a decade the world would see how the country's new masters not only continued but reinvigorated the national tradition of dressing European ideas in distinctively Russian clothing. "Byzantine complications," wrote Sir William Hayter, "have distorted Western ideas of relative clarity, and Western attempts to understand the result are often defeated."

By the mid-1940s, following the "Great Patriotic War," as Stalin decreed the struggle with Germany should be called, *democracy* had become a popular term in Soviet writing and a popular idea in Soviet political thought. If in the West, in general, the idea of democracy meant rule by the majority with due regard for the wishes of the minority, the twist given the idea in Russia produced the concept of democracy as dictatorship— dictatorship by the ruling class. The crucial difference, explained a Soviet political essayist, I. P. Trainin, was that "the bourgeois state exercises dictatorship in the interests of the propertied minority, and the socialist state in the interests of the overwhelming majority of the people." "The people," however, were not all the people but a selected group: "The term is interpreted to mean people devoid of exploiters, people consisting . . . of workers, peasants, and the Soviet intelligentsia."

The sessions at Yalta in February had done nothing to make Roosevelt change his mind about the existence of a Soviet-Western semantic barrier. The most heated discussions had come over the composition of the postwar Polish government. The Western Allies recognized the government-in-exile, set up in London early in the war and led by prewar political figures. But not long before the meeting at Yalta, the Soviets had recognized the provisional government established by the Committee of National Liberation (the so-called Lublin Committee), which they controlled. Unwilling to see the London Poles frozen out by the Lublin Poles acting at Stalin's direction, Roosevelt and Churchill (chiefly Churchill) argued for a new Polish government that would contain representatives of all the democratic parties; the prime minister doggedly called for a government that would be simultaneously independent, democratic, and—to be sure—friendly to the Soviet Union. Handicapped by the inescapable fact that Poland lay behind Red Army lines, however, and was thus utterly in Soviet control, the Western leaders could do no better than win Stalin's assent to reorganization of the Lublin government "on a broader democratic basis."

Democratic parties, Churchill had insisted; *democratic basis,* Stalin had conceded. What did Stalin mean by what he said, and how much did he believe it? The first question still hung in the air at Potsdam, and the second would never find its full answer in Stalin's lifetime. But part of an answer came during a Big Three discussion concerning the proper fate for Bulgaria, which during the war had functioned as a German satellite. On hearing Churchill call for punishment of the erring Bulgars, Stalin offered an provocative reply. After saying that he did not wish to give his colleagues a lesson on policy, the generalissimo declared that he did not think "policy should be based on considerations of revenge." "We wondered," said Hayter, "what he would say it should be based on; justice, the interests of the masses, the preservation of peace?" Stalin went on: "In my opinion, policy should be based on the calculation of forces." Everybody had always known that, Hayter noted, "but it was interesting to hear it from the horse's mouth." But Stalin's view of Bulgaria had more to it than that: though the Bulgars had been allied with Nazi Germany during the war, they now were undergoing energetic communization; therefore, in Stalin's firm opinion, they now merited protection by the Soviet government rather than attack by the victorious Allies.

For instruction in power-related thinking, the Western leaders might have profited from reading Stalin's curt rebuff of a complaint made in October 1944 by the Yugoslav Communist leader, Marshal Tito, that Bulgarian troops in Serbia were hogging booty seized from the Germans instead of sharing it with the Yugoslavs. "The law of war is such," Stalin brusquely told Tito, "that whoever seizes booty, keeps it." Nor had the British and the Americans eavesdropped on Stalin when he said to Tito a few weeks before Potsdam, "This war is not like those of the past; whoever occupies a territory imposes his own social system on it. Everybody imposes his own system as far as his army can advance. It could not be otherwise." Most succinctly, Stalin had told his foreign minister, V. M. Molotov, that now was "the time to grab everything we could."

These views stood in sharp contrast to comments Stalin made to the Western Allies. On July 18, talking with Churchill, the generalissimo declared that in the countries liberated by the Red Army, Soviet policy called for "a strong, independent, sovereign state." He opposed "Sovietisation of any of those countries. They would have free elections, and all except Fascist parties would participate." Indeed, when abstractions seemed called for, the generalissimo, in this conference as in previous meetings with his allies, readily adapted himself to his audience, speaking of Western ideals and beliefs and never introducing Marxist-Leninist visions.

In accordance with what he had told Tito and Molotov, Stalin had moved quickly to establish control in Berlin. Even before the fighting was over, an airplane from Moscow had brought a leading German Communist, Walter Ulbricht, back to the city. Ulbricht had fled Germany after Hitler came to power in 1933 and had spent most of the ensuing years in the USSR; now he and nine other German Communist functionaries had returned with the mission of establishing a party organization. Just a week after the German surrender, the first issue of "an extremely important political and cultural undertaking," as Marshal Zhukov described it, the Communist Party newspaper *Tägliche Rundschau (Daily Review),* appeared on the streets. On June 9 the Kremlin created the Soviet Military Administration for Germany (known variously as SMA, SMAD, and SMAG) to administer the Soviet zone. Next day, well ahead of the schedule for political activities anticipated by the Americans and the British, Zhukov issued an order authorizing the establishment of "antifascist" political parties in the Soviet zone; July 11 saw the revival of the Communist Party of Germany (KPD). On July 18, while the Big Three were conferring at Potsdam, representatives of the Communists, the Social Democrats, and two other parties came to Berlin for a Soviet-sponsored conference of their own. By July 27 the Soviet authorities had presided over the creation of eleven central German administrations, which, though their scope was limited to the Russian zone, could possibly serve as "matrix cells" for the organization of a future German state. After all, the Americans would one day, and perhaps fairly soon, leave the country. "It must look good," Ulbricht said, "but it must be controlled by us."

During the days leading up to the Potsdam Conference, the press also carried news about clashes between the Anglo-American and the Soviet authorities in Berlin. No agreement existed on the vital question of providing food and fuel for the city; nor could reporters see any sign of an integrated three- or four-power administration. By its nature, wrote an American correspondent, the Red Army, wherever it found itself, was a "foraging" army, living off the land it invaded. In Germany, Russian soldiers were seizing cattle, sheep, and goats from farmers and driving them to a grazing land where they stayed until the time came to slaughter them; "even in Berlin herds of cattle and flocks of sheep are driven through downtown city streets in the morning to come back later in trucks as beef and mutton which is distributed at Red Army messes." Red Army soldiers had seized residents from houses in the supposedly British sector, accusing them of political offenses, and the U.S. deputy commander for military government in Berlin, Colonel Frank Howley, conceded that people arrested by German police in the American sector were undoubtedly being handed over to the Soviets. Though attempting to play down the significance of such discord, Howley admitted that Russia's support of political parties ran counter to American views on the occupation. Red Army soldiers had even torn down Howley's posters concerning punishment for civil offenses. In short, Howley said, "The Russians are running all of Berlin." Until higher authorities settled matters, he concluded, that was the way matters would stay. "All the Allies announced that they entered Germany as conquerors," wrote a correspondent, "but the Russians alone act as though they meant it."

Apart from questions concerning the depth and sincerity of Stalin's ideological professions, the Western statesmen could not be sure of the extent of his power. In response to protests concerning Soviet recognition of the Lublin Committee as the government of Poland, for instance, Stalin had told Roosevelt and Churchill at Yalta that the decision had been made by the Presidium of the Supreme Soviet and could not be undone. In his dealings with the Western leaders, Stalin often spoke in this way of his "colleagues" and their wishes, attempting to create the impression that the Soviet government functioned, in accordance with the kinds of charts found in political science textbooks, as a structure capped by an oligarchy in which he counted merely as one member, if an important one.

How much weight did such assertions deserve? The Western statesmen could not decide, but they never tended to credit Stalin with complete dictatorial power. After various fruitless dealings with Molotov, some

Americans—even, at times, such shrewd and experienced observers as Harriman and Bohlen—believed that the slab-faced, inflexible foreign minister headed a hawkish clique in the Kremlin that acted in opposition to the more reasonable faction led by Stalin, or at least kept important information from the generalissimo. These views were not as willfully naive as they might seem half a century later. In the 1940s, for all its size and prominence, the Soviet Union was in many ways a land of mystery. (Much of the geographical information available to the West, for example, actually came from German maps the Allies had captured.) Foreigners found travel heavily restricted and conversation with local people forbidden. American and European analysts attempting to peer through the murk surrounding the Kremlin resembled physicians trying to diagnose a patient from a distance, through a screen, with no questions allowed.

The Big Three at Potsdam faced issues on both sides of the world. The reaffirmation of Stalin's pledge, made at Yalta, to enter the war against Japan held particular importance for the United States—or, at least, it had done so until the time of the conference. Curiously, all the difficulties encountered during the war in dealing with the Russians had not disheartened Admiral Leahy and his JCS colleagues; they presumed that they could carry out combined operations with the Soviets in the Far East as they had done with the British in Africa and Europe. As for Europe, the leaders faced administrative, economic, and political questions concerning control of Germany and arrangements for governing Berlin. They also had to deal with the issue of peace treaties for Germany's satellite countries, fix reparations, and decide what to do with war criminals—and, inevitably, to engage in disputes about the fate of Poland and other Eastern European countries.

Although the foreign ministers and the chiefs of staff had held meetings during Monday and Tuesday, the first plenary session of the Potsdam Conference opened at 5:10 on Tuesday afternoon, July 17. Stalin immediately proposed that, as at Tehran and Yalta, the U.S. president serve as chairman—an arrangement in accordance with protocol, since Truman, as a head of state, outranked the other members of the Big Three. Officially assuming the chair, Truman pointed out the urgency of preparing for European peace settlements and presented a draft proposal for the establishment of a Council of Foreign Ministers to carry this work forward. He further declared that the Allied Control Council for Germany ought to take up its duties immediately, and he submitted a set of principles that, in the view of the United States, should guide the council in its administration of Germany. After a round of sparring, Churchill declared that the British wished to add the "Polish problem" to the brief agenda Truman had proposed for the conference. Stalin countered with a series of items for discussion—the division of the German merchant navy among the victors, reparations from Germany and also from Italy, disposition of Italian colonies, the future of the fascist Franco regime in Spain, and "the question of the present émigré Polish government." There it was: the Polish question, which had consumed time and tempers at Yalta, was back on the table.

Much had changed in Poland during the months since Yalta. As nearly as people in the West could tell—the Russians allowed no Western observers into Poland—the Communist Party, the Red Army, and the Soviet secret police had combined to destroy opposition to the Lublin Committee (renamed the Warsaw government), arresting many non-Communist political figures. Though the Soviets maintained that they were doing nothing more than ensuring security behind their lines as they pushed into Germany, their actions seemed calculated to leave the erstwhile Lublin group unchallenged on top of the heap. These actions also demonstrated the Soviet fear that, left on its own, the new Warsaw group would perish from its profound unpopularity among the Polish people. In pursuing the stated goal of a Polish government that would simultaneously be independent, democratic (in some Western sense), and friendly to the Soviet Union, the Americans and the British clearly were chasing the political version of the impossible dream.

Finally, after Stalin had continued to reject any but the sketchiest token representation of the London Poles in the Warsaw government, the West had acceded. In late June Churchill yielded, grudgingly, to Truman's unenthusiastic wish to recognize the new regime. The prime minister could not, however, resist offering a puckish suggestion: The Western Allies should grant recognition on July 4. Not quite, replied Truman, and the official date became July 5. The problem now became not the makeup of the Polish government but a more physical point: Just where on the map would Poland be? Since the USSR was supposed to receive land in eastern Poland, the leaders had agreed at Yalta that, in effect, the country would be picked up like a piece of luggage, moved westward, and set down again, receiving compensation in the west for what it had lost in the east.

Just before this first session at Potsdam adjourned, Stalin wanted to know why Churchill refused "to give Russia her share of the German fleet." If Churchill didn't want any of it, that was fine, Stalin said in a typical instance of his pithiness: "He can sink his share."

After bandying these generalities about in their first session, the statesmen returned next day to take up an agenda distilled for them by their hardworking foreign ministers. The inevitable wrangle about Poland proved long and inconclusive, and another question also took shape—a question bound up with the Polish problem. The Big Three had to agree on what to do with Germany, but what exactly *was* Germany? Stalin pushed for regarding Germany as "what has become of her after the war," an idea that would grant automatic recognition to Polish absorption of much of eastern Germany; "we cannot get away from the results of the war," Stalin maintained. Truman doggedly argued for the starting point to be Germany with the frontiers of 1937—the Reich before it expanded into Austria and Czechoslovakia, the Germany of the Versailles Treaty; territorial changes, he declared, should be made at the peace conference. Everyone spoke as though anticipating a sort of reenactment of the great peace conference of 1919, which ended with a formal signing ceremony at Versailles. No one—at least in the West—dreamed that no real peace conference would ever take place.

Along with the meetings of the Big Three and the foreign ministers came specialized subcommittee sessions, such as those of an economic group charged with formulating plans for dealing with Germany. Reparations, as was hardly surprising, stood first in Soviet thinking. At Yalta the Russians had pressed for agreement on a specific amount they should receive from the Germans, and against State Department advice to avoid fixing any figure—since nobody at the time had any idea what Germany's capacity to pay might be at the end of the war—FDR had agreed to the desired $10 billion (1945 dollars) "as a basis for discussion"; the Americans quickly found, however, that the Soviets chose to regard the figure as representing a binding agreement, to which they would repeatedly return. In the reparations committee, Ivan Maisky, the chief Russian representative, a veteran diplomat and longtime ambassador to Britain, warned the other members that the tricky Germans would "try to prove that without very considerable imports they can't live and can't export." But "it would be undesirable politically to say that imports have priority over reparations. Everybody would say that reparations come first and imports after because we have suffered so much." Otherwise, it would appear that "capitalists want to have profits from foreign trade and don't care about reparations for those who suffered." But reparations would have to come from somewhere. (As a good Marxist-Leninist, Maisky had previously told Stalin and Molotov that the Soviets should make the United States and Britain understand that reparations would actually benefit them by keeping Germany from becoming a competitor in world trade. But this should be done carefully, Maisky said, "because owing to their intrinsic hypocrisy the Anglo-Americans would not want to openly admit the correctness of this conclusion.")

The representatives agreed on a formula the would give Germans a "minimum subsistence standard" that would not exceed the level for other

European countries, excluding Britain and the Soviet Union. At the same time, American and British representatives pointed to the need for Germany to develop a balanced economy that would enable it to earn credits. Germany should, of course, be prevented from building up any kind of warmaking potential, but its economy would still require a functioning industrial sector. As one of the U.S. representatives, Assistant Secretary of State Will Clayton, pointed out, the American people after the First World War had made the mistake of financing Germany and thus, by this largesse, enabling her to make reparations payments; that is, the United States itself had in effect become the payer of reparations to its allies. President Roosevelt had earlier made it clear, Clayton said, that the Americans would not make that mistake again.

At a subsequent meeting of the committee the Russians, seeking "to ensure control of German war potential," proposed the internationalization of the Ruhr industrial area, which was described by one of the Americans as "25 × 50 miles—all black coal plus much industry." In a discussion with Secretary Byrnes, Molotov commented that, in representing the Soviet point of view on reparations, Maisky had "not done so well." Byrnes thought little about the remark until he realized, much later, that after Potsdam neither he nor any other American representative had ever laid eyes on Maisky again. Byrnes feared that Maisky had continued to do not so well.

The final Potsdam protocol would call for the each of the victorious powers to obtain its claimed reparations from its own occupation zone, and, in addition, for the Soviets to receive from the Americans and the British 10 percent of the capital equipment in these zones not needed to maintain the German economy at the agreed-upon level, together with another 15 percent of production equipment from these zones in exchange for commodities—food, coal—from the Soviet zone. This solution to the reparations tangle came from Byrnes, the old Senate negotiator, who declared himself pleased with his "horse-trade on reparations."

Generally, the Big Three in their meetings tended to argue, at some length, about two or three questions, such as the shape of Poland and the question of German reparations, but then to hand the detailed issues and finer points over to the foreign ministers—often without actually having settled the underlying questions of policy. By July 21, Churchill was declaring that the Big Three had "been here for a week" with few important decisions made. At this session, during discussion of the vexing but inescapable Polish problem, Stalin maintained that the Poles ought to keep and farm the territory they had moved into in eastern Germany. What about the Germans in the area—more than eight million of them? Churchill asked. Stalin proffered a simple answer: They had all run away; none were left.

Even if that were true, Churchill said, they would have to be fed wherever they had fled, since they had come "bringing their mouths with them," and the land claimed by Poland amounted to a quarter of the arable land of 1937 Germany. Of course, neither Churchill nor Truman accepted Stalin's statement that "no single German remained in the territory to be given Poland." In this exchange the Soviet dictator was presenting an outstanding example of one of the techniques that made him a formidable debating opponent— his use of colossal, sweeping assertions that could not conceivably be true but that he would stick to regardless of whatever contradictory evidence his fellow statesmen produced; they could either grumble and quietly disagree, or they could call him a liar, a charge that neither Churchill nor Truman found himself prepared to make. The Western leaders did, however, make it plain that they objected to Stalin's presenting as a fait accompli Polish control of eastern Germany. Finally, the Big Three agreed to invite representatives of the Polish government to join the discussions at Potsdam. The West gained nothing from their appearance except an astounding promise by the premier, Boleslaw Bierut, a veteran Communist who had spent the war years in Russia and had chaired the Lublin Committee, that the country would develop a Western-style democratic government, very likely on the English model; the Poles, Bierut assured Churchill, did not wish to copy the Soviet system. Not one to hesitate in drawing the long bow when it came to playing the democratic game, the premier declared that Poland would be one of the most democratic countries in Europe.

Stalin appeared to have made a fundamental choice. He would stake out his turf, establish his power, and then talk to the West.

CHAPTER 5

"Unmitigated Skepticism and Despair"

By July 21, Colonel Charles Donnelly noted with a touch of optimism, the Big Three had settled down to business. As one of their most important functions, the colonel said, the American strategic and logistical planners had to study all of the implications of any proposal they wished to make or that the British made to them, then draw up recommendations to the Joint Chiefs of Staff concerning the best course of action. In turn, the chiefs briefed the president, sometimes meeting with him personally but usually working through Admiral Leahy. The British followed much the same procedure with their chiefs and the prime minister. But not so the Russians, said Donnelly. "Our policy of decentralizing responsibility enables lower echelons to plan, discuss and often implement some matters, whereas, with the Russians, all decisions seem to be made at the highest level." This approach tended to overwork those at the top, the colonel said, adding shrewdly, "especially Stalin, who does not trust his underlings very far"; Donnelly, indeed, seemed to have a better grasp of the true Soviet command system than did some of his civilian superiors. The working of this system, Donnelly said, meant that "it takes a long time to get decisions, or even answers, from the Russians, unless the matter is one in which they have a special interest." Not only did such delays cause irritation, but "if the Russians do not feel like it, they will not answer at all, courtesy be damned!"

After digesting the information provided by their respective staffs, the heads of government—ideally, at least—came into meetings knowing what was at stake, how far they could go in making concessions, and what constituted the strength or weakness of their own position. Then they engaged in a demanding game. As Donnelly summed it up, "They must be good poker players, concealing knowledge of their own strength or weakness, press their advantages strongly, know when to take their losses and

give up, when to bluff or call a bluff and when to stay tough until the end."
Donnelly considered Stalin "excellent" in this game and Churchill
"erratic"; the skill of Truman, the newcomer to this high-stakes table,
remained to be seen.

In addition to supplying their political masters with information and
advice, the Allied staffs had social duties to perform. During one meeting of
the U.S. Joint Chiefs, an officer informed the members that they had been
invited to attend a review of the British Seventh Armoured Division, which
had figured prominently in Field Marshal Montgomery's famous victory
over the Afrika Korps at El Alamein in 1942. Without stopping to think,
Admiral Leahy told the group in his gruff way that he had seen enough
parades of soldiers to last him the rest of his life. Then, suddenly realizing
that this opinion hardly complimented the army of which General Marshall
was the head, the admiral quickly added, "But I always found these parades
interesting and instructive." Laughing, Marshall said, "Admiral, you remind
me of the young officer who had been on guard duty all night and went into
the mess hall in the morning for some coffee. He took a swallow, spat it out
and said, 'This is the damnedest coffee I ever tasted.' Then, remembering
that it was the custom in his outfit that any officer who griped about the
mess became the mess officer, pronto, he added: 'But I like it.' "

One evening the British and American staffs turned out for a concert at
the New Palace by the RAF symphony orchestra. As the hosts, the British
chiefs escorted their U.S. opposite numbers, with Field Marshal Sir Alan
Brooke, the chief of the Imperial General Staff, beside General Marshall.
An intense man with rapid-fire speech, often difficult to deal with, Brooke
was in many ways the brains of the British high command and had been the
principal maker of British strategy. For the past three and a half years, he
had shown remarkable stamina in standing up to Churchill, with all the
prime minister's constant swirl of schemes and proposals. Presently, accompanied by swarms of guards who spread out over the palace grounds, the
Soviet officers joined the party.

After sitting through an Elgar overture and serenade and a performance of the *Appassionata* sonata, Colonel Donnelly and his group
decided that they had heard their evening's quota of classical music. As
they strolled toward their car, they were stopped by a British officer who
spoke with a note of some desperation: "I say, are you chaps looking for
what I am?" The Americans told him that they were simply going to their
car. "Well," said the Englishman, "I'm looking for a bush to pee behind,
but I'm afraid of being shot."

"If you're shot," answered one of the Americans, a young officer from
Kansas who claimed to be something of an Anglophobe, "we will testify that
you died in a noble cause."

The officer responded with a laugh tinged with desperation and walked between the parked cars in search of his much-needed bush. When the Kansan asked the identity of "that bird," he was told that he had just wised off to no less a personage than the chief of the Imperial General Staff. A colleague later reported to Donnelly that when Brooke returned from his mission, he told General Marshall with some bitterness that he had not been able to find a bush without a Russian guard behind it. Apparently the field marshal had finally concluded that privacy did not hold the number-one priority.

During one of the U.S. Joint Chiefs of Staff meetings, General Brehon Somervell, the army chief of supply, raised a question about priorities of another order. How, he asked, did a certain project rank in importance compared with the Manhattan Project? Keenly interested, Colonel Donnelly noted that this was the second mention he had heard of this mysterious project. Earlier, having heard the term but failing to find it in his list of code names, he had asked his boss what it referred to. "He told me to put it out of my mind," Donnelly said. "It was so secret that even the name was classified," and "we were not even to speculate on what it might be." The significance of the Manhattan Project seemed to be confirmed when the Joint Chiefs told Somervell that it ranked ahead of everything else.

At about noon on July 16, the day after arriving in Potsdam, President Truman had received vitally important news about the Manhattan Project. Word came from Washington that a scientific-military team working at Los Alamos in the New Mexico desert had produced the anticipated successful test of a nuclear device. "Diagnosis not yet complete but results seem satisfactory and already exceed expectations," read the coded message. The message referred to a plutonium bomb, one of the two kinds being produced; the scientists had also created a uranium bomb—literally just one—which would not undergo a test, since no other bomb of that kind would be ready for months. Next day the seventy-eight-year-old U.S. secretary of war, Henry L. Stimson, who for months had devoted much of his attention to the implications of the bomb, joined Churchill for lunch and handed him a sheet of paper bearing the sentence "Babies satisfactorily born." On expressing his bafflement at this message, Churchill was told it meant that the atomic bomb had become a reality. On the following day a complete account of the awesome event arrived; it was, as Churchill said, "world-shaking news."

In the last phases of the war, a heavy bomb—a "blockbuster"—carried a ton or a ton and a half of TNT. The Allies now had one single bomb, weighing about thirteen pounds, with the explosive force of many thousands of individual blockbusters. At a tête-à-tête lunch on July 18, Truman and Churchill talked over the great new phenomenon and agreed that Stalin should be told about it; he would "inform Stalin about it at an opportune time," President Truman noted in his diary.

With the war in Europe now over, discussion of the possible uses of the atomic bomb related to the struggle with the Japanese—which had just produced, on the island of Okinawa, an almost three-month battle of unparalleled ferocity in which the Americans had suffered 50,000 casualties. The contemplated battle for Japan itself would be on a much larger scale and even bloodier. But now, said Churchill, "all this nightmare picture had vanished. In its place was the vision—fair and bright indeed it seemed—of the end of the whole war in one or two violent shocks." This vision brought with it, as its obvious corollary, a realization that the Allies would hardly, as they had long presumed, require much Soviet help to end the war in the Far East. Mighty blows from the air, and not men, guns, and tanks on the ground, would force Japan to surrender. "Believe Japs will fold up before Russia comes in," Truman thought. "I am sure they will when Manhattan appears over their homeland." The statesmen clearly realized the enormous power of the new weapon, but its transformational nature— not that of the existing bombs, of which there was no reserve supply, but that of the nuclear future—had not yet sunk in. Despite Truman's optimism, twelve days after the Los Alamos explosion he and Churchill approved a report from the Combined Chiefs of Staff that gave November 15, 1946, as the anticipated date of the Japanese surrender. The chiefs looked to attacks on the Japanese homeland beginning nearly a year earlier, on November 1, 1945; U.S. planners had earlier expressed the view that the Japanese would never surrender unconditionally because they had no such concept, as was demonstrated by the striking fact that during the entire war no organized Japanese unit had ever surrendered under any conditions whatever.

At the close of the July 24 plenary session of the conference, Truman, with no fuss, left his place at the big table and moved around to Stalin, who stood talking with Pavlov. The president had decided, he had told Churchill earlier, that the best way to tell Stalin about what the prime minister called "the great New Fact" would simply be to approach him in a casual manner. This he now proceeded to do, informing the generalissimo that the United States had developed a new kind of weapon of tremendous power. Showing no strong reaction, Stalin merely commented that this was good news and he hoped the United States would make good use of this weapon against the Japanese.

Truman wondered whether Stalin had grasped the point; in reply to Churchill's question "How did it go?" the president said, "He never asked a question." To Churchill, Stalin's failure to seek any information beyond Truman's brief statement indicated quite clearly that the generalissimo had no knowledge of the great Anglo-American atomic effort, with its array of scientists and laboratories and production facilities. On the other hand, several months earlier Stimson had expressed to President Roosevelt his belief that, through espionage, the Soviets knew about the Manhattan Project; Stimson thought it reasonable to acknowledge the truth at Potsdam, if asked—and also to acknowledge American awareness of Soviet nuclear efforts—but not to share technical information.

Stalin's muted response raised questions not only at the time but through subsequent years. Andrei Gromyko, who stood nearby, professed to believe that Truman was disappointed, the presumable implication being that the president had expected news of the new weapon to intimidate the generalissimo so that the United States could take a hard line on disputed matters during the remainder of the conference. According to Gromyko's later account, Truman gave a description specific enough to leave no doubt that the atomic bomb was the weapon. Indeed, shortly after the conversation with Truman, Stalin himself telephoned Igor Kurchatov, the chief physicist of the Soviet nuclear program, to order a speed-up of the effort, while Molotov, seeming petulant, complained that "the Americans have been doing all this work on the atomic bomb without telling us."

The world would later learn that the Soviets did not need to be told about the Manhattan Project; Stalin and Molotov had abundant information from their own sources, and for the Soviets' own A-bomb project, Molotov told a Soviet interviewer many years later, intelligence operatives "neatly stole just what we needed." Until three months earlier, Stalin had actually known far more about the atomic bomb than had Truman himself—who had heard nothing about it until being briefed by Stimson after he assumed the presidency—owing to the activities of such scientific spies as Klaus Fuchs, Alan Nunn May, and Ted Hall. Truman's news nevertheless had its usefulness to Stalin, because the well-organized espionage pipeline from Los Alamos to Moscow could hardly match the speed with which the report of the successful test reached Truman.

Although Truman came to Potsdam as a novice in dealing with Stalin, Churchill had spent many long evening hours with the generalissimo in meetings between the two in Moscow as well as at the previous Big Three conferences. But in attempting to ascertain from Stalin's visible reactions what Truman's revelation meant to him, the prime minister showed that he had not grasped an essential aspect of Stalin's personality. The Yugoslav Communist politician Milovan Djilas, who knew the Kremlin, paid full tribute to Stalin's genius as an actor. Commenting on a discussion in which

Stalin had criticized Djilas, the Yugoslav wrote that "it is truly difficult to ascertain how much of Stalin's action was play-acting and how much was real rancor. I personally believe that with Stalin it is impossible to separate the one from the other. With him, pretense was so spontaneous that it seemed he himself became convinced of the truth and sincerity of what he was saying. He very easily adapted himself to every turn in the discussion of any new topic, and even to every new personality." Beyond that, said Djilas, Stalin "sized up people quickly" and "particularly distinguished himself by his skill in exploiting people's weaknesses."

Thus Stalin, as a poker player, brought important advantages to the great game at Potsdam, and in addition to his intuitive and histrionic gifts, he had a fear of being cheated, as Molotov put it, and a determination to avoid it. "Stalin often said that Russia wins wars but doesn't know to avail itself of the fruits of victory," Molotov commented. "It was my main task as minister of foreign affairs to see that we would not be cheated."

Truman's conduct at the conference raised questions that would take on importance for the future. If he and the West had intended to use the news from Los Alamos as a hole card that he could now produce to take the pot, his actions showed little sign of it. In the first place, of course, the date of the conference had been fixed before anyone knew whether the atomic bomb would work or how powerful it would prove to be; in fact, Churchill had wanted the meeting to take place a month earlier. The availability of the bomb would certainly simplify matters in the Pacific war, but nobody in the Western camp was proposing to threaten its use to settle matters in Europe—whatever form one might have managed to devise for such a threat. As Molotov said later, even if the Americans had bombs left after attacking Japan, "they could not have played a significant role elsewhere."

Actually, Truman was looking at Russia in quite a different way. Following a "most satisfactory" lunch with Stalin two days after receiving the report from Los Alamos, the president noted in his diary the nature of this satisfaction. (This diary, which Truman wrote on unnumbered pages, was turned up by researchers after his death.) Stalin had expressed his wish "to cooperate with the U.S. in peace as we had cooperated in War" but acknowledged that "it would be harder." After the generalissimo's comment that "he was grossly misunderstood in U.S. and I was misunderstood in Russia," said the president, "I told him we each could help to remedy that situation in our home countries." He would do all he could in the United States, and Stalin, with "a most cordial smile," promised to make the same effort in Russia. In the plenary session later that day, Truman as chairman "banged through" several proposals; Churchill was surprised, but Stalin was "very much pleased." Truman, in fact, had purposely adopted a brisk executive style, partly because with his staff he had developed explicit positions on all the issues and hence saw no value in the kind of discursive discussion Roosevelt had thrived on and also because he wanted to present himself as a "straightforward, hard-hitting trader" with nothing to hide. Churchill's doctor, Lord Moran, likened the president to "a Wesleyan [Methodist] minister who does not know anything about the game and is not very sure whether it is quite nice for him to play at all, but who is determined, if he does play, to make his full weight felt."

When it came to sizing up the members of the Big Three, Truman had concluded at his first meeting with Stalin that the Soviet leader was "honest—but smart as hell," a judgment actually more favorable than the opinion the president had privately formed of Churchill during their lunch the previous day. After some days of the conference, Truman reacted with concern to news that Stalin was sick. If Stalin were to "cash in," who could succeed him? Certainly not Molotov, who "lacks sincerity"—that is, in contrast to Stalin.

Not only had Truman liked what he saw as Stalin's honesty and frankness, he had been conditioned in advance by Jimmy Byrnes to hold a certain picture of the generalissimo. Although Byrnes had no background in foreign affairs, FDR had included him in the U.S. delegation at the Yalta Conference because of his standing in the Senate, where the president needed strong support for the planned United Nations organization. At Yalta, Byrnes had been impressed by Stalin, whom he later described to Truman as representative of types quite familiar to both men—political bosses and senators, men with whom you could do business, with whom you could horse-trade, who might drive hard bargains but whose word you could rely on. As a veteran member of the Capitol Hill club talking with a fellow member, Byrnes likened negotiating with the Russians to deal-making in the Senate: "You build a post office in their state and they'll build a post office in your state."

For Truman, meeting Stalin simply confirmed this advance impression. To a remarkable degree, indeed, "Uncle Joe" reminded the president of his political mentor in Missouri, Kansas City Democratic boss Tom Pendergast, who engaged in all the discreditable practices that characterized big-city machine politics and spent time behind bars but, for all that, could be depended on to keep his promises. "Stalin," Truman told a White House staff member, "is as near like Tom Pendergast as any man I know." Later, Truman expanded on this thought with the idea "that Stalin would stand by his agreements, and also that he had a Politburo on his hands like the Eightieth Congress." (The president clearly did not realize the unhealthful nature of Politburo membership compared with the relative salubrity of service in Congress: of twenty-five persons who served on the Politburo as

Stalin's "colleagues" during his regime, eleven were shot and three more committed suicide or died under suspicious circumstances.)

At Postdam the West and the Russians looked at each other through the haze of their preconceptions. To Molotov, the Polish government established by the Lublin group—an out-and-out Soviet puppet, in most eyes—was "independent but not hostile" to the Soviet Union; the frequently expressed Anglo-American concern for Polish liberties had simply masked the Western desire "to impose a bourgeois government, which naturally would have been an agent of imperialism." Similarly, Gromyko dismissed Western complaints about the Soviets' failure to live up to the Yalta agreements as "Washington's attempts to interfere in eastern Europe which reflected its expansionist aims there and in other areas of the world."

In his own way, Truman viewed the international scene from a similarly limited perspective. Frequently admired for his familiarity with history ("he certainly displayed surprising knowledge of Hannibal's campaigns," commented the British ambassador, Lord Halifax), the president seemed to look at history with something of an antiquarian's eye, regarding the past as a parade of contextless individuals and specific deeds; through no fault of his own, he lacked a university education that could have given him facility in relating events and ideas. Similarly, Byrnes, a bright man with great drive, had been forced to leave school at fourteen, though he had later studied law. Thus the president and the secretary of state could easily identify the United States Senate, with its cozy deals on dams and army camps and tax loopholes, with the governing regime of a vast Eurasian arena in which the masters had shut up ten to twenty million of their own citizens in labor camps and had shot another five to ten million. These facts did not necessarily mean that East and West could not arrive at bargains, but such agreements must not be based on illusions. In its general tone and its avoidance of real communication, the Potsdam Conference, had the participants realized it, would serve as a model for East-West meetings to come in the following years.

Twelve years later, looking back at Potsdam in a private account he never sent to anyone, Truman spoke of Joseph E. Davies as a Russophile "as most of us were" and described himself as the "innocent idealist at one corner of that Round Table" because of his desire for the establishment of free governments in countries affected by the war. The Big Three had reached a number of agreements, he said, but they were broken "as soon as the unconscionable Russian Dictator returned to Moscow!" But Truman conceded, in characteristic vein: "And I liked the little son of a bitch." As unreflecting in his own way as the Russians showed themselves to be in their fashion, Truman had presumed that any clear-thinking person would agree with him on the universal merits and applicability of capitalism, free trade, and the two-party system. Such an outlook made the president a representative spokesman for his people in 1945.

On July 28 a development of a kind unprecedented in Big Three annals shook up the group around the big table. Churchill and Eden had returned home on July 25 to await the announcement of the results of the July 5 election; now Clement Attlee and Ernest Bevin arrived from England to take their places. In Potsdam, British enlisted men had told Colonel Donnelly and others that they would have voted for Churchill himself but did not like the Conservative Party; their officers, however, felt that Attlee lacked the necessary caliber to head the government. Truman and Byrnes were said by a staff member to be confident that Churchill would be the one coming back from London. Confounding most expectations, at least on the part of people outside Britain, the voters in this first general election in ten years had given the Labour Party a sizable majority; "the result came," said George VI himself, as "a great surprise to one and all"; even Attlee seemed to have expected a different outcome.

After putting his government together, the new prime minister, together with Bevin, his foreign secretary, came to Potsdam. The two made a contrasting pair; Attlee, a laconic, compact middle-class one-time social worker and lecturer, had taken a philosophical path to Labour Party membership through the Fabian Society, while Bevin, an ebullient 250–pound hulk of a man, the son of an unknown father who had begun his working life at the age of eleven, had labored as a docker and had risen to create and lead Britain's largest union. The two men, said Byrnes, differed from Churchill and Eden "about as much as it is possible for people to differ." On meeting Bevin, who clearly intended for Britain to sit at the table as a full equal of the United States and the Soviet Union, Byrnes found his style "so aggressive that both the President and I wondered how we would get along with this new Foreign Minister."

Attlee and Bevin did not come ill informed. For the new prime minister, of course, the trip to Potsdam was only a return, since Churchill had included him in the British delegation from the outset. Besides, both Attlee and Bevin had not only had seats in the coalition government's War Cabinet but had served on the influential Armistice and Postwar Committee— although, in an administration headed by so dominant a figure as Churchill, other ministers inevitably tended to revolve as satellites around the leader.

But now Attlee and Bevin had power. With his thorough working knowledge of the British economy, Bevin had expected to become chancellor of the exchequer in any Labour government that might come into being. Instead, seeing the problems with the Russians arising in Eastern Europe and in Germany, Attlee decided to give the Foreign Office to the formidable, popular, and reliable Bevin, who "commanded the confidence not merely of organised Labour but of the great mass of central opinion on which Governments must depend for their ultimate strength," even though he had no more experience in international affairs than his American counterpart, Jimmy Byrnes. (When Bevin telephoned his wife to tell her that a planned brief holiday had to be canceled, saying, "It's not Devon for me tomorrow, it's Potsdam," he received the reply "Potsdam? Where on earth's that?") The appointment pleased Foreign Office professionals, who tended to look dubiously on the Labour Party with its sometimes pacifistic past; the permanent undersecretary, Sir Alexander Cadogan, commented that "we may do better with Bevin than with any of the other Labourites." Despite Bevin's inexperience, Attlee demonstrated enormous faith in him and, unlike Churchill, had no intention of acting as his own foreign secretary. As he later said, "You don't keep a good dog and bark yourself—and Ernie was a very good dog."

The Soviets could draw little satisfaction from the replacement of the capitalists Churchill and Eden by the two socialist leaders, even though one of the two could match proletarian credentials with anybody who had ever held office in any country. During the war Attlee and Bevin had often expressed sympathy with the Soviet Union for "her terrible war losses," Gromyko said, but "now their vocabulary had altered and they were far more sparing in their generosity"; the Russians quickly saw that they had been right in their prediction that if Labour won the election, it would follow the existing policy. At the conference table, Attlee was "quiet as a mouse"—as Gromyko perhaps did not realize, a characteristic Attlee performance in any context. For Molotov, Bevin was simply "a Churchill man. Hostile." In seeing the new foreign secretary as a foe, Molotov made no mistake; to Bevin, the Moscow-controlled Communists and their maneuvers represented an alien and disruptive threat to the well-being of his cherished British labor movement, and Stalin and his ilk were traitors to the left. (Beyond that, Bevin came to detest Molotov personally. He could never meet the Russian, he once said, without thinking of the hundreds of thousands of peasants he had liquidated. Molotov, he felt, "was like a Communist in a local Labour Party—if you treated him badly he made the most of the grievance, and if you treated him well he only put the price up and abused you next day.")

Neither Bevin nor Attlee, however, achieved any greater success than Churchill and Truman experienced in the disputes over the boundaries of Poland and the Polish occupation of eastern Germany. The final conference communiqué acknowledged the status quo, though it made a face-saving bow in the direction of the British and the Americans by declaring that "the final delimitation of the western frontier of Poland should await the peace settlement." The West could not escape the fact that, with the Red Army controlling all of Eastern Europe, the Soviets could do as they liked, regardless of what anybody might choose to say at a conference table. The possession by the Americans of two atomic bombs played no part in decisions concerning Europe. In its lack of real suspense, the Potsdam Conference was like an autopsy; the patient was dead to begin with.

One American observer, a little-known forty-one-year-old diplomat serving in Moscow, read the final Potsdam communiqué with "unmitigated skepticism and despair." He saw the joint four-power arrangement for control of Germany—with its implicit assumption that the great anti-Hitler coalition would continue to function after the common enemy had vanished and the world moved from war to peace—as completely unrealistic. Beyond that, he had a clear view of the semantic fog in which the Western statesmen had labored as they discussed and debated issues with Stalin. "Democratic," "peaceful," "justice"—the use of such terms in agreements with the Soviets, he said, "went counter to everything I had learned, in seventeen years of experience with Russian affairs, about the technique of dealing with the Soviet government." What excuse could the American and the British statesmen possibly offer for putting their names to a document calling for Western collaboration with the Soviets in creating a judicial system for Germany "in accordance with the principles of democracy, of justice under law, and of equal rights for all citizens without distinction of race, nationality or religion"? How could the Western leaders solemnly declare that "democratic" political parties would be "encouraged" to function throughout Germany "with rights of assembly and of public discussion"? Anybody in Moscow, said this observer, "could have told our negotiators what it was that the Soviet leaders had in mind when they used the term 'democratic parties.'"

This dismayed observer, George F. Kennan, had not yet begun to achieve the renown that would make him, for half a century, one of the best-known diplomats and students of international relations in the world. For the moment his ideas concerning the future of Germany had little influence at the topmost levels of the American government. When he expressed such thoughts as "the idea of a Germany run jointly with the Russians is a chimera" and "the idea of both the Russians and ourselves withdrawing politely at a given date and a healthy, peaceful, stable, and friendly Germany arising out of the resulting vacuum is also a chimera," he encountered strong and heated opposition, much of it from persons who held State Department professionals in low esteem as antidemocratic elitists. (Kennan could not know it, but the new president had one day declared his lack of admiration for the "striped pants boys" in the State Department.)

Many years later, however, Soviet Premier Nikita Khrushchev observed: "After the defeat of Hitler, Stalin believed that he was in the same position as Alexander I after the defeat of Napoleon—that he could dictate the rules for all of Europe." In this very vein, when Ambassador Harriman asked the generalissimo whether he was pleased that the Russians were now sharing Berlin, Stalin immediately expressed dissatisfaction: "Czar Alexander made it to Paris." According to Khrushchev, "Stalin even started believing that he could dictate new rules to the whole world. Part of his mistake was to exaggerate our capabilities and ride roughshod over the interests of our friends."

Still more years later, George Kennan, who in his nineties had achieved almost high-priest status among those who concerned themselves with questions of American foreign policy, whether or not they always agreed with him, offered what amounted to a supplement to Khrushchev's point. The many concessions Britain and the United States made to Stalin at the end of the war, Kennan said, encouraged the Soviet dictator to believe that he might easily get his political way in Europe, and it was this trend that the containment policy, born in 1946 and 1947, was created to arrest.

But in 1945 those differing from Kennan's views included high-ranking U.S. Army officers, one of whom, said Kennan, reproached him and "State Department people" in general for their inability to "get along with the Russians." The army, this officer declared, knew how to accomplish the collaboration. He and his colleagues were now going to have the opportunity to show the diplomats what they could do.

CHAPTER 6

The Sinews and the Curtain

ON MARCH 5, 1946, in Fulton, Missouri, Winston Churchill delivered a speech to which he attached great importance; he gave it a resonant title: "The Sinews of Peace." Although he had been out of office for more than seven months, the wartime prime minister—the incarnation of the spirit of Allied victory and already a figure of legend—attracted attention wherever he went. This speech, delivered at a small and obscure college in the American heartland, would put him in the headlines around the world, would stir up clamorous controversy, and in time would rank as one of the framing events of the next half-century.

Churchill had arrived in New York on the *Queen Elizabeth* in mid-January, en route to Florida, where he had been invited to spend a good part of the winter at the residence of a wealthy Canadian friend. Although he had been in poor health and had undergone an operation, he had much more on his mind than vacationing in "the genial sunshine of Miami Beach." Restless out of power and, as always, seeking action to elude the grasp of the depression that constantly threatened him, Churchill had told his friend and physician, Lord Moran: "I think I can be of some use over there; they will take things from me. It may be that Congress will ask me to address them. I'd like that." Frustrated by his lack of power, he felt the need to "do things." What things? Secretary of State James Byrnes learned about some of them when he flew to Miami to pay Churchill a visit.

Some four months earlier, the president's military aide, a loyal alumnus of Westminster College in Fulton, Missouri, had done the college president the favor of bringing him to the White House and introducing him to Truman. The Westminster president, Dr. Franc McCluer (whose diminutive size had won him a decidedly unacademic nickname, "Bullet"), sought Truman's help in persuading Churchill to come to Fulton for "three or four lectures." Seizing McCluer's letter of invitation, Truman picked up his pen and wrote a postscript: "Dear Winnie. This is a fine old college out in my state. If you'll come out and make them a speech, I'll take you out and introduce you." Churchill accepted immediately. This single speech—as it now became—would offer him at least one opportunity to tell an American audience some of the things on his mind. Later, another appearance would be arranged at a reception and dinner at the Waldorf-Astoria in New York.

As Churchill, nursing a heavy cold, lay in bed in Miami, he gave Jimmy Byrnes a brief version of the message he intended to deliver in Fulton. The secretary of state seemed to find nothing objectionable in what he heard, and when Churchill came to Washington to join the president for the train trip west, Byrnes was given the whole speech to read. The next morning Truman turned down his chance to look over Churchill's words; this way, the president said, he could meet any Soviet charge that the United States and Britain were "ganging up" on Russia by truthfully denying that he had read the speech in advance. This reasoning, however, made it obvious that even if Truman had not read the speech, he knew the essence of its message. Shortly before, in fact, Churchill had made a quick trip up from Florida to go over his ideas with Truman. Then, back in Washington on March 3, Churchill had won Admiral Leahy's approval of his planned remarks. Earlier, in a cable to Prime Minister Attlee, Churchill had, somewhat vaguely and mildly, described his plan and within a few days had received Attlee's blessing. Thus, to a considerable extent, the former prime minister had cleared the possible political obstacles from his path to Fulton.

As the preparations for the Missouri expedition were taking place, war-weary Americans were still trying to adjust to a disappointing and puzzling new world. During the war, with heavy official inspiration and encouragement, Americans had developed great admiration and even fondness for the Soviet people. *Life,* the widely read picture-and-text magazine, characterized the Russians as "one hell of a people," who "look like Americans, dress like Americans and think like Americans"; the NKVD was mildly described as "a national police force similar to the F.B.I." These great people had been America's ally in the great crusade against what many saw as absolute evil. Now, few felt animosity to the Russians, but all were weary of conflict. Just a few days before the trip to Missouri, Robert C. Ruark, a newspaper columnist and former war correspondent, had written in response to reports of tensions with the Soviet Union: "I wish Mr. Churchill and Mr. Stalin and Mr. Truman would all go away and leave me a new refrigerator, a dozen new hats, an automobile, and the stranger I was married to before the war."

On March 5 the ten-car Baltimore & Ohio presidential special pulled out of Washington, headed west for Missouri. Half an hour or so after the train had left Union Station, the door of the club car opened and a jaunty President Truman appeared, telling reporters, "Don't get up. I'm just

making an inspection of the train to see if there's any gambling going on."
A while later, the president put on a pair of cotton gloves and took over
the engineer's post, sitting at the throttle for five minutes as the train rolled
across Virginia. After Churchill, fueled by five Scotches, had regaled, or
perhaps bemused, the company by reciting "Barbara Frietchie" (during
World War II he had given the same performance for President Roosevelt), the two statesmen and their companions enjoyed a steak dinner and
then sat comfortably chatting and playing poker until well after two
o'clock. The next morning, after Churchill had made the final changes in
his text, mimeographed copies were handed out. Looking up from his
copy, Truman—according to Churchill's report to Attlee—called the
speech "admirable" but said it would "make a stir."

Arriving at Jefferson City late in the morning, Churchill and Truman
received from Governor Phil Donnelly, respectively, a box of fifty long Havana
cigars and a hickory-smoked ham. After a ride through the capital in convert-
ibles, the eminent visitors then transferred to closed cars for the twenty-five-
mile drive to Fulton, where they were met by vast crowds—people who had
come from miles around to see the man whose voice, as a correspondent said,
was "as familiar in Missouri as it is in Yorkshire." Bands played "The Missouri
Waltz," and the ladies of the Methodist church had prepared an early supper
for visitors. Street entrepreneurs had brought in almost a ton of hot dogs for
the 30,000 potential customers; other vendors hawked sandwiches, candy, and
souvenirs, and red balloons bounced above the heads of the crowd. After a
fifteen-minute ride through town to enable the people to see Churchill and the
president, the visiting party drove to President McCluer's house for lunch.
Afterward the academic procession, featuring Churchill in a red Oxford robe,
moved to the college gymnasium, the site of the ceremonies. Even if the speech
itself should prove nothing more than routine, Bullet McCluer, by producing
the greatest day in the history of Fulton, had scored an impressive public
relations coup for his college.

As has often been the case in history, the truly enduring feature of
Churchill's address was not the aspect that drew most of the attention of
those who heard him that day. A masterpiece of construction, thoroughly
thought out, carefully organized, repeatedly revised, making use of dramatic
suspense, the speech (as always with Churchill) had nothing impromptu
about it. As the former prime minister carefully built up his argument, it
became clear that the "sinews of peace" consisted of the ties that should
continue to bind together the British Commonwealth and the United States
in a "fraternal association"—an alliance—carrying forward into the nervous
postwar world the relationship that had led to victory in World War II.
Churchill paid due and careful attention to the United Nations, which the
public at the time looked on as the world's vessel of hope for a peaceful

future. Only then, two-thirds of the way through his remarks, did the speaker come to the factual situation that had evoked his proposal for a continued alliance. "From Stettin in the Baltic to Trieste in the Adriatic," he declared, "an iron curtain has descended across the Continent. Behind that line lie all the capitals of the ancient states of central and eastern Europe. Warsaw, Berlin, Prague, Vienna, Budapest, Belgrade, Bucharest, and Sofia, all these famous cities and the populations around them lie in what I might call the Soviet sphere and all are subject, in one form or another, not only to Soviet influence, but to a very high and increasing measure of control from Moscow." Summing up developments during the past year, Churchill declared that the Russian-dominated Polish government was making illicit inroads on Germany, Communist parties had been given power out of all proportion to their size, police governments had been established everywhere except Czechoslovakia, Turkey and Persia were being pressed by Moscow, and the Russians were creating a quasi-Communist Party in their zone of Germany. This last-named activity could lead to a Soviet buildup of a pro-Communist Germany in their area and thus give the Germans the "power of putting themselves up to auction between the Soviets and the Western democracies."

Whatever conclusion his audience might draw from these undoubted facts, Churchill said, "this is certainly not the liberated Europe we fought to build up." And, he said, "nobody knows what Soviet Russia and its Communist international organization intends to do in the immediate future, or"—and here the speaker raised the key question of the era for anybody, regardless of his or her views—"what are the limits, if any, to their expansive and proselytizing tendencies." With this neat and typically Churchillian rhetorical balance—"expansive," for Soviet Russia, and "proselytizing," for international Communism—the former prime minister addressed himself to the twin concerns of the people who looked on the Kremlin with uneasy eyes. Although his listeners did not immediately realize it, he had also given the world what would endure as one of the most famous and characterizing phrases of the postwar era. And as for Berlin, even though the Soviet Union was only one of four powers that had legal rights and responsibilities there, Churchill had placed it behind the "iron curtain"—in the Soviet sphere.

Lieutenant General Lucius DuBignon Clay turned forty-seven in April 1945, just as the war in Europe was ending. A slim, compact man whose face was dominated by heavy black brows and a notably long nose, Clay had grown up in north Georgia; he was the son of a U.S. senator and a descendant of a brother of Henry Clay, once voted the outstanding senator in American history. Whether or not fate picked him out for a special destiny, Lucius Clay, the youngest by far of six children, proved to be the only one to escape the ravages of alcoholism, which killed his brothers and his only sister. He told an interviewer that his brothers had enjoyed early success without having had to work for it, and "therefore attached too little value to it." The death of his father when Clay was only twelve meant that he had a harder financial row to hoe than had his brothers; the family's reduced circumstances constituted probably the principal reason Clay went to West Point, to which, as the son of a senator, he readily received an appointment. Reared among families with many Civil War veterans, Clay once observed that he "had to go to school in the North to learn that the North had won the war."

A natural nonconformist—inner-directed, as people would later put it—with no great respect for discipline and little patience with much of the West Point ritual, Clay ranked first in his class in English and history and always near the bottom in conduct. Assigned, against his expressed desire, to the Corps of Engineers, Clay served in a variety of posts after graduating from the academy in 1918. As was true with other engineer officers, the coming of the Roosevelt administration in 1933 had a strong effect on his career, because of the army engineers' heavy involvement in the great array of dams and other building and reclamation projects that characterized the New Deal; for several years in the 1930s, in fact, Clay represented the corps at congressional hearings on river-and-harbor bills, becoming well known and widely connected in Washington, with a reputation for efficiency, decisiveness, and strict honesty.

After the United States entered World War II, Clay's outstanding reputation worked to his disadvantage when he tried to obtain a combat assignment—he spent most of the war as director of procurement for the army. Representing the army on the War Production Board, Clay with his forcefulness and mastery of facts usually managed to get the allocations he sought. A business executive who sometimes clashed with him in the fight for materials and goods paid him a tribute with a special twist: "After I had been battling with Clay for several months," he said, "I concluded that it must have been someone just like him who originally inspired the association of the adjective 'grudging' with the noun 'admiration.' "

Briefly in Europe in 1944, Clay lent an important helping hand to his friend General Eisenhower by unsnarling the shipping situation at Cherbourg; observers credited him with doubling the flow of supplies to the armies in just a few days. Modestly, Clay explained the feat by saying that he had simply got other officers off the back of the port director, who, given the proper authority, proved highly efficient.

After returning to Washington, Clay spent several months as deputy to

Byrnes, who was then wearing his hat as "assistant president" for war mobilization. Still hoping, like any career officer, to see combat, Clay looked forward to duty in the Pacific, since everyone at the time expected the war against Japan to last well into 1946. Instead, thwarted again, he found himself in March 1945 posted to Germany as deputy military governor under General Eisenhower, then still Allied supreme commander. So little thought out were the possible demands of Clay's new assignment that nobody had clearly drawn the lines of authority and responsibility, but the general quickly moved to ensure that he would report directly to Ike and thus enjoy independence from staff control; "military government responsibility," as Clay said, would be separated from "direct military command as soon as the war ended." He saw immediately that, despite the name, the essence of military government was political rather than military. Later he wrote of his amazement that he "did not visit the State Department or talk with any of its officials." Nor did he know much about the debates between the War Department and the State Department (with the heavy involvement of Secretary of the Treasury Henry Morgenthau) concerning policies and programs for governing Germany after victory.

During much of 1945 Clay acted as de facto U.S. military governor, though the peripatetic Eisenhower officially held the position until November, when he went to Washington to become chief of staff of the army. General Joseph T. McNarney, who had served as deputy chief of staff during the war, replaced Ike as troop commander in Europe and, formally, as military governor, with Clay continuing as deputy for military government and head of OMGUS, the Office of Military Government for Germany (U.S.). Everybody on all sides accurately regarded Clay as the actual military governor, although he did not acquire the title until March 1947, when he also succeeded McNarney as commander of U.S. forces. As his official guide in the conduct of his duties, Clay had a top-secret document, known as JCS (for Joint Chiefs of Staff) 1067, issued in its final form two weeks after V-E Day. In the early months this secrecy caused problems for the American commanders, since their own subordinates as well as members of the press tended to presume that U.S. military government had no administrative or procedural plan but simply dealt with the Germans through day-to-day improvisation. In spite of Clay's best efforts, his superiors did not unshroud the directive until October.

JCS 1067 had not come from the minds and typewriters of officials who admired or sympathized with the Germans. Even before American generals and reporters had confronted the horrors of the Nazi camps, the lurid and degenerate nature of Hitler's regime had ensured that the victors would not arrive in Germany with charity in their thoughts. The most vengeful plan was produced by Morgenthau, who as a Jew had kept specially close watch on the

Nazis. "Long before the war and the worst of the pogroms," noted the secretary's biographer, John Morton Blum, "Morgenthau had worried about the European Jews whom politics put at Hitler's mercy." The secretary later referred to the last phase of the war, when he and others had some knowedge of the Nazis' plans for extermination of Jews, as "those terrible eighteen months." Morgenthau at first won the support of Roosevelt, his old friend and Dutchess County neighbor, for a scheme to turn Germany, the industrial heart of Europe, into a land of farmers and shepherds. Though FDR retreated from the plan when commentators of every stripe pointed out its obvious flaws, much of its punitive spirit survived into successive versions of JCS 1067, with the chiefs tending to echo the Morgenthau position and the State Department emphasizing its impractical nature; FDR offered only wavering and self-contradictory guidance (though three weeks before his death, he declared that he did not wish to destroy German industry but did want to see it decentralized).

After Roosevelt's death Truman, accepting the final May 1945 document as part of his legacy from FDR, gave it his approval. One historian has characterized this document as "an agreement glued together with careful phraseology, by avoiding issues or delegating their determination in the absence of agreement." Hence those who wanted to abolish German industry and those who took a more moderate line each gained something; inevitably, this indeterminacy or ambiguity also left a large ground of decision open to the military governor.

No matter what their various points of view, the drafters of 1067, working while the war was still on, could not know the actual conditions under which military government would take up its heavy tasks. Nor could they know how long the occupation might last; in view of the isolationist American past, President Roosevelt and others thought that two years would be as long as the public would support a policy of maintaining forces in Germany. Roosevelt told Stalin the same thing—information that, harmonizing perfectly with the generalissimo's desire to play the part of European colossus like Czar Alexander I after Waterloo, surely made an important contribution to the formulation of Stalin's postwar strategic calculus. Combining the prospects of a brief U.S. presence in Europe and the fresh economic depression he anticipated for the West, Stalin could contemplate the map of Europe in late 1945 with great expectations.

Yet the Soviet premier could never find full satisfaction—perhaps the Americans would not even stay in Europe long enough. In a September 1946 cable from Washington, Ambassador Nikolai Novikov warned that the United States was considering ending the occupation "before the main tasks of the ocupation—the demilitarization and democratization of Germany—have been implemented." Such a move would "create the prerequisites for the revival of an imperialist Germany, which the United States plans to use in a future war on its side."

Telling Roosevelt that the American people would not stand for a lengthy commitment of troops to Europe, Leahy had once suggested that the United States give France its occupation zone and simply bring the troops home; then–Secretary of State Edward R. Stettinius had presumed that the admiral was joking. In essence, in any case, the planners in the European Advisory Commission anticipated a relatively short occupation, which would last only until the signing of the peace treaty.

Speaking for the Americans on the spot in Germany in 1945, Clay said that "if we had then realized the confusion and chaos which existed we would indeed have thought ours a hopeless task. Certainly the authorities in Washington who had prepared our policy directive did not visualize these conditions"—conditions that thoroughly tested the military-government teams that accompanied the armies as they moved into the Reich. Clay's special economics adviser, Lewis Douglas, a business executive and government official (soon to become ambassador to Britain), said that JCS 1067 had been "assembled by economic idiots"; despite Germany's misdeeds, Douglas believed, it was absurd "to forbid the most skilled workers in Europe from working as much as they can for a continent which is desperately short of everything." But Douglas's attempt to win modification of the directive failed. At their backs, coming from across the Atlantic, the military government administrators could hear continuing demands for the "hard" peace they were expected to impose on the Germans; anytime the peace appeared to be turning soft, cries of criticism arose. Many people in the Allied countries felt that if the Germans were hungry and homeless, they had nobody to blame but themselves; having created their own misery, they deserved little in the way of sympathy. Clay later told an interviewer that "you had a tremendous amount of understandable bitterness and hatred that failed to, or wouldn't, recognize that you couldn't have an empty void in the center of Europe, and any efforts that you made to fill that void you knew were going to be met with tremendous criticism and resentment."

Shortly after arriving in Germany and seeing the devastation, which he called "far greater than is realized at home," Clay took care to defend himself against any possible charge of "getting soft" by saying that he realized the need for "stern and spartan treatment." In July at Potsdam, however, Clay had the benefit of some thoughtful counsel from the veteran statesman Henry L. Stimson, who had served as secretary of war since 1940. As Clay recalled the conversation, Stimson told him that regardless of how vindictive the American people might feel at the moment, "just remember that in the long run, unless you restore an economic life to these people under which they have some hope, you will be repudiated by the very people who have given you these instructions." Overall, Clay in later years saw JCS 1067 as "too vindictive a directive to have long suited the American people, because we are not a vindictive people."

In July, as Eisenhower's Allied command was turning control of its portion of Germany over to the individual national forces—which meant that JCS 1067 would now come into effect in the American zone—the U.S. command issued administrative regulations for application of the directive. As modified after the Potsdam Conference (which in effect adopted much of the directive for all the Allies), the rules involved the "five *d*'s": demilitarization, denazification, deindustrialization, decentralization, and democratization. Though divided into zones, the country was supposed to be treated as a single economic unit under the Allied Control Council (ACC), which would be made up of the commanders in chief and would sit in Berlin—which itself would also be divided into four sectors and would be governed by a "Kommandatura" reporting directly to the ACC. Denazification held prime importance for the Americans; the remnants of Nazism were to be pulled up by the roots in preparation for a future civilized and democratic Germany. In October, in pursuit of this aim, General Clay issued Military Government Law No. 8, which forbade Nazis and Nazi sympathizers from holding any job, public or private, above the level of common laborer. The British paid much less attention to denazification, and the Russians not only disregarded it but made heavy use of former Nazi officials in their administration. For his part, General Eisenhower had also put heavy emphasis on nonfraternization—no social relationships with Germans—but, paying no attention, GIs in large numbers eagerly pursued fräuleins; the policy collapsed almost as soon as it supposedly came into effect. Howard K. Smith, the CBS radio correspondent, commented that "there might as well have been laws requiring the moon to rise up square."

On hearing the word that U.S. forces would begin the move to Berlin on June 30, one U.S. officer expressed his pleasure that "the days of waiting, of backing and filling, were over. It was now Berlin for certain, with a full armored division and the 1st AB Army."

This long-awaited move would not mark the first appearance of American forces in the city. Earlier in June, Colonel Frank Howley, the designated military government deputy for the U.S. sector—and an advertising executive in civilian life—had led a reconnaissance party to assess the scene in Berlin. Keenly aware of the importance of appearances, Howley decided that "no non-GI vehicles or equipment would be taken into Berlin on this trip—I didn't want the Russians to see a miscellaneous collection of vehicles representing the American Army. It was my intention to make this advance party a spectacular thing. It would be the first ground party of Americans to go through the Russians into Berlin, and I wanted it to look as such." This group grew into "a formidable party of 114 vehicles including trailers, jeeps and ten-ton trucks."

The full-scale movement begun on June 30 did not go nearly so well as Howley's reconnaissance. The operation proceeded slowly and, "to make matters worse, the rain began to fall as we approached the Berliner Ring. With no billets to go to, we wound up in the Grunewald, that great forest park in the southwestern area of the city. The cruelest blow of all was to have to set up pup tents in the mud and rain and crawl into them for the night." The U.S. high command clearly lacked Howley's psychological insight; to Lieutenant Colonel John Maginnis, assigned to command one of the six boroughs *(Verwaltungsbezirke)* in the U.S. sector, the operation was "undoubtedly the most unimpressive entry in history to the capital of a defeated enemy nation, by the armed forces of a great conquering power. Right then and there in the feelings of the U.S. forces to a man, there was instilled a feeling of resentment against the Russians that was never really to disappear." (This muffing of an opportunity to make a favorable high-level impression did not lack striking historical precedents in Germany. Just seven years earlier, beginning the series of meetings that led to Anglo-French capitulation to Hitler at Munich, Prime Minister Neville Chamberlain, though representing the power and majesty of the British Empire, flew unescorted to Germany in a single small commercial airplane. As uniformed and bemedaled Nazi grandees watched, Chamberlain clambered down from his aircraft, looking like nobody more potent than a salesman arriving in a new town and hoping to fill a page or two of his order book.)

One feature of Berlin made a strong impression on Howley and Maginnis. All around the city the Russians had put up billboards bearing slogans intended to appeal to what a later generation would call the hearts and minds of the populace: HITLERS COME AND GO BUT THE GERMAN PEOPLE GO ON FOREVER . . . THE GREAT RED ARMY HAS SAVED BERLIN . . . THE RED ARMY DOES NOT MAKE WAR ON THE GERMAN PEOPLE. But Maginnis couldn't help wondering whether this devastated city was really worth bothering with. He did not know that an explicit Soviet order directed troops moving out of the Western sectors of Berlin to leave "not even a pisspot" behind.

At the beginning of July, General Clay set up a small temporary office in Berlin, while staff members looked for enough space to establish the U.S. section of the Allied Control Council. As Eisenhower's deputy theater commander and as deputy military governor (in effect, deputy for military government), Clay held broad dual responsibilities. Such overlapping authority was characteristic of the U.S. military at various levels during the occupation; the lines of authority may have looked precise on flow charts, but in practice they were frequently intertwined, though Clay always had the aim of keeping military government to itself, separate from the chain of military command.

To Clay's satisfaction, a Fourth of July parade by men of the Hell on Wheels division proclaimed for all to see that the Americans were on hand to assume official responsibility in their sector. During these days Clay had his first chance to explore Berlin, a city still inert with social and economic paralysis. Cleanup crews continued to haul dead bodies from the rubble of bombed buildings and fish them from canals and lakes. In one borough almost half of the houses had been completely destroyed and only 5 percent had escaped damage. With most of the pumping stations destroyed, outfalls dumped floods of untreated sewage into the canals. Subsisting on a diet of about 800 calories a day—two-thirds of the official ration, itself meager enough—workers hired to repair buildings for use as military government offices were collapsing as they wielded their tools, until the Americans set up a hot lunch program for them. Though he had to battle Soviet officialdom merely to get himself and his men into their assigned portion of Berlin, Colonel Howley immediately set to work around the clock to attack the paralysis, as if confronting and cleaning up the results of a hurricane or any other natural disaster and, Clay said, also bringing the "humanitarian touch of America to the stern task of occupation."

The U.S. settling-in period, which began on July 2, came to its formal end at the unlikely hour of four A.M. on July 12, when, as Russian officers slept, the Americans raised their flag and officially took over their sector. During this ten-day "dawn period," as Howley called it, numerous incidents arose with the Russians. One day the colonel received word that the local Soviet commander in Kreuzberg, one of the boroughs in the sector the Americans were occupying, had declared his intention of tearing down various proclamations U.S. officials had posted. At the same time the Soviet commander coolly suggested that the Americans do the removing themselves, to keep the Germans from witnessing a difference of opinion between the victors. The matter was settled amiably enough, on the grounds that within three or four days, in any case, the Americans would take formal charge of the borough.

In April, Clay had written Byrnes, with whom he had developed a warm relationship during the months they worked together, that "too much of our planning at home has envisaged a Germany in which an existing government has surrendered with a large part of the country intact. In point of fact, it looks as if every foot of ground will have to be occupied." Later Clay commented that he doubted "if there ever had been a complete collapse of government anywhere as there was in Germany. You see, Japan still had the emperor and they still had cabinet members; they still had the machinery of government to work with. We had none. We had to re-create everything from scratch, and it was a rough and difficult job." Just about a week after sending off his letter to Byrnes, Clay declared to Assistant Secretary of War John J. McCloy that "Washington must revise its thinking relative to destruction of Germany's war potential," which the war itself had accomplished; the industry that remained, said the general, "even when restored will suffice barely for a very low minimum living standard in Germany." The American command must have "sufficient freedom here to bring industries back into production for that purpose." In sum, said Clay, "it is going to take all we can do to re-establish government services and a semblance of national economy for many months."

The general believed that the essence of the situation could be simply expressed: If the Germans could not produce for export and thus earn money to pay for imports, they would starve; in the absence of any German authority capable of taking the measures needed to revive industrial production, therefore, military government would have to do it. In May, writing to Major General John H. Hilldring, director of G-5, the Civil Affairs Division of the War Department, Clay vouchsafed the not-altogether-subtle hope that "our directives can be flexible and general rather than specific until we have been able to develop the information that will enable you at home to develop sound policy." He also expressed his consistent desire to make German civilians responsible for their own administration as soon as the occupation had achieved order and stability in the country.

Replying to Clay's request for greater formal freedom, Hilldring stuck by 1067 but added that Clay should allow time for long-range policy to "bubble up out of the facts you uncover in Germany"; Clay himself, Hilldring commented, would certainly not want to be "personally responsible for formulating the U.S. policy in Germany." Hilldring apparently did not realize the importance of two related traits of Clay's character—his high degree of inner-directedness and his faith in the soundness of that direction. Ideally, certainly, Clay would prefer a directive with which he could agree completely; also, given a directive with which he thoroughly disagreed, he would simply resign (as he later proved several times). Left between those poles, however, he would hardly sit and fret while trying to decide what to do. Indeed, taking note of Clay's appointment to Germany, the *Washington Post* had commented that "General Clay's exceedingly high abilities are better suited to the German situation than to our own. The task calls for authoritarianism."

Clay had yet to show the world another important side of his character. But its day would come.

CHAPTER 7

General and Chargé

AT THE ALLIED Control Council meeting of July 7 the representatives of the four occupying powers agreed to create an Allied governing council for Berlin as foreseen in Article Seven of the Allied agreement of November 14, 1944. This council received the name "Kommandatura"—an illegitimate, coined word of Russian-German parentage. (The Russian word is *Komendatura,* the German *Kommandantur.)*

Food for Berlin and reparations for Russia would constitute continuing problems for the ACC. At the July 7 meeting Marshal Zhukov declared that since eastern German territories had been lost to Poland, the area around Berlin could not supply food for the Allied sectors of the city. Temporarily, hoping that a standardized ration would soon be established throughout Germany, General Clay agreed that the United States would bring in food for the people in its sector. The commanders also decided that henceforth the French would take part in the meetings and that the Kommandatura would function under operating procedures detailed in a document presented by the Russians; like the agreements governing the Control Council itself, it called for unanimity—no rule for governing Berlin could be adopted unless all four Allied commandants favored it. This quickly led to something like the freezing of the status quo the Soviets had established in Berlin between early May and the arrival of the Western allies in early July, since nothing could be changed if the Soviet commandant did not agree.

Speaking of the meeting place of the Allied Control Council, a French writer observed that "there are some places marked by destiny." This building in the heart of Berlin, the one-time seat of the Prussian Court of Appeals, had suffered some bomb damage, but Clay's engineers got it into shape for the ACC meeting on August 10, 1945. A large building "not without elegance," five stories and 546 rooms, it had two interior court-yards, with added wings, and in front a park with a circle of trees. Destiny's latest previous act marking this building had been one of the most tragic dramas of the Nazi era, the sessions of the People's Court in which the authors of the July 20, 1944, plot against Hitler had been cursed and reviled before being condemned to hanging with piano wire; the chief judge, Roland Freisler, a merciless cross-examiner, had won from Hitler the admiring appellation "our Vyshinsky." Looking over the building, the French reporter could easily imagine prisoners being led through the long corridors to the many interrogators' offices that opened off them. Coming together every ten days, the delegations of the four occupying powers sat at tables forming a square, each occupying one side. The presidency changed each month, and the delegations moved around the table so that the chairman always sat with his back to the fireplace. The country chairing also had charge of the refreshments, each taking the opportunity to present its national specialties.

Just below the Control Council stood the Coordination Committee, on which sat the deputies of the commanders and which drew up all the specific rules for carrying out decisions of the council (and which often became confused with the council). Below the council and the committee functioned twelve directorates—dealing with areas such as transport, finance, and reparations—and numerous committees and subcommittees on which all the four powers were represented.

The Berlin Kommandatura established itself in a three-story brick building with the flags of the four powers flying in front. This organism, which had direct administrative duties, supervised the affairs of the municipality. Made up of the four commandants with their staffs, it worked through specialized committees (such as public services, economy, and police). In effect, as the French reporter observed, the Kommandatura represented the quadripartite command organism of a fifth German zone consisting of Greater Berlin. Official figures (compiled in the early autumn of 1945) broke down the population of this special zone as: American sector, 905,455; British sector, 581,897; French sector, 406,744; Soviet sector, 1,124,414.

Although Clay immediately found that negotiating with Marshal Zhukov and his colleagues had its complexities and its irritations, he did not come to the four-power table as an opponent of the Russians; instead, he placed a high priority on establishing good working relations with them. A problem solver, a man who produced results wherever he went, Clay took up his assignment in Germany with no particular knowledge of the country or of the Soviet Union; if U.S. policy called for four-power cooperation, then Clay would do his damnedest to achieve it. He was, in fact, the high-ranking officer who, in conversation with George Kennan, had criticized State Department officials for their inability "to get along with the Russians." Relations between the delegates were "truly excellent," noted the

French reporter. According to another observer, Clay and his Soviet counterpart, the elegant and unproletarianly tailored Marshal Sokolovsky, might insult each other during council meetings, but afterward they would stroll out, arm in arm, for a drink. However heated the discussions, members of all the delegations usually met an hour later around the same table in the restaurant or bar of "the Building," and they invited each other to their homes for dinner. Clay even forbade Germans with whom he dealt to criticize Russians in his presence.

Though the Russians frequently violated sector boundaries to assault and sometimes kidnap Germans, this behavior seemed to disturb Colonel Howley—who, as military government chief in the city, had to deal with it directly—more than it did Clay. Thus the general genuinely epitomized the spirit of the army as expressed to Kennan: he was determined to get along with the Soviet representatives and to make four-power control of Germany work. "We are going to have to give and take and do a lot of things which the American public will not believe in," Clay said in a press conference shortly after V-E Day, "but we cannot go in there with four nations without being prepared to give and take." Later, replying to an interviewer who spoke of him as "very self-disciplined with a burning desire to excel," the general responded: "I never thought of it that way. I don't know that I ever thought of anything except the particular job at hand. The job has to be done, and it is up to me in my capacity to do it. In my day you didn't get a choice. I can't remember any job that I ever went on that I asked for." In the military establishment, Clay said, you would "take whatever job you were given and do a good job of handling it." But he conceded that if you acquired a reputation as a soldier who succeeded at the jobs he undertook, you probably had a desire to maintain that reputation and therefore would "work a little harder, a little longer, and be a little more determined."

Like many other prominent commanders, and civilian entrepreneurs as well, Clay had his quirks. A political scientist on his staff spoke of the general's "engineering habit of rushing things through," which sometimes led him to take unwise actions without giving himself time for reflection. After a ride through the countryside, in which various street signs engaged his attention, he returned to the office and ordered that all markers bearing the names of Bismarck, Frederick the Great, and other figures of older German history join Nazi names in municipal dumps. Another day the general, apparently believing that personal titles could cause social problems, issued an order forbidding German officials to use such universally employed distinctions as president, commissioner, and director. More fundamentally, his experience in Washington, while giving him a measure of practical political sophistication, had not called for him to confront and settle complex political issues—and the issues presented by Germany, a foreign country to all the occupiers, were as complicated as such issues could ever be.

As time went on, Clay, for all the talk of his authoritarianism, revealed himself by his actions to be something of an unusual phenomenon—something like the kind of democrat Thomas Jefferson might have been if he had lived in an industrial age. Believing strongly in a free press, for instance, Clay allowed newspapers to flourish uncontrolled, and when his staff sought to shut down a local publication that had criticized him, the general expressed his irritation. How were the Germans going to learn democratic ways if they were not allowed to practice them?

Though determined to work on a friendly and understanding basis with the Russians, Clay found other opponents showing their colors. Hardly had the Big Three left Potsdam and returned to their home countries when Clay, who was dedicated to creating central German administrative mechanisms to stimulate and guide the economy, ran into opposition from the French. Pointing out that the Big Three had turned down his request to take part in the Potsdam Conference, General Charles de Gaulle, head of the French provisional government, declared that he would act as he saw fit with respect to decisions taken at the conference. In notes delivered to his allies on August 7, his foreign minister, Georges Bidault, a historian and journalist who had spent a year as a prisoner of war of the Germans and after his release had played an important part in the Resistance, expressed doubts about the declared Allied plans for Germany; some days later, in a talk with Secretary Byrnes, Bidault clarified French objections. France needed much more in the way of reparations—coal, machinery, labor services by the Germans—than the agreement stipulated. In addition, just as the Russians had acquired territory in the east, the French wanted their share in the west.

Repeatedly the French made it plain that they strenuously opposed the creation (or re-creation) of a centralized Germany. Miraculously, the one-time mighty Reich, their tormentor since Bismarck's day, now lay prostrate and dismembered, able to threaten nobody. Indeed, since the time of Cardinal Richelieu in the seventeenth century, French leaders of all political persuasions had striven to keep the German lands divided, only to meet failure and defeat in the mid-nineteenth century. Contrasting strongly with the picture after World War I, when Germany, though beaten, had remained the greatest country in Europe outside of Russia, the marvelous state of affairs that had developed in 1945 must last as long as possible. And, Bidault had said, the French feared that the Russians would dominate a unified Germany. Certainly, the French declared, they could not accept any administration that presumed to exert authority over the industrial Ruhr and the Rhineland, areas the French wished to see detached from Germany and put under international control.

With the Soviet-sponsored Poles absorbing a large part of eastern Germany and the French trying to stake a claim, if indirectly, on a major part of the west, the result, if achieved, would be a skeletonized Germany shorn of many of its farms and factories. Despite his joke about turning over the U.S. zone to the French, Admiral Leahy, who early in the war had served FDR as ambassador to the rump Vichy French state, had little faith in France; he saw it as occupying "mythical" status as a great power and, in consequence, likely to cause discord among the truly great powers. France might be a necessary partner in the occupation of Germany, but the admiral held no great hopes for the fruitfulness of the arrangement.

Since the French seemed determined to block the achievement of centralized administration, Clay told his superiors in Washington, he believed it "essential" that the Americans bypass them and deal directly with the British and Soviet opposite numbers to establish trizonal arrangements; he also moved to set up administrative structures in the three German states that made up the U.S. zone. (The Soviets had already taken a similar step in their zone.) Back in Washington for meetings in November, Clay pressed his point but found few takers. The split between the War Department and the State Department followed the lines of the earlier discussion between Clay and George Kennan; put another way, the line was drawn between the diplomats, who had past experience with the Soviets, and the soldiers, who were new to this particular arena. The diplomats regarded the soldiers as naive; the soldiers thought the diplomats simply anti-Soviet—and pro-French besides. Well into 1946 Clay and the army generally saw French obstructionism rather than Soviet hostility as the main roadblock to achieving central administration for Germany. They held to this view even while acknowledging that the Russians often caused problems: they forbade travel between their zone and others, for instance, and they did not favor interzonal trade. In their own zone they indulged in frequent harsh and undemocratic conduct: they moved people around like cattle, they allowed no free press, they imposed their own concept of "land reform."

Despite all the stresses, civility continued to mark the sessions of the Control Council. With the Americans in the chair on the first anniversary of the creation of the council, General Clay produced a birthday cake, which he cut in four with a sword. In December the Americans decorated the meeting room with candles and garlands, and at the meeting just before Christmas an American staff member even produced an electric train, which the generals seemed to enjoy playing with but had trouble operating. Some who watched the fun claimed that the Soviet representative caused derailments on purpose; after such an incident he would say "French *maquisards*"—a sly reference to the sabotage activities of the French underground during the German occupation. (Apparently others besides Clay saw the French as impediments to action.)

On April 22, 1946, in a bad augury for democracy—at least, in the Western sense—Soviet pressure forced the merger of the Social Democratic Party in their zone with the German Communist Party; in effect, the Social Democrats, though more numerous, were taken over by the Communists, as if, in the business world, a small company should absorb a larger corporation; the new shotgun entity received the name Socialist Unity Party. One writer termed the process by which the Communists achieved this success "gradual strangulation" of the opposition with the help of the Soviet Military Administration.

Even so, from Clay's point of view, the French still caused more problems. The French behavior actually provided the Soviets with an unearned political bonus: Whether or not they might really want a centralized control structure, they could win favor with Germans by calling for it while secure in the knowledge that they would not have to make good because the French would veto it in the ACC. The Russians could make additional hay by accusing the United States and Britain of hiding behind the French, using them to block centralized control. They might even believe that this was really the case—though, to be sure, Clay had told them otherwise: the Russians would no doubt have been amazed to hear the earnestness with which Clay defended them.

Just a few days before Soviet pressure created the fused Socialist Unity Party, Colonel Howley told Maginnis, justly enough: "I don't wonder that the Americans have finally become fed up with the Russians. We Americans always love people too much or hate them too much. It is a very extreme characteristic which we blame the Germans for having." But then Howley, even after a year of intricate and often frustrating frontline dealings with the Soviets, could go on to say, "Actually I'm always surprised at how well we get along with the Russians. We differ from them in almost everything: ideals, government, wealth, social graces, etc. Yet, here in Berlin we have married the girl before we have courted her. It's like one of those old-fashioned marriages when the bride and groom practically met each other in bed. Now we are discovering our great differences and I for one, am not a bit worried about it, provided we have commandants here who will use a reasonable amount of courage and tact. By tact I mean skill to try and get along with the Russians at every point, and by courage to go and get things done if they cannot get along with the Russians."

Despite his soft words, Howley himself often took very direct action to counter the Russians. Hans-Karl Behrend remembered what happened one day when a Soviet military train made a stop in Zehlendorf. Though "there wasn't much to steal," Russian troops leaped from the train and began to loot stores. When U.S. MPs arrived in jeeps, they "reacted in absolutely undiplomatic fashion," beating back the Russians with their clubs. "This was done without great deliberations," Behrend commented, "and without someone mediating. It was instantaneous action and instantaneous success." Howley, who was not a regular army officer, earned much respect from Berliners, Behrend said, and more than that, "he was liked and, I guess by some people, almost loved. He was not only highly energetic, he was not the snobbish type people sometimes are when they have graduated from one of the famous military colleges in the United States." Here Behrend displayed a measure of psychological insight; Howley's friend Maginnis saw the same point from the other end of the tube: "One thing I had been discovering about him of late that puzzled me was that he was wary, even suspicious of regular army officers. Why this attitude existed I never knew but it was there. It was not a mood; it was an ingrained feeling that evidenced itself from time to time. . . . I believed, unfortunately, that this attitude of his was not lost on the regular officers, especially those whose displeasure one could ill afford to arouse." Among those with potent displeasure was surely General Clay. But Berliners, it seemed, admired the way Howley "did not allow the Russians to push him around in the city Kommandatura."

"We took reparations after the war, but these were trifles," V. M. Molotov told his interviewer some thirty years later. These in-kind reparations consisted of obsolete equipment, the old foreign minister said, "but there was no other way out. Even if it offered only minor alleviation, it had to be used."

After the tremendous devastation wreaked in the Soviet Union by the invading Wehrmacht, nobody questioned the Russians' right to receive compensation—reparations—from the Germans. But what kind of compensation, how much, and how it should be collected constituted continuing questions. At Potsdam, Secretary Byrnes believed that he had arranged a workable compromise with Soviet demands—an arrangement whereby the Russians could take, in the way of dismantled factories and other equipment, what they wished from their occupation zone and a level of reparations from the other zones, part of it in exchange for Soviet goods.

Without a central German administration, however, the Western military governors found themselves in a box, since the reparations were to come from productive capacity beyond the level needed for Germany to maintain a standard of living equal to that of its neighbors, and the Allied Control Council had to decide that level. After pushing for determination of the level for many months, Clay achieved success in March 1946. The powers reached agreement on the twenty-eighth, and three days later the first shipment went off to Russia. But Clay's triumph proved short-lived. Though he clearly favored and had fought for the establishment of a program of reparations, on May 3, in a surprising move, he revoked U.S. participation. This move of course affected the Russians, but more than anything else it represented Clay's disgust both with the French, who received reparations but continued to oppose the creation of a central administration, and with the State Department, for failing to put pressure on the the French to cooperate with the other powers. In a press conference Clay explained himself by saying that that in its zone the United States would not "dismantle any further plants except that ones that have already been allocated." When the powers established the mechanisms that had been agreed to at Potsdam, he said, reparations would resume. In a letter to Eisenhower, now chief of staff, Clay did not completely exculpate the Russians. "Economic integration is becoming less each day," he said, "with the Soviet and French zones requiring approval for practically each item leaving their respective zones." But in other comments he made it clear that he was taking his primary aim at the French.

For all his problems during this troubled year, Clay could yet win an accolade from the economist John Kenneth Galbraith. Viewing the situation with a measure of optimism, Galbraith declared that "General Clay's patient and brilliant bargaining has earned him not only the profound respect (though not necessarily the deep affection) of his Russian, French, and British colleagues but also has won such liberal measures as four-power inspection of disarmament in all Germany, exchange of oil, rubber, dyestuffs, and other basic commodities between the Russian and American zones, and city-wide and genuinely free elections in Berlin—to pick only three examples at random." Galbraith saw such dealings as signs of hope for business in the future. Others saw matters in quite a different light. One such observer soon made his views known in a memorable fashion.

In February 1946 the U.S. embassy in Moscow received a query, originating in the Treasury Department and sent through the State Department, concerning the Soviet government's lack of interest in joining two international financial agencies, the World Bank and the International Monetary Fund. Why, the disappointed officials wondered, were the Russians being aloof? This minor question came to the irritated attention of the chargé d'affaires in Moscow, George Kennan, as he lay in bed fighting a bad cold, sinus trouble, and a toothache. Kennan immediately had a question of his own:

What was the matter with those naive people at Treasury that they persisted in holding on to their unrealistic picture of the Soviet Union? "It was no good," Kennan said, "trying to brush the question off with a couple of routine sentences describing Soviet views on such things as international banks and world monetary funds." Now was the time to tell Washington the whole truth: "They had asked for it. Now, by God, they would have it."

Taking advantage of the department's request for analysis of Soviet policy, with his normal restraint weakened by his complex of miseries and the aftereffects of sulfa drugs, Kennan called in his secretary and, seizing the moment, dictated not merely a thorough answer to the query from Washington but a monumental lecture, an eight-thousand-word disquisition on Soviet attitudes and purposes that would become renowned in U.S. foreign policy circles as the Long Telegram.

He divided the message, dispatched on February 22, into five parts, Kennan later said, so that it would not look "so outrageously long." He began with "Basic features of postwar Soviet outlook, as put forward by official propaganda machine" and continued with "Background of outlook," "Projection of Soviet outlook in practical policy on official level," and "What we may expect by way of implementation of basic Soviet policies on unofficial, or subterranean, plane, i.e., on plane for which Soviet government accepts no responsibility" (front organizations and stooges, as Kennan explained). The telegram concluded with practical deductions for the framing of American policy. Among his many points, Kennan explained that the Soviet Union still nurtured the idea of "antagonistic 'capitalist encirclement,'" with which no permanent peaceful coexistence was possible, and it insisted on "relentless battle with socialist and social-democratic leaders" (such as, indeed, Clement Attlee and Ernest Bevin). This neurotic view of world affairs, Kennan said, arose from inner-Russian causes rather than from events in the external world, and Marxism-Leninism offered "a perfect vehicle for [the] sense of insecurity with which Bolsheviks, even more than previous Russian rulers, were afflicted." Communist dogma with its high-sounding purposes provided "justification for their instinctive fear of [the] outside world, for the dictatorship without which they did not know how to rule, for cruelties they did not dare not to inflict, for sacrifices they felt bound to demand." Hence no one should underestimate the importance of Communist dogma.

When it seemed feasible, Kennan said, the Soviet government would attempt "to advance [the] official limits of Soviet power"—a statement that could have been made by an eavesdropper on the conversations of Stalin and Molotov. Unofficially, through its international organizations, the Kremlin would attempt to "undermine [the] general political and strategic potential of [the] major Western Powers" and to set these powers against each other—British versus Americans, Germans versus both. The Soviets, Kennan declared, constituted "a political force committed fanatically to the belief that with US there can be no permanent modus vivendi." But Soviet power did not take unnecessary risks; hence, if the adversary had sufficient strength and displayed his willingness to use it, he rarely had to do so. American dealings with the Soviet Union, Kennan said, ought to be "placed entirely on [a] realistic and matter-of-fact basis." In addition, in dealing with other countries, the United States should put forward a "more positive and constructive picture of the sort of world we would like to see."

The concision, force, and elegance with which Kennan presented his views ensured that they would attract important attention in early 1946, a time in which the American giant stood uncomfortably on two legs, not yet sure which one rested on solid ground and should therefore bear the main weight of policy. To strive to cooperate with the Russians and to get along with them? Or to recognize them as threats to security and peace and stand up to them? Which should it be? Kennan's magisterial telegram provided a flash of light for Washington, a moment of crystallization. Clearly, irresistibly, he had explained what lay behind the Soviet actions that had divided and distressed American policymakers. Now such actions made their own kind of sense. Now one could see how the Soviets could talk democracy in Eastern Europe and then remorselessly crush democrats.

Kennan's voice did not reach the West as a lone warning from Moscow. The thinking of officials of the British Foreign Office drew much of its direction from the reports of their own expert, Frank Roberts, chargé d'affaires in the Moscow embassy and thus Kennan's opposite number. Some ten months before Kennan's telegram, Roberts had told his colleagues back in London that "there is a fundamental divergence between Soviet political philosophy and totalitarian practices and the way of life of the outside world. Given these facts we should be rash to base our policy upon the hope that in the foreseeable future the Soviet Union will settle down into a country with whom our relations can be normal and easy." So nearly eye to eye did Kennan and Roberts view the Soviet phenomenon that, as Roberts told an interviewer many years later, the two would joke about the needless expense their governments had incurred in maintaining two embassies in Moscow.

Several weeks after Kennan had dispatched his telegram to Washington, Roberts told London that the Soviets' "very lack of moderation . . . the way in which they have pressed their demands simultaneously throughout the world, the impression they have created that there is no limit to Soviet aims and that a concession in one place merely leads to further demands elsewhere—now seem to have alarmed the Americans as much as ourselves"—a development for which Foreign Office officials had hoped for a year and a half. Listening to Soviet political speeches, Roberts said, could lead one to ask "whether the world is not now faced with the danger of a modern equivalent of the religious wars of the 16th century, in which Soviet communism will struggle with Western social democracy and the American version of capitalism for domination of the world." Part of what Roberts sensed at this time was the beginning of an intensely xenophobic phase of Soviet policy that would become known as the Zhdanovshchina, from the name of Andrei Zhdanov, Stalin's spokesman on cultural matters; "bourgeois" culture, Zhdanov declared, was "putrid and baneful in its moral foundations."

Neither in Britain nor in the United States did the ideas of the two foreign affairs professionals translate directly into political action. For the Americans, ideas and action probably had a more tortuous relationship, in good part because of all the different centers of power that expected to have a say in the creation of U.S. policy; besides, important segments of opinion both inside and outside the government opposed the State Department almost on principle. Lord Halifax, the appeasement-minded foreign secretary from 1938 to 1940 in the Cabinet of Neville Chamberlain and ambassador in Washington during most of World War II, spoke of the "sometimes almost unbearable methods" of his American hosts, adding parenthetically, "from which we may educate them gradually but which we cannot hope to change quickly." (For all their flaws, U.S. policymakers might well have expressed surprise, or even a bit of ironic amusement, had they been able to peek into the British diplomatic pouch and glimpse such evidence of condescension on the part of one of the most disastrous English foreign ministers since Henry III established the position of "king's secretary" in 1253.)

After Kennan's telegram arrived in Washington, however, it followed anything but a tortuous course, quickly achieving almost mass circulation. His old chief in Moscow, Averell Harriman, applauding its message, passed it on to the fervidly anti-Communist secretary of the navy, James Forrestal, who distributed hundreds of copies; it was read by many high officials, though probably not by the president himself, as it moved through the corridors of power in Washington. Notable among its readers was an aide to Truman, Clark Clifford, who would soon preside over the drafting of an administration document, "American Relations with the Soviet Union" (with an analysis so "hot" that President Truman ordered all ten copies put under lock and key). In all, a great vacuum in the realm of policy seemed suddenly to have been filled. "Six months earlier," wrote Kennan subsequently, "this message would probably have been received in the Department of State with raised eyebrows and lips pursed in disapproval. Six months later, it would probably have sounded redundant"—although "the realities which it described had existed, substantially unchanged, for about a decade, and would continue to exist for more than a half-decade longer." The point of it all, Kennan decided, was that in Washington a message was heard when people were ready to hear it.

As luck would have it, just four days before Kennan sent his telegram, an American columnist created a sensation by breaking the story of the first Communist spy ring to claim public attention in the western hemisphere. The information about the operation came to the authorities from a defector, Igor Gouzenko, a Soviet military intelligence agent in Ottawa. Not knowing just what to think about the report, and expressing concern for the effect on U.S.-Soviet relations if it should prove greatly exaggerated or even untrue, the American press for the most part hesitated to draw conclusions. But doubt disappeared when the Canadian prime minister, Mackenzie King, confirmed the existence of the espionage ring. Even while the Soviet Union was allied with the West, it inescapably appeared, the Russians had been stealing Western secrets.

Then, on March 5, came the most striking feature of this variegated cluster of trends and events in early 1946, Winston Churchill's speech at Fulton, Missouri.

Although Churchill's identifying and naming the Iron Curtain would make his speech at Fulton memorable ever afterward, this phrase was not what attracted immediate attention; *Life* magazine, for example, quoted the term but did not give it any special emphasis. In this reaction the press was reminiscent of newspapers after the 1929 stock market crash—they knew something had happened but for some time failed to realize just what it was. Churchill's call for an alliance of the English-speaking nations represented a theme and a dream he had held throughout his life; in a private conversation eight months earlier, at Potsdam, Truman and Byrnes had turned down the same idea.

The eloquence and urgency with which Churchill had now publicly presented his great hope created a far greater stir than anybody on the train to Missouri had expected. American and other believers in "UNO," as the United Nations was called at the time, expressed anger and dismay. (Oddly, few of the indignant commentators took issue with the former prime minister's declaration that the national capitals behind the Iron Curtain lay in "what I might call the Soviet sphere" and were subject "to a very high and in some cases increasing measure of control from Moscow.") Days later, wrote Dean Acheson, then undersecretary of state, Washington "was still rocking" and "Congress was in an uproar."

Listening to the hubbub, President Truman, though he had sat on the platform and applauded Churchill's words, "pulled back into his shell," as a reporter said, and even declared that he had not known in advance what Churchill was going to say (hardly a true statement). Retreating, too, Secretary of State Byrnes told the Friendly Sons of St. Patrick in New York that the United States would involve itself in no alliances—"we propose to stand with the United Nations." A few months later, in a dispatch that became available only in the 1990s, Nikolai Novikov, the Soviet ambassador in Washington, told his superiors that while the "ruling circles of the United States" obviously supported the idea of a military alliance with Britain, they had not yet taken the official step, though "Truman by his presence did indirectly sanction Churchill's appeal." Prime Minister Attlee quickly disavowed the speech, and Acheson's State Department colleagues advised him not to attend a New York dinner honoring the illustrious but now unstylish visitor. Acheson's place on the dais at the Waldorf-Astoria was taken by Ambassador Winant; nearby, the seat of former New York Mayor Fiorello LaGuardia remained vacant.

As the West could not know at the time, Soviet diplomats during the last months of World War II had produced their own predictions and prescriptions concerning the postwar world. Maxim Litvinov, Molotov's predecessor at the Foreign Ministry, visualized a Europe under the control of the Soviet Union and Britain, with the United States not directly involved on the Continent but active in its own hemisphere—a world divided into security zones or spheres of influence. (Litvinov occupied a peculiar position with Molotov, who considered him "intelligent, worldly-wise, and knowledgeable about foreign affairs"; but he sometimes talked indiscreetly and he was not trusted. As Molotov saw it, Litvinov's problem was his sympathy for Trotsky, Zinoviev, and Kamenev—three prominent early Bolsheviks who had been done in on Stalin's orders. Indeed, Litvinov had almost joined this condemned trio; as Molotov put it, in his usual brusque fashion, "He remained among the living only by chance.")

Ivan Maisky and Andrei Gromyko set out a vision similar to Litvinov's, all three seeming to foresee a postwar world run by the three victorious powers. In a key difference between Litvinov, on the one hand, and Maisky and Gromyko, on the other, the latter two seemed to believe that all three powers would have a similar view of a "democratic, antifascist Europe," whereas Litvinov, who understood the West better, foresaw that the differing ideas of politics and democracy between the West and the Russians would likely lead to conflict rather than cooperation in Europe. All these documents received Molotov's close attention, and some of the ideas they presented were therefore likely to have reached Stalin.

For such a tripartite division of world power to function in reasonable balance, the three participants would have to be independent from each other and roughly equal in strength. This indeed was the precise picture Molotov's diplomats saw, because it was drawn for them by their Marxist-Leninist ideas: the United States and Britain, instead of acting together, would as imperialist powers inevitably find themselves divided by a "contradiction." Locked in a competition for markets and profits, the two countries would not put up the kind of common front they had generally presented during the war. Looking toward postwar gains in territory and influence, Litvinov even noted: "To knock Britain down from her positions, we would undoubtedly need strong support from the USA." In describing the anticipated sphere-of-interest picture, the diplomats displayed no concern at all for the backgrounds and wishes of the people, such as the Eastern Europeans, who would live under it. In marginalia on a document concerning the Polish question—the most vexing issue at Yalta and Potsdam—Molotov wrote: "Poland—a big deal! But how governments are being organized in Belgium, France, Greece, etc., we do not know. . . . We have not interfered, because it is the Anglo-American zone of military action."

Overall, Molotov and his subordinates appeared to see cooperation with the Western countries as being desirable when possible on the right terms, but preservation of Soviet gains from the war as the paramount consideration; what happened in those territories was nobody else's business. What was not supposed to happen in the broader world, in any case, was the creation of a new Anglo-American alliance. That would be a contradiction, not of capitalism-imperialism, but of Marx and Lenin. But now, at Fulton, Missouri, Winston Churchill had called for just such an alliance.

Churchill's address, said *Newsweek,* had stirred up the "worst diplomatic storm of the postwar period." Calling the speech "shocking," three senators declared that the former prime minister's proposal "would cut the throat of the United Nations Organization. It would destroy the unity of the Big Three, without which the war could not have been won and without which the peace cannot be saved." A few members of Congress supported Churchill, declaring the speech realistic, but the majority brushed off his ideas. Newspapers generally viewed with distaste and alarm the kind of military marriage Churchill proposed, though the *Wall Street Journal* called the speech brilliant, with a "hard core of indisputable fact." By the time he arrived in New York for his Waldorf speech, Churchill—although both a national and a sentimental hero to Americans—had become an extremely hot political potato. Outside the hotel, New York members of the CIO chanted, "Winnie, Winnie, go away; UNO is here to stay!"

Early in his speech Churchill had assured his audience that he had no ax to grind: "Any private ambitions I may have cherished in my younger days have been satisfied beyond my wildest dreams." Since the former prime minister had been hailed around the world as the savior of his country, the second Alfred, this statement rings true; yet it is also true that he was avid for power like all great leaders, and a stirring speech in America could move him back into the center of affairs. He had also given the world a fresh example of the mysterious working of a personal three-year rule by which he seemed to be guided—for decades he had consistently anticipated events by three years. In 1911 he had become first lord of the admiralty and moved with energy to build up the fleet for the war he saw coming and that arrived in 1914. In 1935, although out of office, he had become heavily involved in preparations anticipating a crisis with Germany, which came in 1938, though the appeasement of Hitler at Munich postponed the war for a year. Now in 1946 he advocated the Atlantic alliance that, in the form of the North Atlantic Treaty, would become a reality in 1949.

The contrast in attitudes, at this point, between Churchill and General Clay arose from many causes—differences in personality, in background, and in experience. But they also suggested the difference between the view from the trenches, in which Clay worked daily as a technician of occupation, and the vista from the heights from which Churchill surveyed the scene as an artist working in the medium of history.

For the present, however, the former prime minister would have to take his public lumps. Meanwhile, he could draw comfort, and even amusement, from some of the heaviest onslaughts on him, which came from Joseph Stalin. If one wanted to find real democracy, said the generalissimo, one should come to the countries of Eastern Europe, where not just one party (as in England) but several of them took part in the government. Even the opposition could participate—provided, to be sure, that it was "more or less loyal." Totalitarianism and police state? said Stalin. Absurd!

For his part, President Truman cabled Stalin an offer of equal time, not merely at tiny Westminster College but at the University of Missouri. If the generalissimo accepted the invitation, the president said—giving his home state double emphasis—the United States Navy would bring him over in the battleship *Missouri.* The generalissimo turned the president down.

Reflecting on the Iron Curtain and the beginning of the cold war many years later, Molotov said simply that "we had to consolidate our conquests." Continuing, he declared: "We made our own socialist Germany out of our part of Germany, and restored order in Czechoslovakia, Poland, Hungary, and Yugoslavia, where the situations were fluid." Of course, he said, "you had to know when and where to stop. I believe that in this respect Stalin kept well within the limits." Revealingly, the former foreign minister automatically spoke of the generalissimo as the only Soviet decision-maker, saying nothing about any democratic process. And in the West in 1946 people had almost endless room for debate concerning whether Stalin saw any limits to the expansion of Soviet power. More subtly, did he sense the importance of what, in a very different context, the French writer and artist Jean Cocteau called "knowing how far to go too far"?

CHAPTER 8

Power in the Balance

ON SEPTEMBER 5, 1946, Secretary of State James Byrnes flew into Berlin's Tempelhof airport. After being received with full honors by his close and admiring friend General Clay, the secretary departed for Stuttgart, where he was to deliver a speech the next day. Accompanied by his wife, he traveled in splendor in the train that originally had been fitted out for Adolf Hitler's private use. The Byrneses found themselves occupying the suite that in other days had served for the Führer and Eva Braun—more luxurious accommodations, Byrnes observed, than those offered by President Truman's private car. Not surprisingly, the train attracted great attention whenever it stopped, with crowds of Germans pressing forward waving bits of paper, asking for autographs, seeming as eager to greet the American secretary of state as many of them had once been to acclaim the Führer.

As he walked onto the stage at the State Opera House, the only large building in Stuttgart that had survived the war more or less intact, Byrnes felt some surprise when an army band greeted him with "Stormy Weather," but the director made immediate amends by switching to "Dixie," in acknowledgment of the secretary's South Carolina origin. Byrnes noted with interest that General Clay, "avoiding the spotlight as always," took a seat in the audience among German officials. The speech Byrnes gave that day not only would become famous in itself but would lend fame to the speaker.

Historians have argued for decades about the meaning of the Stuttgart address, with its declaration that "security forces will probably have to remain in Germany for a long period. *I want no misunderstanding* [italics supplied]. We will not shirk our duty. We are not withdrawing. We are staying here and will furnish our proportionate share of the security forces." What did Byrnes mean by this? He had not previously been known in the evolving cold war as what later generations would call a hawk, but was he now flinging down a challenge to the Soviet Union?

If the journalists who reported the story had been privileged to read an internal document written two months earlier by General Clay, they would have noted the similarity of these remarks by Byrnes to statements in Clay's directive. In Clay's view, it was the obstructive tactics of the French that continued to constitute his chief problem. But Byrnes also supported the idea of creating a German national government and specifically declared that the Soviet-sponsored Polish absorption of East Prussia ought not to be taken as final. In presenting this view and thereby bidding for German favor, the secretary produced the second act of a diplomatic drama that had begun two months earlier, when Molotov had in effect acknowledged the shortsightedness of the exploitative Soviet policy on reparations. The spirit of revenge, "a poor counselor in such affairs," should not be the guiding motive in dealings with Germany, the Soviet foreign minister declared—the country should be allowed to become "a democratic and peace-loving state" with its own industry and foreign trade. (Molotov did not acknowledge that the dismantling of German factories and their removal to the Soviet Union had produced nothing like the economic rewards the Russians had counted on.) One historian, writing a few years later, characterized this pair of speeches by Byrnes and Molotov as "the unofficial funeral of the Potsdam agreement and the overt beginning of a race for Germany between the Western Powers and the USSR."

Such complexities hardly made themselves evident to the immediate commentators. In any case, what Byrnes was believed to have said possessed more importance than what he may have meant, and whatever the relative emphases he had placed on France and Russia, he had plainly declared that the Americans were in Europe to stay for the foreseeable future. Byrnes himself considered this address his "most effective speech." A month later, in succinct remarks made to the American Club in Paris, the secretary carried the point further. "The people of the United States have discovered," he said, "that when a European war starts, our own peace and security inevitably become involved before the finish. They have concluded that if they must help finish every European war, it would be better for them to do their part to prevent the starting of a European war."

In the months following Byrnes's speech, nature took a cruel hand in the fate of Europe. During the winter of 1945–46, the people of the Continent had suffered from chilling drought; now, in January 1947, a winter of freezing blizzards struck. "Since the surrender of Germany," Dean Acheson wrote, "the life of Europe as an organized industrial community had come well-nigh to a standstill and, with it, so had production and distribution of goods of every sort," with agricultural production "lower than at any time since the turn of the century." Especially severe blows fell on Britain, as the frigid weather exhausted coal stocks, leading to deep cuts in the output of electric power. In bringing industrial production almost to a halt for three weeks, the weather accomplished a feat beyond anything achieved by German bombing; unemployment zoomed from 400,000 to 2.3 million. The government slashed food rations to levels worse than those during the war, and of perhaps special significance, the Treasury was nearing the end of its financial reserves.

In Germany the beginning of the year saw Western frustration at the economic logjam produce the economic (not political) fusion of the American and British zones into an entity dubbed the "Bizone" or "Bizonia"—a fledgling development disliked by the French and bitterly opposed by the Russians. In Berlin that winter the Allies and the Soviets wrangled over endless questions, especially the relationship of the Socialist Unity Party (the result of the forced marriage between the Social Democrats and the Moscow-controlled Communists) to the labor unions—the Free German Trade Association (FDGB). Having lost the local elections in October, the Communists, according to the report of a U.S. diplomat gifted with a measure of foresight, saw the unions as "perhaps the last means short of blockade" of maintaining Soviet military government control in Berlin, because the FDGB had the power of co-decision in most economic enterprises in the city. Labor leaders in Bizonia opposed the creation of a Communist-controlled national union but could not long survive if they appeared to be fighting against national unity; hence "Berlin is apt to prove [a] key point." Thus, by the beginning of February 1947, the blunt word *blockade* had appeared in an official U.S. report.

On February 25, while the foreign policy leaders in Washington grappled with a major new political challenge, Marshal Sokolovsky, the Soviet commander in Germany, denounced the U.S.-British fusion of their zones, declaring that it would lead to the partition of Germany and would threaten European security by enabling the old Prussian Junkers to regain control of the country; not only the Junkers, he said, but "U.S. and British monopolists" would dictate Germany's future. The British representative on the Control Council, Lieutenant General Sir Brian Robertson, commented dryly that he "had not had the pleasure of meeting" these U.S. and British monopolists and pointed out that all the iniquities the Russians professed to see in Bizonia could be remedied by four-zone fusion, as the British and the Americans had earlier proposed. The American diplomatic adviser told Washington that Sokolovsky's bitter attack might well provide a foretaste of the approach the Soviets would take in the Council of Foreign Ministers' conference in Moscow, which would begin the following week.

In Washington, during the afternoon of February 21, the first secretary of the British embassy in Washington had appeared at the State Department with two "blue pieces of paper"—formal diplomatic notes—one concerning Greece, the other Turkey. These communications painted a stark picture. In six weeks' time, said the first note, the British, who maintained some 40,000 troops in Greece, would pull their forces out; they could no longer afford to keep up their aid to the Greek government in its war with the "Democratic Army of Northern Greece," as the Communist-led guerrilla forces were called. News of the desperate nature of the situation arrived as no surprise to Washington; nor had the British move come suddenly. For several months Foreign Office officials had pondered the possibility of seeking greater U.S. involvement in Greece and Turkey, and the Americans had dispatched a fact-finding economic mission to the area. Already this group had sent back disturbing reports stressing the danger of imminent collapse in Greece.

Further, the Russians had been exerting outward pressure along the southern edge of their empire, refusing to evacuate northern provinces of Iran as required under a World War II agreement, seeking the return of border territory lost to Turkey in the aftermath of World War I, and pressing for a naval base on the straits between the Black Sea and the Aegean, as well as supporting the Greek insurgents (which they did mostly indirectly, through Soviet-dominated Yugoslavia and Bulgaria). Victory in Greece, with the establishment of a Communist regime, and the creation of a Soviet base on the Dardanelles, with its threat to the independence of Turkey, would markedly change the strategic situation in the Mediterranean and the Near East.

But why should the United States involve itself in areas as far away from home as the eastern Mediterranean, supporting one faction or government over another in Greece or in Turkey? Just two years earlier, President Roosevelt had made his statement about the duration of the American military presence in Europe; now, according to the late president's timetable—which did not express his desires but represented his view of political realities—the moment for departure had almost arrived. The president was, of course, thinking of an orthodox military occupation following the conclusion of a peace treaty. But no peace conference had taken place and no treaty had been produced. Now, complicating matters, here came the British, plainly saying that, with exhaustion forcing them to surrender their traditional responsibilities in the eastern Mediterranean, the Americans must take their place.

These notes from London carried the implicit message that for many years now—almost a century and a half—the Americans had hidden behind British skirts, enjoying the benefits of the European balance of power that British efforts had maintained while remaining aloof from the dirty work of actual maintenance. (Somewhat disconcertingly, a British historian once found twenty different meanings of *balance,* sixty-three of *of,* and eighteen of *power,* leaving us with an awesomely great number of permutative meanings for the whole phrase. Its standard meaning, however, derives from the eighteenth-century idea of a rational balance among states, a healthy situation in which peace is the norm and, sometimes, when it gets out of balance, may need war to restore it.)

For avoiding these day-to-day labors, however, the Americans had during the twentieth century been forced to pay a heavy price. Because the decline in its strength meant that Britain could no longer by itself, or with France, limit or defeat the leading continental power, the Americans had twice come onto the scene as firefighters. Having played little part in events as the conflagrations developed, they had reached across the Atlantic in 1917 and again twenty-five years later to bring about the two defeats of Germany. American tradition, to which President Roosevelt gave reluctant acknowledgment, now called for the United States to pack up its soldiers and equipment and go back home.

Yet despite the hopes of most people in the West, the very war in which Germany had met its second and complete defeat had not removed from Europe the threat of domination by a single country. Instead it had produced a new leading continental power—now, in real terms, the only continental power—the Soviet Union. This power, however, would not move on from its agreements with the West by bluster, hysteria, and open attack, as had been the case with German aggression under Hitler. Instead, as George Kennan explained, the Soviet Union would act as "a fluid stream which moves constantly, wherever it is permitted to move, toward a given goal. Its main concern is to make sure that it has filled every nook and cranny available to it in the basin of world power." Further, and tellingly, Kennan declared that he saw "no trace of any feeling in Soviet psychology that the goal must be reached at any given time."

Discord among the World War II partners had begun sounding just six weeks after the end of the Potsdam Conference. In their first meeting, held at Lancaster House in London, the Council of Foreign Ministers could make no progress toward settling the array of problems assigned them at Potsdam in the areas in which the Big Three had confined themselves to issuing generalities, in particular the creation of peace treaties for Germany's defeated satellites. The Balkans, North and East Africa, Trieste, Italy generally, Greece—all became arenas for contests between the Americans and the British on one side (though not by design), and the Russians on the other. Continuing sarcasm from V. M. Molotov brought flushes to the fleshy face of Ernest Bevin, but neither his table pounding nor the suave rejoinders of James Byrnes affected the course of what amounted to a nondiscussion. "It was our first experience with the extraordinary ability of Molotov to frustrate and delay," Chip Bohlen later noted.

While in general favoring efforts to get along with the Russians, Bohlen, who had come to the conference as Byrnes's special adviser on Soviet affairs, saw Molotov's obstructionism as "another revelation, however faint, of Soviet policy toward Germany. It looked as if the Soviets were going to seal off their zone and block any moves toward treating Germany as an economic whole." A magazine correspondent cabled home from London that "the pessimism which had pervaded informed opinion has now developed into complete hopelessness." On October 2 the conference broke up with nothing accomplished. *Newsweek* in its analysis ascribed this failure chiefly to problems of perception—the "lack of common understanding of the meaning of basic terms." But already the editors saw something more than misunderstood words at work: the Anglo-Americans, they concluded, had failed to understand that Russia had set for itself the role of continuing the historic expansion that characterized the czarist empire.

These developments raised three great questions with which President Truman and his advisers had to contend: Did the Americans consider it necessary to maintain a classical balance of power on the continent of Europe and in its neighboring areas? Was the United States prepared to take up the unglamorous work required to maintain such a balance? And in view of the timelessness with which the Kremlin was believed to look on events, if the Americans gave any kind of affirmative answer to the first two questions, would they—or could they—develop something that would be new to them, the political stamina to follow consistent long-range policies instead of, as usual, engaging in "sporadic acts which represent the momentary whims of democratic opinion"? Long disillusioned with respect to Congress and what he saw as its unenlightened, parochial, and often trivializing interference in matters of foreign policy, George Kennan wrote those words as no great friend of democratically inspired diplomacy. He hardly stood alone in such leeriness of Capitol Hill; James Reston of the *New York Times* expressed a similar view in saying, "If you tell Congress nothing, they go fishing; if you promise nothing, they go fishing; if you tell them all, they go wild."

Prejudiced or not, Kennan nevertheless raised the inescapable questions that confronted the makers of national policy. "Nations must rely on the quality of their diplomacy to act as a catalyst for the different factors that constitute their power," observed the political scientist Hans J. Morgenthau, adding that "constant quality is best assured by dependence upon tradition and institutions rather than upon"—and here Morgenthau used Kennan's word—"the sporadic appearance of outstanding individuals." Truman and his officials did not tend to speak in such terms, but they faced the realities those terms represented. Historically, while American diplomacy lacked "the institutional excellence of the British, it had the benefit of material conditions that even poor statecraft could hardly dissipate."

In any case, James Byrnes in his Stuttgart speech had given at least a partial answer to the three great questions. If the people of the United States had to help finish every European war, surely they should do their best to prevent the starting of such a war.

At midday on March 6, 1947, an airplane carrying a new secretary of state, General George C. Marshall, landed at Orly airport outside of Paris. The general, who had succeeded James F. Byrnes just a month and a half earlier, was on his way to Moscow for the foreign ministers' conference; it would be his first appearance in this contentious circle.

After all his labors as U.S. Army chief of staff through the six years of World War II, the widely admired "organizer of victory" had not enjoyed even a single day of retirement. Immediately following Marshall's resignation as chief of staff in November 1945, President Truman, who esteemed him above all other Americans, had called on him to take on the extraordinarily unpromising task of mediating the years-long conflict in China between Chiang Kai-shek's Nationalists and Mao Zedong's Communists. In January 1947, after a year of dogged and demanding effort, Marshall had acknowledged that he had undertaken a mission impossible and had asked to be recalled. Still having no intention of allowing the general to retire, Truman then chose him to go to the State Department to succeed Byrnes, with whom he had long had strained relations. Though the state of Byrnes's health provided the official reason for his resignation, Truman resented the secretary's continuing reluctance to accept the relationship of subordinate to president and his consequent way of acting in international negotiations almost as a freelance operative. Once, questioned by Bohlen about his failure to keep in touch with the White House, Byrnes answered with some acerbity that he knew when it was necessary to report to the president and when it was not; for Truman, apparently, Byrnes had too often thought it was not.

No American since General Marshall's time has occupied a comparable place in public life. Hence, as the historian Robert H. Ferrell has commented, it is difficult today to convey the potent effect Marshall's personality exerted on his contemporaries: "American generals revered him. Civil leaders held him in similar high regard." The military historian S. L. A. Marshall (not a relation of the secretary's), who as soldier and journalist spent time with a great variety of notable persons, gave a one-word description of his reaction to General Marshall: "Awe." Admired for his integrity, his knowledge of his profession, his remarkable gift for being able to look at situations as they would appear to civilian colleagues and the public, and his ability to get the best out of those who worked for him, Marshall also possessed an almost indefinable quality that won him the devotion of all who knew him. Dean Acheson, undersecretary of state during Marshall's first months at the department, observed that the general had "no military glamour about him and nothing of the martinet. Yet to all of us he was always 'General Marshall.' The title fitted him as though he had been baptized with it."

Before leaving for the Moscow conference, Marshall appeared at a full-dress meeting with President Truman and an array of congressional leaders to make the State Department case for aid to Greece and Turkey. As chief of staff during World War II, Marshall had come to occupy a unique position in the esteem of Congress with his thoroughly deserved reputation for unflinching candor. Speaker Sam Rayburn told a friend early in the war that Marshall had more influence with a committee of the House than anybody else he had ever heard, "because when he takes the witness stand, we forget whether we are Republicans or Democrats. We just remember that we are in the presence of a man who is telling the truth, as he sees it, about the problems he is discussing." This quality, together with the general's lucidity in exposition and his refusal ever to condescend to legislators, made him an acknowledged master at dealing with Congress even before he acquired the towering reputation that came to him as the result of his leadership during the war.

State Department representatives generally, however—most especially the career officers—enjoyed no such standing on Capitol Hill. Many of the legislators, self-conscious exemplars of a straightforward, no-nonsense American heartland ethos, looked on professional diplomats as little more than partygoers in striped pants, effete Ivy League elitists who at heart probably even favored Britain over America. A hostile observer characterized them as "a class of stoopnagels with Oxford accents and glib French."

The congressmen and senators who disliked the predominance of Ivy Leaguers in the foreign service, however, had only themselves to blame, since the meager salaries dictated by the State Department budget meant that only persons of some private means could afford to enter the service. In addition, in an era in which homosexuality not only had nothing gay about it but was, if practiced, illegal, critics of the department liked to mutter about the alleged proclivities of diplomats: "Where you desperately need a man of iron," it was said, "you often get a nance." With no natural domestic constituency and no dams, tax favors, or crop subsidies to bestow on possible supporters, the State Department traditionally had suffered step-child status in relation to Congress. In nurturing this image of the department, Congress not only hampered the work of the diplomats but also did itself no favor by reinforcing its own native insularity. In recent years President Roosevelt, though a product of Groton and Harvard, had made matters worse by his clear distrust of the State Department and his consequent reliance on personal representatives overseas; FDR's confidential adviser, Harry Hopkins, sounded the two popular themes with his characterization of members of the Foreign Service as "cookie-pushers, pansies—and [more idiosyncratically] usually isolationists to boot."

Thus, at the best of times, policy recommendations created in the State Department encountered hard going in the outside world. Now Marshall and Undersecretary Acheson faced the formidable task of selling congressional leaders not only a wholly new kind of policy but one that pertained to an area of the world never before considered an American concern. Declaring that "we are at the point of decision," Marshall produced an impressive presentation of the kind of reasoning that later, in the Eisenhower era in relation to Asia, would become known as the domino theory. If Greece and Turkey went, said the secretary, "Soviet domination might extend over the entire Middle East to the borders of India. The effect of this upon Hungary, Austria, Italy and France cannot be overestimated." The Greek-Turkish crisis, the secretary declared, might ultimately "extend Soviet domination to Europe, the Middle East and Asia." (Though Marshall probably did not know it, the domino theory had deep roots in American history. George III, who pioneered it, feared that if the Americans won their independence, the West Indies and Ireland would soon follow them, and then "this island would be reduced to itself and soon would be a poor island indeed.")

Domino reasoning would never prove wholly convincing in relation to Asia, but coming from Marshall, it made an impact on the congressional leaders gathered in Truman's office that February day. Acheson, who feared that Marshall had spoken too calmly and soberly, followed the secretary's remarks with a more fervent statement designed to win an immediate favorable verdict from the congressional jurors who sat before him. "These congressmen had no conception of what challenged them," Acheson said later; "it was my task to bring it home." The Soviet Union, he told his audience, was "playing one of the greatest gambles in history at minimal cost. It did not need to win all the possibilities. Even one or two offered immense gains," and only the United States had the strength to "break up the play." Thoroughly impressed, Arthur H. Vandenberg of Michigan, a

Republican power in the Senate, pledged his support and declared his belief that most of his fellows would join him.

On the morning of March 7, two days after Marshall left Washington on the first leg of his trip to Moscow, Truman explained the situation to the members of his cabinet. Acheson, acting secretary of state while Marshall was away, brought the news that the Greek government had formally asked the United States to replace the support previously given by Britain. (As Acheson later noted archly, Greece made this request "with the support of kind friends and their guidance of a feeble hand.") No one appeared to have trouble grasping the revolutionary aspect of the proposal. As Admiral Leahy commented in his diary, the members fully understood that "projection of the United States into the political problems of Europe" represented "a direct and positive change in the traditional policy of the United States." Favoring the Greek request, the members wanted the administration to tell the people "fully and frankly" that the purpose of supplying the aid was "to prevent Soviet domination of Europe and the resulting destruction of what we consider democratic government in that part of the world with a future danger to our own safety." Leahy noted, however, his fears of "a very active adverse reaction by domestic political opposition if not by a majority of the people of the United States." But, said the admiral, the president would be "sustained by a sense of righteousness, and he has plenty of courage."

On Monday, March 10, however, Truman's more detailed appeal for aid to Greece and Turkey evoked little enthusiasm from an enlarged group of congressional leaders. The legislators generally agreed that the United States ought to take some kind of action to "prevent the submergence of free government by Communism," Leahy wrote, but they did not agree on details and expressed doubt that Congress would supply the needed money; even Vandenberg, so positive in the earlier meeting, began talking about the greater relative importance of China as compared with Greece. But the conference approved the president's plan to address a joint session of Congress two days later. Still concerned about the proposed "reversal of the traditional American policy to avoid involvement in the political difficulties of European States," Leahy felt the meeting with congressional leaders and Truman's forthcoming speech might hold supreme importance for the freedom-loving peoples of the world, but that they also might be "milestones on the way to another world war." The next day he declared himself "unable to make a reasonable estimate as to the probable effect of this message on our political relations with the Soviet government."

While the leaders in Washington were taking practical steps to produce a presidential speech and a program of action, Marshall and Bohlen departed for their mission to Moscow. The secretary of state thus found himself in the diplomatically difficult position of entering upon a confer-ence while his associates back home were drafting a public program to counter the actions of the country playing host to the conference. No more than Leahy could Marshall forecast what effect Truman's message might have on Soviet conduct, but he had told Acheson to press ahead with the proposed program "with utmost vigor and without regard to him and his meeting."

In Bohlen, Marshall had as an adviser one of the two stars to emerge from a Soviet-affairs training program the State Department had conducted in the late 1920s and early 1930s. Bohlen's career since those days had been intertwined with that of his fellow star, George Kennan, and the two had long had a close friendship. Though their similar-sounding two-syllable names gave Bohlen and Kennan wide identification almost as the State Department's twin Soviet experts, they had their marked differences in personality: in an Elizabethan comedy of humors, Bohlen would have represented the sanguine temperament and Kennan the melancholic. The two also held divergent views, not so much with respect to the Soviet Union, about whose nature and motives their experience had given them similar conclusions, as in relation to their own country. Enlisted in 1944 by Harry Hopkins to serve as liaison between the White House and the State Department—a wholly unique assignment—Bohlen had closely observed political as well as diplomatic realities and had developed a tolerance for Washington give-and-take that Kennan never shared. In addition, though a St. Paul's and Harvard alumnus, Bohlen with his easy affability and his casual, unpressed style did not conform to the Ivy League image dwelling inside many hostile congressional brains. Hence he had uniquely appropri-ate qualifications to serve as diplomatic adviser to a nonpolitical secretary of state; he had quickly won the general's confidence and now accompanied him as special assistant. Kennan, more intense and more given to theory, would soon become head of Marshall's departmental innovation, the Policy Planning Staff.

During his one-day stay in Paris, Marshall dined with President Vin-cent Auriol and, following the standard procedure for a visiting statesman, laid a wreath at the Arc de Triomphe. The French president seized the opportunity to explain to his guest how deeply his countrymen feared the resurgence of a united Germany and the revival of the Ruhr's industrial might in German hands—the fears that had led the French representatives in Germany to do their best to block General Clay's efforts to create the centralized economy called for in the Potsdam protocol.

While in Paris, Marshall and Bohlen had to deal with another and very important item of business. From Washington came the text of the speech that President Truman intended to deliver to the joint session of Congress on the situation in Greece and Turkey. The secretary and his adviser read the message with mounting concern at its rhetoric and cabled back to Washington asking that its "flamboyant anti-Communism" be softened. Since he was going to ask Congress to give its support to an entirely new kind of American policy, however, the president turned Marshall and Bohlen down; he and his advisers felt that they had to have the rhetoric in order to get the money they needed; Acheson, in particular, favored a general rather than specific approach. In the following week, on March 12, the president delivered the speech that outlined what would become known as the Truman Doctrine.

In January General Clay had written the War Department suggesting that General Marshall make a stop in Berlin on his way to Moscow. "Psychologically we believe it would be of advantage to our position in Germany," Clay noted, adding that "we would not interfere with opportunity afforded for a brief rest." Perfectly aware of the possible importance the Moscow conference held for the future of Germany, Clay and his staff prepared, in addition to normal reports, thirty-one separate papers on a variety of subjects from aviation to financial reform; the general also had experts ready to go along and data available "covering all possible subjects." But Clay himself decided not go to Moscow; not fond of lengthy, talky meetings, not really at ease with Marshall, and sure that he would be needed in Germany if unrest arose as a result of news from the conference, he wanted to stay away—even though his absence would mean that the unwisely pro-French views (as the general regarded them) of one member of the U.S. delegation, the prominent Republican foreign affairs specialist John Foster Dulles, would go without the refutation Clay might be able to give them.

As it would turn out, however, within days Clay would find himself in Moscow continuing his heated debate with Dulles. Though Dulles held no government office at the time, this quarrel represented the schism, now almost institutionalized, between the State Department and the War Department—the world of George Kennan versus the world of Lucius Clay. On a practical level in this many-layered quarrel, Clay tended to act the part of a lawyer who had Germany for his client and German economic survival and development as his aim—a hardly surprising outlook, since the War Department, and hence the army, held the responsibility for the success of the occupation. The State Department, on the other hand, looked to broader European concerns, one of the most important being the need to build up France as an important power. This consideration enabled State to bear with some equanimity the French obstructionism that exasperated and frustrated Lucius Clay.

Unfortunately, the general had developed few personal mechanisms for dealing with tensions and frustrations, whether caused by the French, the Russians, the Germans, or the U.S. State Department. A sense of duty, not desire, kept him on the job in Germany, and maintaining his calm and courtly exterior exacted a high price. He worked every day, usually eleven or twelve hours, and for the first year of the occupation, until his wife came to join him, he had spent his limited evening off-duty hours alone in the house (large, but no grand mansion) he occupied in Dahlem, in southwestern Berlin. He drank coffee all day and went through three or four packs of cigarettes. His personality and routine presented a perfect prescription for ulcers, which he had duly developed. One of his associates gave this assessment: "Clay is a fine fellow when he relaxes. The only problem is that he never relaxes."

Coming events would give the general little opportunity to change his ways.

CHAPTER 9

"Irrevocably Divided . . . Two Hostile Camps"

An IMPRESSIVE GROUP of dignitaries, including the Soviet deputy foreign minister, Andrei Vyshinsky (but not V. M. Molotov, the foreign minister), and ambassadors from countries represented in Moscow, gathered at the Moscow airport in the frosty, windy afternoon of March 9, 1947, to greet the American secretary of state, whose four-engine C-54 touched down at three-thirty. The warmest welcome of all came from the U.S. ambassador, Lieutenant General Walter Bedell Smith.

A native of Indianapolis, Smith had entered the army from the National Guard in World War I; later, while attending the infantry school at Fort Benning, Georgia, he had caught the eye of the army's greatest talent scout, then-Colonel George C. Marshall, whose fabled "little black book" held the names of promising officers who would rise to stardom in World War II. Smith worked for Marshall as secretary of the General Staff and then moved to the Anglo-American Combined Chiefs of Staff as U.S. secretary. Highly valued by Marshall, Smith had other admirers, including General Eisenhower, who, with Marshall's reluctant blessing, stole him away from Washington to head his own Allied staff. So fond of his nickname, "Beetle," that he had his personal stationery engraved with a small black bug, Smith in style and even in appearance had more of the quality of a bulldog; much of his renowned irascibility, friends said, came from the ravaging pain caused by stomach ulcers. As an executive, he won from Eisenhower the honorary title "general manager of the war." Though he expressed interest in the military governorship of Germany and had Marshall's support, the post had gone, de facto, to Lucius Clay; Secretary Stimson appears to have felt that Smith's personality did not quite fit this particularly complex bill.

After returning to Washington in January 1946 following eight postwar months spent on occupation duty in Germany, Smith had hardly begun work back at the War Department when Secretary Byrnes asked him to go to Moscow as successor to Averell Harriman, who, after more than two arduous years in the Soviet capital, had been rewarded with appointment to the London embassy. While conceding that U.S. ambassadors were normally civilians, Byrnes explained that in his view the Moscow assignment called for a soldier, because Stalin had often shown distrust of professional diplomats and appeared to look with favor on military men. The secretary also seemed to feel that Soviet generals, who had become important figures during the war, would continue during peacetime to influence Soviet policy; hence Smith, with his wartime military experience in Europe, could speak their language or, as the secretary said, could get "under the Russian skin."

Surprised at the whole idea, Smith took a few days to think it over and discussed it with Ike, who advised him to take the job and try for a year or two to "break through the crust"; if this effort did not succeed, he could turn the post over to somebody else. Convinced by this reasoning with its tinge of optimism—the possible permeability of the Moscow crust—Smith returned to Byrnes and agreed to take the job. He felt, he wrote later, that the State Department officers who then began briefing him took too gloomy a view when they maintained that the United States and the Soviet Union might arrive at a relationship of reasonable stability but saw little likelihood of genuine collaboration. Perhaps more might be possible: "the first essential was an effort to restore confidence and mutual understanding"; Smith seems to have said "restore" rather than "establish" quite reflexively. He left Washington for Moscow on March 24, 1946, and arrived there four days later, in a C-54 loaded with packages from Americans to relatives and friends in the Soviet capital—"everything from fur coats down to altar candles." His impedimenta also included his own morning coat, striped trousers, and silk hat, which even in this citadel of the proletariat he would wear for the formal presentation of his credentials to the chairman of the Presidium of the Supreme Soviet, Nikolai Shvernik.

When the March 1947 Council of Foreign Ministers conference began, Smith had spent almost exactly a year in Moscow. "The main issue, it was already established," Smith said, "would be Germany and, with it, the future of Europe." Before General Marshall arrived, diplomats in Moscow "had been speculating on how the Secretary of State, without previous experience in international conferences, would be able to deal with what one of them called 'this group of tough, Middle-Eastern bazaar traders.' " But the ambassador had no fears for his chief. He had seen General Marshall "under all conditions of stress and strain" and had "never seen him fail eventually to dominate every gathering by the sheer force of his integrity, honesty and dignified simplicity." Smith knew how Marshall would play the game: "He would say little until he had the situation and all the facts well in hand," and "he would make no mistakes." (During the conference, Ernest Bevin would describe Marshall as "quiet and firm and very direct.")

Delighted to be the host of his eminent boss, Smith felt a pang of disappointment when Marshall failed to admire the "diplomatic" bowler hat he had picked up in Paris. When, later, he saw a photo of himself wearing the hat, Smith said, he understood Marshall's reaction. But in the realm of style Smith would soon have worse problems. Shortly after the American party arrived in Moscow, the ambassador became involved in a flap with a local barber, who misunderstood Smith's acquiescence in the use of hair tonic and instead administered a henna rinse. Smith, often considered testy even when nothing went wrong, fumed as he stared in the mirror at his newly pink hair—which retained its distinctive tint for the life of the conference.

Apart from such diversions, Smith quickly felt at home again with the general. "I want you to do this and this," he heard the secretary of state say, and "I said, 'Yes, sir,' and thought, 'Here we go again.'" (Marshall's resumption of his old relationship with Smith was typical of him; the assumption of command in most situations had become so automatic as to be almost instinctual. Once, when told by Dean Acheson that he could not have the services of a certain Colonel Davis in G-5 [military government], Marshall, though no longer chief of staff, found the idea of his choice's unavailability "novel and puzzling"; without hesitating, he proceeded to telephone Davis's boss, Major General John Hilldring, and order him to provide the officer the next day—as Hilldring duly did.)

The conference, which opened on March 10 with the customary panoply of big table, clusters of aides on their chiefs' right and left hands, and smaller tables at which advisers sat with notes and documents, took one action concerning Germany so rapidly that, Smith said, "it left most of us rather breathless." On Foreign Secretary Bevin's motion, the foreign ministers adopted a resolution declaring the abolition of the Prussian state, "the core of German militarism." (This action approved a February 25 law adopted by the Allied Control Council for Germany.)

From that point on, however, harmony on any but minor questions vanished from the conference chamber. Weeks slipped into following weeks as the ministers wrangled over a series of deadeningly familiar issues—the economic unification of Germany, the creation of a German provisional government, the kinds of reparations the Soviet Union should receive, and the makeup of the peace conference that would produce the long-awaited peace treaty for Germany. At one point, Bevin engaged the French foreign minister, Georges Bidault, in an exchange of asides. (A bit unnervingly, the shrewd but rough-and-ready Bevin tended to refer to Bidault as "Bidet.") "Where are we?" Bevin asked.

"God knows," Bidault replied.

"I didn't know," Bevin said, "He was a member of the Council of Foreign Ministers."

Brushing aside General Clay's reluctance to join in the doings in Moscow, Marshall summoned him almost immediately after the meetings began. During the conference Clay produced for Marshall a memorandum outlining his view—and, he said, that of the American delegation—of the conditions for considering the economic treatment of Germany. This document made it plain that Clay still looked to the creation of a peace treaty to guarantee security to Germany's neighbors and establish a democratic German national government. "We can discuss economic unity as an isolated problem," Clay commented; "we can solve it only as a part of our overall solution of the German problem." Yet, of course, creating such a treaty would depend upon achieving agreement among the four occupying powers. On the last day of March, having breathed as much of the conference air as he could endure—and having expended considerable energy in his continuing feud with John Foster Dulles—Clay sent Marshall another memorandum, this one requesting permission to return to Germany, where, he made it plain, he was really needed.

In Clay's recollection, Dulles believed at the time that "the resources of the Ruhr were needed by all of Europe, and that if we formed them as an independent state like Switzerland they would be used to serve Europe and not simply to serve Germany." Dulles also appeared to see the internationalization of the Ruhr as a way the Western allies could leave Germany "and at the same time get the Russians out of Germany"; Dulles was "very active," Bohlen commented, "putting forth his views and his opinions very vigorously." Clay felt that Marshall, new to the job of secretary of state and thus lacking a clear outlook with respect to Germany, was "tempted to accept the Dulles idea," even though such acceptance "would have made Germany a dependent nation on the rest of the world forever." (Stalin saw the situation the same way. A year earlier he had told Walter Ulbricht that German unity must be the paramount aim and that Germany could not survive without the Ruhr district; French demands for shared control must be rejected. But in the generalissimo's view, as reflected in Ulbricht's notes of an earlier meeting, unity must come "through unified KPD/unified Central Committee/unified party of the working people." This approach had led to the creation of the Socialist Unity Party—hardly the prescription Clay had in mind for unifying Germany.)

Bohlen noted that Dulles took advantage of his position as the Republican Party's representative on the scene to gather American reporters together and give them his views on the subjects discussed at the conference. The worldly Bohlen saw this practice as probably "a little bit of a bother" for

Marshall, but readily conceded that it "seemed to be part of the general political structure of the United States." It was untidy, maybe, but it was just the way Americans did things, that was all. Bohlen's calm acceptance of this kind of behavior could hardly have come from George Kennan.

Aside from his weariness with Dulles—how could he not see that without the Ruhr, Germany would have no hope of supporting itself?—and his general dislike of such conferences, Clay missed the closeness and the influence he had known with Marshall's predecessor, Byrnes, and he seemed to feel that Marshall was allowing the State Department professionals to lead him up an anti-Soviet garden path. Having received the desired permission, Clay left his fellow delegates to soldier on. As he departed for Germany, the general even carried with him the belief that his fervid opposition to internationalizing the Ruhr would quickly lead to the end of his tenure in Germany; the first thing Marshall would do when he returned to Washington, Clay thought, would be "to get General Smith in General Clay's place."

Just two days after the conference opened, President Truman in far-away Washington went before Congress to make his call for American aid to Greece and Turkey. The delegates in Moscow learned not only that the president had asked for $400 million for these two countries but that he had placed this specific proposal in a far broader context. Imposing no limitations of time or place, Truman declared: "I believe that it must be the policy of the United States to support free peoples who are resisting attempted subjugation by armed minorities or by outside pressures." Bevin and others questioned the president's timing—at that moment, should he really have drawn such a strong distinction between Western values and an opposing way of life "based upon the will of a minority forcibly imposed upon the majority" that relied on "terror and oppression, a controlled press and radio, fixed elections and the suppression of personal freedoms"? In its turn *Izvestia* dutifully denounced the speech. Yet neither Stalin nor any other Soviet representative spoke of it, at least in public. Along with many other Westerners, Bevin had not yet grasped the fact that Stalin did not make foreign policy on the basis of pique and ruffled feelings.

Believing that the fate of Germany hung in the balance between action and inaction, and frustrated by five painful weeks of vain talk, Marshall decided to take a direct approach to the Soviet summit. On the evening of April 15, accompanied by General Smith and Bohlen, he went to see Joseph Stalin. Though the interview served as a formal call as required by protocol—Marshall's British and French counterparts had already paid their respects to the generalissimo—the secretary wished to express to Stalin face to face, as Smith put it, the position of the United States and emphasize its "willingness to cooperate and its determination not to be coerced." And he would assure Stalin that the Americans had no intention of trying to dominate any other country in the world.

The generalissimo received his callers in the paneled conference room next to his office. Cordial to General Marshall, as always, and seeming relaxed, Stalin listened quietly, puffing on cigarettes and doodling his inevitable wolf's heads on a pad, while the secretary summarized the situation and expressed his fears for the prosperity and security of Europe, which seemed unable to recover from the ravages of war and weather. But Stalin's answers, though delivered calmly, shook Marshall. "It is wrong," the generalissimo said, "to give so tragic an interpretation to our present disagreements." The differences between the sides had no great importance but resembled a quarrel within a family; the arguments at the conference amounted to nothing more than "skirmishes and brushes of reconnaissance forces." Compromises on all the issues would sooner or later become possible; meanwhile, he seemed to say, why worry? The hour and a half of talk produced nothing more definite than this casual unconcern with the plight of Germany and Europe; Marshall felt forced to conclude that Stalin approved of matters as they stood—chaos in Europe suited the Soviet Union and provided recruits for Communism. The United States must act, if not with the Russians, then without them. Even so, Marshall continued to look to Stalin for gleams of reasonableness; like other Western representatives before and after him, he for a time nurtured an illusion that the generalissimo was more reasonable than his blunt, unyielding foreign minister, Molotov—an illusion created by Stalin's extensive repertoire of acting skills that would appear over and over in his dealings with the West.

Summing up his conclusions from the conference, Bedell Smith commented that the West "at long last" understood Soviet aims in Germany: "The alternatives of a divided Germany, or a Germany under the effective economic and political domination of the Soviet Union had become unmistakably clear." To prevent the development of the latter alternative, the Western powers must now take appropriate action in their zones. Many of those attending the conference, Smith said, would surely wonder whether this would not be the last meeting of its kind. Bevin wrote Attlee that "the Russians clearly want to create a situation in which everyone will forget what they have done in their Zone"; they wanted to "rehabilitate their Zone at our expense and then on top of that get reparations from current production": the reparations question simply would not go away but remained central among Soviet desires. For Bevin, the Soviet rejection of the American proposal for a four-power forty-year treaty (originally proposed by Byrnes "to ensure that neither Germany nor Japan again threatens the peace of the world") represented a tragic mistake, "as bad as when she linked up with Hitler in 1939." For Smith, the inconclusiveness of the conference set the stage for a new East-West crisis. All of the Western representatives had to wonder how well and how long, in a Germany heading for division, a divided Berlin could stand.

The Kremlin, however, took an optimistic view of the situation. An editorial in *New Times,* an ostensibly independent labor publication that actually served as a vehicle for Stalin's ideas and was written and edited in Molotov's office (sometimes actually by the foreign minister himself), declared that in clarifying the positions of the two sides, "the Moscow conference performed a work of no little value." Given good will on all sides, the parties could now proceed to the "necessary, if exacting work of reconciling the different points of view and arriving at agreed decisions." Thus, if Stalin still saw a chance for a degree of cooperation between his country and the West, provided that his position in Eastern Europe was recognized, he might by his policy of delay have been attempting to win better terms in Germany rather than waiting for Western Europe to collapse. But that was not what Marshall and Bevin heard.

In a radio address delivered April 28, a few days after returning from the six-week ordeal in Moscow, General Marshall expressed his hope that Stalin had been correct in speaking of skirmishes and reconnaissance forces. But he feared otherwise; certainly, "the recovery of Europe has been far slower than had been expected." Marshall identified the vital fact: "The patient is sinking while the doctors deliberate." Something had to be done—action could not await "compromise through exhaustion." As General Clay had feared—and foreseen—Marshall put German recovery squarely in the center of European recovery, which meant that the secretary would, for instance, see German coal from the Ruhr as, in effect, European coal. Contrary to Clay's strong desire, decisions affecting Germany would be made in Washington.

On the way home from Moscow, Bohlen said, Marshall had talked about the need to find a course of action that would prevent the complete economic collapse of Western Europe. Thus it was that the State Department's new Policy Planning Staff, directed by George Kennan, took up its first assignment. The secretary of state considered the matter urgent.

On March 31 Admiral Leahy received an eminent caller in his White House office. With public discussion swirling about the issues raised by the Truman Doctrine, Colonel Charles A. Lindbergh, the most idolized figure of his generation, wished to make a contribution to the debate.

Lindbergh's defeatism in the 1930s with respect to Germany had lost him much of the adulation he had won by his solo flight across the Atlantic in 1927 and the sympathy that the public had poured out after the kidnapping and murder of his baby son in 1932. The colonel pointed out to Leahy, however, that his public opposition to U.S. involvement in World War II, which had lasted until the Japanese attack on Pearl Harbor, should cause the American people to pay attention to his pro-Truman Doctrine views. Lindbergh's thoughts "were not expressed with great clarity," Leahy noted dryly, but the colonel seemed to believe that the United States "should openly announce all out opposition to further open or secret expansion of the Soviet form of government beyond the boundaries of Russia." Unfortunately, such a decision "would bring on a world war between Russia and the United States," a development Lindbergh believed "essential to the preservation of democratic government." The old admiral contented himself by replying simply that in his opinion the administration was following a correct policy that should receive the support of all Americans.

Some two weeks later, Leahy reacted much more strongly to another set of opinions concerning foreign affairs, expressed not in his office but in speeches in England. Henry Wallace, who had preceded Harry Truman as vice president of the United States and would have been sitting in the Oval Office that very day had President Roosevelt not allowed him to be dropped from the 1944 Democratic ticket, had launched a series of vigorous attacks on what Leahy was already calling the "bi-partisan foreign policy" of the United States. (This term would within a year become standard.) These broadcast addresses, the admiral felt, offered "convincing evidence of mental unbalance that will in my opinion, permanently remove him from political participation in American affairs." The thought that Wallace might have succeeded FDR in the White House was "appalling." The admiral could not have imagined that little more than a year later Wallace, on his own third-party ticket, would be campaigning against Truman in one of the most remarkable presidential seasons in American history.

Despite the—slowly—developing bipartisan American foreign policy, Leahy a few days later recorded an interesting response to Marshall's report from Moscow on his evening conversation with Stalin. "It appears to me," the admiral noted, "than an agreement as to peace terms with Germany might be reached if Russia is permitted to assess ten billion dollars worth of reparations." But such reparations would have to come from current production—the problem that had festered since Potsdam. Fortunately for his blood pressure, no doubt, General Clay was not in Washington looking over Leahy's shoulder as the admiral wrote his diary entry. But if Leahy had seemed to be considering the idea, he clarified his thinking a few days later. On April 25, noting the adjournment of the Council of Foreign Ministers conference in Moscow, he saw the reparations problem as one of the points of "definite disagreement" between the West and the Soviet Union. The admiral reacted to Marshall's April 28 broadcast speech with disappointment and a measure of disapproval, observing, in a prickly diary note, that the radio report on the Moscow sessions would not "attract widespread interest by the people of the United States"; it "lacked dramatic appeal and was not a sufficiently positive statement of principle to be adhered to by the United States."

Marshall got off easily, however, compared with a Republican congressman from Ohio who in a speech in the House chamber compounded an attack on Truman's request for aid for Greece and Turkey with the implication that as the president's chief adviser, Admiral Leahy had been heavily involved in developing the Truman Doctrine as part of "a conspiracy to draw America into warfare on the side of reactionary Fascist elements everywhere in the world." Remembering his service as FDR's ambassador to Vichy France, Leahy commented that "having for two years in Europe been maligned by Goebbels's Big League experts, attacks by amateurs from the local Bush Leagues are in comparison not even complimentary." Bipartisanship was not developing easily in Washington; it would not really come into its own until further problems arose in Europe.

During the evening of June 5, as the British foreign secretary lay in bed listening on his little table radio to the BBC's American commentary, he suddenly began giving the broadcast his full attention. Secretary of State Marshall, it appeared, had just delivered the kind of speech Ernest Bevin had long been waiting for. As the European postwar economic crisis continued, people had talked here and there, in America and in Europe, about some possible new initiative for large and direct U.S. involvement in European recovery. Now, it seemed, General Marshall, without fanfare or advance publicity of any kind, had proposed such a program. Though the speech had received no advance buildup, Dean Acheson had not left the outcome wholly to journalistic chance. The undersecretary had made a special point of explaining the potential importance of the speech to British reporters, one of them the BBC correspondent who had broadcast the account Bevin heard on his little radio.

Next morning Bevin arrived at the Foreign Office determined to act with no delay—to take what he had heard as Marshall's offer and run with it. Sir William Strang, who had become permanent undersecretary, suggested that the British ambassador in Washington might ask the State Department just what kind of action Marshall contemplated. "Bill," said Bevin, "we know what he *said.* If you ask questions, you'll get answers you don't want. Our problem is what *we do,* not what *he meant*"—the

Europeans must go ahead. What statements had Marshall made that sent the British foreign secretary into immediate and decisive action, with no cabling back and forth across the Atlantic, no summoning of panels of experts, no huddling with staff members trying to read the secretary's mind?

Marshall had used for his forum the commencement exercises at Harvard, at which he was presented an honorary degree. The university president, James B. Conant, had asked Marshall to come to Cambridge in 1945 and 1946, but both times the general had begged off, pleading the pressure of his obligations. Earlier in 1947 Marshall had turned down a third invitation from Conant, but in May, as a result of the evolving U.S. policy for Europe, the general decided to take advantage of the proffered platform; he would not only come to Harvard next month, he told Conant, but as the university president wished, he would make a speech to a gathering of alumni.

In the month since George Kennan had assumed the position of head of the new Policy Planning Staff (established on May 5), he and his group had managed to produce a report containing, as Kennan had urged, a key idea: the United States should not only offer its help in the restoration of Europe's economic health, but it should do so not by a program created in Washington but through plans made by the Europeans themselves: "the program must be evolved in Europe" and "the Europeans must bear the basic responsibility for it." The report also contained the specific point that U.S. aid under the proposed program should not be directed to the combating of Communism as such, even though Communists were seeking to turn the European economic crisis to their own ends. Hence Soviet-controlled countries should be regarded as eligible for participation, though in order to do so they would naturally have to loosen up their economic systems.

An important contribution to the swelling stream of thought came from Will Clayton, undersecretary of state for economic affairs. A rags-to-riches Houston businessman who owned the largest cotton brokerage firm in the world, Clayton held strong beliefs in free enterprise and free trade. Returning from an eye-opening trip to Europe, he gave his colleagues a potent memorandum on what Bohlen called the "invisible damages of war."

In response to the rapid deterioration of the situation in Britain and on the Continent, the secretary of state and his advisers decided to use the Harvard commencement as the platform from which to present these ideas to the world. In a quiet speech, mostly drafted by Bohlen, Marshall described the administration's analysis of the European crisis, declared that the Europeans needed help from outside and that the United States ought to supply it, and then delivered a description that was to be widely quoted: "Our policy is directed not against any country or doctrine but against hunger, poverty, desperation and chaos." Its purpose was "the revival of a working economy in the world so as to permit the emergence of political and social conditions in which free institutions can exist." The United States, said the secretary, would give full cooperation to "any government that is willing to assist in the task of recovery," but "any government which maneuvers to block the recovery of other countries cannot expect help from us." Those governments or political groups that sought to exploit the misery of Europe would encounter the opposition of the United States. Thus, at least conceptually, the door swung open for everybody.

In the sentence that would be seized on by Ernest Bevin, Marshall said simply, "The initiative, I think, must come from Europe." Marshall had forbidden any publicity buildup, Bohlen said, because "he was concerned lest the American reaction would be that this is another give-away program, Santa Claus, etc." He was counting heavily on the reaction of the Europeans, and he would not be disappointed; Bevin "caught this on the bounce and moved it forward." All the work now had to be done, but, led by the British foreign secretary, the Europeans were preparing to do their full and necessary part. Within three weeks of Marshall's speech, they were meeting in Paris to discuss what actions to take. (In a marvelously offhand diary entry, Admiral Leahy noted reports from Paris about "a conference between the foreign ministers of France, England and the U.S.S.R. with the purpose of studying an informal statement made by Secretary Marshall of the necessity of rebuilding the industrial capacity of Europe without delay." Reports indicated, said Leahy, that Molotov was "attempting to delay or prevent any useful effort by Europe to cooperate.")

Molotov had not only come to the foreign ministers' sessions, he had brought with him a large and varied delegation of experts, even including nutritional specialists; he had also brought a large load of suspicions and questions. Novikov, his ambassador in Washington, had suggested that Marshall's proposal amounted to nothing more than a quietly phrased, politically subtle and shrewd version of the Truman Doctrine, intended to gain Western European support for anti-Soviet policies. Nevertheless, the USSR should be represented in Paris, Novikov thought, to see what concrete ideas might lie behind Marshall's rather vague words: What kind of aid, and how much of it, did the Americans have in mind?

Ideological considerations aside, the West for its part had to face the practical problems Soviet participation would present. Dealing with the Russians always involved protracted bargaining and haggling and voicing of suspicions; if the Soviets should participate in the plan, the likely result would be endless delays in the development and execution of any program for recovery—a reality suggesting that Stalin's most effective way of sinking the Marshall Plan would simply have been to take part in it. But American insistence on a joint European effort proved the decisive point: Congress would approve no series of aid packages to individual countries, and Molotov rejected the idea of a common approach to the United States— each country should determine its own needs and priorities. After he and his delegation went home from the conference, easing many Western minds, the British, the French, and other Western Europeans proceeded to develop economic plans. Not only did Stalin withdraw the Soviet Union from the discussions, however, he forced the Czechs and the Poles to retract their acceptance of the invitation to the follow-up conference; the lure of American aid was too powerful, the attraction that could develop might raise the Iron Curtain dangerously high. The Kremlin now began to redefine the Marshall Plan as not only an American anti-Soviet effort in Western Europe but a program to undermine Soviet control and influence in Eastern Europe.

One more factor played a part in these decisions. "Throughout this period," said the Russian historian Mikhail Narinsky, "the Soviet leadership had well-placed informants of a special nature in the British Foreign Office"—the famous Cambridge spy Guy Burgess, for one. This source passed on to Moscow the news that U.S. and British officials wished to move ahead immediately with Western European participation and hoped that Soviet satellites would also join in the effort, even if the USSR did not. This intelligence should have come as no surprise, but sometimes the Soviets seemed not to realize that other people could hear their rhetoric and could hardly be blamed for taking it seriously—rhetoric that for thirty years had committed the USSR to class war and the destruction of international capitalism by any and all means, including violence. Such convictions and declarations not only made it hard for the Russians to come to any kind of general arrangements with the West but, beyond that, tended to keep them from believing that such accommodations were even possible.

In 1946 Maxim Litvinov, the former foreign commissar and ambassador to the United States, had put this ideological and psychological point plainly in the quite un-Soviet, direct style he sometimes displayed. Identifying the underlying cause of trouble between the West and the Soviet Union as "the ideological conception prevailing here [in the USSR] that conflict between communist and capitalist worlds is inevitable," Litvinov said in response to a question that if all the expressed Soviet foreign policy desires were met, "it would lead to the West being faced, in a more or less short time, with the next series of demands"; ideological and institutional paranoia thus appeared quite as insatiable as the individual variety. On another occasion Soviet wiretappers recorded a conversation with an American correspondent in which (according to Molotov in his late interviews) Litvinov declared: "You Americans won't be able to deal with this Soviet government. Their positions preclude any serious agreement with you."

In July 1945 the victorious Allied "Big Three" met in the Berlin suburb of Potsdam to make plans for war-devastated Europe. Harry Truman had been U.S. president for three months. Winston Churchill would be replaced as British prime minister by Clement Attlee before the conference ended. Though Joseph Stalin, who had been master of the Soviet Union for two decades, met his fellow leaders with smiles, he would prove unshakable on the issues.

After pledging at Potsdam to foster a new, democratic Germany, the Allies quickly found themselves divided by differences over small details and major questions. The lines defining sectors of Berlin hardened into borders even as the city tried to rebuild from war damage.

Many Western diplomats believed that Joseph Stalin's obstinacy was forced on him by hard-liners in the Communist Party Politburo, led by Foreign Minister V. M. Molotov (left). Only gradually did the West realize who made all the decisions in the Kremlin.

Marshal Vladimir Sokolovsky, Soviet military governor, kept firm control over the eastern zone of Germany while he and Soviet political officers sought to create a united country under Communist influence. After finishing his service in Germany, Sokolovsky would move up to become chief of the Soviet General Staff.

When he declared at Westminster College in Missouri in 1946 that "an iron curtain has descended across the Continent," Winston Churchill gave the world a famous phrase. But his call for a postwar Anglo-American alliance ignited widespread protests in America and Europe.

As U.S. military governor, General Lucius D. Clay had the chief
responsibility for helping Germany back onto its feet. In carrying out this
duty, he often spoke as an advocate for the German people, thus putting
himself at frequent odds with officials in Washington.

U.S. ambassador Lewis W. Douglas, Secretary of State George C.
Marshall, and British foreign secretary Ernest Bevin (left to right) enjoy a
rare laugh in a troubled time. American and British leaders developed
increasingly close relationships in the early postwar years, and when
Marshall proposed his plan for European economic recovery, Bevin
became the first foreign statesman to respond to this new kind of
initiative.

In February 1946 the U.S. chargé
d'affaires in Moscow, George F.
Kennan, cabled the State
Department an 8,000-word
warning of Soviet hostility to the
West. This "long telegram," which
would become famous in
diplomatic circles, set Washington
"vibrating with a resonance that
was not to die down for many
months."

When the Soviet authorities closed the highways, railroads, and waterways into the Western sectors of Berlin in June 1948, the Americans and the British fought back by flying food and fuel into the city. A small effort in the beginning, this airlift demonstrated the West's resolve both to the USSR and to the citizens of Berlin. Lieutenant General Curtis E. LeMay, U.S. air commander in Europe (above center, with Stuart Symington, secretary of the air force, and General Hoyt Vandenberg, air force chief of staff), supplied the first planes.

Flour and coal (being loaded into a truck, opposite) formed the most important cargoes; they would leave the insides of planes coated with dust, white or black.

Press and public in the West hailed Operation Vittles in its first summer months, but most experienced observers, East and West, did not expect this success to last. They knew that the task of the airlift would only grow harder as the city's stockpiles ran short, cold weather increased the demand for coal, dense fogs shut down the airfields, and pilots grew weary. How many more crashes like this one could the airlift survive?

Not until December 17, after much discussion, debate, and lobbying, would Congress grant the administration funds for short-term aid. The European Recovery Act, as the establishing legislation for the Marshall Plan would be called, would not come for more than three further months, until dramatic events had changed the picture in Central Europe and profoundly shaken the western democracies. Paradoxically, the Communists themselves would provide the final push that would bring the plan into being.

Despite the failure of the spring 1947 Moscow conference to make progress toward a German peace treaty, the four foreign ministers met in London on November 25 to have one more try. In the interim a significant political event had occurred in Eastern Europe. In late September, in response to a summons from the Kremlin, representatives of European Communist parties had presented themselves at a small town in Poland, where they heard an important address by Stalin's ideological specialist and spokesman, Andrei Zhdanov, whom many observers also considered the dictator's heir presumptive. Like many of Stalin's other close associates, Zhdanov, a veteran of the nine-hundred-day German siege of Leningrad, faced the world with a "Kremlin complexion," as Milovan Djilas called it—a pale, unhealthy skin resulting from late nights, no sunlight, considerable vodka, and the unrelenting strain of close association with Stalin; as another dubious perquisite of his participation in life at the top, Zhdanov also suffered from asthma.

In August, Stalin and Zhdanov had developed the ideas that Zhdanov presented to the representatives at the September meeting, none of whom apparently knew that they were to receive a new and fundamentally important Communist line. Reporting on international developments, Zhdanov declared in his speech that since 1945 the world had become irrevocably divided into two hostile camps, imperialist and progressive socialist, led respectively by the United States and the Soviet Union; Communists must uncompromisingly oppose the imperialists. The Soviet representative also in effect ordered those present to join the new organization he had planned at Stalin's bidding: the Cominform, the Communist Information Bureau, which he described as a response to the Marshall Plan (still unfunded by the U.S. Congress). As was often the case in the Communist world, the new emphasis on doctrine had not arrived wholly unheralded. Just a few months earlier, Stalin's favorite economist, Eugene Varga, had won approval for his 1946 book in which he foresaw no major crisis for capitalism for the next ten years; now the winds reversed direction as the new Soviet line began to emerge. A month later Zhdanov had attacked a leading work on the history of European philosophy, which soon received party condemnation on the ground that it gave objective treatment to Western philosophers; glorification of all things Russian would now be the companion of denunciation of the works of the West. Ideologically, Stalin had decided to circle the wagons; practically, he now aimed at direct control over the nations and local parties of Eastern Europe.

When General Marshall left for London in November, he took with him some doubts on the part of colleagues that U.S. intelligence had made a proper effort to be of service to him. With the Central Intelligence Agency just two months old as a body established by law, American intelligence was still inchoate. The United States had entered the postwar era with no consensus on what kind of intelligence organization it should have or even what purpose intelligence should serve. Some thought any effort in this field should not be "central" at all; one World War II intelligence officer working with the State Department recommended, vainly, that "if we are going to do secret intelligence, we should not advertise the fact." State Department officials and members of the armed services met, discussed, and debated, sometimes taking broad views, sometimes defending time-honored turf. These meetings paid considerable attention to clandestine intelligence gathering but seemed to ignore the other side of the coin, covert operations.

In January 1946 President Truman issued a letter of instruction (not as strong as an executive order) authorizing State, War, and Navy to establish a Central Intelligence Group. In April, not long before the end of his brief tenure, its temporary director, Rear Admiral Sidney Souers, described one very important job for the new agency. An interdepartmental planning group, he said in a top-secret memorandum, recognized the "urgent need to develop the highest possible quality of intelligence on the U.S.S.R. in the shortest possible time"; a working committee was to establish and coordinate a system that could produce a digest of all types of "factual" strategic intelligence on the Soviet Union. (The specification of "factual" represented a bow to Secretary of State Byrnes, who agreed that everybody needed information but regarded interpretation as the province of his department.)

When Lieutenant General Hoyt S. Vandenberg replaced Souers on June 10, 1946, he "inherited a going concern but a small one" and moved immediately to extend the responsibilities of the Central Intelligence Group, with the aim of transforming it into an "independent, entirely self-sufficient, national intelligence service" established by legislation rather than simply by presidential order. Knowledgeable in the worlds of politics and bureaucracy, the general, nephew of Senator Arthur Vandenberg, built up the staff of the Central Intelligence Group from about a hundred to four hundred, explaining that "if I didn't fill all the slots, I knew I'd lose them"; actually, he looked toward an establishment of two thousand. In July 1946 Vandenberg directed the preparation of "Soviet Foreign and Military Policy," the forerunner of the later National Intelligence Estimates. After shepherding the CIG toward statutory status as the CIA (which came on September 20, 1947), Vandenberg went to the air staff, being succeeded by Rear Admiral Roscoe Hillenkoetter.

On November 12 an official of the new CIA declared in a memorandum that staff intelligence, though adequate with respect to some parts of the world, was "decidedly inadequate" on the USSR, Britain, France, and Germany, "the very crux of the world situation." U.S. intelligence had developed no general analysis of Soviet aims and strategy since the Vandenberg assessment in July 1946, which (suggesting the pressure Vandenberg could put on subordinates) had been "produced by one man over the weekend to meet an unanticipated and urgent requirement." As for Germany, the single paper the staff had produced, which had come the previous April, contained only a review of the objectives and policies of the occupying powers. Even the document the staff was working on at the moment, said the memo, was "too slight and superficial" to give Marshall and his associates the analysis of the actual German situation they needed to prepare for the London meeting.

In London, as in Moscow and at earlier conferences, the foreign ministers wrangled over a wide range of questions and made limited progress on a few. But they reached a complete dead end on the question of the structure of the German state that the treaty would create. The decision on the structure stood first in importance, because it would determine the political alignment of the new government. Three weeks of talks around the table saw the ministers further apart than they had been when they arrived in London. Having no intention of enduring a replay of the barren ordeal in Moscow, Marshall had told an aide that if he saw no possibility of serious negotiation, he intended to end the conference, though if any possibility of progress developed, he would stay as long as it took to achieve an agreement.

Before Soviet Foreign Minister Molotov left Moscow for London, he had been given a memorandum on Germany drawn up by a deputy foreign minister, Andrei Smirnov, who concerned himself with German affairs as head of the ministry's Third European Department. Smirnov warned Molotov about "practical steps taken by the United States and Great Britain in Germany to pave the way to a settlement of the German issue." He was speaking, Smirnov said, "not about a propaganda maneuver or political blackmail" but about the threat of Germany's dismemberment and the inclusion of West Germany in the Western bloc. In conformity with directives formally approved on November 21 by the Politburo, Molotov presented to his fellow foreign ministers in London a plan calling for the establishment of a "united democratic Germany" and the socialization of basic industries; he also stressed two of the original occupation *d*'s, denazification and demilitarization.

Secretary of State Marshall, while agreeing with the idea of a centralized government, insisted that such a government had to be effective and, in the words of the U.S. official historian, "genuinely democratic"— individuals must have basic freedoms, as was not the case in the Soviet zone, and ideas, people, and goods must be able to move freely throughout Germany.

Molotov retorted that such resistance to his proposals came from the Allied wish to prevent German economic recovery, out of fear that the country might become a rival in the European and world market (the dialectical point made by Ivan Maisky before the Potsdam Conference). Seeming to some observers almost to be seeking the breakup of the conference, Molotov spoke savagely of his fellow foreign ministers as representatives of countries that needed "one or other piece of German territory as a base for the development of a war industry, and Germany's reactionary forces as a support for a policy ... opposing the development of the democratic movement in the European countries liberated from fascism." In London, as in all other East-West dickering and dealing, the word *democratic* obfuscated much and clarified nothing.

Concerned about appearing to have made plans based on the anticipated failure of the conference, Marshall had discouraged advance discussion among the Allies of alternatives to a central government for all of Germany. But Robert Murphy, General Clay's political adviser, cabled Washington that he believed "most intelligent Europeans would take it for granted that we had made our plans in view of lack of 4-power unity." Clay, who found both Marshall and John Foster Dulles now in philosophical accord with him on the importance of German recovery in itself, cabled the War Department shortly before the beginning of the conference that the Allies "must have courage to proceed with the Government of West Germany quickly if CFM fails to produce an answer for all Germany." On the basis of his wartime dealings with the Russians, Clay later said, Marshall had earlier believed that he might be able to get along with them. But the chaos at the London conference, with Molotov's denunciation of the United States, convinced the secretary of the need for the Allies to establish a separate policy for western Germany. Here Clay may have mistaken Marshall's opposition to open discussion of alternatives to a central government for all of Germany for opposition to the alternatives themselves. If a break came, the secretary wanted Congress and the American public to see plainly what had caused it.

The session came to its bitter end on December 15. The Russians did not, however, accept any responsibility for the fiasco. "By making use of the sharp differences in discussion on the issue of German reparations," said one Soviet account, "U.S. State Secretary G. Marshall interrupted the session and refused to continue its work."

Observing in his telegram to Washington that "the resentment of the Germans against colonial administration is increasing daily," Clay offered a succinct summary of the central issue: "Two and a half years without a government is much too long."

CHAPTER 10

"... With Dramatic Suddenness"

EARLY IN THE new year an FBI agent ushered into Admiral Leahy's office a caller with astonishing news. The visitor, a "Circassian" named Boudikine, had supposedly had a remarkable career in World War I, having served in the Russian army, been captured and tortured by the Germans, and finished the war as an officer in the Italian navy. In the second war, the admiral was told, Boudikine had been associated with the British army "in an advisory capacity." On this January day Boudikine enjoyed the attention of a high-level audience—not only Leahy but General Dwight D. Eisenhower in his last month as chief of staff of the army, and the president's military and naval aides, summoned for the occasion. "He is an intelligent man, a Moslem," noted the often skeptical Leahy, "and he appears to be telling the truth."

While strolling in a London park one evening, Boudikine told his listeners, he had overheard a conversation between a Soviet admiral and a Soviet general, who seemed to speaking quite openly in a kind of drunken confidence that nobody within earshot would be likely to understand Russian. Their talk concerned the details of a gigantic forthcoming military operation; the officers described how massed Soviet bombers, taking off from airfields in Canada, were going to attack the United States, striking at lines of communication, nuclear facilities, and ammunition depots. Coordinated with the attack would be a wave of sabotage, to be carried out by 50,000 Soviet agents already in the United States, assisted by "disaffected Negroes" and by Armenians belonging to the Soviet underground apparatus. The plan also called for the assassination of three American leaders—President Truman, "who is clever"; General Marshall, "who is intelligent"; and General MacArthur, "who is a dangerous opponent in war." General Eisenhower was of no concern to the officers, Boudikine reported, because they believed that he "could be controlled"—a possible implication being that Ike might be allowed to survive so that he could preside over the postwar puppet American government. Perhaps Boudikine did not recognize the general sitting nearby; frequently a man of few words, Leahy did not record Ike's response to the caller's unflattering judgment.

Worst of all from the admiral's point of view, perhaps, Soviet submarines and "speed boats" would simultaneously seek out and destroy all the ships of the United States fleet—a prospect to which Leahy, as the senior U.S. naval officer, could hardly be insensitive only a handful of years after Pearl Harbor. J. Edgar Hoover's seeming endorsement of Boudikine could have involved personal sensitivities as well, since the FBI director had rejected an authoritative warning about the Japanese plan in the summer of 1941, some four months before the day of infamy came.

Leahy and Hoover clearly gave a measure of credence to Boudikine's story, though it sounded like nothing so much as an updated version of *The Riddle of the Sands* and other fantasies of overwhelming German invasion with which British novelists used to frighten their compatriots in the first decade of the century. Thus, at the beginning of 1948, some three weeks after the breakup of the London foreign ministers' conference, the inner councils of the FBI and the White House gave serious attention to a story that Leahy, at least, would have snorted at even a year earlier: Stalin's Russia, like Kaiser Wilhelm II's Germany in its day, now loomed as the tricky as well as formidable adversary of a liberal Western power. The reception Boudikine received offered unmistakable proof that the U.S. government badly needed an effective high-level intelligence agency.

The year that lay ahead would hold nothing so apocalyptic as an overwhelming Soviet assault on the United States from mysteriously acquired Canadian bases or assassination of the nation's leaders, with the heavy involvement of dissident minority citizens and wily fifth columnists. But the developing conflict between East and West would undergo a complete transformation. Just in the next weeks, Communists in Central and Eastern Europe would produce real, not imagined, events that would confirm many Western attitudes and change others. As had been the case before World War II, the arena would be Czechoslovakia, a country that the West had sponsored at Versailles after World War I and that, as a liberal democracy, had been an object of continuing solicitude on the part of the West until it was abandoned at Munich in September 1938. When the country was restored after World War II, with its 1938 president, Edvard Beneš, back in his post, the government, under Beneš's leadership, sought a close relationship with the Soviet Union. The foreign minister, Jan Masaryk, son of the country's founding president, also worked for friendly relations with Russia but retained his lifelong Western orientation, suffering a humiliating blow when his bid to bring his country into the Marshall Plan was vetoed—after he had accepted the offer—by Joseph Stalin. In November 1947 Masaryk told a journalist friend in New York that the Communist authorities at the recent Comintern meeting in Poland had ordered Czech Communists to liquidate the opposition parties, the kind of development that had already taken place in Poland, Hungary, and Romania. "I begged him, in vain, not to return to Prague," the friend said, "but he was unwavering. He said that he could not leave Beneš to cope alone."

But Beneš, a man who had once been called the only "permanent minister" in Europe but was not a national leader in the heroic mold, found his coping skills exhausted. On February 25, 1948, fearing bloodshed, he yielded to heavy pressure and appointed a Communist-dominated cabinet; party figures already controlled the police, the militia, and other agencies that held direct power over the people. Because of Beneš's acquiescence in this coup-by-reluctant-assent, direct Soviet intervention did not become necessary, though a Soviet deputy foreign minister, Valerian Zorin, was on hand in case the local Communists needed outside help. Beneš remained in office for three further months, but he had ceased to hold any actual power; he left politics with the doubly tragic fate of having been driven from office, in turn, by both Nazis and Communists, and died within a few months. Shortly before his death, Beneš had said, "My greatest mistake was that I refused to believe that Stalin lied to me cynically"—in declaring that the Soviet Union had no intention of interfering in the political life of neighboring countries—"and that his assurances were an intentional deceit." But Beneš himself had actually given the game away during the war, when he told Stalin that Czechoslovakia "would always speak and act in a manner agreeable to the Soviet government." Ten years after the appeasement of Hitler at Munich, Beneš, with tragic unwisdom, had appeased Stalin in advance.

Even without visible direct intervention by Moscow, the coup in Prague rattled the windows of chancelleries across Europe and sent a shock wave across the Atlantic to the White House and Capitol Hill. During the first weeks of the year, Foreign Secretary Bevin, seeing the great need to buck up the Western Europeans after the acrimonious breakup of the London Council of Foreign Ministers conference, had devoted much of his attention to promoting his imprecise but strongly held idea of a closer relation among the liberal European states. The Marshall Plan had called for the European countries to cooperate and submit an integrated economic program rather than separate national shopping lists. With the Soviets refusing to allow the Eastern European countries, and even Czechoslovakia, to take part—and trying, through strikes and political subversion, to keep the American initiative from succeeding in Western Europe—the foreign secretary declared on January 22 in a speech in the House of Commons that "the free nations of Europe must now draw together." As a working term for this concept, he used the phrase "Western Union" (which did not in Europe, as it would have done in the United States, call to mind a giant telegraph company). No one knew what Stalin and his associates had in mind concerning Western Europe, whether they planned subversion and disruption or military advance and war. Bevin did not expect Stalin to run the risk of starting a war, but nobody who had high responsibility for the destiny of a country, either in Britain or on the Continent, could be sure that he would not.

As important as Bevin believed his idea—and as clearly as he saw the vital necessity of winning American support for it—he knew such overtures and discussions would have to wait. On December 17, 1947, after an appeal from General Marshall, who saw the specter of coming European collapse while senators and representatives dithered through another winter, President Truman won from Congress an act providing special short-term aid for Western Europe. Just two days after signing this measure, while legislative committees were still investigating and debating Europe's needs, Truman presented the worked-out Marshall Plan proposal itself. (At one point, said the president's aide Clark Clifford some years later, a staff member proposed that the program be called the "Truman Formula," but the president vetoed the idea. "Anything that is sent up to the House and Senate with my name on it," he said, "will quiver a couple of times and then turn over and die.") Treading carefully to avoid making any public move that might spook congressional conservatives and thus damage the bill's prospects, Bevin never linked the United States to any kind of contemplated organization of European states, instead concentrating his rhetoric on praising the Marshall Plan.

Americans who opposed the plan might have been surprised to learn that a number of British politicians and economists, especially in Bevin's own Labour Party, likewise objected to it. The Americans had designed it to serve their own interests, said the dissenters; it would only make Britain an economic vassal of the United States. In the United States, which functioned as the world's stronghold of militant capitalism, the conservative Republicans controlled the Congress, while in Britain an administration professing a socialist program ruled over the economy; in these circumstances wrangling over economic ties between the two countries had nothing surprising about it. "Problems of fundamental political and economic policy, of sovereign rights, arise and are not to be easily resolved," said an economist at Harvard, and "these may jeopardize the position of the [Marshall Plan] administrator caught between the British Labour Government (say) intent upon nationalization and the supporters of private enterprise here." When a Republican congressman who supported the program asked

Marshall in a hearing whether the U.S. offer of aid to European countries might not bring accusations of American interference with their sovereignty, he received a characteristic answer. If the United States were engaged in a conspiracy to commit economic imperialism, said the secretary, the effort would require "a more Machiavellian approach than is exhibited here with public hearings and public discussions on every side with regard to every issue."

Marshall expected general approval by the Europeans, even though Congress wanted to attach so many strings to the aid that problems would inevitably arise. At one point, the budget-cutting Representative John Taber of New York, the almost antediluvian chairman of the House Appropriations Committee, spoke of the Marshall Plan as "this world-wide relief program" based on nothing more than "a series of after-dinner conversations in which Administration economists let their imaginations run wild." Marshall made energetic efforts to counter such views, traveling all over the country to meet with "tobacco people, cotton people, New York, eastern industrialists, Pittsburgh people, the whole West Coast." He worked, he said, as hard "as though I was running for the Senate or the presidency."

For his part, Bevin, despite his strong attachment to socialism, brushed off all philosophical or doctrinaire objections to Marshall's initiative. Of course the plan would serve American interests, he said, "but it is to everybody's interest as well." It was, he declared, "much better to spend money now on rebuilding a healthy and self-reliant Europe than to wait for the devils of poverty and disease to create again conditions making for war and dictatorship." Marshall made the same point: "We can act for our own good by acting for the world's good," succinctly adding, in January, "Dollars will not save the world—but the world today cannot be saved without dollars."

Though the late February shock wave from Prague surprised political leaders and diplomats less than ordinary citizens, it disquieted everybody. Americans had a special interest in Czechoslovakia, not only because many of them had ancestors or were themselves from that area but because the union of Czechs and Slovaks could trace its founding to a declaration produced in Pittsburgh during World War I by Thomas Masaryk, Jan's father, together with Slovak leaders. In Europe Ernest Bevin, already discussing a common defense with frightened ministers of the Low Countries and France, spoke of "the critical period of 6–8 weeks" that "would decide the future of Europe," and in a little more than three weeks he led the way to the creation of the Treaty of Brussels, signed on March 17, which established the West European Union.

Just a week earlier, the fate of Czechoslovakia had taken shape in a personal tragedy that seemed in the West to symbolize the workings of Stalinist Russia's drive for control of the Continent. On March 10 the authorities in Prague announced that Jan Masaryk had been found dead in the courtyard of the Czernin Palace, beneath his bedroom window. Suicide, declared the authorities—the foreign minister had deliberately plunged to his death. Few in the West thought it likely, but however he died, the tortured Masaryk was a victim of the February coup. (The former Czech ambassador in Washington gave reporters a lurid account of the tragedy: Masaryk had been bludgeoned to death, after shooting two of his assailants, and his body had been dumped out of the window. "Fairy tales," retorted a Czech government spokesman. "Hollywood yarns." The U.S. ambassador in Prague, Laurence Steinhardt, at first accepted the official story of suicide but within a few weeks had changed his mind; the Kremlin hated Masaryk because of his "jocular contempt for the Soviets," Steinhardt said, and after all, they had murdered Trotsky; most important, if Masaryk had killed himself, as a true patriot he would have left a statement explaining his action to his countrymen.) On the day of Masaryk's death, General Marshall told a press conference that, concerning Czechoslovakia, "there are great fears as to the developments" and a "considerable passion of view on the part of a great many in this country." Speaking calmly, the secretary nevertheless declared that the earlier fate of other non-Communist officials, and what had just happened to Masaryk, marked "a reign of terror and not an ordinary due process of government by the people."

Although Representative Taber and other conservative Republicans would whittle away at some of its provisions during the process of fixing the appropriation, the authorization of the Marshall Plan now won passage in the Senate within three days and in the House of Representatives on March 31; President Truman signed the act on April 3. The prime motivator, Joseph Stalin, who more and more displayed a remarkable gift for producing reactions opposite to those he sought, had now succeeded in frightening European and American leaders into creating the beginnings of an Atlantic economic and military community aimed at the political, industrial, and agricultural recovery of the Continent and the containment of the Soviet Union.

On March 31 General Clay dispatched an "eyes only" telegram from Berlin to the Army Security Agency at the Pentagon for delivery to General Omar Bradley, who had now succeeded Eisenhower as army chief of staff. The Soviets had sent the U.S. command a "peremptory letter," Clay said, giving twenty-four hours' notice that they were imposing restrictions on U.S. military and civilian personnel and freight proceeding by rail through the Soviet zone to Berlin. Since these trains had always had the right of free access as "a condition precedent to our entry into Berlin and to our evacuation of Saxony and Thuringia," the general said, he did not propose to give it up. He asked for a prompt reply, because he had to take action that very day: "It is my intent to instruct our guards to open fire if Soviet soldiers attempt to enter our trains." Obviously, Clay said, "the full consequence of this action must be understood."

The announcement of the new Soviet traffic regulations accelerated the rising curve of tensions in Allied-Soviet relations in Germany during the first half of 1948. In January and February, Clay had been disturbed by reports that Soviet authorities, in Berlin as well as in the Soviet zone, were seizing printed matter produced in the Western zones. These actions, which the four-power agreement for free interchange of published materials prohibited, were highlighted by a notable act of lèse majesté: the Russians confiscated copies of *Speaking Frankly,* a memoir by no less a personage than Clay's old boss, former Secretary of State James F. Byrnes. The Soviets also seized labor-union newspapers produced in the U.S. zone and burned Western magazines. This anti-Western campaign crystallized in the creation of official companies licensed to distribute only Soviet-approved materials in eastern Germany, which thus became walled off from the western zones by a paper curtain.

Interzonal traffic in people and freight as well as in ideas encountered Russian interference. In January, Soviet inspectors, asserting that they had the right to check the identity of passengers, boarded U.S. trains. To stop this activity before it could become a trend, Clay put guards on the trains with orders to turn away such inspectors. The inspectors kept on trying, through February and March, with the result that American trains frequently sat for hours on sidings.

The new Soviet traffic regulations of March 30, contained in a letter from the Soviet deputy military governor, Lieutenant General Mikhail Dratvin, to his U.S. counterpart, Major General George P. Hays, required Americans traveling through the Soviet zone by rail or road to present documentary proof of their identity and their affiliation with military government; freight shipments had to possess similar documentary evidence; and all baggage except personal luggage would be inspected at Soviet checkpoints. Thus, in one bureaucratic-sounding message, the Russians struck at the West's most vulnerable point in Germany. Archivists in London and Washington searched files in vain for agreements guaranteeing the United States and Britain access to Berlin. No such documents had ever been produced, although, as General Clay observed, the right of occupation clearly implied the right of access. (Since nobody favored midair collisions, the situation in the air was different—traffic control and the management of air corridors required written understandings. The occupying powers had readily reached agreement on these points in 1945; at that time nobody put much emphasis on air traffic to Berlin.)

Clay did not dismiss the Soviet letter out of hand, however: "I propose to have Soviet Deputy Commander advised today that we are prepared for our train commandant on arrival at entry points to furnish to the Soviet representatives a list of passengers together with their official orders, and that likewise we are prepared to present a manifest covering freight shipments in our trains when they arrive at entry points." But this compromise would be the limit, and the guards would be under instructions to open fire if Soviet soldiers tried to enter the trains themselves. Otherwise, American personnel would find it impossible to travel between the U.S. zone and Berlin except by air, and, the general declared, "it is undoubtedly the first of a series of restrictive measures designed to drive us from Berlin." In teleconferences between Clay's headquarters and Washington, Secretary of the Army Kenneth Royall and General Bradley approved Clay's proposed reply and won the president's endorsement. Though Clay was authorized to move trains as he saw fit, his bosses added a word of caution: "It is important that our guards not fire unless fired upon."

In a teleconference with Royall, Bradley, General J. Lawton Collins, the deputy chief of staff, and Lieutenant General Albert C. Wedemeyer, the army's director of plans and operations, Clay told Washington that he was working in full harmony with the British commander, General Sir Brian Robertson. (At that time the most efficient and reliable medium for long-range communication, the teleconference, essentially a form of teletype, used screens on which rapidly decoded messages were flashed.) Like Clay, Robertson was an engineer officer and had not held a combat command; suitably enough for the new Berlin situation, he had long experience in supply and logistics. The British had declared that they would not allow Soviet officials to search their trains, and, Clay said, "I think their decision relative to shooting will depend almost entirely on our own." Worried that gunfire might bring on war, Royall asked Clay whether the general would agree with a proposal for Truman to inform Stalin that trains would continue to move "pending discussions as to any proper regulations." Or should the trains simply move but in no case engage in shooting? Clay saw both ideas as indicating weakness: "I do not believe this means war but any failure to meet this squarely will cause great trouble." Rather than endorse either of Royall's suggestions, he said in his blunt way, "I would prefer to evacuate Berlin and I had rather go to Siberia than to do that."

In another conference later the same day Clay took care to make his own view plain and at the same time to stiffen the resolution of the men at the other end of the transatlantic conversation: "Please understand we are not carrying a chip on our shoulder and will shoot only for self-protection. We do not believe we will have to do so." But the integrity of the trains, he said, stood as "a symbol of our position in Germany and Europe." He also reassured his superiors that he would instruct the train guards not to fire unless fired upon, but he could not resist registering a protest: "I do not agree that this is a fair instruction to a man whose life may be in danger."

In an attempt to discover just how far the Soviets intended to go, Clay sent a train with a few armed guards across the zonal border, ordering it not to stop for the newly announced inspection. It proceeded unimpeded for some distance into the Soviet zone but was finally switched off the main line onto a siding, where, Clay later wrote, "it remained for a few days until it withdrew rather ignominiously. It was clear the Russians meant business." What was not so clear to Clay was how much business Washington meant; the cautious nature of Royall's reply left him with no choice but to order the train back to the West. British trains met the same fate.

In this developing situation, General Bradley took a look at the disconcerting disparity between what the Americans could say and what they could back up with force. They did not have to speak softly, if they chose not to do so, but they did not have a very big stick to carry to Berlin or anywhere else. "Had I had enough hair on my head to react," Bradley said, Clay's March 31 cable "would probably have stood it on end." Actually, this message was not the first shocker the U.S. commander in Germany had sent Bradley during this exceptionally eventful month. On the fifth, just a week and a day after the coup in Prague, the chief of staff had received a cable that, he noted, "lifted me right out of my chair." Preceded by no warning and making no reference to any specific event or communication from the Soviets, Clay's "special report," as its author later described it, seemed more like a general alarm:

> FOR MANY MONTHS BASED ON LOGICAL ANALYSIS, I HAVE FELT AND HELD THAT WAR WAS UNLIKELY FOR AT LEAST TEN YEARS. WITHIN THE LAST FEW WEEKS I HAVE FELT A SUBTLE CHANGE IN SOVIET ATTITUDE WHICH I CANNOT DEFINE BUT WHICH NOW GIVES ME A FEELING THAT IT MAY COME WITH DRAMATIC SUDDENNESS.

Coming so soon after the coup in Prague, this message received wide circulation in Washington. Actually, however, this kind of generalized speculation did not represent a typical production by the hard-headed Clay. Since the beginning of the year—as currency reform was debated, expectations grew for the Marshall Plan, and the trend was clearly moving toward the creation of two Germanys, east and west—the Allied and Soviet commanders had engaged in a continuing demand-and-response chess game, in which cause and effect were sometimes difficult to distinguish. In the days leading up to the dispatch of the "dramatic suddenness" message, Clay later said, he had noted in Soviet officers from Marshal Sokolovsky down "a new attitude, faintly contemptuous, slightly arrogant, and certainly assured." And the days of comradely drinks after working hours had definitely vanished; disputes and quarrels now marked the sessions of the Allied Control Council. Sokolovsky claimed, accurately enough, that the Anglo-Americans were aiming at associating western Germany in a Western bloc—"a dangerous course"—though the marshal chose to gloss over Soviet policies in eastern Germany, which he always presented in any forum as purely democratic and therefore above capitalist reproach. With effective four-power control of Germany a vanished illusion, Clay the good soldier now devoted himself to a different task.

But Clay's message nevertheless raised a central question: Why had he sent it, since other messages from him at the same time conveyed no such fears? The general explained himself many years later by saying that this message, which he "did not consider . . . alarmist," had been written to help the army make its case to Congress for reinstituting the military draft. He expressed indignation that his secret warning had soon appeared in the *Saturday Evening Post*; he intended it, he said, only for tactical use by friends. Coming from a man who had spent more than a decade in Washington, where policy making by leak had long been established, such ingenuousness could only seem a bit less than convincing. Less surprising, perhaps, was Clay's readiness to exaggerate what he saw as the truth in order to influence Congress, a difficult body with which he had been forced to deal through the years in depression and war. In any case, he seems to have failed to warn General Bradley to take the message with a large grain of salt. It may be true, as well, that Clay, who had done his best to make the four-power occupation succeed, later regretted having been the author of the message that presented him as a commander waiting for war. To add to the confusion stirred up by this telegram, Clay's special assistant for intelligence dismissed the general's own explanation.

To George Kennan, Clay's March 5 message had constituted a misreading of Soviet actions, which to Kennan represented not moves toward war but "Moscow's attempt to play, before it was too late, the various political cards it still possessed on the European continent." Nor, for that matter, did Kennan believe that the facts justified Ernest Bevin's thrust toward military organization for Western Europe: "Further military advances in the west could only increase responsibilities already beyond the Russian capacity to meet," and hence were not to be feared. Chip Bohlen remembered an observation made by Clay in 1945 that "the key to getting along with the

Soviets was that you had to give trust to get trust"; Bohlen had replied that within a year at most the general would become one of the U.S. officials most opposed to the Russians, because "anyone who started with too many illusions about the Soviets came out totally disillusioned." And, said Bohlen, "my forecast was right."

General Bradley, who saw the Soviets holding plenty of cards in Europe and thus had ample reason for feeling his hair standing up and his body being jolted from its chair, had only recently come to the post of chief of staff, after serving an outstandingly successful term as director of the Veterans Administration. During World War II the general had commanded the largest field armies in American history, but now, in this new kind of struggle, he saw the United States attempting to "contain" Soviet expansionism with forces woefully inadequate for the task. Holding the Russians in check around the globe, the proclaimed goal of the Truman Doctrine, clearly demanded a buildup of U.S. military strength; instead, with the postwar demobilization—disintegration, as soldiers saw it—the armed forces had shrunk to only 1.6 million, with a total annual budget of some $10 billion. Nor was this the worst of it. Looking to the forthcoming presidential election, the Republican 80th Congress passed, over Truman's veto, a large tax cut that caused the president to make fresh reductions in military spending. The budget ceiling had resulted in an army only 552,000 strong and still shrinking.

The facts behind the numbers told a more depressing story: The army had little combat readiness, with half its troops overseas on occupation duty, "serving as policemen or clerks." Though the troops scattered around the United States were not needed as policemen, they had no greater effectiveness than those overseas; only one division, the famous 82nd Airborne, could be considered at all ready for action. When State Department planners proposed that ground forces be sent to Greece to oppose the guerrillas, the Joint Chiefs replied that they had no troops to send. "We are playing with fire," said General Marshall, "while we have nothing with which to put it out." (Instead of troops, in this case, the army dispatched a general, James Van Fleet—whom Bradley believed to be worth two divisions; aided by political developments, Van Fleet performed so well that within a year the Greek army had won a total victory.)

Britain, the only consistent American ally, could make no better showing. Ernest Bevin pursued his active policy for European defense in the awareness that his country's army, in infantry strength, numbered only two-thirds of even the small force that had entered the war against Germany in 1939—90 infantry battalions compared with 141. Unlike the Americans, the British had retained the draft, but members of Bevin's own Labour Party had forced the government to cut time in service from eighteen months to twelve, and the overall numbers were going down; the last remaining armored division faced deactivation. As for the Royal Navy, lack of oil had forced it to cancel the autumn maneuvers.

The combination of Western moves toward greater unity and the military weakness of these powers made French Foreign Minister Georges Bidault speculate gloomily in March that now was surely the time for the Russians to strike, before the Western plans had produced any actual new strength. Another French minister declared that the Russians would be in Paris by August; the French chief of staff expressed his agreement with this despairing view.

Unfortunately for General Bradley and his American and British colleagues, the public and most politicians felt little concern over Western military weakness. Since August 1945 the popular picture of war in the contemporary world had featured, not infantrymen with rifles and machine guns, not even columns of advancing tanks, but enormous mushroom clouds rising in the sky over two Japanese cities. What need did the West have of divisions? If truly serious trouble arose with the Soviet Union, American atomic bombs could settle matters in a day. So widespread was faith in the efficacy of nuclear force that even the eminent British pacifist Bertrand Russell declared that if the Russians rejected American proposals to internationalize the control of nuclear weapons, they should be brought to heel through the threat of nuclear attack. (Actually, at this moment of increasing international tensions, the world had few fiercer conflicts than the internecine American brawl between the navy and the recently created independent air force over control of the delivery of atomic bombs. If they should ever be used, should they be dropped from long-range bombers flying from land bases or by planes off aircraft carriers, which themselves could go anywhere?)

For General Bradley and other presidential advisers, the choice between responding to a challenge by launching a nuclear attack, on the one hand, or taking no action at all, on the other, represented an unacceptable restriction on the nation's freedom of action. Strategists and experts at think tanks began looking at the idea of "calibration," a way of responding to a presumed Soviet threat without having to decide whether to "capitulate or precipitate a global war"; the United States needed to develop the ability to oppose aggression at the level of that aggression. In addition, the country had not entered the postwar arena with a bulging atomic arsenal. In January 1947 the Los Alamos atomic laboratory had only one bomb, which David Lilienthal, chairman of the Atomic Energy Commission, regarded as no better than "probably operable"; a few months later the commission still had no bombs ready for immediate use. By the spring of 1948, however, the stockpile had grown to some fifty. The situation had further complexities, with the top officers of the air force and the navy spending much of their energies in the doctrinal and territorial battle over the control and delivery of strategic weapons that would become known as the revolt of the admirals. The air force pushed the development of the gigantic B-36, dubbed the Peacemaker, the largest warplane ever built, powered by six pusher piston engines and widely criticized as obsolete even before it entered service; the navy hoped to counter with a supercarrier, which, however, died in the budgeting process.

Still, Clay's "war" telegram sent U.S. intelligence agencies into a stir of activity. On March 16, as a result, the CIA was able to give the president no cheerier a forecast than that war was not probable within sixty days. (Top secret behind-the-scenes documents, available only half a century later, show that the still-fledgling CIA's handling of this assignment gave rise to considerable criticism. The eleven-day time required to produce an authoritative estimate, explained Secretary of Defense Louis Johnson, came in part from "the fact that an 'Eyes Only' message did not come immediately to the attention of appropriate intelligence agencies, and in part [from] the lack of established procedures for dealing with such matters.")

The next day, amid the general swirl of doubts, fears, and apprehensions about Soviet intentions and Western abilities—while the European foreign ministers were meeting in Brussels to frame Bevin's "Western Union"—President Truman went forth to do St. Patrick's Day battle on Capitol Hill. The Joint Chiefs had agreed on a small increase in ground-force strength and had also recommended the renewal of the draft. Gamely, in this election year, the president asked Congress for legislation to reinstitute selective service; he also called for the immediate passage of the Marshall Plan. He received the latter prize at the end of the month, and despite the widespread lack of congressional faith in Truman's leadership, accelerating events in Germany produced the selective service legislation in June. This renewal of the draft, however, could yield no immediate increase in U.S. military strength. As before, the small Western garrisons in Germany could only serve as symbols of the potential might of the countries they represented. If the Soviets should decide to move into the Allied zones, they would meet no ground forces capable of stopping or even seriously delaying them. Of necessity, one way or the other, the Allies had only one true asset: the air.

CHAPTER 11

A Salami for the Slicing

IN FEBRUARY, GENERAL Clay flew to London for a meeting with the British and French on long-range policy for Germany. This conference proved to be a major point in the flow of events in 1948. Held in the drafty solemnity of India House, a potent symbol of one-time imperial glory with its great viceregal portraits, the meeting ran in two sessions, from February 23 to March 5 and from April 20 to June 2. During the first session came the news of the Communist coup in Prague. In the interval between the two sessions, the British and French held the meetings with the Benelux countries that produced the Treaty of Brussels, signed on March 17.

Just three days later, at the March 20 meeting of the Allied Control Council in Berlin—a special session called at Marshal Sokolovsky's request—the Soviet commander told the Western military governors that he must be given full information about Allied decisions reached in London concerning western Germany. While conceding that the request was reasonable enough, the Western representatives told the marshal that since this was a meeting between governments and they themselves had not received the "directives" he sought, they had nothing to pass on; when they received instructions, they said, they would keep him fully informed. Sokolovsky barely waited for the translators to finish. Making it obvious that he had not expected a satisfactory answer—and perhaps had not wanted one—he began to read a vitriolic prepared statement accusing the Western representatives of concealing a decision reached at London to jettison the Potsdam agreements and thus prevent the establishment of a peaceful and democratic Germany.

To the surprise of the others, Sokolovsky, the chairman for March, then announced, "I see no sense in continuing this meeting, and I declare it adjourned." He rose from his seat in front of the fireplace, the members of his delegation all stood up, and the entire group walked out of the meeting room. As General Clay observed later, no meeting of the council had ever before been adjourned without unanimous agreement or without fixing the date of the next meeting—"and, significantly, no chairman had hitherto left a meeting without inviting his colleagues to join him for coffee and light refreshments." The Western representatives saw the walkout as no impromptu affair but a deliberate warning not to proceed with their plans for western Germany. Although the three Western powers would go through the motions of calling subsequent meetings, Sokolovsky's departure meant that the Allied Control Council was dead. It would never meet again.

If the Western commanders had been able to look into the offices and conference rooms of the Kremlin, they would have found full confirmation of their belief that Sokolovsky's theatrical actions had nothing spontaneous about them. But why, exactly, had the marshal wanted a meeting so that he could deliver a public diatribe and then walk out?

On March 9 Moscow had summoned Sokolovsky and his political adviser, Vladimir Semyenov, for urgent discussion of steps to counter Western policies for Germany as they emerged from the Allied conference in London whose first session had concluded just four days before Sokolovsky received his summons to Moscow. In secret meetings in the Kremlin, with participation confined to a tight circle and no involvement of the Politburo as such, the Soviet leaders developed ideas for a sustained counterattack on the Allies in Berlin. This thinking found its reflection in a comprehensive memorandum, "On Our Measures to Be Adopted with Respect to Germany in the Near Future," drawn up for Molotov by Andrei Smirnov. With the Western powers departing from the Yalta and Potsdam agreements, as Smirnov saw it, and "transforming Germany into their strong point," the USSR should take action to thwart them. If the Western representatives should refuse to discuss the issue at a meeting of the Council of Foreign Ministers, then it would become clear that they had "renounced the idea of settlement of the German issue on the basis of the Potsdam decisions." Then the Soviets would have grounds for declaring that the Allied Control Council was dead and that, consequently, all agreements on control mechanisms and occupation zones had died with it. The Soviet Union could then announce that it was obliged to close its occupation zone "in order to ensure the respective financial measures, protection of the borders, etc."

A week and a day later, Marshal Sokolovsky banged the gavel on the Allied Control Council, rose from his seat, and walked out of the chamber, thereby setting the whole process in motion. Symbolically, he had put a pistol to the head of the council and pulled the trigger.

The Allied commanders and their political chiefs lacked other information that could have come to them only if the West had planted a spy in Stalin's inner circle. On March 26, less than a week after Sokolovsky's walkout, the generalissimo would play host to a delegation from the German Socialist Unity Party (SED), led by Wilhelm Pieck. Pieck had presided over the forced merger in 1946 of the Communists and the Social Democrats in the Soviet zone, a move that had found some Social Democratic support in the East at the time. Russian actions in the intervening two years had, however, caused the fused party to lose much of the support it could originally claim. Nor had anyone forgotten the behavior of Soviet troops in the early days of the occupation—most women in the Soviet zone detested the country these soldiers represented.

In talking with Stalin, however, Pieck attributed the SED's loss of support to anti-Soviet agitation on the part of the West; the German masses, it seemed, were beset by "great confusion" and thus readily succumbed to enemy influence. In fact, Pieck confessed to Stalin, things were so bad that the party might well lose the election in Berlin scheduled for October; the German leader did not have to spell out for the generalissimo that not even all the repressive measures the party could call on could guarantee a victory. Nevertheless, all might turn out well "if one could remove the Allies from Berlin."

Stalin did not hesitate. "Let's make a joint effort," he said. "Perhaps we can kick them out."

Actually, the kicking had already begun without Pieck's contribution. Just the day before, Marshal Sokolovsky had issued the internal order that constituted the first step in executing the Soviet plan for Berlin.

In mounting the Berlin operation, Stalin took a calculated risk. The term *brinkmanship* would not exist for another eight years, when John Foster Dulles would use it to describe to an interviewer how national leaders had to be able to go to the brink of war without falling over the edge; such dexterity, Dulles said, was the "necessary art." In decreeing the blockade of Berlin, the generalissimo engaged in his own version of this dangerous art. He contemplated no direct attack on Western forces in Germany, and his army made no preparations, engaged in no maneuvers, with such an end in view. Interviewed many years later, General S. P. Ivanov, chief of staff of the Soviet occupation forces in Germany in 1948, declared that Russian political and military leaders "were not suicides." The American monopoly of nuclear weapons meant that Stalin would not indulge any temptation to solve the Berlin problem by military attack. Instead, he would use the overwhelming Soviet military superiority in Berlin and in Germany to get his way by pressure—by "military-political blackmail," as one Russian historian called it. Stalin did not intend to topple over the brink into disaster; he did not even appear to believe that he was walking close to any edge.

"There is a change in spirit over here now," an officer in Berlin wrote on March 29 to General John Maginnis, who had returned to the States and entered the race for a congressional seat in Massachusetts. "Appeasement of the Russians is apparently ended as is babying the Communist Party and their front organizations." But sharing General Bradley's concerns, this officer added that "unfortunately also our Army and Navy and Air Corps are ended and most all we have now are big words to back up our intents instead of the greatest Army, Navy and Air Corps the world has seen." He described the situation in Berlin with a bit of understatement as "hotter than usual. It reminds me very much of the Summer of 1945. In those days when we stood up to the Russians, threw them off installations in our Sector, shot them when they didn't stop wholesale murder and rape in our Sector, the Russians backed off and behaved themselves." At that time, of course, American statements and protests had had the tangible backing of such resources as the Second Armored Division. But at least Americans today could take a measure of comfort: "One good thing about our past back-breaking efforts to please the Russians and win them over is the fact that nobody can say we didn't try."

At the beginning of April, General Clay's political adviser, Robert D. Murphy, reported to Secretary of State Marshall that developments toward fusion of the three Western zones of Germany had made the Kremlin dissatisfied with its own position and image. Soviet charges that the West had destroyed the Allied Control Council, as Murphy saw it, might therefore represent a bold effort to induce the Allies to end discussions concerning the trizone and even to liquidate the bizonal administration. These charges, Murphy said bluntly, also constituted an important element in the Soviet plan to force the Western powers out of Berlin in order to liquidate this "center of reaction" east of the Iron Curtain. In working toward this end, the Soviets might try to "make it increasingly impossible or unprofitable for western powers to remain on," through the use of such tactics as interfering with the communication lines between Berlin and the West. Already the Soviets were waging a propaganda campaign concerning the alleged invasion of their zone by "organized bandits and refugee workers from western zones." The next move might be to clamp regulations on the railroads and highways that connected Berlin and western Germany. "Our position in Berlin is delicate and difficult," Murphy conceded, but "our withdrawal, either voluntary or involuntary, would have severe psychological repercussions which would, at this critical stage in [the] European situation, extend far beyond the boundaries of Berlin and even Germany. *Soviets realize this full well.*"

Holding the rank of ambassador, the fifty-three-year-old Murphy—the "diplomat among warriors," as he later styled himself—brought an unusual background to his assignment with Clay as the top State Department member of the U.S. command team in Germany. As military governor, however, General Clay held undisputed first place, in accordance with the standard American procedure of appointing a commander in chief for an area and leaving him in full charge, to perform the task at hand or to be replaced, but not to be managed from home; this arrangement contrasted with General Robertson's situation, which reflected the British practice for a commander of "yoking him with a senior civil official and subordinating him to the usual cat's-cradle of committees in Whitehall."

A lanky man, given to jokes and quips and devoted to high-stakes poker, Murphy seemed to attract controversy, but he also had the kind of origins that should have endeared him to the senators who had trouble finding common ground with State Department prep-school types. Born in Milwaukee, the son of a railroad worker, Murphy as a teenager dropped out of school to go to work in the Milwaukee Road roundhouse, and with the money he earned from this and other jobs, he put himself through Marquette University; later, while working as a clerk at the Treasury Department in Washington, he took night classes at George Washington University, received his law degree in 1920, and on graduation went straight into the foreign service. In that era the weightiest advice a recruit received had to do with conduct; Murphy's twenty-minute indoctrination ended with "Above all, young man, be circumspect with the ladies!"

Murphy served as a vice-consul in Zurich and Munich and consul in Seville and Paris, until his ability and his desire to perform more significant tasks than issuing passports and granting visas won him the post of counselor of embassy, second only to the ambassador to France himself, William C. Bullitt. Murphy stayed on in France representing the United States after the armistice with Germany and, through his friendships with various members of the government established by Marshal Pétain in the spa town of Vichy, acquired in some quarters a reputation as pro-Vichy.

In late 1940, paying no attention to negative reports about Murphy, Secretary of State Cordell Hull chose him to make a survey of political, economic, and military conditions in North Africa while expediting the distribution of American food to the local people and supposedly inspecting consulates. Murphy then organized a team of twenty American experts in various fields who, under his direction, went to North Africa ostensibly as consular officials. "By the exercise of infinite patience and tact," wrote one journalist in 1943, "Murphy finally created one of the ablest groups of intelligence agents ever assembled by Americans. The task of these men was not only to learn and report on everything of importance which happened in North Africa but also to make those contacts which enabled them to swing to our side almost all the tribal headmen and a large proportion of French officers before our expeditionary forces under General Eisenhower arrived." Murphy's genuinely strong Catholicism, which had contributed to the view that he was pro-Vichy, gave him a bond with French officials and military leaders, whom he often accompanied to mass, and thus contributed to his political efforts.

Coming to light after the Allied landings in North Africa in November 1942, Murphy's efforts to weaken the allegiance of the local French officials to Marshal Pétain's regime and to prepare the way for the arrival of the Allies—an assignment involving the coordination of subversive activities, political warfare, military factors, and propaganda—and his involvement in the subsequent negotiations with Admiral François Darlan, who agreed to work with the Allies, immediately made him one of the best-known U.S. diplomats. Performance of these varied and complex tasks brought Murphy criticism as well as praise, since some of his predictions proved ill-founded and many in the press and elsewhere objected to Ike's and Murphy's dealings with the Vichyite admiral as a sellout to fascism. One writer declared that Murphy had "earned the undying hatred of French democrats," but defenders pointed out that since General de Gaulle had few followers in Algiers, the Americans had had to deal with Darlan or nobody. (Murphy himself had arranged the escape of the much more acceptable General Henri Giraud from France to North Africa, but Giraud also lacked followers.)

Some of the critics made it plain that, regardless of the military advantage the Anglo-Americans gained from the "Darlan deal," they would have preferred dealing with nobody. The columnist Walter Lippmann accused Murphy of having "bungled a delicate and difficult responsibility," but many in Washington gave Murphy credit for selling "the idea of cooperating with the United States to the French at a most critical time," and one reporter called him "Lawrence of North Africa." FDR gave him the Medal of Freedom and the rank of minister to North Africa. Certainly Murphy had gained wide and unusual experience from all these activities, and, whatever the criticisms, his mission would forever have a unique distinction: it marked the first U.S. use of diplomatic status as a cover for significant secret activities. It also gave him valuable training as political associate of an American commander.

In September 1944 Murphy received his assignment as U.S. political adviser for Germany, an appointment that continued his relationship with Ike. One afternoon in March 1945, back in Washington for conferences at the State Department, Murphy paid a call on General Clay, then James F. Byrnes's deputy director of war mobilization and reconversion. As Murphy introduced himself, he said, to Clay's surprise, that he had come by to offer congratulations to the general on his appointment as Eisenhower's deputy for military government—an assignment that meant, of course, that the general and the visitor would be working together. Murphy must be mistaken, Clay said; he had heard nothing about any such appointment. But just a few minutes after Murphy left the office, Clay received a summons to Byrnes's office, where he learned to his considerable surprise that the news Murphy brought him was accurate.

Even before meeting Murphy, Clay had admired him for his work in North Africa "in saving many American lives at the expense of much unwarranted criticism." In his German assignment one of Murphy's earliest—unfortunately, unsuccessful—efforts was his attempt to influence Ambassador Winant and the European Advisory Commission to reach explicit agreements with the Soviets guaranteeing Western access to Berlin. And with respect to the German economy, Murphy from the outset shared Clay's view that its recovery held vital importance not only for the sake of Germany but for Europe as a whole.

When Murphy spoke to Marshall of the situation in Berlin as "delicate and difficult," he had, consciously or unconsciously, used the phrase Walter Lippmann had applied to Murphy's responsibility in North Africa more than five years earlier. Perhaps that was even truer now for a diplomat among warriors in a cold war that was heating up.

In describing how he destroyed Hungary's post–World War II coalition government, the Hungarian Communist leader Matyas Rákosi gave the world a memorable phrase: he said he had sliced off the non-Communist parties "like pieces of salami." That an adaptation of these "salami tactics," as the method became known, was being used in Germany now seemed evident as the Soviets progressively sliced away at the Allied position in Berlin. On March 25 Marshal Sokolovsky issued an order, "Strengthening Protection of and Control Over the Demarcation Line of the Soviet Zone," aimed at cutting down on the amount of Allied highway and railroad traffic. Two days later the marshal issued a second order; this one called for strengthening Soviet control over the borders of Greater Berlin. In the first few days of April, acting on an April 1 Sokolovsky order, the Soviet command stopped outgoing westbound trains and closed freight lines to Munich and Hamburg. To Western observers, who did not know the discussions that lay behind these actions or the in-house orders that had given form to them, the marshal appeared to be acting in accordance with the advice proffered by one of his favorite—and quite challenging— proverbs: "I want to skin this bear before I shoot it."

Progressively skinning the Berlin bear, the marshal's troops expelled U.S. and British signals teams from their posts at Weimar and Magdeburg in the Soviet zone; these teams, which functioned under a 1945 agreement, maintained the repeater stations for communication lines between Berlin and the Western zones. Worried members of Congress began pressing army officials to bring families home from Berlin. When such pressures reached Clay, he replied that the evacuation of Americans would be "almost unthinkable." When officers in Berlin themselves made the same request on behalf of their wives and children, Clay declared, quaintly, that it was "unbecoming to an American to show any signs of nervousness." Of course, he went on, those who felt uneasy could certainly leave if they wished, but he wanted nobody with him in Berlin who had sent his family home; hence any request to leave would apply to all members of the family—the officers would go home with their dependents. As a commander, Clay clearly knew how to get the attention of his subordinates at all levels: this declaration brought about the hasty withdrawal of almost all the applications that had come in.

On April 2 Clay and Murphy saw no immediate crisis facing them. "Despite the imaginative reporting of some correspondents in Berlin," the ambassador told General Marshall, "Clay reports that the Americans are calm and continuing their everyday life normally." Murphy also said that remaining in Berlin would call for a large-scale increase in air-passenger lift. Clay himself cabled his army superiors that "our women and children can take it." The "immediate evacuation of dependents," he told General Wedemeyer, "would be considered a Soviet success." But looking at the situation tactically, Vladimir Semyenov took the opposite view. Allied commanders might prefer for the dependents to leave, he commented to the Foreign Ministry, in order to have greater freedom in "offering resistance to our pressure"; thus, without the families in the city, "dislodging" the West might become harder than it would be otherwise.

On April 5 the Western commanders, who depended increasingly on the sanctity of the air corridors to Berlin, encountered what seemed a brutal new reality. About two miles from touchdown at Gatow airfield, in the British sector, a British Viking civilian passenger aircraft was buzzed by a Soviet Yak fighter, which then smashed into it, ripping off the starboard wing. Both planes went down, the British aircraft landing just inside the

Soviet zone near the airport, the Russian fighter crashing in the British sector. All nine passengers—seven British, two American—on the British plane were killed, along with the five-man crew. For some hours after the crash, the Soviet military guard refused to allow the British to remove the charred bodies of the passengers and crew; when Soviet soldiers attempted to take the body of the fighter pilot and also portions of the wreckage, the British retaliated with a similar restriction.

Robertson and Clay immediately ordered fighter escorts for all Western aircraft traveling in the air corridors, and after trying for more than three hours to locate Sokolovsky, Robertson had a meeting with the marshal. Ill at ease, Sokolovsky denied that the fighter pilot had been following orders to molest the aircraft; the Soviet command had not directed and would not direct any interference with British aircraft in the corridor. But Sokolovsky also denied that the presence of the Soviet plane, which appeared without warning, had represented a violation of the established safety regulations. Beyond that, he declared—"as ridiculous as it may seem," Clay told Bradley—that the Viking had caused the problem by ramming the Yak. Robertson and Clay agreed that, regardless of the absurdity of Sokolovsky's attempt to put the blame for the crash on the lumbering British transport rather than on the swooping fighter, his assurance that the incident had been unintentional was almost certainly true. Clay added, less presciently, "We may expect that this accident will slow down their use of pressure tactics in [the] Berlin area." He and Robertson then revoked their orders calling for fighter escorts of U.S. and British aircraft.

In a teleconference with Clay on April 10, General Bradley displayed a good intuitive understanding of salami tactics. Were the Western Allies actually on the point of being driven out of the city? "With our passenger trains completely stopped," Bradley said to Clay, "Russians in effect have won the first round unless [there is] some way to get this changed. Do you see any such likelihood? If not, will not Russians restrictions be added one by one which eventually would make our position untenable unless we ourselves were prepared to threaten or actually start a war to remove these restrictions?" Although the British and French were weakening—particularly the French, who had no capacity to supply their people in Berlin by air—the only Soviet action that could force the Americans out of Berlin, Clay said, would be the complete Soviet cutoff of food shipments to the western sectors of the city. If the Russians should go that far, then perhaps the Western occupiers might have to leave, but surely that would not happen, because such a drastic move would alienate the Germans. The Americans should not leave Berlin, therefore, "short of a Soviet ultimatum to drive us out by force if we do not leave."

Then Clay, as if confirming Bohlen's 1945 prediction of his reversal in attitude, sounded a true transatlantic clarion call: "Why are we in Europe? We have lost Czechoslovakia. Norway is threatened. We retreat from Berlin. . . . After Berlin will come western Germany and our strength there relatively is no greater and our position no more tenable than Berlin. If we mean . . . to hold Europe against Communism, we must not budge." While George Kennan would have rejected this analysis, when thinking back to his own 1945 conversation with Clay he could only have smiled at the attitude that had produced it.

A few days after Clay made this declaration to Washington, the Soviet authorities in Berlin, in a cheerful and clearly accurate report, assured their superiors in Moscow that the plan "of control and restrictive measures to be adopted on the communication lines connecting Berlin and the Soviet zone with the Western zones . . . has been carried into effect undeviatingly since April 1." These measures had "dealt a strong blow at the prestige of the Americans and British in Germany. The German population believe that 'the Anglo-Americans have retreated before the Russians' and that this testifies to the Russians' strength."

Having assured Moscow that they had many more tricks up their collective sleeve, the Soviet authorities in early May imposed "new and impossible" documentation requirements for Western freight trains. "The situation here is very tense, very grave," a U.S. officer still in Berlin wrote on May 11 to his old friend, General Maginnis, back home in Massachusetts. Kommandatura meetings had become "little else than vituperative accusations and charges one against the other (or should I say one against three and vice-versa). The Russians shoot at us with all they have; at the British with medium and occasionally heavy artillery; and snipe at the French with small arms."

The writer then presented a grim scenario of the developing drama in Berlin as he saw it. Though the Western representatives had finally "taken off the gloves and begun to fight with bare knuckles," the change had come too late—not because a shooting war looked imminent but because the Soviets seemed likely to realize their aims without one: "Their primary objective, as I see it, is at the moment to force us to leave Berlin and the hell of it is that I believe they can succeed if our next show of ungloved diplomacy does not call their bluff." Rail traffic out of Berlin had already become "nonexistent," and the Russians seemed likely to place additional restrictions upon surface transportation to such an extent that the Allies would find it impossible to supply food to the people in the western sectors of the city. Taking an insightful but dubious look ahead, the writer added, "I do not see how we could do it 100% by air."

If the squeeze on food and fuel should become acute, the Germans themselves would complain bitterly to the Allies—they would "scream"—

despite "the awareness of what awaits them if we leave." Thus the question would become: "Can we stay here and see them starve and freeze?" The answer was no: "I believe we will have to go." The Russians would win without having to fire a shot—they could say, "We did not cut off military supplies. The Western powers were so inefficient that they could not take care of their sectors and the Germans themselves asked that they leave."

From this catastrophe for the West, the writer said, would follow the defeat of the Marshall Plan in all of Germany, and the people of the Benelux countries would lose whatever confidence they had had in the determination of the Western powers to defeat Communism. The Russians were embarking on a reign of terror, and "the Germans are scared and understandably so," with street kidnappings—"snatches"—increasing and more and more threats being made against people friendly to the West.

Working as a secretary for a corporation and reading Western newspapers, Alice Sawadda kept in close touch with developing events. When things started turning bad, she was not surprised: "We felt very scared that the Russians would take us again." Karin Hueckstaedt remembered that "there were a lot of threats. They tried to coerce the people that live in the West to side with them, with their regime. They threatened to cut you off everything."

Concerned about such threats and worse, Maginnis's resourceful friend had developed a back-door method (outflanking General Clay's staff) for giving travel priorities to "a few people who otherwise would be in extreme danger if we leave here and are unable to take them with us." Murphy expressed strong concern to the State Department about the "strength of determination in Washington to maintain the position"; it was, he said in what resembled one of Clay's efforts to stiffen the resolve of his superiors, the only thing that worried him about the U.S. position in Berlin. The dissolution of the Allied Control Council, the high cost of maintaining the position, with its obviously unfavorable logistics, and the "lack of a specific purpose for our presence here" might combine to weaken American determination to hold fast. General Robertson and the French commander, General Pierre Koenig, both considered the Control Council finished, Murphy reported; however, "most of the French here have never liked the selection of Berlin as seat of Control Council in any event and would not go into mourning, I am sure, if Berlin were abandoned." For that matter, Murphy added, the French would not deplore the partition of Germany.

The Control Council was not the only four-power agency to become a dead letter. In the increasingly charged atmosphere, wrote a French chronicler, it became clearer and clearer that the Soviet delegation intended to sabotage the Berlin Kommandatura. Without prior notification, it withdrew its experts from the various committees, and at meetings of the commandants the Soviet member, General Alexander Kotikov, read declarations, prepared in advance, that often had nothing to do with the subjects that were supposed to be on the table: "It was clear that he was speaking less to his colleagues than to Berlin and even world opinion. The Kommandatura became the last theater of quadripartism, which meant that the delegates regularly went from administrative territory to that of politics. In this game, speeches became more and more aggressive, accusations of bad faith multiplied, and there were even personal attacks."

The Soviets had developed new tactics designed to irritate and confuse, said Warren Chase, one of Murphy's deputies. Without giving any adequate reason or any warning, they would simply change established Kommandatura procedures. At one point the Russians suddenly reversed the procedure for translators so that each interpreter had to translate his commandant's remarks into the two foreign languages instead of translating remarks made in the foreign languages into the commandant's own language. Contrary to custom, they rejected items proposed for the agenda by other delegations, as had always been the custom, and refused to approve meeting schedules. The Soviets were using these methods, Chase believed, to "create a situation which is so confused that eventually an opportunity will be created for the break-up of the Kommandatura in circumstances so obscure that the break-up cannot be laid to them."

"It would take a wheelbarrow," Colonel Howley said in one session, "to bring here all the insults published about the Americans in the Soviet sector."

"A ten-ton truck wouldn't be enough," Kotikov retorted, "to haul all the insanities and calumnies the press carries in your sectors." In one bizarre exchange, Kotikov accused American MPs of having beaten an old woman; Howley was furious, especially because the interpreter made matters worse by translating "beaten" as "bitten."

Personal attacks, avoidance of discussion, refusals to shake hands with colleagues from the other countries—instances of such Soviet behavior, often of minor importance in themselves, demonstrated the "completely farcical character" of Kommandatura proceedings, Chase said. His superiors could understand those proceedings only if they "clearly realized that Kommandatura no longer has the least significance as a governing body for Berlin, but is merely one segment of a much broader battlefield on which a war of nerves and a propaganda war is being waged. All statements at the Kommandatura are made now with an eye to the German newspapers of the next day." In a meeting at the end of May that dragged on more than an hour past midnight, Kotikov for the final two hours "went out of his way," Murphy reported, to "bait" the current chairman, Major General E. O. Herbert, the British commandant. Part of this behavior, Brigadier General Jean Ganeval told Murphy, came from the presence of a new political adviser—"a 'killer' who sits at Kotikov's elbow and leaves him no discretion whatever."

On June 10, as the Soviets continued to slice away at the Berlin salami, the Allies had to call in armed guards to keep Western-sector locomotives and cars from being hijacked into the East. In another tactic, the Russians held up traffic "to force furnishing of comprehensive info of contents of each car," as Clay put it. A British spokesman rejected as unreasonable the Soviet condition that each car should have its contents indicated on the label—a stipulation suggesting that the Soviet border authorities were claiming the right to select what freight would be allowed to proceed to Berlin; the British refused to list military supplies. After two days the Russians allowed eight trains to leave Helmstedt for Berlin. Speaking at a press conference, General Clay declared that in an emergency the United States would use airplanes to bring freight to Berlin but that this method of supply would hardly work on "a permanent basis."

The final break in the four-power Kommandatura came on June 16, at eleven o'clock in the evening, in a session that had begun at ten in the morning. Howley wanted to put off pointless debates, observed the French chronicler, but "the Russians replied with a harangue." The U.S. commandant (sometimes known as "Howlin' Mad" Howley) then said that in view of his heavy schedule on the next day, he was going home to bed; his deputy, Colonel Babcock, would stay and listen to the discussion. When he left the room, Howley "perhaps closed the door a little too abruptly." Prodded by his Communist Party political adviser, the Soviet deputy commander, Colonel A. I. Yelisarov (representing General Kotikov in the latter's absence), immediately began collecting his papers, at the same time uttering rapid-fire and sketchily translated comments about Howley. He then stood up and declared that he would not set foot in the room again until the U.S. commandant had "presented his excuses" for slamming the door. At this point, following Marshal Sokolovsky's March example in the Allied Control Council, the entire Soviet delegation walked out. Calling after Yelisarov to try to arrange a date for the next meeting, the chairman, General Ganeval, received no response. He then declared the meeting adjourned.

Two days later Soviet authorities began stopping Berlin-bound freight cars for vaguely worded violations of regulations; twenty-seven trains loaded with coal were turned back because "the cars are defective." Finally, on June 19, declaring that technical difficulties had created serious problems, the Soviets stopped all rail traffic between the West and Berlin, telling would-be passengers that "the stations are congested"; Hans-Karl Behrend, who had become a reporter for a Berlin newspaper, recalled

Russian statements that they had been forced to cut railroad connections because the ties of the tracks were rotten.

On June 23 the Soviet Military Administration, which controlled the main power plant feeding western Berlin, cut off electricity to the Western sectors—as Colonel Howley observed, "both that which had been imported by Allied agreement and paid for at the rate of $.85 of hard coal per kwh and that produced in the Soviet Sector from our joint stockpiles of coal." All deliveries of coal, food, milk, and other supplies ceased. "Nothing was allowed on the surface to move East or West across the Elbe," while authorities told drivers that the autobahn bridge was closed "for urgent repairs." "The [river] barges couldn't continue coming," said Behrend, "because the huge elevator on the Elbe—it's not a system of locks but a tremendous elevator that lifts up the barges—wasn't working. British and American engineers offered to help, but they were turned down."

The next day this extraordinary simultaneous collapse of all land and water facilities brought traffic between western Berlin and the West to a stop—the blockade now stood complete—and the Soviets announced that the Western powers no longer held any rights in the administration of the city. Thus far in the anti-Allied project, Marshal Sokolovsky had applied the Kremlin blueprint with professional precision.

In stopping all food trains at the Elbe, the Soviets apparently presumed that, with no supplies coming into the city, the people of the Western zones would within days pour into the streets demanding the withdrawal of the Western powers, if that was what it would take to get food again. The Berliners who had thanked God when the Americans and the British arrived now faced with dread the prospect of a new Soviet occupation—the rapes, the kidnappings, the arbitrary arrests, even the endless political indoctrination. Particular horrors threatened those who had joined in political association with the Allies. "It was really scary," Karin Hueckstaedt said. "They were bombarding us on the radio from the Russian sector: 'Give up, you will starve'—all that."

But the Allies fought back. As Howley noted, they had previously stockpiled in western Berlin a six weeks' supply of food, which was immediately frozen for use in the Western sectors only. The colonel was even able to reassure parents with infants needing fresh milk: two months earlier, in a just-in-case move, he had brought in 200 tons of condensed milk and fifty tons of whole powdered milk. In a public appeal, he called on the people to show their courage: "There are evil forces at work whose sworn and ordered mission is to create chaos," he said, but "the people of Berlin will not be permitted to starve." In a daring riposte to Soviet radio announcements that western Berlin was about to run out of water, U.S. authorities made their own radio declaration: "Give your baby a bath." There was plenty of water, the people were told, and thus reassured, like nervous depositors finally convinced that the vaults of their bank actually hold ample cash, they abandoned their incipient panic. But the blockade remained an inescapable fact.

Many currents, conflicting and combining, ran beneath the series of East-West events that led to the Soviet imposition of the blockade on western Berlin—this attempt, remarkable in the modern world in peace-time, to force national states to take certain political actions by threatening the starvation of more than two million people for whom these states were responsible. But one particular question, seemingly lacking in any drama at all, had continued to stimulate action and counteraction. It took on more importance than many of the more visible persons and events, and it even developed its own cloak-and-dagger side. General Clay believed during the spring that when the "real crisis" came, it would turn largely on this question, and that Russian fears in connection with it probably lay behind the salami slicing in Berlin. The question concerned money.

CHAPTER 12

A Matter of Money

In the early months of 1948, one word ran as a leitmotiv through Allied-Soviet relations in Germany: currency. Issues relating to the money supply preoccupied both the Western powers and the Russians. With their strong economic position, resting ultimately on the resources of the United States, the Allies developed positive ideas about the course to follow; the Russians, economically inferior, gave apprehensive attention to these developments.

To begin with, the military governments of the great wartime coalition, as administrators of a country, held the responsibility for the money supply as for other aspects of economic life. When the victors took control in 1945, the German marks in circulation, having almost nothing backing them, had little more value than blank paper—hence the spontaneous public adoption of cigarettes as a medium of exchange. This hyperinflation demonstrated beyond question the desperate need for reform of the monetary system, but the difficult relations between the West and the Russians—there being no "Germany"—made agreement on such a development unlikely. Besides, some authorities felt that with the German economy nearly prostrate, currency reform might prove to be the kind of operation that would kill the patient.

Even so, in 1946 U.S. authorities presented the Allied Control Council with a proposal calling for "the financial rehabilitation of Germany," providing for the exchange of old marks for new at the rate of ten for one, together with a new schedule of taxation, reorganization of the banking and insurance industries, and various other fiscal measures. Despite some differences of approach among the Western powers as well as disagreements with the Soviet representatives, the discussions seemed to make progress—until the Russians declared that they must have their own plates to print some of the new currency in their own zone; they would do the job at a small plant in Leipzig. But the Western powers—most emphatically, the United

States—wanted the currency printed under four-power control at the former Prussian *Staatsdruckerei*—the government printing plant—in Berlin; without such control, the Western Allies would have no guarantee concerning the amount of money printed or actually put into circulation.

Already, in fact, the Western Allies had been bitten by an open-ended currency arrangement they had previously made with the Soviets. In the latter phase of the war, the Western authorities had given the Russians printing plates for Allied military marks, identical to those to be used in the West, so that all the armies moving into Germany might have the same currency. The Soviets "printed these occupation marks by the billions and spread them like fall leaves over the country." They were handed out to Red Army soldiers for as much as six years' worth of accumulated back pay, and given to purchasing squads assigned to roam the country picking up all kinds of assets; the Russians themselves had no idea how many of these marks they had put into circulation.

In one of its many unintended consequences, that operation had provided a bonanza for GIs who sold cigarettes, candy, wristwatches (a particularly desired item), and every other kind of Western gimmick and device to Soviet soldiers in exchange for their occupation marks, which, under the rules—and though backed by nothing—were convertible into dollars. By the end of 1946, when dollar scrip replaced these military marks, enterprising GIs had exchanged more than $200 million worth of them (at 1946 values) for American dollars. (Indeed, some observers believed that manipulation by entrepreneurial GIs accounted for more of the monetary loss than did anything done by the Russians.) Unhelpfully, the U.S. Treasury, which had first promoted the plan, now declined to cover the conversion of the military marks into dollars; General Clay and his staff had to find ways to make up the loss.

The Russians' insistence on their Leipzig plan at the Allied Control Council meeting brought this round of currency negotiations to an end. It had probably served as nothing more than an excuse to forestall the reaching of any currency agreement, so General Clay's financial adviser believed—the Soviets "no doubt feared that economic recovery in Germany would ill serve the purpose of first bringing the people into a state of economic chaos." In a January 1947 memo, however, the Soviet finance minister maintained that the Western Allies were trying to "impose control over the amount of our expenditures on the occupation and reparations."

"Judging by past experiences in monetary matters," Colonel Howley observed, "if the Soviets had been allowed to print the new currency at Leipzig, we would never have known how much was printed, nor would they have given us any important information about the currency situation in the Eastern Zone."

Throughout the first six months of 1948, the currency problem demanded much of General Clay's time. On January 13 he told Washington that he intended to introduce the question in the January 20 Control Council session; as the first meeting since the breakup of the London foreign ministers' conference, this session loomed as "critical." Reacting to Clay's proposals at the meeting, Marshal Sokolovsky proposed that the Control Council condemn any separate currency reform in any zone and agree to establish a central German finance department and bank of issue; however, Clay told Washington, such a central department and bank could not function without German economic unity. The advantage of the type of currency conversion the United States was proposing, Clay said, was that it was "based on the absence of economic unity." Later, when Clay commented that the Soviet proposal was not clear and that reform had been debated for two years while the German financial situation grew steadily worse, Sokolovsky expressed his belief that "new printed money is already in Clay's pocket."

On February 12 something new happened in the Control Council: the Soviets agreed to the printing of the new currency at the *Staatsdruckerei* in Berlin, under four-power control, and they also more or less abandoned— or shelved—their insistence on the establishment of a central finance administration. Clay took a pragmatic view of this development. The West had to accept the proposal, he reported in a cable to Undersecretary of the Army William H. Draper, Jr., "or else be forced into position before German people of making the next step toward partition without specific cause." If it should work out, well and good, but if the Soviets failed to agree on the necessary technical details, nothing would be lost, because the Americans and the British would proceed with their plans for Bizonia; these plans would be ready to go into operation in mid-April; thus Clay had included a sixty-day timetable in his acceptance of Sokolovsky's proposal. From the Western point of view, the seeming Soviet agreement posed the danger of hindering reform in Bizonia by offering the Russians opportunities to exercise various obstructive and delaying tactics. Now that the Western representatives, through three years' experience, had developed a thorough familiarity with the Soviet style of operating, they found themselves in the paradoxical position of hoping that their own proposals would not find formal acceptance.

Robert Murphy noted in early March that the tone of Berlin Kommandatura meetings had changed. For some time, even after the breakup of the London foreign ministers' conference, the commandants had conducted their meetings in a generally friendly atmosphere. But since late January the atmosphere had "steadily deteriorated and the Commandants have been brought to a point at which it appears that agreement is impossible on even the most routine questions." The West knew, Murphy commented, that "Soviet tactics frequently serve only a temporary aim and they may well be reversed tomorrow. Their present tactics, however, seem designed to irritate, confuse and tire the other three delegations," perhaps to trap them into making unwise decisions "out of sheer exhaustion and impatience" or to goad them into hasty action that would give the Russians a pretext for breaking up the Kommandatura while, at the same time, putting themselves in a favorable light. Further, since "the Soviet Government (like the Nazi Government) charges the other person with those things which it itself intends to do," the West might well ask itself whether the Soviets intended to break up the four-power administration of Berlin. Often, it seemed that, like a paranoid person, the Russians would keep raising the irritation level as though trying their best to earn a kick in the teeth and thus prove themselves correct in their view of the world.

Then came the special March 20 meeting of the Allied Control Council, at which Marshal Sokolovsky demanded full information about the London meeting and launched into his series of denunciations of the West. The latest proposals for a currency agreement—including making the *Staatsdruckerei* an international enclave under four-power guard—seemed ready to founder under Soviet objections, but the issue had not come up for a vote before Sokolovsky led his delegation in the Soviet walkout from the council.

Now that all chance of a four-power agreement on currency reform had vanished, with the Control Council no longer meeting, the Western Allies finally decided that they must proceed on their own if western Germany, at least, was ever going to climb out of its desperate situation and move toward recovery from the war. As analyzed in early 1948 by a prominent economist, the severe problems of Bizonia, the fused U.S.-British zones, included being hampered not only by the disorganized currency system but "by the breakdown of European trade, by inadequate production and consumption. Incentives are lacking; and because of Germany's central position in Europe her impoverishment seriously affects the rest of Europe." Further, "that Germany is not a free agent, that she is subject to drains on reparations account, that she has been dismembered, that the pressure of population on resources has greatly increased, that no strong German government exists, that morale is at a record low—all these intensify her difficulties."

In spite of the grimness of this picture, the tireless General Clay had begun 1948 in a spirit of optimism: production was increasing, if slowly; exports were rising; and raw materials were being made available in satisfactory quantities. But, for eminently sound reasons, nobody had any faith in the currency; barter and the black market took much of the place of legitimate financial dealing. Before an effective currency could be established, however, Bizonia must have a sound banking system, with a central bank; on February 15 the bizonal authorities enacted a law establishing the Bank deutscher Länder (German States Bank), which could issue currency and control credit. Just a week later Clay went to London for the conference with the British and French on long-range policy for Germany—with an agenda that included among its items the political and economic organization of the three Western zones. At this conference the French representatives agreed to join the new banking system and to take part in the consequent currency reform without waiting for agreement on all the principles and details involved in the establishment of a "trizone." None of these negotiations were easy, however, and at any moment an American-French split would not have shocked anybody.

Acknowledging the extinction of hope for a German government supported both by the West and by the Soviet Union, the London conference instructed the military governors of the three Western zones to take an anticipated but fateful step: they were to call together the minister-presidents of the German *Länder* and empower them to convene an assembly that would draw up a German constitution.

This decision had a number of delicate and controversial aspects. Western German leaders had to face criticism from compatriots that the creation of a united western Germany meant the renunciation of an overall German government that would include the Soviet zone. (Some seven months earlier, in June 1947, representatives of all the German state governments, east and west, had met in Munich to discuss the establishment of a German national government. Delegates from the states in the Soviet zone had stayed only for a day, however, leaving after the others rejected their proposed agenda for the meeting.) In January, Murphy had reported to Washington with some admiration that the German leaders who met with the Allies to discuss the economic reorganization "took the rapid-fire treatment to which they were subjected . . . manfully. They were handed an extremely large package and their response was good. You can well understand [the] delicate position they are in vis-à-vis their own population and particularly their political opponents."

As representatives of the country next door, French diplomats had deep domestic worries as well as fears about the impact of a united western Germany on both the Germans and the Russians. An official of the Foreign Ministry told the U.S. ambassador in Paris, Jefferson Caffery, that establishing "a German economic administration" might well lead the Soviets to set up a countergovernment in Berlin. Georges Bidault, the foreign minister, seemed on the verge of desperation: "I beseech you to persuade your people to make it a little easier for me. What happened [in the meeting] is being exploited in such fashion here as to make my position well-nigh untenable; and you know that I have cut my bridges behind me." But, though never sure how the French would react to particular developments, the Americans and the British pushed ahead. For Clay, the French attitude continued to produce its old-time irritation. On January 12 he expressed his pique in a message to Undersecretary Draper: "In point of fact, we are getting somewhat tired here of always having the finger pointed at us for offending French pride by taking Bizonal actions without French approval, instead of having the finger pointed at the French for wanting to be a partner in planning but independent in operation."

In contrast, the Anglo-American allies had reached a high level of agreement on policy in January, as appeared in an exchange between Lord Inverchapel, the British ambassador in Washington, and Secretary of State Marshall. On January 8 Inverchapel sent the secretary a British Cabinet document, approved that same day, that listed the aims of British policy toward Germany: to "proceed as rapidly as possible with the establishment of a stable, peaceful, and democratic Germany and to avoid the creation of a situation which could eventuate in the emergence of a Communist-controlled Germany." If the four powers should reach no agreement, Britain would cooperate with other Western powers in undertaking a variety of needed economic and political measures. Expressing his general acquiescence, Marshall endorsed the expressed idea of setting up a "western German administration" that would perform certain limited functions but not be constituted as a government for western Germany. "We feel," he said, "that there should be an evolutionary development in this regard, dependent to some extent on which action is taken in the Soviet zone." A few days earlier Murphy had reported to Marshall that some of the German minister-presidents "express alarm over the tempo at which we are moving and plead for more time." But, sanguinely, the ambassador also detected a "growing eagerness on the part of the French ... to participate in bizonal affairs."

In addition to the interlaced issues of a West German government and a new currency for Germany, the United States during these months confronted a new kind of problem in relation to the Soviet Union. The Russians, said a memorandum produced in the still-new National Security Council, were "conducting an intensive propaganda campaign directed primarily against the US," using "psychological, political and economic

measures designed to undermine non-Communist elements in all countries," while the United States, in effect, simply stood in the international
arena with its hands behind its back and allowed the Russians to punch
away. The Soviet campaign had as its aim "not merely to undermine the
prestige of the United States but to weaken and divide world opinion" to
such a point that Soviet designs could no longer be opposed. Satellite
regimes, national Communist parties, and organizations susceptible to
Communist influence all had parts in the Soviet effort. The United States,
however, had a good case to make and needed to set about making it. Much
of the world knew little or nothing about American aid to foreign countries,
and nobody in Washington had the responsibility for spreading such information. The government must therefore strengthen and coordinate all
foreign information activities.

In a later memorandum—May 4, 1948—George Kennan's Policy
Planning Staff called for the United States to wage political warfare,
describing the concept as "the logical application of Clausewitz's doctrine in
time of peace." Broadly defined, political warfare would include every kind
of effort short of a shooting war, using operations both overt and covert:
political alliances, economic measures (like the European Recovery
Program—an example Kennan might not have offered a year earlier),
"white" and "black" propaganda, clandestine support of friendly foreign
groups, and encouragement of underground activity in hostile countries.
Two years previously, one official had opposed "black" propaganda operations in foreign countries, saying that conducting them "would be contrary
to the fundamental premises of our own Governmental system and would
be honoring the totalitarians by imitating them." And just in November
1947 the secretary of state himself had shown concern about the proposed
"psychological warfare" campaign: Would it conflict with his policy of
telling only the truth on the Voice of America? But under the pressures of
cold war, State Department ideas were evolving rapidly.

The Americans, Kennan said, must learn from the British, whose
success through the years owed much to their understanding and use of the
principles of political warfare. The Russians, too, offered a striking example
in this realm: "Lenin so synthesized the teachings of Marx and Clausewitz
that the Kremlin's conduct of political warfare has become the most refined
and effective of any in history." The Americans needed to get a grip on
themselves, because they had always been handicapped by "a popular
attachment to the concept of a basic difference between peace and war, by a
tendency to view war as a sort of sporting contest outside of all political
context, by a national tendency to seek for a political cure-all, and by a
reluctance to recognize the realities of international relations—the perpetual rhythm of struggle, in and out of war." These views could already be

recognized as vintage Kennan, and in following them with the explanation that what he and his staff were proposing was an operation in the traditional American form—"organized public support of resistance to tyranny in foreign countries"—he displayed a well-timed anticipation of events.

Several eventful months later, Kennan took a direct hand in the application of his ideas. In a letter drafted by him for Undersecretary of State Robert Lovett to send to Secretary James Forrestal, he asked the secretary of defense to give a helping hand to Frank Wisner, a CIA official being sent to Germany, where, said Kennan in a covering note, he would encounter, "as one of his first major obstacles, the problem of cooperation with the Army." Would Forrestal kindly instruct General Clay to work with Wisner?

On a visit to Washington in October 1947, General Clay had reported rumors in Berlin that the Russians, at their plant in Leipzig, were printing new currency they might put into circulation at any time. Not wanting to be caught short if the Russians should pull such a surprise, the general won agreement from the State and Treasury departments to prepare a supply of new money for the Western powers to use as a defense measure; without new Western currency to counter the new Soviet issue, the West would have to continue using reichsmarks after they had officially lost all value in the East. Clay's financial adviser expressed his horror at the prospect: "Billions of these outlawed notes would have quickly crossed the borders into the West and they would have so greatly increased the already superabundant currency as to make it almost unusable." In addition to that, the Americans saw the prospect of the Soviets' using money that would now have become worthless in the East to finance the activities of the German Communist Party in the West.

Word of the American contingency plan had leaked to newspapers in the United States and also in Germany, but nobody outside of a tiny circle knew that the Treasury Department had moved with remarkable dispatch to produce the currency itself. To speed Operation Bird Dog along, the Bureau of Engraving and Printing in Washington went on day and night shifts, and before the end of the year, the new blue-backed notes had begun arriving in Germany, where they disappeared into the vaults of the old Reichsbank building in Frankfurt.

Though only a handful of persons knew that thousands of cubic feet of space in the Reichsbank basement were stuffed full of new banknotes waiting to be issued if the need arose, ordinary German citizens for the past three years had heard rumors about changes in their money: obviously, sooner or later the authorities would take steps to deal with the situation caused by the highly inflated currency. Because of all the talk, fresh rumors in the spring of 1948 drew little attention. But now, night after night, army trucks were backing up to the Reichsbank, then driving off loaded with wooden cases marked "Clay" and "Bird Dog," spreading the new money across the country. (Displaying the customary GI level of insight into what was actually going on, one driver managed to connect Operation Bird Dog with an utterly unrelated if prominent issue of the time. He was heard to say to another: "Know what we're carrying in them boxes? Ammunition for the Israelites!" His friend had a different view. "It's ammo, all right, but something tells me it's going to the A-rabs.") Finally, anticipating imminent anti-inflationary reform, in which they would receive something like one new deutsche mark for ten of the old reichsmarks, the German public let themselves go in a spending spree, buying everything from racetrack tickets to cemetery plots; people even settled up old accounts with doctors.

The Allied military governments announced the reform—the first for German currency since the remedial measures taken after the great inflation of 1923—just after the close of business on Friday, June 18. Beginning on June 20, the people of the Western zones could turn in their reichsmarks, which would no longer have any value. At first, citizens would receive merely enough of the new money to meet their current expenses, on the basis of one new mark for one old one (actually, they initially received forty of the new marks for sixty of the old, with more to come later); the rate of exchange for the bulk of the currency turned in would be announced within a week. Experience in other countries had shown, said U.S. authorities, that this two-stage process was the most effective way to prevent black marketeers and others from bypassing the limit on the amount of currency that could be redeemed by shifting some of their wealth into the hands of stooges, who would declare it as their own. The overall hope, observers said, was that after reform a cigarette would once again be something people smoked.

When the Allies and the German state governments drew up their regulations for reform of the currency in the Western zones, they could not include Berlin in these plans, since laws governing the city could come only from agreement of all the occupying powers. At a meeting on June 23 of economic specialists representing these four powers, the Russians advocated making the new currency they intended to put into circulation in the Soviet zone also the money for Berlin; they maintained that they should control the money supply, and banking and finance as well, for the entire city. Having no intention of yielding the financial management of western Berlin, the Allies proposed the creation of a new special currency just for Berlin, to be issued and controlled by the Kommandatura—at this point still officially the supreme authority for the city. Rejecting this proposal, the

Russians declared that Berlin must be considered economically as belonging to the Soviet zone. The Allies offered a compromise; perhaps the new Soviet money could serve as Berlin's currency, but under quadripartite control: "The possibility was suggested that the Kommandatura or some other special four-power body might determine the amount of new money from the East to be issued in the city, the terms upon which the new money would be exchanged for the old, and the general banking and credit policy for the city." This suggestion received only a quick *nyet*; the Western powers, said the Russians, were not to have any financial power in Berlin. Then, just before the meeting adjourned, a courier arrived with news for the Soviet delegate and thus for all the others as well. The Soviet authorities had just proclaimed a new currency and a new financial structure for the Soviet zone and for Berlin; it would take effect the next morning.

Not entirely surprised that the meeting had failed to produce harmony, the Western powers had their own plan. Several days earlier they had secretly stocked their sectors of the city with two tons of the new money— 250 million deutsche marks—each bill specially marked with a *B* for Berlin. They also had prepared their own proclamation, telling residents of the western sectors of the city that the Soviet announcement did not apply to them. The Allies had given twelve German financial and economic experts the assignment of "solving the problems of a Western Berlin reform" and then locked them in a special "cage" in York House, a British Berlin headquarters, where they lived, ate, and worked while performing their task. So secret had this project been kept that the families of the experts had been told that they were going to Frankfurt on another task, and their cars had even set off in the direction of the airport before doubling back to York House.

The Allies proceeded more deftly than the Russians, who "apparently were caught off guard by the Western Germany decision, despite the fact that they must have known of our preparations and should have known that we would not give in on the basic principle of currency reform for Germany." Rushing into action before their new currency had become available, the Soviets stuck thumbnail-size stamps to the corners of old reichsmarks with cheap potato glue; some of them fell off within a few days. These easily copied stamps, which bore the numbers of the new denominations, stimulated a lively counterfeiting business; the Germans called the new notes *Tapetenmark* (wallpaper marks).

Marshal Sokolovsky ordered the city government of Berlin to begin planning immediately for converting old reichsmarks to the new Eastern marks; anybody caught possessing the Western D-mark would be subject to arrest and punishment. Anybody who accepted it in a transaction of any kind would be regarded as "an enemy of the German economy" and "a traitor to German unity." In the midst of the accusations back and forth between governments, Berlin's *Scheiber* (large-scale black market operators) promptly went into the currency business; on the first morning the "rublemark," as the Soviet note was nicknamed, opened at five for one deutsche mark, and by the end of the day a trader needed thirty of the Soviet marks to obtain one D-mark. Noting that rail lines would have to accept Russian currency in the Soviet sector and the D-mark in the others, a streetcar collector commented cheerfully that he should "have a good time of it in rublemarks" by substituting his own Soviet marks one for one for the D-marks he collected.

In spite of these major financial developments and the dramatic events pitting the Allies against the Soviets in Berlin, as the blockade developed through its successive stages, the Allied financial authorities still held out a measure of hope that somehow the occupying powers could avoid the division of the city into "separate monetary camps with an inevitable trend toward complete division." Hence for the next nine months the Eastern mark continued to be accepted at par in the Western sectors, even though it caused great confusion to western Berliners, who favored the Western mark over its wallpaper competitor but for a long time could never be sure they might not wake up one day to find that the four occupying powers had reached some sort of agreement that would make the Eastern mark the official currency for Berlin.

On the busy day of Wednesday, June 23, the city assembly of Berlin had the daunting task of debating Marshal Sokolovsky's order to the city government to introduce the new Ostmark (Eastern mark) and enforce its use as the only currency permitted in the city. Should the assembly members obey this command, or should they follow the opposing order from the Western powers, which declared the Soviet action a violation of the city constitution and of Allied agreements concerning Berlin?

"It is impossible to over-emphasize the general confusion which the Russians attempted to create," wrote Colonel Howley—they were trying to stage "a Czechoslovakian putsch in Berlin." On their way to the meeting at the city hall, which was situated in the old heart of the city in the Soviet sector, the assembly members had to run a gauntlet of "professional" Communists who had been brought to the scene in trucks—trucks, Howley noted with bitterness, that had been sent to Russia under U.S. wartime lend-lease. Unchecked by the Soviet-controlled police, bands of these Communists, wearing SED (Socialist Unity) badges, surrounded the assembly members in the streets, the halls of the building, and the assembly chamber itself.

Outside the building, loudspeakers harangued the crowd with raucous messages threatening the city government.

After the officers of the assembly finally managed to clear the floor of the chamber and get the session under way, the Communists, some 18 percent of the membership, attacked the West and demanded the immediate adoption and implementation of the Soviet order. Despite the menace crackling in the air, the members of the three democratic parties—the Socialists, the Liberal Democrats, and the Christian Democrats—defied the Communists, insisting that the assembly follow the city constitution, which had been signed by the Russians as well as by the other occupying powers. Acting Oberbürgermeisterin (mayor) Louise Schröder won cheers by introducing a resolution declaring the citizens' loyalty to the four-power occupation; as Soviet observers watched, the resolution passed by a large margin. A Christian Democrat declared: "Anyone who leaves Berlin is a traitor!" In rejecting Sokolovsky's order, the Berlin assembly had thereby expressed its refusal to have the city incorporated into the Soviet zone.

As the democratic leaders left the meeting, which ended at about seven o'clock in the evening, some of them were pounced on and beaten by thugs. Most of the Berliners had now gone, but, trying to incite those who remained against the assembly members, a "goon squad" followed one assemblyman to his car, pushing him. At this cue, a young man in the crowd bent down to pick up a rock, but an older man nearby said, "Don't do it, boy." This statement, mild in the circumstances, was enough to persuade the boy not to attack anybody. Attempting to evade the goons, another assembly member ran to a car driven by a friend and leaped into the back seat. Before he got his leg inside, one of the thugs slammed the door on it, causing a deep cut. Thugs also attacked Jeanette Wolff, a one-time governess whom the Nazis had sent to a concentration camp a decade earlier for being Jewish. Though she was beaten, she managed to get away. "They are mad," she said, "this is 1933 all over again." Yet despite the pressure from the Russians, the presence of the crowd of 50,000 around the city hall—which had followed orders to appear—and the activities of the goons, the city government did not resign, the assembly rejected the Soviet order, and the crowd refused to erupt into an antidemocratic riot.

June 23 itself marked a Soviet defeat. But the next day, Thursday, was the day all traffic between the Western zones and Berlin came to a stop, completing the blockade. The American, British, and French military governors and commandants now had to deal with a new kind of paradox, a peacetime siege. "This is not Prague, this is Berlin!" Jeanette Wolff declared to a rally of some 60,000 anti-Communists. "We shall not bend till freedom is secure."

CHAPTER 13

A Few Days' Grace

O<small>N</small> J<small>UNE</small> 26, two days after the Soviets halted all traffic from the West into Berlin, Winston Churchill expressed a somber view of the issues created by the blockade. They were as grave, he told a gathering of Conservative Party voters, "as those we now know were at stake at Munich ten years ago." The world had surely learned, declared the man who had identified and named the Iron Curtain, that it could not find safety "in yielding to dictators, whether Nazi or Communist." The only hope of peace was "to be strong, to act with other great freedom-loving nations, and to make it plain to the aggressor, while time remains, that we should bring the world against him, and defend ourselves and our cause by every means should he strike the felon's blow."

Some two months earlier, speaking in private, the former prime minister had expressed considerably more explosive views. Though out of office for three years now, Churchill still held the leadership of the Conservatives, and in any case remained a great figure whose views would always win attention. When the Soviets developed nuclear weapons, Churchill told the U.S. ambassador to Britain, Lewis Douglas, war would become a certainty; therefore, now was the time to tell the Russians that "if they do not retire from Berlin and abandon Eastern Germany, withdrawing to the Polish frontier, we will raze their cities." This idea, Douglas commented in his report, had its "practical infirmities," but in his underlying thought Churchill was right. The West could not "appease, conciliate, or provoke" the Soviets; they would respond to no outside influence except the vocabulary of force.

What part had the Western currency reform played in the Russians' clamping the blockade on western Berlin? They had first cited "technical difficulties" as the reason for holding up rail traffic, but then these supposed difficulties had spread to water routes and to highways. Had the creation of the Deutsche mark provided the reason, the excuse, or something of both?

Currency clearly constituted an important issue, but how much more was involved? How and with what intensity did Joseph Stalin and his colleagues view the Western moves toward trizonal unity? Behind such questions stood the Allied need to find a policy and a course of practical action for Berlin. Unfortunately, Western intelligence agencies did not have access to such documents as Andrei Smirnov's March memorandum.

Across the Atlantic in the United States, the dramatic and ominous events in the old German capital did not immediately evoke from politicians the kind of rhetoric that might have been expected. Domestic politics now held the American stage. It was a presidential election year, and, as it happened, the crisis week in Berlin coincided with the gathering in Philadelphia of eager Republicans sure that now, at last, after all those defeats at the hands of Franklin D. Roosevelt, the opportunity to pick America's next president was theirs. On the evening of June 24 the convention delegates, to no one's surprise, rewarded New York Governor Thomas E. Dewey's well-fueled drive for the nomination by giving him the prize. Four years earlier, in a wartime presidential contest, the governor had lost to the champion, FDR. The picture this time looked utterly different. Roosevelt's successor would be fighting for his political life.

President Truman, in fact, had already begun the battle. On Friday, June 18—the day the Western powers announced the currency reform for their zones in Germany, the day before the Soviets cut off railroad passenger traffic into Berlin—the president returned to Washington from a fifteen-day trip that had taken him almost 10,000 miles through eighteen states, to the West Coast and back. Weary, with sunburned nose and cracked lips, he nevertheless seemed far cheerier and more optimistic than when he had boarded the westbound *Ferdinand Magellan* at Union Station on the evening of June 3. Officially, Truman had had as his purpose the delivery of the commencement address at the University of California, which had been moved up a week from its original date of June 19 to enable him to fit the visit to Berkeley into his schedule. The press could sniff out no representatives of the Democratic National Committee on this "nonpolitical" trip, because the presence of such partisans was strictly forbidden. But the trip had profoundly political purposes; Truman had called it nonpolitical so that the government would have to foot the bill—the Democratic National Committee had almost nothing in the bank, for travel expenses or any other purpose.

This spring of Democratic discontent saw money and morale both at low levels. In all his decisions and actions in the three stressful and uniquely challenging years since April 12, 1945, Truman had suffered from an inescapable handicap: he had not won the presidency himself but had simply inherited it from his illustrious predecessor. In the view of many Americans, he had done little with his legacy. The victory in World War II had delivered not a golden peace but a new kind of struggle with a new foe that seemed mightier than the Axis powers combined. The president and his administration had produced remarkable new ideas and initiatives to meet this challenge but could point to no victories (although it was only at the beginning of April that Congress passed legislation creating the Economic Cooperation Administration to administer the Marshall Plan). With the Soviet Union thus far looming as the winner in the developing postwar competition between the two great powers, fear of the spread of Communism overseas and of its influence in the United States itself grew from day to day.

Though the country had reached the greatest level of prosperity in its whole history, the president received little credit for this achievement; the public saw an economic scene shadowed by strikes and inflation. In combating strikes by seizing the industries in question, Truman had won no new friends but instead had alienated old supporters in the labor unions. An index of his influence on Capitol Hill was offered in June, when Republican majorities overrode three presidential vetoes within four days—the most reversals in such a short period that any president had ever suffered. For all his efforts to promote civil rights, Truman had succeeded only in losing support in the South (notably, among the region's representatives in Congress), not in keeping the support of New Dealers. People everywhere spoke of "the mess in Washington"; a punning variation on Alexander Pope's famous line summed up the popular discontent: To err is Truman.

In addition to all his perceived deficiencies as a statesman and leader, Truman was a poor speaker; Democrats heard the painful contrast between his flat, twangy, regional voice and the lustrous tones of FDR. Beyond that, though some may have been put off at times by Roosevelt's lordliness, that quality now seemed far preferable to the inappropriately humble demeanor that Truman often displayed, as if he shared with his critics the opinion that he did not belong in the great office in which fate had placed him. Hardly anybody of importance in the Democratic Party believed he could win the coming election. Despite the long-established tradition that a party renominated a one-term incumbent president—even in the bleak Depression summer of 1932 Republicans had done it for Herbert Hoover—Democratic paladins had concluded that the only hope for the party lay in finding another nominee.

Seeing himself as the loyal standard-bearer of the continuing New Deal, Truman felt with particular bitterness the defection of prominent liberals. In 1946 Eleanor Roosevelt and others had founded Americans for Democratic Action, a group that frequently criticized him as not measuring up to liberal standards. Now, in the spring of 1948, Representative James Roosevelt of California, the oldest son of Eleanor and Franklin, had placed himself at the head of a nationwide group of liberals, with an admixture of big-city political bosses, who sought to dump Truman and draft General Eisenhower. No one knew whether Ike, who was in transit from the Pentagon to the presidency of Columbia University, was a Democrat or a Republican or neither, but everybody knew he was the most popular public figure in America. During the war Eisenhower had devised the stylish Ike jacket, a fly-fronted army blouse that ended at the waist; to Democratic candidates, this chopped-off sartorial creation seemed to offer far more in the way of political coattails than anything the harried onetime haberdasher could produce from his own wardrobe. Truman himself had once flirted with the idea of Ike as president, but that sentiment had come from early postwar gratitude and now had no place whatever in the president's view of things. "Doublecrossers all," Truman, in the black-and-white style he liked to use in his intimate writing, called the defectors in his diary. "But they'll get nowhere—a double dealer never does."

Responding to reports of Truman's pique with the Roosevelt family, Mrs. Roosevelt wrote him in March noting, in her own direct fashion, that while she did not presume do tell her children what to do, "there is without any question among the younger Democrats a feeling that the party as at present constituted is going down to serious defeat and may not be able to survive as the liberal party."

During his stop in Los Angeles, Truman took the ringleader of these "younger Democrats" aside and expressed his feelings directly. "Your father asked me to take this job," he told Jimmy Roosevelt, jabbing his finger into the younger man's breastbone. "I didn't want it. I was happy in the Senate. But your father asked me to take it, and I took it." If Jimmy's father could see what his son was doing, Truman declared, he would turn over in his grave: "But get this straight: whether you like it or not, I am going to be the next president of the United States. That will be all. Good day." Jimmy had nothing to say.

As that interview suggested, Truman had finally started to shed his cloak of excessive humility. In public appearances he had begun to spend less of his time laboriously reading a prepared text and more of it delivering extemporaneous remarks, a change met by a marked surge in the enthusiasm of his audiences. In particular, just three weeks before leaving Washington on his western trip, he had brought roaring applause from an audience of the Young Democrats when he declared: "I want to say to you that for the next four years there'll be a Democrat in the White House, and you're looking at him!" Such signs that he might not be quite as hopeless an orator as everyone had believed led Truman and his advisers to decide to make the June trip to the West Coast; he could bypass the nay-sayers in his party and in the press and talk directly to the people. He had as his central aim, he told one of his assistants, Ken Hechler of West Virginia, to "convince the people that their self-interest was bound up with Democratic success," and he also sought to persuade the state and city bosses that they could not get their local candidates elected unless they built up stronger support for the presidential ticket. He took as his models Andrew Johnson and Woodrow Wilson, each of whom had made a tour of the country to explain controversial and misunderstood policies. But, Hechler protested, both of these earlier presidents had failed in their missions. Snappily, Truman dismissed the objection. Johnson hadn't covered enough territory, he said, and Wilson had been cut down by sickness.

As a shakedown for the actual presidential campaign, Truman's trip had its errors in planning and execution, but these were far outweighed by his reception in cities and towns across the West. When the conservative Republican senator Robert Taft of Ohio urged people to fight inflation by eating less, Truman told the crowd in Butte, Montana, that he guessed the senator would let them starve. Furious, Taft hied himself to the Union League Club of Philadelphia, where in a speech (nationally broadcast that evening in a condensed version) he attacked Truman and gave the political world a lasting expression. The president, said Taft, was "blackguarding Congress at every whistle station in the West." This attitude rendered cooperation between Capitol Hill and the White House impossible, the senator declared—Congress should simply adjourn until the new president (presumably not Harry Truman) was elected. Editing Taft's railroad term, Truman declared in response that Los Angeles was the biggest "whistle stop" he had visited, and in this form the expression would become standard for Truman's later campaign travels.

Now, back in Washington, Truman, a sturdy, energetic figure in his neat double-breasted suit, struck reporters as "full of bounce." These observers had not missed the import of Truman's tour. The theme of the campaign, *Time* declared, would be "the Plain People's President Against the Privileged People's Congress." Truman had "denounced the 'rich man's tax bill'; he bedeviled 'the special-interest boys'; he warned of 'special privilege against the interests of the people as a whole.'" Declaring his intention to keep the pressure on Congress, he was going to "veto some more bills." (This remark drew from Andrei Gromyko, now the Soviet representative to the United Nations—where he made heavy use of the veto—the crack that "it seems [Truman] is well ahead of me.")

Four days after Truman's return to Washington, the Republican convention would open in Philadelphia. Three weeks later the Democrats would follow. It was the quadrennial American high political season, a time when even popular presidents did their best to walk carefully, avoiding adventures and evading commitments. Unfortunately, however, the world refused to turn tame for the sake of U.S. domestic politics. Truman could return from the West full of bounce but could still be lacking prestige and authority, with no visible constituency, fighting off opposition to secure his party's nomination and an almost certain loser if he succeeded in winning the nomination. But president he was, and commander in chief as well, and he had to face the problem that was turning into a crisis thousands of miles away.

The day after Truman returned to Washington, Robert Murphy reported that the Soviets had suspended all rail traffic between their zone and the others. When General Robertson suggested to General Clay that the British and the Americans make a vigorous protest, Murphy told the State Department the American commander had given him a mild answer: the Western Allies should wait two or three days to see just how far the Russians intended to go. The new Soviet regulations in themselves were "not immoderate" but a natural defensive reaction to protect the Soviet zone from an influx of old reichsmarks; if the United States had found itself in the same position, it might have taken the same action. At this point the State Department took the view that developments in Berlin offered a great opportunity for propaganda. The Allied military governments should "utilize all media an all-out effort to expose current Soviet strategy"—which it defined as the attempt to undercut the government of Berlin by cutting off supplies to the civilian population in order to achieve Soviet expansionist aims. The campaign was needed, the State Department told Ambassador Douglas in London, to "offset Soviet propaganda blaming [the] western allies for [the] Berlin situation." Certainly the people of Berlin themselves should be left in no doubt as to who was responsible for their plight.

Clay favored making a protest to Moscow for the sake of the record—he did not expect it to produce results—and on June 25 he told Undersecretary Draper that he had proposed to Robertson a joint conference with Sokolovsky, in which the Western commanders would "point out the seriousness of the present situation" and suggest the possibility of resolving it through trade agreements. Clay thought it unlikely that such a meeting would produce a solution, but it might reveal Soviet intentions, and in any case, "our effort to meet with him will at least indicate a desire on our part to reach a solution which will prevent suffering by a helpless German population caught between us."

This day, the day after the Russians had halted all land and water traffic between Berlin and the Western zones, saw Washington receiving many other opinions from the commander in Germany. Secretary Royall wanted to know the circumstances surrounding the introduction of the new Western D-mark into Berlin. The army already had plenty of information on the subject, Clay replied politely but with perhaps some between-the-lines acerbity, but he went on to explain that the new mark had been brought into Berlin in response to the Soviet declaration that Soviet currency and complete Soviet control would be installed in Berlin. The real point of the blockade, Clay suggested, was probably not to drive the West out of the city by starving its people but to frighten them away from the Western mark.

The relationship between Clay and his civilian superior in Washington, Secretary Royall, had its complexities. Earlier in the spring, when the Soviet restrictions on traffic had begun appearing, the general had sensed the secretary's hesitancy to take the kind of firm action Clay advocated. From his vantage point on the front line, Clay saw little danger of war but feared the erosion through inaction of the Western position; in particular, he saw American prestige and influence in both Germany and Europe at stake. Taking a longer view from across the Atlantic, Royall and other officials tended to regard the U.S. stake in Berlin as limited, not worth a war, not even worth the risk of war. Later on June 25, after Clay had cabled his answer to Royall's question about the introduction of the D-mark, the two discussed the Berlin situation in a lengthy teleconference. Royall ordered Clay to take no action in Berlin that could possibly lead to armed conflict, even if that should mean delaying the issuance of the D-mark in the city. Too late, Clay said—the new money had already been passed out to food offices in the three Western sectors, and the city government had taken a stand in support of the West. Besides, Clay added, though he and Robertson realized that their governments wished to avoid armed conflict, "we cannot be run over and a firm position always involves some risk."

In Kenneth Royall, Clay had an agent of administration policy who at the moment might insist on caution in Berlin but who also knew the army thoroughly and had had firsthand experience of war on low and high levels. Appointed undersecretary of war by Truman in late 1945, Royall had succeeded Judge Robert Patterson as secretary in July 1947, just before the reorganization (if not the true unification) of the armed services transformed his title into secretary of the army, a post in which he served under the first secretary of defense, James Forrestal. A fifty-three-year-old North Carolina lawyer from very old families that included a colonial governor, the square-jawed Royall could hardly be "overlooked," a columnist commented, since he stood six feet five inches tall and weighed 250 pounds. At the end of the war, when soldiers demonstrated for faster demobilization, Royall had shown little sympathy, brushing aside senatorial criticism to declare that the "hysteria to get the boys back home" posed dangers to U.S. occupation policy. In no sense a pacifist, Royall declared in a 1947 speech aimed at "demolitionists" of the army that "the potential warlike strength of America is the greatest guarantee of tranquillity among the nations of the world."

But potential power, including possession of the atomic bomb, did not translate into immediate strength in a trouble spot like Berlin. Once again American policymakers had run up against the unpleasant reality that the postwar demolition of the army had left the United States with very limited strength to mount any kind of military action anywhere without considerable delay. In Berlin itself, U.S. forces amounted to only about 2,500—the strength of a regiment—out of a Western total of some 6,000; 90,000 Soviet troops surrounded them, with endless reinforcements almost within arm's length.

That morning's *New York Times* had carried a page one story with an arresting headline: CLAY DECLARES U.S. WON'T QUIT BERLIN SHORT OF WARFARE. The Russians, said the general, were exerting their "final pressure to drive us out of Berlin," but the Western Allies would consider nothing short of war as a sufficient reason for withdrawal; further, the Soviet blockading tactics would not delay the creation of a German government in the Western zones. On the other hand, reported the *Times* correspondent, observers had a general impression that "the Western allies would consider leaving the former German capital if the suffering of the populace became too great." During his teleconference with Clay, Royall, on behalf of both the State and Defense departments, grilled Clay about his statements: Washington wanted no more comments that suggested American policy until it had developed such a policy. Well, Clay said in effect, he had simply responded to a reporter's question with a factually accurate statement: "The Americans could as far as they were concerned remain indefinitely in Berlin short of war."

Besides the caution imposed by the administration's lack of a contingency plan, Royall did not, so to speak, believe that Berlin was well worth a mess; he saw the Berlin currency question as a minor matter, not "a good question to go to war on." But, Clay replied, if the Soviets decided to go to war, they would do it because they believed the time was right, and the currency controversy would simply provide the excuse.

Closing the teleconference with praise for General Robertson's cooperation (he had been "splendid throughout"), Clay could not resist taking a dig at his old bêtes noires: "Neither he nor I get any support even moral from the French." In a telegram sent the same day, in which he informed Royall and General Bradley that he proposed to meet with Sokolovsky to discuss practicable solutions to the Berlin problem, Clay added an earlier thought that still had no more appeal for his superiors than before: "I am still convinced that a determined movement of convoys with troop protection would reach Berlin and that such a showing might well prevent rather than build up Soviet pressures which could lead to war." But Clay went on to concede that if a convoy set out from the West for Berlin, "once committed we could not withdraw."

Reacting to such ideas, Bradley saw in his mind's eye a disquieting sight: a series of local political dominoes. If putting armed convoys on the autobahn leading to Berlin should bring about a firefight between Allied and Soviet troops and the Western forces won, the Russians could not accept such a setback; they would have to respond with counterattacks until they won. The same would be true in reverse if the Soviets prevailed in the first brush—the West would escalate, but of course only to the limited extent that the small Allied forces made possible. Sooner or later, Bradley feared, the shooting would grow into all-out war. Since the convoys would be moving through Soviet-controlled territory, Bohlen observed, the Russians could put up tank barriers or remove bridges and thus force the Western powers to make the first hostile move. Robertson had the same thought. While paying tribute to the British general, Clay apparently had no inkling that Robertson saw him as a sort of cliché American cowboy who had to be restrained "in his wilder moments" from sending convoys dashing up the autobahn. Actually, Robertson had no grounds for such fears, since he was privy to much of the cautious White House and Pentagon thinking.

General Ivanov, chief of staff of the Soviet occupation forces in Germany, later observed that he and his fellow generals had not overlooked the possibility of an American attempt to send an armored column to Berlin. But they had not devoted much attention to devising countermeasures, Ivanov said, because Soviet intelligence found no evidence of any actual preparations for such an operation. Had such evidence existed, it would have had the most serious implications, because the demarcation lines between the Eastern and Western zones were "holy Soviet borders." Russians were not supposed to cross to the West; the Allies were not supposed to cross in the other direction. If a convoy had appeared, the Soviets might simply have erected barriers to stop it.

But, a Russian historian speculated, what would have happened if U.S. personnel on such a convoy failed to maintain their self-control and opened fire? And even before that could occur, what would junior Soviet officers do when they saw Western tanks and armored cars rolling across their holy border? Americans were attacking Russians, they would think—they would not wait for the invaders to shoot but would open fire themselves. According to Ivanov, the third possibility—"that the Soviet leadership would have yielded to the U.S. pressure and let the convoy go free"—was ruled out in the first discussions of the situation by the Soviet General Staff and the occupation forces staff. The sending of a convoy would have led to unpredictable results, most likely including armed conflict. What the Soviet leaders could surmise but did not know definitely was that General Bradley took a similar view. He and his colleagues on the Joint Chiefs had quite effectively summed up the possibilities in a top-secret memorandum to the secretary of defense: "Soviet passive interference, such as road and bridge obstruction or destruction, could make the armed convoy method abortive, while Soviet interference by military action, whether simply for prevention or deliberately as a result of war decision, would not only make the convoy method abortive but would shift the stage from one of local friction to that of major war involvement."

In spite of his widely circulated telegram of March 5, Clay did not believe that the Soviets were looking toward war. With many views vastly different from those of George Kennan, he nevertheless saw Russian moves in essentially the same way, as efforts, in reaction to Western actions, to achieve political objectives or to retain positions of political control. Like Kennan, he tended to see the Soviets as responding not to provocation but only to their own inner calculations. Individually, however, he played a variation on this theme, crediting Marshal Sokolovsky with considerable scope for independent action and regarding him, beyond their differences on policy, as a personal friend and not simply as an agent of the Kremlin's will whose affability or hostility constituted nothing more than a feature of a political line. One day in late June, after U.S. MPs had stopped what turned out to be Sokolovsky's car doing 80 in a 25 m.p.h. zone and one American had warned off the marshal's pistol-waving guards by jamming his gun into the pit of Sokolovsky's stomach, Clay went to make his apologies—not because the MPs had done anything wrong but simply because he regretted the incident. Instead of reacting in "his usual humorous fashion," Sokolovsky was "cold and indignant and charged that the arrest had been made as a plan to humiliate him." Clay, who had thought he was paying a call on an old friend, let it go at that. A conversation that took place early in the occupation illustrates Clay's thinking about the marshal. When Sokolovsky told Clay that the Soviets would not use the Red Army to promote Communism, Colonel Howley had scoffed at this assurance. "But I know Sokolovsky," Clay protested. "He wouldn't lie to me." As Howley put it, Clay, a scrupulously honest soldier himself, could not understand an unprincipled one.

In his recommendations Clay did not always appear consistent, sometimes seeming to favor compromise, sometimes managing to see matters from what he took to be the Soviet viewpoint, and sometimes—as in his proposal for convoys—advocating measures involving the threat of force. Even if he saw the purpose of running armed columns to Berlin as demonstrating the unlikelihood of war, Clay as a soldier knew the danger involved in bluff and counterbluff. He had also worked sincerely to carry out his mission in Germany, at first for the entire country and then for the three zones after four-power agreement proved impossible. In any case, he had a policy for Berlin, and he had proposed tactical measures to support it. What, aside from its fears and reservations, did Washington have to offer?

The discussion at a cabinet meeting on June 25 revealed that the impact of the total blockade of Berlin had not yet sunk in on Washington's highest policymakers. Questioning Forrestal about "the German currency squabble with Russia," President Truman received the reply that the situation was not as serious as it seemed in the press. Fresh from his teleconference with Clay, Royall expressed disagreement with Forrestal's judgment, but the president, absorbed in his desperate battle for political life, moved on to describe how he had sat up the night before watching the Republicans nominate Thomas E. Dewey. After the governor's smooth-running convention machine had routed a "Stop Dewey" movement, the convention had chosen him unanimously; even so, Truman gleefully noted, the delegates had given their nominee only a chilly reception. This switch to presidential politics in the discussion gave support, presumably unwitting, to a point made in the *Times* report that had quoted Clay's "short of war" statement. The U.S. military government in Germany, said the story, felt that the Berlin situation had long since moved from the local level to the higher realms of government, yet the view from Germany showed that the Republican convention had absorbed the attention of Washington.

In James Vincent Forrestal, President Truman had a defense chief who, though an Ivy Leaguer like many of the president's other associates, was hardly typical. The son of an Irish immigrant who had established a contracting business, he had worked as a reporter for several years before going to college and had managed to survive and flourish at Princeton despite being an exotic creature in those surroundings, a Northern Democrat. Later, more typically, he had joined the 1920s bond-salesman trek to Wall Street, and by 1938 he had become president of Dillon, Read and Company. During World War I he became a navy flier (Naval Aviator No. 154) but saw no combat. In 1940, having gone to Washington to work directly for FDR, he became the navy's first undersecretary, with a monumental immediate assignment. "Congress has just passed the two-ocean-navy bill," Secretary of the Navy Frank Knox told him. "And, Jim, it's up to you to build it."

Throughout World War II Forrestal served as the chief figure in navy procurement; as Walter Millis, the editor of his papers, put it, if nobody could be said to have *built* the great wartime navy, Forrestal was the person most responsible for *buying* it. When Knox died of a heart attack in 1944, Forrestal moved up as the automatic successor. Atypical even in appearance, Forrestal stood out in a group of smooth, comfortable types, with his lips compressed into a tight line—as if clamping inner tensions into place—and his splayed nose, broken in a sparring match at the Racquet Club. "The suggestion of a tough fistfighter which it left on him," Millis commented, "probably did him no disservice in the rough-and-tumble of wartime Washington." Forrestal had few illusions about himself, however, believing that "you can't make a hero out of a man in a blue serge suit."

Like Royall and other defense officials, Forrestal expressed concern at the rapid U.S. demobilization after the war; strongly anti-Communist (to the level of obsession) but seeing himself as neither a warmonger nor a pacifist, he argued for a level of American strength sufficient to "make it clear to any possible group of enemies that the risks of engaging us are too great to make it worth while." But, he added, those who possess strength must also have patience. Everybody recognized Forrestal's outstanding ability and accomplishments, but, although functioning in a political context, he often seemed to regret the association of politics and government and would urge the administration to try to solve important problems by removing them from politics—an approach Truman found impracticable as well as unappealing.

After the June 25 cabinet meeting, Forrestal, Royall, and Undersecretary of State Robert Lovett (who had succeeded Acheson in the post just a year earlier and was representing Marshall, undergoing tests at Walter Reed Hospital) stayed with Truman to talk further about Berlin. Approving Royall's instructions to Clay, the president expressed concern that trouble might erupt in the classic way—in this case, from individual action by a "trigger-happy Russian pilot or a hothead Communist tank commander." Much of the discussion concerned the legal basis of Western rights to access to Berlin; nobody seemed very sure about it, and no document existed to make everything clear. With reference to the 1945 letters between Truman and Stalin, General Wedemeyer's staff believed that this correspondence could be regarded as a contract guaranteeing Allied access, but they conceded that "there has been some difference of opinion as to whether the documents in question do, in effect, contain a specific agreement on transit rights."

Not only had nobody seemed to anticipate serious trouble on the railroads and the autobahns, nobody in high authority seemed to have given Berlin much concentrated attention at all. No National Security Council document, no contingency plan existed. If the Americans pulled out of Berlin, Truman said, the supporters they left behind might suffer at the hands of the Russians. But should the Americans stay when their presence would mean great difficulties for the people? On the whole, the president felt that the Americans should remain, but how? No immediate decision seemed required—the stockpiles of food and coal should last for several weeks. But the decision could not wait a comparable time. The Western leaders should certainly have a few days' grace, but they would soon have to make up their minds: to try to stay in Berlin, or to give up and go.

CHAPTER 14

Anatomy of a Response

"THE WESTERN COUNTRIES have blundered into this crisis and are only beginning to realize the intensity of the dilemma with which they are faced," declared the usually sober and measured *Economist* of London. "They have every right to be furiously angry with the so-called leaders who put them there. But anger will not get them out. Only hard thought and high courage will do that." Lacking any plan for meeting the developing crisis, the U.S. authorities began the required process of hard thought with what General Bradley called "a series of hastily arranged emergency meetings," starting with a Sunday-afternoon session of something over four hours in Royall's Pentagon office, in preparation for a meeting the next day with Truman. Bradley later summed up the alternatives succinctly: "get out; fight; or try to stand on quicksand, hoping for a diplomatic solution or another sudden change in Soviet policy."

With respect to Soviet policy, the president himself had confused matters just days earlier, while on his western trip. In remarks at Eugene, Oregon (a town somewhat too large to be considered a whistle stop), Truman for some reason decided to share with the crowd a few thoughts on Joseph Stalin. Looking back to the Potsdam Conference, the president produced some startling statements. "I got very well acquainted with Stalin there," he told his audience, "and I like old Joe. He's a decent fellow." Unfortunately, however, Stalin had an extremely serious problem, the president said: "But he's a prisoner of the Politburo. He can't do what he wants to do. He makes agreements, and if he could he would keep them. But the people who run the government won't let him keep them." Anyway, someday "that great country and this great country" would come together on the basis of their mutual interests, Truman said.

What kind of pondering had produced this analysis of the Soviet power structure? Aside from its barbershop tone, and the inappropriateness of a head of state's offering such views in public, Truman's view could not truly be considered wholly idiosyncratic; not long before, for instance, Forrestal had written routinely of "the gang who run Russia," though he had said nothing implying that Stalin was anybody's prisoner, and a highly sophisticated observer who had once served as political editor of the *Berliner Tageblatt* took it for granted that the blockade had been instituted by "the men around Stalin."

These opinions reflected some of the West's continuing puzzlement concerning the scope of Stalin's authority. Certainly, with his quiet, often friendly demeanor, the generalissimo puzzled Westerners; he lacked the bluster and bombast the world had come to associate with dictators. But a prisoner of his associates? No one familiar with the Georgian's use of power in the 1920s and 1930s could share that opinion. When reports of Truman's curbstone comments reached Foggy Bottom, Undersecretary Lovett and Bohlen, the department counselor, turned their shock into immediate intervention. Aside from the dubious accuracy of the president's opinion, the two saw this as no time, with a Soviet noose being tightened around Berlin and trouble with the Communists simmering elsewhere, for the U.S. chief of state to lull the home folks with chatter about the decency of old Joe. Lovett and Bohlen contacted Truman's entourage with the very strong suggestion that the president utter no more such idle thoughts.

The group in Royall's office on Sunday afternoon, June 27, unhesitatingly proceeded on the premise that neither Stalin nor the other members of the Politburo could be considered affable chaps full of goodwill toward the United States. They batted back and forth the three possibilities Bradley said: fighting, getting out of Berlin, and doing something in between—maintaining, as Forrestal put it, "our unprovocative but firm stand in Berlin, utilizing first every local means, and subsequently every diplomatic means, to obtain recognition and assertion of our rights while postponing [an] ultimate decision to stay in Berlin or withdraw." Royall disagreed, arguing that the Americans should not delay deciding on their ultimate position, since actions taken right away should be designed in accordance with this decision; on the whole, the secretary of the army favored withdrawal. Along with the possible policies, the group discussed other actions, steps that might be taken "on the one hand either to minimize or cover our withdrawal from Berlin, and on the other hand to augment our position vis-à-vis the Russians." Perhaps two squadrons of B-29 bombers then based at Goose Bay, Labrador, should go to Germany; it also might be advisable to base two B-29 groups in England. (B-29s carried great symbolic weight, their last missions of World War II having been the atomic bomb flights to Hiroshima and Nagasaki.)

The group came to no decision and formulated no recommendation for the president; the next day Forrestal, Royall, and Lovett would lay before him the three possible policies. These options, which came from discussion among only a handful of officials, made no mention of trying to stay in western Berlin and supplying the Allied sectors by air. "The Berlin crisis had been long in the making," Millis observed; "but when finally it broke, the response was this ad hoc meeting . . . which bypassed the formal machinery of the Security Act to take large (if rather vague) politico-strategic decisions." Where were the CIA, the National Security Council, the War Council?

At the meeting early Monday afternoon, June 28, in the Oval Office, Lovett summed up for the president the Sunday discussion, leading to the central question: Were the Americans going to stay in Berlin or not? Before Lovett finished his sentence, Truman broke in to say that there was no discussion on that point—"we were going to stay period." Royall said with due deference that he wanted to be sure that the problem had received thorough consideration, since the United States ought not to be committed to a position under which "we might have 'to fight our way into Berlin' unless the possibility was clearly recognized and its consequences accepted." Truman met this hand on his sleeve with the comment that the United States "would have to deal with the situation as it developed" but that the Americans were in Berlin as the result of an agreement, and the Russians had no right to use pressure to get them out. Thus Truman's "we're staying" declaration seemed to mean that, in any case, the Americans must wait and see—if they were going to go, they were not going yet. (That same day a memo approved by General Bradley summed up the army's essentially bleak view of the situation: "Only future developments can determine whether we must leave in one month or in one year. Eventually, however, we will have to withdraw unless present indicated Soviet policy undergoes a radical change.")

Afterward, bringing Clay up to date on the high-level deliberations in Washington, Royall reported everybody's acceptance of the general's judgment that the controversy over currency probably represented only a phase in a "major Soviet effort to drive Western Powers from Berlin" and endorsed Clay's proposal to meet with Sokolovsky to try to feel out Soviet intentions. Since the Russians had claimed that they had imposed the traffic stoppage as a protective measure against, in effect, contamination by Western currency, Royall authorized Clay, in conjunction with the British and the French, to reopen the currency discussion with Sokolovsky but to make it clear that "agreement cannot be reached on currency except in conjunction with lifting traffic ban."

On this same day the Berlin situation received some detached diary commentary from Admiral Leahy, who noted that the Americans did not have "sufficient force to hold our zone in Berlin and an evacuation would probably result in Soviet action to eliminate the German residents who have been friendly toward the Western Allies." The president, Leahy said, had told him that U.S. policy concerning Berlin had not changed—"he desires to remain in Berlin as long as possible"—but the United States would be making no commitments in forthcoming meetings with the British chiefs of staff. Army Undersecretary Draper and General Wedemeyer had been dispatched to Berlin to make an estimate of the situation; however, as Leahy summed matters up, in Berlin the United States had a "hopeless" military situation, because the country had no force available anywhere and no information that the Soviet Union was "suffering from internal weakness." Hence, "it would be advantageous to the United States prospects to withdraw from Berlin." But, Leahy's conscience reminded him, withdrawal would guarantee a grim fate for Germans who supported the Allies.

Despite the excitement stirring in Washington, London, and Berlin, President Truman, like Admiral Leahy, seemed not to have breathed deep of crisis atmosphere. On the evening of June 28, he noted how he and Bess ate supper on the south porch of the White House, facing the Jefferson Memorial across the lawn. Kids were playing ball in the park, and a robin hopped around looking for worms, found one, and pulled with all his might to unearth him; airliners landed and took off at National Airport. "It is a lovely evening," Truman said. "I can see the old Chesapeake and Potomac Canal going across the Washington Monument grounds, barges anchoring west of the Monument. I can see old J. Q. Adams going swimming in it and getting his clothes stolen by an angry woman who wanted a job. The old guy did not have my guards or it wouldn't have happened." But the reverie had to come to its end: "I wake up, go upstairs and go to work and contemplate the prison life of a President. What the hell!"

With all Truman's preoccupations, Berlin had to prove itself a true crisis to get the attention it needed. Although one of the least duplicitous of men, the president frequently managed to bring trouble on himself by engaging in or approving of actions that gave American policy a cast of double-dealing. Just in the previous month, two U.S. moves in the international arena had made the world question the nature of American leadership. Their importance in relation to the Berlin crisis lay not in their substance but in the harm such diplomatic styles could do to personal relationships at the highest level.

Early in May an American initiative, minor in itself, had turned into a fiasco that left the British—particularly Ernest Bevin—irritated and suspicious, the Americans embarrassed, and the Russians chortling. Responding to Kennan's and Bohlen's concern at the course of events in Germany, Undersecretary Lovett, after discussing the idea with President Truman, had arranged with Marshall for Ambassador Bedell Smith in Moscow to be directed to meet with Molotov—informally, at Smith's suggestion—to make it clear to the Soviets that the United States firmly intended to maintain its rights in Berlin and to resist "any further act of aggression" by the Soviet Union. Marshall in his instructions also told Smith to assure Molotov that the United States sought peace and wished to avoid any actions that might lead to war. In a conciliatory touch, Molotov was to be told that "as far as the United States is concerned, the door is always wide open for full discussion and the composing of our differences." On May 4 Smith duly had his meeting with Molotov. Then the foreign minister and his colleagues made their move.

Far from keeping the talk private, the Soviets pounced on the opportunity, releasing an edited version of Smith's remarks that made the United States, with its individual approach, appear to be bypassing its allies. The story, when it broke, incensed Bevin. How could the United States deal directly with the Soviet government without telling him about it? But they had made no proposal, offered no program, the Americans said; nevertheless, a bad taste lingered. Then Henry Wallace, the former vice president who was preparing to run for the presidency on his own third-party ticket, seized on the Smith-Molotov interview to write an open letter in the *New York Times* asking Joseph Stalin to cooperate in a meeting with American representatives, the ultimate aim being the building of a "Century of Peace." Within a week Stalin had replied, praising Wallace's initiative but questioning whether the U.S. government would back it up. The U.S. government, of course, had no desire at all to back up anything Henry Wallace did, and its repudiation of his proposal left the way open for the Kremlin to accuse the Americans of launching a move toward U.S.-Soviet understanding and then quickly backing away from it. "Whether the episode was taken to show the duplicity or the clumsiness of American diplomacy," wrote Bevin's biographer, Alan Bullock, "it immediately revived European lack of confidence in American policy."

Statesmen rarely have the good fortune to confront problems in sequence instead of in clusters. On May 11 Bedell Smith's interview with Molotov provided the subject for a fiery session Bevin held with Ambassador Lewis Douglas. Only three days later came the second diplomatic disturbance of the month; this one concerned the Middle East. All during the development of Anglo-American policy toward the Soviet Union after the end of the war, as the two powers worked more and more closely together, their differing views on Palestine put the most serious strains on their relationship.

In the postwar years the British, who had controlled the area since the end of World War I, found themselves in an increasingly unrewarding situation as they struggled to keep a measure of order while Zionists warred against them. As the months went by, Bevin and his colleagues increasingly resented American criticism, as well as the American refusal to play any active part in the area. Early in 1947 Britain, announcing that it would withdraw from Palestine when its mandate expired on May 15, 1948, handed this hotter and hotter potato over to the United Nations; in November the United States and the Soviet Union joined a UN majority in voting for partition of Palestine between Arabs and Jews. But heavy fighting between the two groups quickly made American leaders wonder whether partition was actually feasible; perhaps a UN trusteeship would be the best recourse until the Arab and Jewish communities could reach some sort of accommodation. At the urging of the United States, the UN Security Council called a special session of the General Assembly to take up the trusteeship question—an idea opposed, quite remarkably, both by the Arabs, who saw it as a bridge to partition, and the Jews, for whom it loomed as a barrier to independence. American Zionists reacted to this push toward trusteeship by subjecting the president to political pressure so intense that, in his annoyance, he for a time refused to see any Zionist leaders.

Without Truman's approval, no American initiative could have been taken. Yet the president either did not see the implications of trusteeship or did not realize that he had approved the U.S. initiative in the UN. With the Zionists in Palestine determined to proclaim the state of Israel the moment the British mandate expired, this complex and tangled drama quickly became a confrontation between two unlikely opponents, Secretary of State Marshall and Truman's young assistant Clark Clifford. In a White House meeting on May 11, the normally seductive-voiced aide gave the secretary of state a stiff lecture on the importance, with respect to the coming presidential election, of granting immediate recognition to Israel in spite of the U.S. move in the General Assembly for trusteeship. Marshall, in what Clifford years later termed "a righteous God-damned Baptist tone," declared that to take such a position "to win a few votes" was unworthy of the great office of the presidency: "The counsel offered by Mr. Clifford was based on domestic political considerations, while the problem that confronted us was international." Marshall added that, if Truman followed Clifford's advice, if "I were to vote, I would vote against you."

This uninspiring debate, which continued by telephone and at lunch tables, came to its climax in one of the more remarkable moments in the annals of the United Nations. At a few minutes after six o'clock on the evening of May 14 (just past midnight in Tel Aviv), the White House followed the news of Israel's declaration of independence with the announcement of U.S. recognition. At that same moment the U.S. representatives at the UN were engaged arguing the case for trusteeship. The various delegations at first dismissed the news from Washington as some sort of silly rumor. But as the subsequent reports confirmed the story, the skepticism among many delegations quickly turned to anger at American duplicity, and to consternation and embarrassment among the American representatives themselves; Ambassador Warren Austin, summoned from the floor to receive the news by telephone, found it so disconcerting that he did not even return to the assembly hall but walked out of the building and had himself driven home.

When he heard the announcement of recognition, Marshall immediately rose above any personal feelings to telephone Dean Rusk, assistant secretary for UN affairs, and order him to New York "to keep our UN delegation from resigning *en masse.*" Truman then went ahead to appoint a special representative to the new Israeli government without consulting his secretary of state. When the appointee, James G. McDonald, stopped in London, he ran into an explosion of frustration over the whole situation from Ernest Bevin. As the British statesman and Truman biographer Roy Jenkins observed, the issue of Palestine "probably was the factor which most inhibited the growth of real respect, let alone affection, between Truman and his most powerful European auxiliary, Ernest Bevin." And, Jenkins added, "it certainly strained the President's relationship with his much admired Secretary of State more than every other issue put together."

Unleashing his political point man on General Marshall, publicly embarrassing the State Department and its representatives in New York, and then bypassing the secretary in the appointment of a representative to Israel all suggested an insensitivity on Truman's part to the feelings of his associates and, perhaps more importantly, to those of Marshall, the cornerstone and absolutely indispensable member of his administration. For the universally admired secretary of state to resign in a huff during the campaign season could do far worse than simply offset whatever political gains the Clifford approach was supposed to produce. And internationally, as Eleanor Roosevelt wrote, the United States was destroying its capacity to lead by changing its position with great frequency and without consulting other countries. Thus the president appeared duplicitous in his dealings not only with foreign leaders but with his own associates.

What was at work in this presidential executive style? A leading student of the presidency, Erwin C. Hargrove, commented some years ago that, in becoming president accidentally, Truman had been driven by "none of the psychological needs . . . tied to skill" that characterized his activist predecessors. He definitely venerated the presidential office, viewing it as the two Roosevelts and Wilson had viewed it, but he lacked their skills of leadership. Though he liked to make decisions, "he had no sense of strategy but made [them] as they came to him without considering their relationship to other decisions. . . . He took each case as it came. He seldom prepared the public in advance for policy departures." Overall, he had the proper conception of the presidential office, Hargrove believed, but "he was not a completely 'political man' in terms of his needs and drives and his political style revealed this." Clinton Rossiter, an admirer, said of Truman: "At times he had the look of greatness, at times he gave off the sound of meanness." But such contradictions hardly marked Truman as unique among political leaders.

Although Joseph Stalin did not have to concern himself with allies and public opinion and elections—or with the feelings of subordinates exposed to public embarrassment—his own kind of "prison life" at the top presented him with serious problems in these same spring weeks. Whether he had originally aimed at a united and communized Germany (on the model of Poland), a united but weak Germany that could be subjected to some degree of Soviet influence, or simply a divided Germany strong in the East and weak in the West, events during the past two years had progressively moved otherwise: toward a united and flourishing West Germany associated with the Western Allies.

But Stalin also had a serious problem in his ideological house. The Cominform, created only eight months earlier to serve as a direct vehicle for Soviet control of the people's democracies, already faced a schism, with Yugoslavia's Marshal Tito as the head heretic. Unlike other national leaders in Eastern Europe, Tito had come to power on his own and had won victory mostly with his own army; his regime supported itself rather than resting on Red Army bayonets. Though a loyal Communist and an admirer of Stalin, Tito saw Yugoslavia as an independent country and himself as an independent agent capable of developing his own policies; in particular, he wished to establish a Balkan federation made up of his own country together with Albania and Bulgaria. Since the creation of such a federation would necessarily make Belgrade a center of Communist power—with some degree of lateral relations among the three Balkan states instead of mediation of all dealings by Moscow—Stalin forbade the enterprise. To his astonishment, the Yugoslav marshal refused to confess his sins, thereby earning from Stalin, on March 27, 1948, a letter denouncing his conduct and policies. On June 28—the day Truman told his associates "we're staying" in Berlin—the Cominform announced the expulsion of the Yugoslav Communist Party.

Rather than leading to the expected overthrow of Tito by his own associates, however, this act of excommunication evoked defiance from Belgrade. The Yugoslav party Central Committee accused the Cominform of trying to overthrow the party and announced that it would talk with the

Soviet Union and other Communist countries only on a "basis of equality." The committee also reaffirmed Tito's proposal for the "unity of the Bulgarian, Albanian, and Yugoslav peoples." Stalin had declared, according to a later account by Nikita Khrushchev, that all he had to do was "move his finger, and there will be no Tito." But with his finger and, indeed, the whole might of the Soviet Union proving powerless to punish the heretic in Belgrade, Stalin had much on his mind this last week of June.

Could the developing situation in Berlin now be considered a genuine crisis? If so, was it a major one? As summed up by Avi Shlaim, a student of crisis decision-making, to qualify as a crisis a situation must be perceived by the highest-level decision makers of a country as meeting three conditions:

1. It offers a threat to basic values, with a simultaneous or subsequent
2. high probability of involvement in military hostilities, and the awareness of
3. a finite (not necessarily extremely short) time for response to the threat.

Other students of the subject require a crisis to come as a surprise, a limitation that would rule out the situation in Berlin. Since December 1947 U.S. policymakers had seen the increasing likelihood—or at least, the possibility—of a Soviet move to push the Western powers out of Berlin. Clay and Murphy had repeatedly warned Washington that the Soviets could at any time sever land links between the Western zones and the Allied enclave more than a hundred miles to the east. Even so, despite the buildup, the actual blockade, when it came, had to force its way into attention at the highest American levels. So in some ways, the Berlin situation could be classed as a surprise—a surprise that came with advance publicity, perhaps—and thus would be all the more a proper crisis in anybody's definition.

Basic values were at stake: some of the U.S. policymakers saw the blockade as a threat to the entire Western position vis-à-vis the USSR in what had become the contest for Germany and Europe. In a June 26 message that seemed intended to stiffen the resolve of his superiors in the State Department, Robert Murphy put the basic values case in strong terms. The Western presence in Berlin had become "a symbol of resistance to eastern expansionism. It is unquestionably an index of our prestige in central and eastern Europe. As far as Germany is concerned, it is a test of US ability in Europe." Hence, if the Americans "docilely" withdrew,

"Germans and other Europeans would conclude that our retreat from Germany is just a question of time. US position in Europe would be gravely weakened, and like a cat on a sloping tin roof." Some American leaders saw the blockade as a test of the credibility of U.S. commitments to its allies. But no true and strong consensus had yet appeared. On the other hand, the existence of western Berlin could be said to represent a threat to Soviet values as perceived by Stalin, Molotov, and their associates; however, they were the ones who had pushed the buttons that set the crisis in motion.

The probability of military moves—Shlaim's second requirement—also seemed on the June 25 weekend to be clearly involved here, because to stay in Berlin the West must make some show of force, whether of the kind General Clay advocated or in another form, and the "Russian reaction," as Truman said, "might lead to war." Further, as the president also said, some hothead could on his own ignite hostilities.

Shlaim's third point likewise counted, although the limited time for reaction was not a matter of hours or even, perhaps, a handful of days. Still, the United States and the West could not wait to move until supplies in Berlin ran out. Aside from this practical consideration, Berlin's symbolic importance required reasonably prompt action.

Hence the United States and the West faced a genuine crisis, by the strictest academic definition of the term. Basic values seemed to be at stake, and a response to the challenge had to come within a clearly finite time period; the West should stay in Berlin, and it had to formulate a way to do it. The possibility of military action existed, the threat of it had been suggested. But the Americans wanted no armed clash, no possibility of war. Without at least the threat of force, how could the West stay in Berlin? What would happen to the cherished basic values, when, in the words of a CIA report, Western withdrawal would "constitute a political defeat of the first magnitude"? But unless somebody came up with a way to stay that did not involve force or the threat of it, the United States and its allies, for all the talk and perturbation, would be leaving Berlin. Was there an answer, and if so, what could it be?

When the Soviets slammed the final door into Berlin on June 24, they put an abrupt end to a holiday Ernest Bevin was enjoying on the Isle of Wight. A torpedo boat came across the Solent to pick up the foreign secretary and start him on his way back to London for conferences about the crisis. The next day, in a two-hour session, the Cabinet heard a firsthand account of events in Berlin from Major General Neville Brownjohn, the British deputy military governor in Germany, who had been dispatched to London by General Robertson. The visiting general offered his listeners little cheer, expressing doubts about the feasibility of supplying blockaded Berlin by air or in any other way. Bevin left the meeting to appear in the House of Commons, where he declared that the people of Berlin were "showing great calmness and show no signs of being intimidated." Without denying the seriousness of the situation, the foreign secretary said that the West could not yield to the Soviet insistence on economic control of Berlin without surrendering Berlin itself. What course would Britain and the West follow now? Bevin chose not to say, because of the "delicate state of affairs," but despite the lack of a ringing affirmation of a strong Western position, reporters readily inferred that the British intended to stay in Berlin.

The best piece of evidence that Bevin and his colleagues intended no dramatic change in policy came from the schedules of ministers, many of whom were as usual going to the country for the weekend; Prime Minister Attlee himself would be out of town until Sunday evening. Bevin, however, would remain in London, with Brownjohn at his elbow.

By Saturday the twenty-sixth, Bevin and his colleagues had evolved an approach, which he and Strang explained to Lew Douglas. In the first place, Bevin wanted to streamline inter-Allied communications—to go into a crisis mode. As reported by Douglas to Washington, the foreign secretary felt that in the coming days the Western Allies would face a series of issues requiring prompt decisions; he therefore proposed, for the sake of efficiency, to deal directly with Douglas instead of communicating with the Americans through the British embassy in Washington and to have London as at least one clearinghouse with full information from all sources. Bevin also wanted the British and American chiefs of staff to develop a joint appreciation of the military side of the Berlin crisis, and though the French were going through one of their frequent cabinet crises, he advocated including the French ambassador in London, René Massigli, in the discussions about Berlin. The Allies should study ways of supplying the city, Bevin thought, and he found himself in step with the Washington decision-makers in liking the prospect of having more U.S. B-29s in Europe. He saw no particular military effectiveness in an operation, but believed it would "tend to refute the view held by the Soviet that we are not determined."

Tägliche Rundschau, the newspaper the Soviets had launched almost as soon as they arrived in Berlin in April 1945, had declared that the Attlee government was not prepared to remain in Berlin and was discussing with the Americans and the French the abandonment of the city. The story was completely untrue, said the British government. "The statement that we intend to stay in Berlin holds good. The opinion of the whole world will condemn the ruthless attempt by the Soviet Government to create a state of siege in Berlin, and so by starving the helpless civilian population, to seek political advantages at the expense of the other Allied Powers."

Bevin's desire to streamline communications between London, Washington, and Berlin did not arise wholly from the pressure of the moment but reflected his displeasure with the Truman administration's dealings during the previous month at the United Nations and in the Kremlin. In his reply to Douglas, sent on June 27, Marshall agreed with Bevin's ideas, including the proposed arrangements about sharing information. Borrowing Forrestal's phrase, the secretary declared the American intention to "continue to maintain the present unprovocative but firm stand in Berlin." But aside from sending B-29s to Europe and encouraging Clay to discuss the currency situation with Sokolovsky, what action did anybody advocate?

CHAPTER 15

"The Air Force Can Carry Anything"

ONE DAY IN late May, a U.S. Air Force officer, Major General William H. Tunner, addressed a group of New York business executives at a boosterish meeting celebrating the so-called Air Commerce Day. Speaking on the topic "Transportation by Air," the general paid generous tribute to the business of shipping goods in airplanes—it was not only an important activity in itself, he declared, but it held vital importance for the national security of the United States. Although just forty-two, Tunner had unchallengeable expert knowledge of his subject: during World War II he had directed the Air Transport Command operations in which Douglas C-47s and C-54s and Curtiss C-46s carried supplies from India through the towering Himalayas to keep China in the struggle against Japan. Tunner had not created the operation but had taken over "an enterprise running on the last margins of original creativeness, and stabilized it swiftly, remorselessly."

"Flying the Hump," as this famous supply campaign was called, had demonstrated "the tremendous potential in military air transport," Tunner told his audience. During its last year, in the face of difficulties of politics, logistics, and weather unknown in aviation elsewhere in the world—with "fog, heavy rain, thunderstorms, dust storms, high mountains, a necessity for oxygen, heavy loads, sluggish planes, faulty or no radio aid, hostile natives, jungles, and one-way airfields set in mountainous terrain at high altitude"— the operation had delivered 550,000 tons of all kinds of cargo; in the last month alone, Hump fliers carried 78,000 tons to China. A plane took off every two and a quarter minutes throughout the twenty-four hours of the day.

Now, in the postwar spring of 1948, the U.S. Air Force, barely six months old as an independent service, had just established a new arm, combining the Air Transport Command with the Naval Air Transport Service to create the Military Air Transportation Service (MATS). Although this new arm was only a skeleton, the general conceded, he nevertheless called it "a complete service, ready for whatever air transport mission may arise in the national interest." He did not know what such a mission might be, but fortunately the service was "capable of rapid expansion."

As events would soon show, General Tunner had his finger on the pulse of the time. Or, perhaps, his unusual and successful experiences had given him a sense of destiny.

On June 26, just two days after Soviet occupation forces completed the blockade of Berlin, General Clay called the U.S. air commander in Wiesbaden, Lieutenant General Curtis LeMay, to ask a blunt question: "Curt, have you got any planes that can carry coal?"

"Carry what?"

"Coal," Clay repeated.

"We must have a bad connection, General," said LeMay. "It sounds like you're asking me if my planes can carry *coal.*"

"That's just what I said. Coal!"

Not one to display limited faith in any aspect of the air force, LeMay rallied quickly. "General," he said, "the air force can carry anything. How much coal do you want us to haul?"

Clay's answer was characteristically terse. "All you can haul."

On the previous day two B-17s based in Wiesbaden had each ferried five tons of food and medical supplies to Berlin; now Clay was proposing something much bigger. General LeMay immediately summoned his staff to an assessment and planning meeting. At that moment the Americans had only two transport groups in Europe. This modest fleet included 102 C-47s, called Skytrains, and just two of the larger, four-engine C-54s, dubbed Skymasters and known in their civilian version as DC-4s, together with a small number of B-17s and other aircraft used for passenger runs and administrative purposes. One of the all-time great aircraft designs and loved by fliers as the Gooney Bird, the C-47, which dated back to the mid-1930s, had become obsolete; it could carry only about three tons of cargo, and few spare parts were to be found anywhere in Europe. Most of the available C-47s were battle-worn veterans of the war. Under their peeling paint some even displayed identifying stripes from the Normandy invasion four years earlier, while others bore pits and scars from encounters with the elements over the Hump. "It was," LeMay said later, "a pretty modest start."

Actually, Clay had turned to air transport almost three months earlier, at the beginning of April, following the March 31 Soviet clampdown on railroad traffic into Berlin. In his rebuff of suggestions from Washington that perhaps the wives and children of U.S. personnel ought to be evacuated from the city—when he said that he regarded such a move as "unbecoming"—Clay assured the Pentagon that a very small airlift could keep the Americans in Berlin supplied indefinitely. In addition, the general saw no cause for concern because he had "sufficient airlift to evacuate dependents and noncombatants rapidly if it becomes essential."

Carried out by C-47s of the 53rd Troop Carrier Wing, this "little airlift" served as a demonstration of American intentions not to give in to Soviet pressure. Some of that pressure came in direct form, as Yak-9 fighters buzzed LeMay's C-47s on their 275-mile path from their Rhein-Main base along the southern air corridor to Berlin. The little airlift delivered up to 100 tons of supplies a day, but after ten days the Soviets eased their restrictions and rail traffic resumed. The April operation mounted by "Clay's pigeons," as the fliers were perhaps inevitably called, existed strictly to maintain U.S. personnel; at no point did the Western commanders contemplate an operation to sustain the people of the western sectors of Berlin. Now in June Clay was calling on LeMay and his airmen to haul 500 to 700 tons of cargo a day to the city. The operation would not last long, Clay assured LeMay—maybe three or four weeks. This amount would make the U.S. forces self-sufficient, but it would not support the civilian population. The U.S. commander did not yet regard the blockade as much more than a particularly threatening Soviet harassing tactic; surely the Russians would not seriously threaten the 2.5 million people of western Berlin with starvation.

"I never dreamed how consequential this could become," LeMay said, nor did other observers, West or East, anticipate a major effort in the air; Soviet intelligence reported no such possibility to Stalin. Observers in Berlin had the general impression, wrote the local *New York Times* correspondent, that the Western Allies "would consider leaving the former German capital if the suffering of the populace became too great"—the probable outcome if the Russians should maintain the blockade, because the Allies simply could not supply 2,000 tons of food and other supplies daily by air. Hence, the correspondent said, an Allied decision to leave Berlin could be viewed as a diplomatic sacrifice undertaken in the interest of the people of the city.

The views reported by the *Times* correspondent could not be considered unrealistic: a metropolis of 2.5 million had enormous needs. On the day Clay telephoned LeMay, western Berlin had on hand, thanks in part to the efforts of Colonel Howley, stocks of grain and flour good for seventeen days; a thirty-two-day supply of cereals; a forty-eight-day supply of fats; meat and fish supplies for twenty-five days; potatoes for forty-two days; skim and dried milk for twenty-six days. Before the blockade, Berlin had imported 15,500 tons of supplies every day. Now, just to keep the populace on a tight but adequate diet, 5,000 tons of food would have to arrive every day—much more than the correspondents or the public realized, though the tricks of this particular specialized trade could include such weight-shaving tactics as deboning meat and dehydrating vegetables. But Clay had not yet called for such an effort.

In turning to the air force theater commander, Clay was acquiring the aid of a quite exceptional officer. Stocky (he stood just five foot eight), with a flat face and a downturned mouth ornamented with a cigar or, occasionally, a pipe, Curtis LeMay could seem the walking cliché of a more-guts-than-brains soldier, perhaps a frontier Indian-rousting cavalryman who had managed to survive intact from General Custer's day into the middle of the twentieth century. This appearance was completely deceptive.

A native of Ohio, LeMay had entered the army after putting in time in the Reserve Officers' Training Corps at Ohio State. In 1930 he became an air corps second lieutenant, and two years later he received an engineering degree from his alma mater. In the late 1930s he pioneered a new field at the time, navigation over water; most notably, he won praise and a measure of fame by locating an Italian liner six hundred miles out at sea.

During World War II LeMay's innovative mind and technical background combined to make him a tactical trailblazer. Assigned as a lieutenant colonel to command an Eighth Air Force bomb group based in England, he developed the "box formation" that became the standard for air groups; this wedge-shaped deployment, with the bombers staggered at different heights, allowed his B-17s to make the most of their firepower, and at the same time, as he said, it "wasn't too difficult for non-veteran pilots to manage in their positioning and spacing and speed." LeMay also caused a stir by ordering his pilots to cease zigzagging on their bomb runs in their attempts to avoid enemy flak; his own mathematical analysis showed him that such evasive maneuvers offered the B-17s no special protection and merely resulted in scattering bombs across the landscape. This move drew heavy criticism as a prescription for aircrew suicide. On his group's next mission after he had issued the order, to clinch the point, LeMay piloted the lead bomber himself. His method proved to be sound and became the standard practice.

LeMay flew lead several more times. "Pilots, navigators, and bombardiers are happier," wrote a correspondent, "when they see his black head, wreathed with smoke from his eternal cigar, climb into the lead plane at the start of a tough mission." LeMay's stern insistence on preparation and efficiency produced results that were more than simply enviable: on twenty-five missions from October 1942 till November 1943, his group averaged the loss of only one bomber per mission. Reporters gave the credit to the "youthful, burly, critical LeMay."

Sent to the Pacific after the German surrender and placed in charge of the air campaign against Japan, LeMay developed new tactics for this new situation. Under pressure to get results, he dispensed with formations altogether and even with guns and concentrated on the use of incendiary bombs. He also reorganized aircraft maintenance, putting it on virtually an assembly-line basis, thus increasing significantly the proportion of planes ready for action at any time.

After putting in time at a Pentagon desk, LeMay had come to Germany in October 1947 to take command of U.S. Air Forces in Europe. Newly arrived, he "shuddered at the trance-like conditions. The war had been over for more than two years, but the Germans were still in a state of utter shock. They looked like zombies, like the walking dead. They went unheeding and aloof across the streets. An automobile would be coming . . . they didn't care, didn't look, didn't even turn their heads when the screech of brakes exploded behind them. There was an eternal nothingness about the place." LeMay saw the same kind of blankness in the stores: "shop and office windows seemed just as empty and dust-covered as those human visages." But then came a miraculous change, as the general saw it, after the new currency went into effect. People could bring in approximately twenty-five dollars in the old currency and swap it for the new; they did this twice, and that was the limit. If you had more than the prescribed amount, you had to prove that you had come by it legitimately. "It amounted to each citizen starting with fifty bucks," LeMay said, and that "was the best thing which could have happened." As soon as the money was changed, "things began to appear from hiding places; they'd be offered for sale in the markets. Everybody began to work"—because people could now get paid for their efforts in "currency that amounted to something." But now the Soviet blockade threatened to stall the progress of this "incredible endeavor."

Although professing in his bluff way to have little interest in policy—"political aspects aren't my concern," he liked to say—LeMay during the earlier months of 1948 had taken a striking personal initiative. Realizing that, if trouble broke out, the Russians with one armored thrust could cut the supply lines between the U.S. zone and the North Sea port of Bremerhaven on which the Americans in Germany depended, he proceeded on his own to negotiate arrangements with the French and Belgian air chiefs for use of a series of airfields. Working through the back door, he stocked these bases with ammunition, bombs, aviation fuel, and maintenance equipment; U.S. airmen wearing civilian clothes staffed each field. If trouble arose, this network would be ready to receive and support combat aircraft. "I was breaking other nations' laws into bits," LeMay said. "You couldn't have any foreign troops stationed in France in peacetime. Nothing was more illegal to the French mind or the French code. Same thing for Belgium." Casually

LeMay mentioned that he had informed General Clay of his activities. He professed not to know whether Clay had told anybody else about them. For their part, the French and the Belgians kept the secret well.

On the day he received Clay's phone call, LeMay sent twenty-five C-47s to Berlin's Tempelhof airport with eighty tons of milk, flour, and medicine. Although these flights on June 26 have generally been considered the inauguration of the airlift, a little-known civilian mission actually beat them out by three days.

At six-thirty in the evening of June 23, as Jack Bennett, European operations director and chief pilot of American Overseas Airways, sat at his desk in the civilian terminal in Frankfurt, the telephone rang and a "clipped, military" American voice said, "Captain Bennett, we'd like to charter a Skymaster from you to fly to Berlin right away."

As a civilian, Bennett did not have to take orders from the military. "Just a minute," he said. "What're we going to put on that airplane?"

"We're going to put coal on it."

"Coal?" His feet came off his desk with a crash, Bennett recalled. Yes, the officer assured him, it was an emergency. Were the Russians playing cat-and-mouse with the autobahn again, Bennett asked, closing it, leaving it open? Yes, the officer said, they were.

But Bennett still rejected the proposal to have any of his planes carry coal. "You can't put coal dust in a passenger airplane," he told the caller. "It will ruin the controls, it will ruin the seats and everything else."

Well then, how about potatoes?

Bennett still refused, until the officer said they could put the potatoes in sacks. "Maybe," Bennett said.

"You might be making history today," the officer said. Bennett assured him that he wasn't interested in making history—he just didn't want to ruin the company's airplanes. When Bennett said that he had to find a pilot, the officer suggested that he fly the plane himself. After thinking over the idea for a few moments, Bennett agreed but pointed out that he had to find a copilot and an engineer. Sounding relieved, the caller agreed to have the potatoes bagged by eight o'clock, which became takeoff time. Bennett and his crew with their load of potatoes rolled down the runway and off for Berlin, and the airlift thus logged its first flight.

Next morning the Russians officially isolated Berlin with their an-nouncement that "the transport division of the Soviet Military Administra-tion is halting all traffic because of technical difficulties." The Russians also cut off supplies of food to the Allied sectors and, in an act having fundamental importance for the airlift, cut off the flow of electricity to western Berlin from generating plants in the east. This move automatically gave coal first place on the list of commodities to be delivered to the city by the Allies.

Bennett followed his first flight with others—"the cajoling conversations were repeated"—and on June 26 "the USAF," as he put it, "officially implemented the airlift with a few aircraft of their own." But as charter fliers, Bennett and other civilians, American and British, continued to play a part in the great effort.

General LeMay realized that his first flights represented only a token effort, and as he began to believe that General Clay would "buckle down and support the city of Berlin entirely by activity in the air," he looked around for more aircraft. Clay, no flier, obviously "never realized that when he talked in tonnages of such prodigious amount, it was far beyond our capacity to operate."

LeMay told Clay, "We'll have to get some help from home." On Sunday, June 27, Clay reported to the Pentagon that he had arranged for a "maximum airlift" to begin the next day. He intended to use seventy C-47s but added that LeMay wanted two new C-54 groups. What Clay considered a maximum effort at this point was only 600 to 700 tons a day, far below what would be required to supply Berlin with the food and fuel it needed, but that had not yet become Clay's purpose. The 600 tons would "substantially increase the morale of the German people" and would "seriously disturb the Soviet blockade." So at this point the airlift would serve primarily as a riposte, a tactical response to the Soviet initiative. This response would have other elements as well; Clay wanted the immediate dispatch of a fighter group already scheduled to arrive in August and called for building up a B-29 group in Germany. If possible, Washington should send other B-29s to Britain and France.

For his part, LeMay, sensing a long haul ahead, moved to set up a special command for the airlift, with Brigadier General Joseph Smith, headquarters commander at Wiesbaden, in charge; Smith's first orders called for him to plan a forty-five-day operation. As commander of U.S. Air Forces in Europe, LeMay himself had to face concerns beyond hauling coal, flour, and medicine, important as this mission was—he had to be ready for trouble of a more than logistical kind. If things should go wrong, for any of myriad knowable and unknowable reasons, and shooting should break out between the Russians and the Western Allies, he had to have bombers and fighters ready for action.

It was the presence in Berlin during the preceding days of General Albert Wedemeyer, who along with Army Undersecretary Draper had come to see the situation at first hand, that perhaps had the most influence on Clay's turning to air supply for the city. An outstanding planner, commander, and military diplomat, highly respected in the army, Wedemeyer had attended the German Kriegsakademie for two years in the late 1930s, where he received a kind of intellectual training rare among U.S. officers at the time. (At the academy he became a good friend of a fellow student, Claus von Stauffenberg, who in 1944 would die in front of a firing squad after his attempt to assassinate Hitler failed.) After returning to America the general had worked closely with General Marshall (initially, the chief of staff spoke of the six-foot-six Wedemeyer as "that long-legged major") and had commanded U.S. forces in the China Theater during the last year of the war. When Clay pondered the advisability of attempting to send an armored column into Berlin, Wedemeyer turned his thoughts in a different direction. Drawing on his firsthand knowledge of the achievements of Bill Tunner and his Hump fliers, Wedemeyer told Clay, "There is no question of your being able to support your position in Berlin by air if enough airplanes are made available."

Despite General Brownjohn's pessimistic June 25 report to the British Cabinet, Ernest Bevin pressed ahead with plans for British and Allied resistance to the Russians. General Robertson, more optimistic than his deputy, favored the idea of a large-scale airlift to supply not only the Allied garrison but the civilian population; he even believed later that he had given the idea to Clay. On June 28 Ambassador Douglas appeared at Bevin's office with two visitors to London, Wedemeyer and Draper, who were continuing their tour. The Americans had decided to hold fast in Berlin, Douglas told Bevin. Describing the airlift as he envisioned it, Draper assured the foreign secretary that the U.S. Air Force was prepared to fly 1,500 tons a day into Berlin. Far from applauding this news, the forthright Bevin fired back that the figure was too low—he was sure the United States could do better. This reply "made a very favourable impression on his visitors."

In Germany the Royal Air Force Transport Command, for its part, made a somewhat confused entrance into airlift activity. Following strict bureaucratic procedure, the only British C-47 squadron in Germany left for home as previously scheduled on June 25, the day after the blockade became absolute. On the previous evening, however, another squadron based in Cambridgeshire received orders for Germany; it was to be prepared to begin operations to Berlin within forty-eight hours. Three days later a second squadron was put on orders for Germany; these Dakotas (as the RAF called C-47s) departed during the morning of June 28. At this point the RAF planned to ferry about sixty-five tons a day, all to support

British forces; like Clay, General Robertson contemplated an operation lasting no longer than a few weeks. But like General LeMay, the RAF commanders saw the endeavor growing very rapidly; two more groups were quickly summoned, giving a total of about fifty-eight Dakotas; the squadron that had left for home on June 25 quickly returned to Germany.

At this time the Americans had only 102 C-47s available in all of Europe, and the RAF thought it might ultimately be able to furnish 150 aircraft of various kinds. Claiming that all their aircraft were needed in their far-off war in southeast Asia, in Vietnam, the French had no help to offer. By June 30 the snowball had begun to grow; old C-47s gathered at the Rhein-Main and Wiesbaden airfields "like crows on a cornfield." Watching these planes fly into Tempelhof, "coming down clumsily through the bomb-shattered buildings around the field, a sight that would have made a spick-and-span air parade officer die of apoplexy," Colonel Howley called them "the most beautiful things I had ever seen." Seeing these flights as the way to crack the blockade, Howley went back to his office "almost breathless with elation, like a man who has made a great discovery and cannot hide his joy."

LeMay's calls for more transports quickly yielded the first C-54s, which came across the Atlantic from stations in Texas and Panama, and then from Alaska and Hawaii. The worldwide call for these aircraft produced dismay when urgent orders required an Air Transport Command base on Guam to give up half of its twenty-six Skymasters. What for? the men asked. Berlin lay a world away and the fledgling airlift was only an abstraction, while Guam, Saipan, and the other bases in the Pacific needed all their planes to keep themselves supplied and to ferry passengers around the vast area. As was often the case, members of maintenance teams tended to personalize an aircraft for which they were responsible, becoming in many ways closer to it than to each other. Jim Harrison, an eighteen-year-old mechanic from Kentucky, and the other members of his maintenance crew looked on resentfully as they saw departing for Germany not only *Bozo,* their regular plane, but also *Mary Lou,* another C-54 for which they sometimes provided maintenance services. (Some thirty-five years later, watching a television documentary on the Berlin airlift, Harrison had the great pleasure of recognizing an old friend when the cameras showed a heavily laden *Bozo* coming in for a landing at Tempelhof.)

Although *Bozo, Mary Lou,* and the other Skymasters, representing a prewar design just a few years younger than the Skytrain, could hardly be called the latest word in transports, these larger, faster planes—originally intended for transcontinental passenger service—offered enormous advantages over the C-47. Compared with the C-54, as one commentator analyzed it, "it would take more than five times as many C-47's with more than four times as many crews flying four times as many hours, at nearly double the cost in gasoline, to put down in Berlin for one month 4,500 tons a day."

In the first days of the airlift, rushing to bring as much tonnage into Berlin as possible, the British decided to make use of the wide lake formed by the Havel River, just inside the southwestern border of the U.S. sector. The United Services Yacht Club offered to make temporary moorings, and on July 5 the first flying boat put down on the water. Soon eight RAF Sunderlands were engaged in the work; they were joined by two civilian flying boats. These aircraft flew out of a former Luftwaffe station at Finkenwerder, on the Elbe River near Hamburg.

The most striking aspect of the Havel operation was its method of handling coal. After taking on coal at dockside, laden trucks climbed up onto a specially built structure resembling a bridge, which stood fifteen feet high and extended for 435 feet. As soon as the trucks got into position, workers would open their sides and a cascade of coal would slide down chutes into waiting barges underneath the structure. These barges, amounting to about forty, had an ironic history. Many of them were in Berlin, available to help out in the airlift, because German occupiers had stolen them during the war from Belgium and the Netherlands and they had not yet been returned to their owners.

Boats and canoes often seemed to cover the surface of the Havelsee, one of the most popular lakes in the Berlin area. With the full cooperation of the citizens, the various police agencies succeeded in keeping the landing channels open, yet nobody had to miss a cherished Sunday outing on the water. The flying boats in themselves proved a great attraction, especially to children. To adults, their comings and goings showed the Western Allies at work, supplying Berlin instead of abandoning it. (The Sunderlands operated for twenty weeks, until winter icing put an end to their contribution. During their service they brought in more than 6,000 tons of supplies.)

Thus, through hour-by-hour, day-by-day evolution rather than by any great design, the airlift began to establish itself. The operation represented a remarkable attempt by the Western powers to redeem a bankrupt political situation through technical and mechanical means. It also had a special appeal for Americans: after what seemed endless months of talking and quarreling with the Russians and getting nowhere, now came a chance to move, to show what people could do when they decided they were tired of being pushed around.

Toying with possible names for the operation, some of the U.S. brass suggested the rhetorically appealing Operation Manna. Others wanted Operation Lifeline and Operation Airlane. The GIs had their own ideas, however, as did General Smith. "Hell's fire," he declared. "We're hauling grub. Call it Operation Vittles." This name with its informal tone harmonized perfectly with the thinking of the men on the line. For their part, the British gave the operation—or intended to give it—the punning name Operation Plane Fare. Regrettably, however, a clerk somewhere along line missed the joke and in his misinterpretation produced the drably uninspiring Operation Plainfare. The name stuck.

Despite the early and energetic Anglo-American efforts to counter the Soviet blockade, Admiral Leahy maintained his detached attitude toward the crisis, noting on June 30 that in a meeting at the Pentagon "Secretaries of Army and Defense seemed to be unnecessarily concerned about future prospects." No positive action would be taken, the group decided, until "the possibilities of relief by diplomatic action" had been exhausted.

On this same day, however, other high Allied statesmen responded more resoundingly—and in public. Ernest Bevin's declaration included an interesting reference to the citizens of Berlin, who were officially people of a defeated enemy country under military occupation. In a statement to the House of Commons, the foreign secretary declared: "We cannot abandon these stouthearted Berlin democrats who are refusing to bow to Soviet pressure." Accordingly, the Western powers had launched the airlift, and Bevin went on to say, "We recognise that as a result of these decisions a grave situation might arise," but the Western Allies "can see no alternative between that and surrender, and none of us can accept surrender." The House responded to these words with cheers, followed by more cheers for the Conservative Party spokesman, Harold Macmillan, who bluntly declared: "We must, if we are frank with ourselves, for this is a serious and solemn moment in this house, face the risk of war. Grave as that risk is, the alternative policy—to shrink from the issue—involves not merely the risk but almost the certainty of war." The Conservatives, he said, stood squarely behind Bevin's policy.

Bevin most emphatically would not have shared the view of a British political adviser in Germany—had he been aware of it—that the Western Allies should immediately withdraw from Berlin. Such a move would admittedly shatter Western prestige and produce corresponding gains for the Russians, the adviser admitted to an American journalist, but, he said, "a good general never tries to hold a hopeless position, nor does he engage in battle with the enemy on a ground of the enemy's own choice. In Berlin every factor is in favor of the Russians." The Allied position was sure to get worse and could not get better: "Sooner or later, we are likely to be forced out of Berlin, so it seems to me better to cut our losses quickly." This view, though full of logic and realism, found no echo in Bevin's thinking, nor in that of most of the adviser's colleagues in Germany.

French officials approached the question from a different angle. The Allies had not consulted France about the choice of Berlin as the seat of the occupation of Germany, they pointed out, and certainly the French had never liked the idea; for them the capital symbolized the arrogant German armies that had marched into France three times in seventy years. "I could never hope to be elected to Parliament again," said one French politician, "if I supported any warlike measure to protect Berlin from the Russians."

Speaking from Walter Reed Hospital, through the State Department's press officer, George Marshall said succinctly, "We are in Berlin as a result of agreements between the Governments on the areas of occupation in Germany and we intend to stay." The West, said the secretary of state, would "deal promptly" with the basic questions raised by the Soviet blockade, and meanwhile maximum use of air transport would be made to supply the civilian population. This was clear enough, and also clear in its import was the news that the United States was sending twenty more B-29s to German bases—double the number already there—even though the air force chose to characterize this dispatch of the big planes as part of the regular training program. Not only did the air force announcement declare that the number of Superfortresses in Europe overall would be trebled, it also revealed that a wing of jet fighters would join them.

Despite the impact of this wing flexing, Marshall's words also suggested that he looked to immediate negotiation with the Russians. Though he had spoken firmly, at this moment the true militant Western opposition to the Soviet blockade seemed to be centered in the foreign secretary's room in Whitehall.

Divided Berlin:
The Four Sectors

City limits

Tegel
Lake

FRENCH
SECTOR

Reinickendorf

Havel

Tegel Airport

Wedding

Spandau   Spree

Olympic
Stadium   Tiergarten

Brandenburg Gate

SOVIET
SECTOR

Spree

Charlottenburg

BRITISH
SECTOR Wilmersdorf   Schöneberg

Gatow
Airport

Tempelhof   Neukölln

Steglitz   Tempelhof
Airport

Havel

Zehlendorf

U.S.
SECTOR

Grosser
Müggelsee

City limits

Dahme

Potsdam

Babelsberg

Seddinsee

0   2.5   5
Miles

N

PART II: THE RAISIN BOMBERS

CHAPTER 16

"Gigantic Tonnages in a Max Effort"

In the days before World War II, the Rhein-Main airport, about seven miles southwest of Frankfurt am Main, built up a place for itself in history as a center for experiments in lighter-than-air craft and as home port of the dirigibles *Graf Zeppelin* and *Hindenburg.* Shielded from winds by the Taunus Mountains, the field made an ideal home for the famous zeppelins, whose mooring required calm weather. But this same relative windlessness meant that, during the winter, fogs tended to shroud the area instead of moving out, and thus the airport might be forced to shut down for several days at a time. Serving as a Luftwaffe fighter base during the war, the 2,000-acre airport suffered such extensive damage from Allied bombing and strafing attacks that the American occupation forces almost had to rebuild it from scratch before it could become a U.S. Air Force base. It later became the European terminal for the Military Air Transport Service. On June 26, 1948, the prime mission of the base became support of the Berlin airlift.

During the last days of June and the beginning of July, a remarkable phenomenon occurred at Rhein-Main. Germans crowded the terminal to "gaze in rapt wonder" at this demonstration of American determination and resourcefulness. "Give our military a big thing like this," said a U.S. civilian employee described by a reporter as normally contemptuous of the military, "and they can do it better than anyone in the world." The press described the operation in dramatic tones, with its "definite warlike atmosphere." In the operations room pilots received their instructions from bulletin boards that read like war briefings. Only code was to be used for communication during flight; pilots were to radio their locations only when asked for the information, radio silence being considered desirable if not mandatory. For the aircrews already on occupation duty in Germany, all this excitement came as a welcome change from tedious routine and limited flying hours.

"Today at the Rhein-Main airport," wrote a correspondent, "a pilot who was 'snoozing' yesterday in Panama was supervising the stacking of flour sacks in a huge, silver, gleaming C-54." Already the operation involved some four thousand officers and enlisted men, not including those who brought the supplies to the field and loaded them onto the planes. Awed by the spectacle, the crowds were taking heart: "the worried look on the Germans who doubted the United States would stay in Berlin is beginning to disappear." Already, it seemed, the Americans were winning this phase of the long-continuing battle for Berlin.

But everything did not go with triumphant ease. Berlin required coal for generating electricity and for supplying homes with gas, and the need would grow as winter came on, but hauling coal posed problems for others besides Captain Jack Bennett. Since neither the sending nor the receiving airports had facilities for loading and handling cargo of this kind, the airlift managers had to experiment. The air force devised the idea of loading coal into the bomb bay of a B-29, which flew low over the once-glorious Olympic stadium to drop its utilitarian load on the field in free fall like thousands of tiny bombs. Unfortunately, as soon as the coal hit the ground, the impact transformed it into clouds of useless coal dust. The airlift managers then decided to improvise with barracks bags.

On June 29, replying to a letter from General Robertson, Marshal Sokolovsky declared his "hope" that the rail line from the West into Berlin would be opened before the city's food stocks ran out. More explicitly, however, the marshal insisted that the "protective measures" against the influx of Western currency must remain in force "for the time being." The Soviet news bureau put the letter into circulation a few hours after the Berlin city assembly, in continuing defiance of the Russians, voted unanimously—except for the Socialist Unity (Communist) members—to appeal directly to the United Nations for intervention "within the next month, or help will be too late." On June 30 Ernst Reuter, who would have been the mayor of Berlin if the Soviets had not overridden his election, asked General Ganeval, as current presiding officer of the truncated Kommandatura (the Western representatives still met), to forward the request to the United Nations. The French government gave the request a cool response; Bidault, in his last days at the Foreign Ministry, deftly summed up his contempt for the UN, saying that even if the organization had not been "created to do nothing up to the present, that had been its principal occupation."

Despite his strong feelings about Berlin, Ernest Bevin responded to the conciliatory tone of Sokolovsky's letter—the marshal actually expressed "regret" over the stopping of traffic on the autobahn—by pressing for a meeting of the four military governors. Murphy read Sokolovsky's words as a "typical Soviet example of vague and implied promises" that was "well equipped with escape clauses," but in response to Bevin's strong desire Clay reluctantly agreed to the meeting; on this topic he saw eye to eye with the French commander, General Koenig, who had equally little faith in the idea.

The commanders came together in Sokolovsky's office in Babelsberg on July 3, with General Roger Noiret sitting in for Koenig, who was said to be "unavailable." Still thinking about the friendship he believed himself to have had with the marshal, Clay observed that the Soviet commander greeted his callers "politely but coldly." When Robertson spoke about the Western desire to resolve the currency issue, Sokolovsky broke in to say that "the technical difficulties would continue until we [i.e., the Western Allies] had abandoned our plans for West German Government," Clay reported. "This was the first admission of the real reason for the blockade. He did not even discuss the currency issue which was later given as the reason for the blockade by his government. It was evident that he was confident we would be forced to leave Berlin and that he was enjoying the situation." Clay added: "We were not."

Sokolovsky did say that the Russians were making repairs on the railroad, noted Jacques Tarbe de Saint-Hardouin, the French political adviser, but he "could not guarantee that others might not become necessary later, somewhere else on the line." Given the "clarity of the discussion," Clay made no reply, and Robertson said, "Everything is now very simple." The atmosphere became stiffer as the meeting progressed, Noiret reported, and at the conclusion "there were none of the buffets of earlier days waiting for us."

To the Allied governments, the situation relished by Marshal Sokolovsky seemed to call for some form of diplomatic initiative with the Soviet Union. On June 30 the London Committee—the U.S. and French ambassadors, Douglas and Massigli, and Sir William Strang—had begun working on drafts of notes for Moscow. Though the hope had been to produce a document that all three powers could sign, the French still had reservations about the Anglo-American view of the Berlin crisis. Here the various political leaders reflected the feelings of their respective citizens. A French public opinion poll showed that only 43 percent believed that the Allies would succeed in staying in Berlin, while a comparable poll in the United States gave a figure of 80 percent—incidentally, a far more optimistic result than a survey of the members of the National Security Council and the Joint Chiefs of Staff would have produced. Massigli managed to have recourse to the UN ruled out as a possible suggestion in the notes, but his government also felt less concern than the Anglo-Americans with the juridical position of the Allies in Berlin and more concerned with sounding conciliatory about settling the currency question.

Thus, on July 6, when the Allies entered on the first of the four stages into which their diplomatic efforts to deal with the Berlin crisis would eventually fall, they handed essentially two notes to Soviet ambassadors, similar but not identical, demanding that the blockade be raised. The U.S. note declared that Western rights of occupation derived "from the total defeat and unconditional surrender of Germany" and were embodied in international agreements that "implied the right of free access to Berlin." No one had any great hope that this message would bring a conciliatory Stalin to the conference table; Chip Bohlen, for one, expected the Soviets to continue what one scholar neatly capsuled as "Sokolovsky's illogical approach of blaming technical problems while offering to end them in exchange for political concessions."

On July 9 came the first casualties of the airlift when a C-47, shortly after taking off from Wiesbaden on its way to Berlin, crashed into a low peak in the Taunus Mountains and plunged into a forest. The resulting fire completely destroyed the aircraft, and the two pilots and an American civilian were killed. Just a little over two weeks later, a C-47 coming into Tempelhof smashed into an apartment building, killing both crew members. The collision demolished balconies on three floors of the building but, remarkably, left the top one intact; debris littered the street in front. Mayors of the six boroughs in the American sector paid a formal condolence call on Colonel Howley, and Berliners put up a plaque at the site of the crash with the message: YOU GAVE YOUR LIVES FOR US; every day from then on, people brought fresh flowers to put beside the plaque. Allied politicians and generals might question the soundness of the airlift idea, but the people of Berlin displayed no doubts.

The Soviet reply to the Western notes, which came on July 14, offered no apologies but blamed all the trouble in western Berlin on "errors" committed by the Western powers. It declared that the West had no "right" but merely an "opportunity" to enter Berlin, which "lies in the center of the Soviet zone and is a part of that zone." No negotiations could take place, the note said, unless they dealt with "the general question of four-power control in regard to Germany"; Berlin could not be considered separately. Commenting on the note in his diary for this day, Admiral Leahy observed that Truman had received the Soviet government's reply to a message in which the president had complained of the "error and injustice" of the Soviet command's imposition of the "virtual blockade" (as Leahy mildly called it), "which has necessitated providing the inhabitants of the American and British areas in Berlin with necessities by air transport which, up to date, has been successfully accomplished." Did the West have the willingness and the ability to defend their position by force of arms? From a purely military point of view, Admiral Leahy said, the Western powers should remove their noncombatant citizens from Berlin, reinforce their military personnel, and increase their "air-borne support of the friendly German inhabitants of their area." Though expensive and politically dangerous, Leahy said, such action would be comparatively safe for the forces in the U.S. sector of Berlin. True, it might precipitate a third world war but, the admiral noted cheerfully, it would leave the West "in an advantageous position for responsibility for starting the war." President Truman, less cheerful, told Bohlen that the Soviet note, which not only said no but said it in angry tones, amounted to a "total rejection of everything we had asked for."

That evening, moving from the international to the domestic political stage, the president took the train from Washington to Philadelphia to appear at the closing session of the Democratic convention. In his fiery acceptance speech in the wee hours of the morning, Truman talked like anything but a certain loser, declaring "Senator Barkley and I will win this election and make these Republicans like it—don't you forget that." He created a political sensation by calling Congress into special session for July 26. "My, how the opposition screams," Truman noted with satisfaction. "I'm going to attempt to make them meet their platform promises before the election." In discussing the date for the opening of the session, Truman gave currency to an idea new to almost all of the public. July 26 was "turnip day" in Missouri, he said; turnips should be sown on that day "wet or dry"; this homey reference delighted some of his followers but only exacerbated the dislike of those who saw "plain Harry" as altogether too plain. He returned to the White House at five-thirty and after three hours' sleep appeared at his desk ready for work.

Two days later the presidential picture took on new complexity as the States' Rights Democratic Party (popularly known as the Dixiecrats), made up of Southern Democrats disenchanted with Truman's views on civil rights, chose Governor Strom Thurmond of South Carolina as its nominee. On July 27, the day after Turnip Day, the odds on Truman would grow even longer when the new Progressive Party nominated Henry Wallace; Truman now faced competition from former Democrats on both the right and the left. Joseph Stalin appears to have believed that Wallace, far from being a fringe candidate who at the most would cause a measure of trouble, would in fact become the next president of the United States. The generalissimo could take great, if temporary, pleasure in Wallace's declaration that, in the interest of peace, the West should get out of Berlin.

As the airlift developed through July, one officer in Washington found himself increasingly restless, eager to get into the action in Germany. Bill Tunner, who had been appointed deputy commander of the new Military Air Transport Service, told his superior, Major General Laurence Kuter, that "if there was any air transport activity going on anywhere in the world, this activity automatically became our responsibility." Tunner wanted Kuter to propose to the Joint Chiefs that MATS become involved in the airlift right away and "all the way." That, after all, was why Congress had created MATS. Generals LeMay and Smith had outstanding records, to be sure, but air transport was a specialized field, differing from combat in every respect—in rules, methods, attitudes, procedures, results. (One thoroughly prejudiced advocate of air transport later observed that combat pilots know only that when you push the stick forward, the houses on the ground get bigger, and when you pull it back, they get smaller.) No false modesty kept Tunner from the realization that in air transport experience he outranked everybody else. He was also an innovator—in pioneering the highly successful Air Corps Ferrying Division, he had been first to see the value of women pilots.

One of five children of a solid but not well-off German immigrant family, Tunner at seventeen had won an appointment to West Point, making the highest grade on his congressman's competitive examination. In his senior year the academy gave the class a week at Mitchel Field on Long Island, where they learned something about the air corps and went up in several planes. The experience decided Tunner's future; years later he wrote, "I still remember each flight as a thrilling experience." Although Charles Lindbergh's solo transatlantic flight and other exploits of the era gave aviation the kind of glamour that would characterize space flight a half-century later, cavalrymen and other old army hands looked on the air corps as a lunatic-fringe enterprise. But to Tunner, graduating in 1928, service in the air corps offered not only the excitement of flying but extra pay. The experience of flying school only increased his enthusiasm: "I just plain loved flying," he said.

In 1932, during Tunner's early years as a pilot, the air corps established its first air transport group, an organization that became permanent in 1937, and as World War II approached, the air corps began ordering C-46s and

C-47s. In 1941 the need to deliver aircraft from American factories to Britain brought the creation of the Air Corps Ferrying Command, which became the Air Transport Command; Tunner became the third officer assigned to the new body, which faced a considerable challenge: no airplane had ever been delivered by being ferried across the ocean. By 1944 Tunner had become commanding general of the Ferrying Division of the ATC, with some 50,000 military personnel and civilians under his command, including 8,500 pilots. He then went off to the Hump, where he would make his name as the expert of experts in air transport.

All Tunner's success had not left him a man who found it congenial or even tolerable to sit on the sidelines when a great game like the one being played in Germany cried out for his contribution. As press and public were celebrating the remarkable achievements of the airlift—by mid-July combined U.S.-British daily tonnage had reached 2,250, an unimaginable figure less than three weeks earlier—Tunner the air transport efficiency expert shook his head at "some of the features of Operation Vittles which were most enthusiastically reported by the press," seeing them as "contraindications of efficient administration."

General Kuter, a veteran of high-policy circles and a one-time acting chief of the air staff, attempted to cool Tunner's ardor. "That's not the way to do it, Bill," he said. "Let's just sit tight and see what happens." This wait-and-see approach lacked any appeal for Tunner, but when the chief spoke, the deputy had little choice but to comply. Seeming to see no great urgency in the situation in Berlin, Kuter himself left Washington on a long-planned trip to inspect MATS bases in the Pacific. Tunner then tried again, pointing out to General Vandenberg, chief of the air staff, and other officers that the ATC had been designed for the very kind of job that had to be done in Berlin, and that the commanders on the spot "knew how to fly airplanes, but the organization of a transportation unit requires certain things and certain know-how."

Days passed, and nothing seemed to change. General Wedemeyer, however, kept himself in the airlift picture. Still marveling at his discovery as commander in China that "he could live by virtue of an airlift," he proposed in a message from Europe to General Vandenberg that the man who had crafted the remarkable success of the Hump operation be sent to Germany to direct this new air transport campaign. Wedemeyer conceded that General Clay disagreed: he felt that he had everybody he needed to do the job. As Wedemeyer's recommendation continued to evoke no response from the air force, it became clear that, with the airlift now functioning, Clay saw no reason to change horses, least of all to bring in a new one from across the Atlantic. Like anybody else, Clay tended to have the defects of his virtues, and along with his thoroughness, determination, and solidity came a frequent reluctance to accept outside advice, especially if it came from Washington—a reluctance that had led to his frequent declarations of his intention to resign. As for LeMay, Tunner thought he simply had no desire to see "some hot-shot come in to throw his weight around"; after all, headlines in America and Europe were proclaiming the amazing achievements of the "LeMay Coal and Feed Delivery Service." Nor could one necessarily expect Vandenberg or any other military commander in such a situation to rush a new commander across the Atlantic to supersede one of his most acclaimed officers (though it was true that LeMay had delegated the actual supervision of the operation to General Smith).

When Wedemeyer, not only an officer of intelligence and attainments but a man of remarkable charm and persuasiveness, returned from his travels he paid a call on General Vandenberg. Yet, even with all his reputation and talents, Wedemeyer did not immediately carry the day. Vandenberg felt, as Wedemeyer later said, that "any of his best officers could easily handle the matter," a view that revealed the air force chief's own failure to understand the challenges posed by air supply. Given time, any good officer could perhaps grasp the transport business, at least reasonably well, but Berlin in July 1948 hardly constituted the time and place for such an officer to begin his education. Nor would such an officer possess Tunner's carefully worked-out philosophy. Wedemeyer simply talked on, extolling Tunner— so effectively that shortly after this meeting the air force chief of staff summoned Tunner and greeted him with the words: "O.K., Bill, it's yours. When can you leave for Berlin?"

General Tunner's speculations about LeMay's negative attitude toward "hot-shots" may have been a bit less than fair. Later, recalling the situation as it stood in early July, LeMay said he had done some hard thinking when "it looked like we were going into a long-term aspect—that we were really going to have to haul gigantic tonnages in a max effort." That meant, he said, that the United States must build an even larger and more precise organization than anyone had foreseen. "That was when we yelled for Bill Tunner to come over and take the chore," LeMay said. "He was the transportation expert to end transportation experts." Indeed, "it was rather like appointing John Ringling to get the circus on the road"—the best possible move. But, LeMay commented, it took a while before Vandenberg "was prevailed upon to send Tunner to Europe."

General Vandenberg's attitude became clear at a high-level meeting on July 22. Mid-July was a period of many such meetings, with President

Truman alternating between matters of high international import and questions of party politics. On July 15, the morning Truman returned from Philadelphia after making his acceptance speech, the National Security Council formally approved the dispatch of B-29s to England, as sought by Clay and advocated by Ernest Bevin; having accepted the desirability of this move, the council deemed it wise to go ahead immediately, while the British were in a welcoming mood. Who knew how attitudes might change if the situation in Europe should worsen?

On July 19 General Marshall summed up for Truman the courses of action he saw available to the United States and its allies. The Soviet blockade of Berlin, said the secretary of state, actually offered proof of the success of American policy, which during the past year had stabilized the situation in Greece, Italy, and France; the United States must now either follow a firm policy in Berlin or see its overall European policy collapse. Marshall even seemed to believe that the West might well manage to repel a Soviet armed attack if one should come in Western Europe, though Secretary Forrestal, who was present at this meeting, pointed out that the United States could commit little more than one division to the effort.

"We'll stay in Berlin—come what may," Truman wrote in his diary. Impatient during a subsequent meeting with Forrestal, Royall, and Draper, Truman wrote, "I have to listen to a rehash of what I know already and reiterate my 'Stay in Berlin' decision." (The president also put down a testy description of another event of the day. General John J. Pershing, the most venerated U.S. military figure since his days as commander of the American Expeditionary Force in France in World War I, had died at the age of eighty-seven. Truman had gone to the funeral in the "marble amphitheater" at Arlington, "the hottest damn place this side of hell and Bolivar, Mo." This was the fifth time he had prepared to attend the long-ailing general's funeral, Truman said, and he noted with relief that "it came off this time.")

When General Clay arrived in Washington two days later, in response to a summons to discuss the situation in Berlin, he appeared reasonably optimistic. He put the chances of war as no more than one in four, he told Forrestal, and declared that "twenty good divisions" could stop the Russians at the Rhine, thus sparing France yet another invasion from the east. But the general did not take note that those twenty divisions did not exist in Europe; all the West could really call on, in case of overt war, was however many atomic bombs the United States had stored in its larder. The B-29s at British bases would serve as the tangible reminder of their existence—not because anyone would know whether this group of Superfortresses actually carried the bombs but because three years earlier B-29s had inaugurated the nuclear age. How strong an effect would this symbolism actually have? It was not easy to know. In their tweaking of the West, the Soviets had not hitherto displayed any fear of evoking a nuclear reaction.

At the July 22 meeting of the National Security Council, General Clay delivered an assessment of the importance of Berlin similar to the analysis Marshall had made for Truman three days earlier. Specifically, if the Western Allies surrendered the city, the general said, they would thereby destroy their plans for the development of western Germany. Abandoning Berlin would also hamper European economic recovery, which depended on increasing German production. As for the attitude of the Berliners themselves, Truman noted that Clay described it as "unbelievable"—they had an utter determination to stand firm regardless of the hardships they might have to endure.

The 2,400-to-2,500 daily tonnage delivered by the airlift could meet Berlin's food requirements, Clay reported, but it could not meet the need for coal; the minimum tonnage necessary to sustain Berlin without extreme hardship was 4,500, though during the remainder of the summer 3,500 might be enough. Operation Vittles was currently employing eighty C-47s and fifty-two C-54s, each of which made two round trips a day, which meant more than 250 daily planeloads arriving for Berlin. Clay now wanted more aircraft, to bring the tonnage up to 3,500; he needed 160 more C-54s, with their carrying capacity far greater than that of the C-47s.

Truman now turned to General Vandenberg. What problems would be involved in sending those additional aircraft to Germany? Answering very much as a cautious and conservative service chief mindful of established doctrine and conscious of his varied responsibilities, Vandenberg said that ordering more aircraft to Berlin would disrupt the worldwide Military Air Transport Service and would put planes at risk if hostilities broke out. The loss of these aircraft would seriously affect the ability of the United States to supply its forces and hold its bases—it would thus affect U.S. strategic warfare capability. If the United States concentrated its aircraft in Germany, it would find itself naked elsewhere if an emergency arose; as an overall commander, Vandenberg shrank from putting all of his eggs in the Berlin basket.

His answer had about it a striking echo of the reply the air force chiefs had given General Eisenhower just four years earlier when, as supreme commander of the Normandy invasion forces, he had called on the air forces to attack railroads in France to hinder German troop concentrations and transport. The air chiefs had responded that the best contribution they could make to winning the war would be to continue the great project nearest their hearts, the strategic bombing of factories, oil facilities, and other targets in the German homeland—that was their doctrine and that was their desire. Eisenhower, whose high and unique responsibilities placed him in a strong position with the U.S. and British governments, had won the day, but only after prolonged argument. Four years later, when the air force—less than a year old as an independent service—and the navy were engaged in an all-out struggle to determine their strategic roles, doctrine still dominated. Hence Vandenberg's reply (as recounted by Truman) was exactly what any observer might have expected to hear.

Vandenberg could have been chosen to be chief of the air staff on the strength of his looks alone. Hollywood handsome, with clean, lean features, he fitted the image of a flier established by Charles Lindbergh two decades earlier; a writer even spoke of him as "dashing." During World War II Vandenberg served in staff positions, taking part in the planning of the Normandy invasion. But not content to serve as a desk-bound planner, he would frequently sneak out of the office to fly as copilot, gunner, or observer on missions, coming back with notes for improvements in tactics, techniques, and discipline. In the summer of 1944, General Eisenhower gave Vandenberg command of the Ninth Air Force, the largest Allied air fleet operating against the Germans, an assignment in which he demonstrated his mastery of air-ground cooperation; the Ninth played an important part in stopping the enemy in the Battle of the Bulge. After the war Vandenberg first served as assistant army chief of staff for intelligence and in June 1946, after a somewhat desperate search by the administration ("We are unable to find any available officer of the Army other than General Vandenberg who fully meets [the] specifications," said Admiral Leahy), took over the post of director of central intelligence.

In early 1947 the general went to the air staff, and in October he became vice chief of staff of the brand-new independent U.S. Air Force under General Carl Spaatz, who had commanded strategic air operations in Europe and in the Pacific. Early in 1948 Vandenberg succeeded Spaatz in the top job. Though his long-term career did not lie in intelligence, Vandenberg had proved an able and aggressive director of the CIG and, as one of his first actions, had called for the assessment of Soviet policy. Yet curiously, in viewing the situation in Berlin, he displayed little concern for preserving the city as a listening post and contact point behind the Iron Curtain.

In objecting to building up the C-54 fleet in Germany, Vandenberg, the former intelligence director and dashing flier who now looked at matters as a conservative service chief, had in essence told the president that he did not favor the dispersal of his reserves from the center to a peripheral operation (a view that perhaps partly accounted for his reluctance to send Tunner, the MATS deputy commander, off to Germany as well). Countering this orthodox opinion, Truman cut to the heart of the matter. What, indeed, was peripheral? The West was going to do its best to supply Berlin—that was the fact. Would the air force chief of staff prefer to see the task carried out by ground convoy? Russian resistance to that effort would certainly mean war, and war would require the air force "to contribute its share to the defense of the nation." The airlift, Truman said, involved less risk, and therefore the air force must give this effort the fullest possible support.

After a private conversation with Truman, General Clay later wrote, he left the president's office "inspired by the understanding and confidence I received from him." But, for all that, the airlift raised far more questions than it provided answers. It was not only General Marshall who felt that time was on the side of the Russians. So the Russians themselves believed. So the people of Berlin feared.

CHAPTER 17

"We Stand Here on the Soil"

DURING HIS FIRST evening in Germany, Bill Tunner decided he knew just how he stood with his superiors. Having arrived in Wiesbaden after office hours on July 29, he immediately headed for General LeMay's residence, a mansion with 102 rooms (greatly impressed, Tunner gave it credit for only fifty-five) and a staff of fifteen; the former home of a champagne magnate, it was the most elegant of the eight hundred houses that had been requisitioned for the use of air force families. LeMay, who customarily spoke tersely and rarely raised his voice, proved to be no chattier than usual on this occasion. He showed no sign of rancor, Tunner noted, but "he was very cold. He said, 'Well, you'd better get started.' So I said, 'Tell Smith I'm here and taking over.' " LeMay told Tunner that he was expected to produce, and added a short "Good-bye." Essentially, Tunner felt, he had been ordered by higher authority to come to Germany and run the airlift, and both he and LeMay, as veteran officers, accepted the fact at face value and let it go at that.

On leaving LeMay's mansion with its antique furniture and its paintings and Oriental rugs, Tunner sought out his own quarters, which turned out to be a single room, a third-floor walkup in a hotel overlooking a block of burned-out buildings. When he opened the door, Tunner found himself in the bathroom; he could get into the room itself only by squeezing between the bathtub and the toilet. "It was pretty obvious," he commented wryly, "that I was in Germany at the command of General Vandenberg, not at the request of anyone in Europe."

Yet LeMay or anybody else who took a look could see that the airlift had already become a giant, dwarfing the rest of the mission of the U.S. Air Forces in Europe. USAFE, created as an occupying force, operated at the leisurely pace characteristic of such forces throughout history; as Tunner commented, "You can occupy by sitting on your butt." They "flew a little bit for fun, and there was a great deal of scrounging." But after June 26 men and material began "to be sucked up precisely as if a giant vacuum cleaner had passed over the depots and airfields." In the first two weeks the demands of the airlift had consumed a normal six-month stock of windshield wipers. Next to go into short supply were propellers and engines; on one particular day MATS flew seven engines and eighteen tires over from the United States, but such efforts still could not build up a reserve supply of either. Aviation gasoline, which came down to Frankfurt in railroad tank cars from Bremerhaven, went to work immediately on arrival. At one point in July, the authorities had to divert three fuel tankers on the high seas to keep the whole airlift from being grounded. By the end of June, the airlift appeared to have established itself as a going concern, although a variety of problems persisted. Having become officially a transport service, with the designation of task force, the airlift would take on almost independent status, like a business with its own highly experienced—and thoroughly self-assured—general manager.

Anybody who had witnessed Bill Tunner's arrival in India in 1944 would have known what to expect when he came to Germany. As his first move in his Hump assignment, he had personally taken a plane over the mountains to see for himself the conditions his pilots faced—in many ways a foolhardy move for a newcomer unfamiliar with the weather and the forbidding corridors through the towering Himalayas. What had first caught Tunner's eye on takeoff were black blotches on the runway, each a somber reminder that a plane had crash-landed there and burned; he realized on the spot the double nature of his mission: get the cargo through and reduce the accident rate. The new commander set to work, concentrating on organization and morale, seeing that the crews wore fresh clothing and cleaned up their quarters, getting them better food, and insisting on military discipline. He tightened procedures in large and small matters, especially putting maintenance and repairs on a precisely organized and scheduled basis. Though Tunner's approach at first drew the expected complaints from some of the crews, on Christmas Eve the men of the command, not acting on any special orders, set a new record with eighty-one trips over the mountains. In a letter to the general, they told him, "We did it as a Christmas present."

Having quickly rounded up a top echelon of fellow Hump veterans and other associates who had various kinds of expert knowledge, Tunner had left Washington almost immediately after his meeting with General Vandenberg. As he recalled it, "I took twenty people I knew, loaded up a C-54, and we took off just as fast as we could." (Vandenberg, fully cooperative, had simply told him, "Don't denude the outfit.") Like everybody else, Tunner did not expect the airlift to become a long-lived affair—he left his car parked outside the office and told his housekeeper he would be back home in ninety days. A widower, he assured his children that he would return in time to put them in school.

The team Tunner took with him to Germany included, as chief of staff, Colonel Theodore Milton, a young officer who had not served in the Hump operation but had commanded a B-17 group in Europe. Milton had last seen Germany from 25,000 feet up in the great and deadly August 1943 coordinated Schweinfurt-Regensburg raid (his group made up part of the Regensburg force, commanded by then–Colonel Curtis LeMay, who got his planes over the target on time because he had insisted that his men learn blind flying in order to cope with bad weather; other commanders had not displayed such foresight and drive). The foremost Hump veteran accompanying Tunner was a prewar friend, Colonel Red Forman, who would serve as operations chief. The party also included another associate from prewar days, Katie Gibson, who was "most proficient and intelligent, not to mention independent" and who served with Tunner at home and abroad, "whenever it was possible for me to have a secretary." On the flight across the Atlantic, these and the other members of the group engaged in what amounted to an almost continuous staff meeting, with Tunner outlining each person's duties. Before the flight ended, the general said, "we were even writing directives there on the plane. Miss Katie filled her notebook with shorthand."

On the morning after his bare-bones interview with General LeMay, Tunner and his staff went to take a look at the building assigned to them as headquarters for the airlift task force. A war-battered apartment house, it had filthy walls, floors covered with debris, no furniture, and no telephones. While one officer went off to forage for desks and chairs and another arranged for telephones and teletypes, a "fresh-faced airman" arrived to tell everybody to appear at the adjutant's office that afternoon to pick up PX and commissary cards. This seemingly innocuous mission triggered something of an explosion in Tunner. "We came here to work," he declared to his staff. "I'm not asking you men to put in twenty-four hours a day, but dammit, if I can do eighteen hours a day, you can do fifteen. We didn't come to Germany to go shopping at the PX or the commissary, so I think we can just skip that little ceremony this afternoon." The members of his team of course had known this without being told, he later said, but he wanted to put his point of view on the record. While the staff officers were waiting for desks and phones, he dispatched them not to the PX but to the local air bases, so that they could start learning the details of the situation.

Tunner's own first look at the operation confirmed the doubts he had developed while still in Washington. This apostle of order and planning and scientific management saw "a real cowboy operation," with neither flight crews nor ground crews working to established schedules. After watching the comings and goings at the Wiesbaden airfield, Tunner hopped a plane for the hour-and-a-half flight to Berlin, where he found a similar scene—"confusion everywhere"—probably the most derogatory description this particular observer could have fashioned. Pilots, a dozen of them at a time, crowded around the Tempelhof operations desk, waiting for clearance. In the snack bar next door, more pilots and other crew members, talking and laughing, occupied themselves with coffee and doughnuts. Observing this scene, Tunner spent no time admiring the spirit and spontaneity of the young aircrews whose feats were amazing the whole world. Instead, he wondered how the crews could get their planes in the air on time. A quick check of the records showed that they frequently did not.

The airlift in its first month had brought together people with all kinds of skills from around the world: mechanics from MATS shops, technicians from air force bases in both hemispheres. "Thanks to their genius for improvisation," wrote a reporter describing the first weeks of the airlift, "what began as a haphazard nine-day wonder—a 'serum-to-Nome' proposition—swiftly took form as the most brilliant single air operation of our times." But, utterly unmoved by all the glamour and excitement, the new director of the airlift quickly decided that the operation owed its effectiveness thus far simply to its newness—the fact that it had just started. The commanders had picked up planes from every base and had done the same thing with the people, taking officers away from their desks so that "administration practically stopped in all of USAFE." Officers would "get a couple of days on the Berlin Airlift and back to their desks. Maintenance people were swiped from the different squadrons." The operation could not have lasted more than a month longer, Tunner concluded; as one of its major flaws, it was failing to make progress. "They were all working like hell"—idleness hardly constituted the problem—and everyone was exhausted. General Smith was attempting to run the operation with a staff of only three or four; that, Tunner declared, was impossible. He called the airlift he saw in his first days "just a hodge-podge, put together outfit."

Tunner's Berlin round trip took him on the standard triangular course: along the southern—American—corridor from the zonal boundary opposite Frankfurt to Tempelhof, then westward on the outbound corridor shared by the Allies, and down the third leg back to the Frankfurt area. As he flew along these courses, a number of navigational points struck him. The U.S. corridor was not only much longer than the others, but included a line of mountains—"just a pretty green foothill compared to the Himalayas," but still requiring his plane to climb to 5,000 feet—whereas the others covered flat country.

The air space over Berlin loomed as dangerously claustrophobic, in contrast to the situation that had prevailed in the Hump operation, in which

Tunner's aircraft operated from thirteen bases in India and flew into six bases in China, while having "practically all of Southeast Asia to maneuver in." In Berlin the airlift had the use of only two landing fields, Tempelhof in the U.S. sector and Gatow about ten miles due west in the British sector. These fields lay amidst what Tunner called a "checkerboard" of Russian air bases. British flights coming into Gatow had to make sharp right turns to avoid Soviet fighters operating from Schönwalde, which sat in the mouth of the corridor from Hamburg; American planes headed for Tempelhof flew within four miles of Johannisthal, another Soviet base. Planes delayed in landing had only the area above Tempelhof and Gatow in which to maneuver. Air controllers assigned specific altitudes to inbound and outbound flights, but even so, Tunner was told, the operation had seen a number of near misses. "For a mass air operation of the present scale," the general commented to an interviewer, "the Berlin airspace presents the trickiest traffic problem that aviation has yet produced."

Just as Tunner and his team arrived in Germany, Gatow was beginning to undergo a transformation. Originally a Luftwaffe training field, this airport had grass runways and ten good-sized hangars but no other facilities for handling large planes. Until the spring of 1948, it saw light duty, with only a small number of flights a day by RAF Dakotas and fighter aircraft using a new steel-plate strip, which did not sit firmly on the sandy Brandenburg soil; its concrete replacement had not yet been completed when the blockade began. Following the Allied decision to mount the airlift, the Royal Engineers rushed this job through during July and then proceeded, together with the RAF Airfield Construction Wing, to prepare Gatow for unprecedentedly heavy traffic by renovating and extending the steel-plate runway and building an asphalt-surfaced 74,000-square-meter offloading apron and other facilities.

Back in Wiesbaden that first evening, Tunner summoned his staff for a nine o'clock meeting. The staff members, who had spent the day doing their own exploring, came in "full of observations and suggestions." Maintenance loomed as the first big question, since, as Tunner put it, "airplanes require constant maintenance" and the existing situation could not continue; routine maintenance must be separated from major checks and overhauls. A central depot must be set up, perhaps at the World War II air force facility at Burtonwood, England; routine maintenance must be speeded up, with less time being lost in the repair docks. Secondly, the frequency of flights must be stepped up. Perhaps before long the Americans could mount some flights from the British bases, which were much closer to Berlin; "two planes based at Fassberg," said Tunner, "could do the work of three based at Rhein-Main." The aim, very simply, was to produce maximum ton-miles per airplane.

In transforming the airlift into a transport operation, Tunner would bring in or develop "highly experienced communicators, highly experienced loaders as well as crews." His description of these crews summed up much of his philosophy and approach: "unlike tactical crews"—regular air force pilots—they would "fly exact speed and exact altitudes and do exactly what they were told on departures and takeoffs, landings." His fliers were "highly skilled men who were accustomed to carrying our most precious commodity, people, around the world, not bombs." Tunner would bring to Germany as many such men as he could get, as quickly as he could get them.

Reacting to what he had seen at the operations desk and in the snack bar, Tunner took several direct steps to cut turnaround time at Tempelhof. On just his third day in Germany, he issued an order requiring pilots and other crew members to stay by their aircraft after landing instead of strolling into the terminal. An unloading crew would appear immediately to begin work; an operations officer would come speeding up in a jeep to take care of necessary paperwork, followed by a weather officer in another jeep. Then would come what would prove to be the most popular jeep of all—a rolling snack bar staffed by "some of the most beautiful girls in Berlin," supplied by the German Red Cross, to pass out the coffee and doughnuts. These measures slashed the turnaround time of a plane to just thirty minutes.

The concentration on maximizing ton-miles, the rationalizing and streamlining of maintenance procedures (taking them far away from the personalized craftsman's workshop of Pfc. Jim Harrison with his friends *Bozo* and *Mary Lou*), the tightening of scheduling, careful checking of airspeed indicators—all these served to produce the essence that distinguished the airlift from any other air operation in the world. The general sought to "get the entire procedure down to a steady, even rhythm, with scores of airplanes doing exactly the same thing all the time, day and night, at the same persistent beat." Beat—that was the key word. "It is this beat," wrote Tunner, "this precise rhythmical cadence, which determines the success of the airlift." He personally lacked much of a natural sense of rhythm, he said, but rhythm constituted the essential characteristic of the airlift. Instead of romance and flying heroics, it must be marked by a cadence as sustained "as the thunder of jungle drums."

Berliners who would never know General Tunner personally or hear him discuss his plans soon intuitively understood his guiding idea. "Our apartment was in Britz, just a few miles south of the airport," said Karin Hueckstaedt, "and I remember a plane came in every three minutes. They turned and came in over Neukölln, and it was terrible because they had to go between houses to land. And, you know, if an airplane or two didn't come you actually woke up because something was missing. You knew something was wrong. The noise of the planes didn't bother us at all. As a matter of fact, we felt secure. As long as we heard those planes flying, we felt like everything was all right. But I remember waking up sometimes and thinking something was wrong. There was no plane."

"There was noise all of the time in the air," Alice Sawadda said, "and we were glad to hear it. Always, if you looked to the sky, you saw many planes." Like Karin, she would wake up if the noise stopped. "The number of planes in the air from which help came is the most memorable picture for me—the feeling that thank God, they are still there." Uwe von Tschammer, who was just ten years old during the airlift, recalled one night when the noise stopped: "Nobody heard anything, so the neighbors started asking each other what was going to happen. Then somebody came in and told us not to worry. The planes were flying in the other way because the wind had changed."

But few human activities enjoy unqualified applause. Charlotte Beelitz, though herself hardly able to believe in the possibility of such a marvelous feat as the airlift, worked with two men who declared that the only negative feature of the airlift was the noise from planes landing and taking off right over their heads. "We don't have a single silent moment," they would say. "Our chairs that we sit in constantly shake because of the planes." Charlotte, however, made the key point: "We had to stand this or otherwise we would starve."

Tunner established the three-minute rhythm at the outset of his command, even though he did not have enough planes to maintain this schedule around the clock. When he had the needed people and planes, his crews would be ready; he chose three minutes as the time most efficiently fitting the existing control equipment. On a twenty-four-hour basis, this schedule would produce 480 landings at Tempelhof and the corresponding 480 takeoffs; thus a plane would be coming or going every ninety seconds. A crash would of course produce the kind of gap spoken of by Karin Hueck-staedt, but a far more common situation—serious weather problems—could also cause a break in the beat. Seeking as much as possible to remove changing weather patterns as a concern for the pilots, Tunner attempted to defeat the rain, clouds, and fog by ordering his crews to follow only instrument flight rules regardless of the weather. On a rainy, nasty day in August, circling over Berlin, the general created another rule: If a plane missed its landing, whatever the reason, it was not to make another pass but was to fly straight on out, then down to Frankfurt, get in line, and return to Berlin.

On this particular August day—it happened to be Friday the 13th—

the general had flown to Berlin for an unusual occasion. The weather, unpleasant but still acceptable at Wiesbaden, turned into heavy clouds as Tunner's C-54 climbed to clear the mountains; ahead and behind the plane stretched a line of Skymasters, separated by neat three-minute spaces, each doing 170 miles an hour. As they approached the Berlin area, the ceiling over Tempelhof dropped like a collapsed tent. In just a few minutes the clouds were squatting on the roofs of the towering apartment buildings forming the avenue to the airport; rain squalls wiped out any view of the runway from the tower, and even the radar turned blind. Desperately the controllers began to stack up the incoming planes—a new arrival every three minutes; soon the stack reached a height of 12,000 feet. Lost in the fog and gloom, pilots called desperately for bearings. Later the general learned that one C-54 had overshot the runway, crashed into a ditch, and burst into flames; another, by hard braking, had managed to avoid smashing into the wreck, escaping with two burst tires; a third had tried to land on an auxiliary runway under construction and had sloshed its way into a ground loop. Planes ready to take off on the three-minute principle had to hold their places to avoid colliding with the madding cloud of aircraft overhead.

As his C-54 moved into the 8,000-foot slot assigned to it, Tunner felt his frustration turning to fury. "This is a hell of a way to run a railroad!" he burst out to his pilot and copilot, both Hump veterans. They "wisely said nothing"; at that moment, the general said later, "I'd have snapped my grandmother's head off." The flight organization had displayed a basic flaw: the personnel in the tower and the ground-control-approach operators had not been able to stay on top of the situation. Remarkably, no midair collisions had occurred yet, but God alone knew why, with the stacked-up planes squeezed into the tight box over the city, unable to extend their circling into any of the Soviet-controlled air space outside the urban island.

As commander of the entire operation, Tunner took immediate action. Seizing the microphone, he ordered the tower to send every one of the circling aircraft back to its home base. It was simple—the planes either had to land or they had to leave. A puzzled voice from the tower said, "Please repeat." Tunner repeated emphatically, making it clear that he was the commander and at the same time making it clear that his plane was the exception—he would be landing at Tempelhof. Once on the ground, he suspended traffic for three hours while he drilled the operators in their procedures. At noon flights resumed, and even after all the confusion and delay, the lift managed to deliver 1,300 tons that day. But Tunner assigned his operations chief, Red Forman, and another officer to stay in Berlin until they devised ways to make sure "this mess" could never happen again. Tunner's chief operational contribution was his decision to allow one landing attempt per plane only; Tempelhof and the tempo of the operation had no space or time to spare. The general lamented that "air-traffic control, at which the wartime air forces had no peer in the world, had become a lost art in the peacetime military establishment." That same day he sent General Kuter in Washington a direct teletype call for help. The MATS chief responded so quickly and effectively that within only four days twenty civilian air controllers, all reservists with World War II experience, found themselves rushed back into uniform and aboard an airplane crossing the Atlantic.

The timing of "Black Friday," as Tunner and his staff labeled August 13, would in most eyes have excused a far worse burst of temper than the general displayed, because he had come to Berlin to attend a special celebration of the efficiency and the effectiveness of the airlift. In an action emblematic of the growing spirit of the Berliners, an elderly German had declared his desire to donate a gold watch—his only valuable possession and a family treasure with associations going back to his great-grandfather—to the men of the airlift. To take full advantage of this public relations opportunity, Tunner had flown to Berlin to make the presentation personally to the pilot who, to that point, had flown the highest number of missions. But as the dignitaries on the ground marked time and tried to stay dry, the commander of the airlift "was flying around in circles over their heads. It was damned embarrassing."

While General Tunner concerned himself with technical problems and deficiencies, many Berliners saw the airlift in a profoundly emotional way. A remarkable intensity of feeling suffused a letter that came the office of the Tempelhof air base commander and was preserved by the commander's secretary. "Yesterday afternoon I have been standing for awhile on the Railroad Station, Tempelhof," said the writer, who declared himself "an inhabitant of the Russian Sector of Berlin"; he had been "watching the coming and going of the two and four motor airplanes. Everytime when one of the big planes appeared on the western horizon and started to land there was a light in the faces of the people. Probably you can't imagine what every single plane means to us people, who are strictly separated from the western sectors because of the will of our occupation forces. We could shout with joy when at night the big birds fly back to the Bizone in order to get new supplies for Berlin." The writer wanted the base commander to give the fliers the personal thanks of the people in the Soviet sector, who, like many in western Berlin, listened "with great joy to the noise their planes are making." He even suggested that the planes "fly a little further sometimes so that in our sector the people will know too: 'The Western Powers don't let us down.'"

It was not "our fault that we in the Russian Sector and Russian Zone got this government and not another one," wrote the Berliner. "Is it our fault that they will not grant us the smallest rights? What did we do that we cannot dare to say a word on the street because spies are watching and listening everywhere; maybe your best friend is only a spy? What did we do that people disappear from the streets forever; that we are not able to visit our friends in the Western parts of Germany, nor to talk of visits to foreign countries; that our letters and telephone conversations are controlled?" The writer asked the Americans to remember that "the inhabitants of the Russian zone are happy about each plane, which in spite of all SED propaganda brings food for a sieged city, which is not a fortress but a helpless heap of stones. We stand here on the soil, which is going to be 'Democracy,' but right now is nothing but the worst terror."

The writer requested anonymity, "because the Russian secret service is quick on hand if it means to let someone disappear forever."

Bedell Smith had not expected that summer would see him still U.S. ambassador in Moscow. In January, General Marshall had announced that on July 1 the U.S. administration in Germany would switch over from military to civilian control, with the State Department replacing the army. To succeed Clay as U.S. proconsul, in this new climate, Marshall had tapped Smith, one of his favorites. On March 8 Smith had written Clay, "Much against my inclination, and, indeed, against my better judgment, I have agreed to take the German assignment under the State Dept. when you leave." General Marshall, he said "finally put the thing in such a personal way that I could not refuse although the prospect seems very gloomy to me." Smith made one reason for his gloom quite plain: "I doubt if even you could have very easy sailing with the personnel the State Dept. is likely to provide." Smith felt so certain of the coming change that he asked Clay for a plane ride to Washington and back in April, and he wanted to use Clay's guest house as temporary quarters.

The rising tensions in Berlin and then the blockade itself, however, had changed General Marshall's plans. On March 23, following Marshal Sokolovsky's walkout from the Allied Control Council, Secretary Royall and General Bradley told Clay that military government was going to remain in charge of the occupation, "in view of the many changes in the international situation the last sixty days." Bradley later wrote Clay that he hated to ask him to stay on till the end of the calendar year but that they could hope for "a lull in this cold war sometime this fall and winter" that would permit the sending of a successor. In his reply, Clay suggested that his departure should be timed to accord with the establishment of a German provisional government, which should bring a period of stability if it was accomplished "without precipitating a Soviet crisis." Early 1949 seemed likely. Accepting this idea, Bradley wrote back on June 8 that he hoped Clay's plans would not be thwarted by any "further crises with the Russians." Before Clay had received the letter, the Soviets, as part of the salami-slicing procedure, had cut off bus traffic between the Soviet and Western zones. Further crises were indeed at hand.

Thus, still at his post in Moscow, Bedell Smith would now have a prominent part to play in the diplomacy of the airlift. What had quickly become by far the greatest air cargo operation ever seen was buying time for the West during July—as everyone agreed with varying degrees of faith— but no one knew how long this purchasing act could last. Sooner or later, it seemed obvious, the Berlin situation would have to find resolution in a Western withdrawal, a Soviet lifting of the blockade, or war—but the Western leaders had made no long-range decision. "Like presidents before and since," Truman "would take matters one day at a time and hope for the best."

Following the harsh Soviet note of July 14, which denied the West any legitimacy in Berlin, the Western powers found themselves looking for a next step to take. Feeling that "the Politburo" had not resolved on war and had not committed itself so irretrievably to maintaining the blockade that "some face-saving retreat on their part" would not be possible, the State Department launched the second phase of postblockade diplomacy by dispatching Chip Bohlen to Europe to coordinate action with the British and the French; Truman wished to bypass the fruitless note-writing stage of negotiations and make a direct approach to Stalin. Bohlen flew to Germany with Clay, who was returning to his post after his sessions in Washington (and was almost immobilized with an attack of lumbago). The two were joined in Berlin by Smith, who flew in from Moscow, and Ambassador Lewis Douglas, from London. After preliminary talks Bohlen and the two ambassadors went on to London to meet with René Massigli and Ernest Bevin.

Sounding less militant than he had appeared just three weeks earlier, the foreign secretary at one point turned to Bohlen, saying in the kind of half-joking way that can reveal deep feeling behind the laugh: "I know all of you Americans want a war, but I'm not going to let you have it." The remark startled Bohlen. The only ground he could imagine for Bevin's having such an idea was Clay's earlier proposal for sending an armored convoy to Berlin—an idea predicated on the general's belief that it would *not* lead to an armed clash. In any case, such a contingency was one any commander would consider, if only to discard it, and the suggestion had won no support in the Pentagon or the White House. The British government knew that perfectly well.

A few days before Bohlen's departure for London, Marshall had dismissed a British draft of a possible Allied note to Moscow as "redolent with appeasement." Bevin explained to Douglas, however, that he simply did not favor Truman's "oral" approach, which took the negotiations out of the hands of the foreign ministers. The Americans, on the other hand, wanted to make an oral approach because it could leave unsaid points that would have had to appear in a written note. In this phase of postwar history, many leading British officials liked to console themselves for the decline of their country's power by playing the game of British Greeks (weak but wily) versus American Romans (stupid but strong). Now it seemed that "the Americans were generally wrong on the big issues," partly because they had "no machine for working out long term plans"; it was therefore up to the British to take the initiative.

On July 22, after the foreign secretary returned from a meeting in The Hague of the foreign ministers of the five Brussels Pact countries, State Department officials sensed "a definite weakening" in his outlook, as if timorous Continentals had further influenced him. It was true that in discussing the issue with the French, Bevin was talking with people who tended to believe that because productive negotiations were desirable, they were therefore possible. Apart from any Continental influence, Bevin had to beat off attacks, often bitter, from the left wing of his own party. He had also had discussions with General Robertson, in from the front, who, though not arguing for Allied evacuation of Berlin, nevertheless maintained that since the airlift was "not practicable" for winter, the Allies should use the brief time it could buy to seek agreement with the Russians on a four-power administration for all of Germany with its headquarters in Berlin. Essentially, the general seemed to believe that the Russians might actually undergo a change of heart whereby they would lift the blockade in exchange for a united, anti-Soviet Germany. Bevin, softening or not, could not agree. One obvious point against Robertson's view was that if the airlift seemed "not practicable" to the general (and indeed to many other Allied officials), it would also seem impracticable to the Russians; they would see no reason to pay a high price for the pears instead of merely waiting for them to fall from the tree later in the year.

Yet the Allies had to try negotiation of one sort or another. "The United States had no expectation that negotiations in Moscow would be productive," in the view of an American diplomat, "but two factors induced agreement to that course of action. One was the need to meet the French and British insistence on that procedure. The other factor seems to have been to prepare for ultimate resort to the United Nations"—a move the

British and French abhorred. During these discussions the cabinet of French Premier Robert Schuman resigned, being succeeded on July 26 by a government led by André Marie, who would serve as premier only seven weeks. Such instability provoked fearful memories of the Third Republic, but the change of government produced an important bonus. Instead of leaving the scene, Schuman replaced Georges Bidault at the Quai d'Orsay, the foreign ministry; thus this sad-faced but forward-looking statesman came to the position in which he would make unrivaled contributions to Franco-German reconciliation.

Despite all the undercurrents swirling around the sessions of the London Committee, Bohlen managed to shepherd his charges to an agreement under which the Western ambassadors in Moscow, led by Smith as the senior envoy, would ask for a meeting with Stalin. Smith actually held enhanced senior status, since the French had just sent a new ambassador to Moscow, Yves Chataigneau (who had the distinction of wearing the U.S. Distinguished Service Cross, won as the result of his outstanding service as liaison with the American forces in World War I), and sickness kept the British ambassador, Sir Maurice Peterson, in England; Bevin replaced him for the occasion with his own private secretary, Frank Roberts, the able former chargé (later minister) in Moscow who had been George Kennan's close colleague.

The complexity of the national and personal motives that had led to this new démarche in Moscow did not imply anything less than firm determination on the part of the three Western representatives to produce results if any such possibility existed. They began their efforts by telephoning for an appointment with Molotov, at which they would hand him an aide-mémoire intended to serve as the general reply to the Soviet note of July 14 and thus as the starting point for conversations. But Molotov, the ambassadors were told, was on vacation; Andrei Vyshinsky, the foreign minister's chief deputy, was also away, attending a conference in Belgrade (an extremely hot spot from the Soviet point of view). Molotov's principal secretary, V. I. Erofeev, suggested that the ambassadors meet with Valerian Zorin, a junior deputy foreign minister (though by no means a clerk—in February he had been the Kremlin's man on the spot during the coup in Prague). "I pointed out," said Smith, "that the matter on which we asked to see Mr. Molotov was of great importance and I asked if the Foreign Minister might be available within a few days." He would try to find out, Erofeev said, and later that same day telephoned Smith to report that Molotov had just begun his vacation and would therefore not be available; the ambassadors would have to see Zorin.

Not unduly downcast at what he took to be Molotov's substitution of the diplomatic "vacation" for the traditional diplomatic cold—he and his colleagues felt sure the foreign minister had gone no farther afield than his nearby dacha and simply wanted to see what the game was before committing himself to taking part in it—Bedell Smith presented himself at Zorin's office at six o'clock on the evening of July 30. On this same day, as it happened, General Tunner took charge on the U.S. front line of this battle and began transforming the airlift into a professional operation. Handing over the memorandum to Zorin, Smith expressed the desire of the three Western representatives "to discuss the situation in Berlin and its wide implications" in a face-to-face meeting with Stalin and Molotov.

The exercise had as its object a direct talk with Stalin, but this would only come about by way of Molotov. Zorin, however, seemed to see no point in any such meeting—his government had made its position clear in its July 14 note—but he agreed to pass the request along. Since the Allies had not come with an ultimatum but instead might well be looking for an opening to talk their way out of their Berlin dilemma, Molotov surprised nobody by immediately managing to interrupt his holiday; the next day his office informed the ambassadors that separate appointments had been made for that same evening for each of the envoys—Smith came first, at seven o'clock. In that meeting Molotov tried to elicit from Smith what "wider questions" (as the Allied aide-mémoire had put it) the West was prepared to discuss; the ambassador did his best to avoid any substantive discussion and pushed for the meeting with Stalin, which Molotov said he "hoped" would come about—wording that meant the meeting would indeed take place.

CHAPTER 18

On Kremlin Evenings

TRUE TO HIS custom, Joseph Stalin received the Western ambassadors in an evening meeting, this one at nine o'clock on August 2, the Monday following their conversations with the foreign minister. When the generalissimo greeted his callers with the affability he often brought to such occasions, Bedell Smith thought this good humor needed little explanation, since Stalin seemed to have "confronted us with the flat alternative of getting out of Berlin in ignominious defeat or of staying on under sufferance and abandoning our announced plan of setting up a separate government for Western Germany." Taking a deeply skeptical view of the airlift and its capabilities, which had rapidly become the conventional wisdom, the U.S. ambassador privately doubted whether this effort could continue meeting the needs of Berlin, particularly during the winter months. But the Allies nevertheless held a few good cards, he thought: General Clay was a master of logistics, and the Berliners seemed to be in the fight to the finish. Smith had little reason at the time to know much about a forty-three-year-old major general who specialized in hauling people and goods by air.

During the bulk of the ensuing conversation, the different aims of the Allies and the Soviets continually recurred in various forms. The ambassadors wanted to bring about the end of the blockade; Stalin and Molotov wanted to deal with Germany overall before discussing any other question. As previously agreed by the Western governments, Smith, as the leading spokesman, declared the Allies' right to their presence in Berlin "unquestionable and absolute"; they could not be coerced "by any means whatsoever" into abandoning it. The Soviet government had no need to impose the restrictions on communications, the ambassador declared, if its purpose was to affect the currency situation in Berlin or to bring about four-power negotiations; the Western powers always stood ready to discuss questions relating to Germany. If, however, the Soviets intended by the restrictions to drive the West from Berlin, then they could not be allowed to succeed. Then

Smith called on Stalin: What did the generalissimo have to say about these points?

As the result of their creation of a "separate state" in Germany, Stalin replied, the Western powers had lost the juridical basis of their right to maintain forces in Berlin; if two separate states existed in Germany, one with Frankfurt (as Stalin seemed to expect) as its capital, then Berlin could not be the capital of the whole of the country. Nevertheless, the Soviet government had no intention of forcing Allied troops from Berlin; he had simply wanted, Stalin said, to put Soviet juridical thinking on the record. He added, surprisingly, "After all, we are still allies." As for the restrictive transport measures—the blockade—they represented an attempt to defend the Soviet zone from economic disruption caused by the currency reform and the introduction of the Western mark into Berlin, which sat in the middle of the Soviet zone. Behind the currency question loomed the London program, authorizing the establishment of the German Federal Republic. If they could settle the most acute questions concerning Berlin, Stalin asked, were the ambassadors prepared to deal with Germany as a whole?

Smith explained that the steps being taken toward a German government in the Western zones were not exclusive but could be fitted into a central German government whenever the four powers could produce an agreement. He saw two "artificial conditions" exerting pressure on the powers—on one side, the Berlin currency, and on the other, the interruption of communications. He urged the simultaneous announcement of the resumption of negotiations on Berlin and four-power discussions of other problems concerning Germany, together with lifting of the blockade (which, in the discussions, was never actually called a blockade). He would then recommend, Smith said, an immediate solution of the artificial currency problem.

Stalin offered a two-part proposal: (a) the Soviets would lift the transport restrictions while the West removed the B-mark (Berlin mark), which would be replaced by the Russian zone Ostmark; (b) the moves toward setting up the new government in western Germany would be suspended pending the convening of a four-power meeting to deal with all fundamental German questions. Could the blockade be lifted, Smith asked, if the Allies withdrew the B-mark and promised to take part in talks on the overall German question? No, Stalin said, the promise could not serve as the key; the key would be the actual suspension of developments in western Germany. Smith could hardly agree to this proviso, with all the opportunities it offered for delay and dilution in western Germany—he would in effect be swapping the developing German government for the lifting of the blockade; he merely said in reply that he thought "implementation of the London decisions had reached a point at which it would be extremely difficult to hold it up."

As the hours passed, and not in an unfriendly atmosphere, the discussion went around and around these points, with the ambassadors declaring that the blockade had no justification if it was supposed to be related to the currency problem and also pointing out that technical experts had to be called in on such questions. Chataigneau expressed his hope for some form of agreement that would lead to future discussions, and all three Western representatives let Molotov know that they found the results of the meeting disappointing.

Stalin finally leaned back in his chair, pulled a cigarette from his pocket and lit it, and said, smiling: "Would you like to settle the matter tonight?"

He would like nothing better, Smith answered immediately.

"I can meet you on this proposal," Stalin said. "There should be a simultaneous introduction in Berlin of the Soviet zone Deutsche mark in place of the Western B-mark, together with a removal of all transport restrictions." The generalissimo then modified his previous proposal, saying that "while the Soviet Government will no longer ask as a condition the deferment of the implementation of the London decisions for setting up a Western government in Germany, this should be recorded as the insistent wish of the Soviet Government."

Smith was elated, and his British and French colleagues likewise acclaimed the great news. Next morning the U.S. ambassador followed up his initial report to Washington with a glowing message in which he described Stalin's and Molotov's eagerness for a settlement and commented on the foreign minister's striking cordiality, though he did not believe this behavior meant in any way that Soviet objectives in Germany had changed. Chip Bohlen, who now chaired an ad hoc State Department committee called the Berlin Group, shared Smith's pleasure, telling colleagues in Washington that, in his view, the Soviet fiasco with Marshal Tito, the success of the airlift, and other factors had greatly changed Russian attitudes. Even after years of rise-and-fall dealings with the Kremlin, it seemed, such an old Soviet hand as Bohlen could still be carried away by soft words from its master and reported smiles from its foreign minister. He may for the moment have forgotten Molotov's landmark obstructionism at the first meeting of the Council of Foreign Ministers, three years earlier, or a memorable confrontation between the British and Soviet foreign ministers one evening at the second session of the group the following summer, when the hulking Bevin, after hoisting a few dinnertime drinks, responded to a run of Molotov sarcasms by getting up from his seat, clenching his fists, and starting toward the almost implausibly tiny (five-foot-four) Russian, saying, "I've had enough of this, I 'ave!'"; security officers had quickly moved in. Bohlen did, however, advise Marshall and other State Department officials to be leery of agreeing to any suspension of the measures for western German government, and he warned that Stalin's objectives remained unchanged.

In London the Foreign Office definitely favored pursuit of the conversations in Moscow, but one of its officials told René Massigli that his government would not favor the kind of negotiation under compulsion represented by linking the withdrawal of the B-mark to the raising of the blockade. As for Smith, his euphoria led him to express his regret that he had failed to take advantage of such a promising moment to obtain from Stalin a guarantee of future access to Berlin. He suggested to Marshall that such a demand become part of an American acceptance of Stalin's proposal, though, he acknowledged, "it will be harder to negotiate with Molotov alone." But that, indeed, was the task to which the Western ambassadors now had to turn. Stalin's brief proposal had to be fitted out with specific details—and that, as everybody knew, was where the devil dwelled.

When the Americans took over Tempelhof as their Berlin air base, they had worked one special transformation. A great black Nazi eagle with a white swastika on its breast had stood above the main entrance of the elegant terminal building, which had served as an important center of operations for Hermann Göring's Luftwaffe. Resisting a natural impulse, the Americans did not pull the eagle down; instead, they naturalized it, removing the swastika and replacing it with an American striped shield. They completed the process by applying white paint to the bird's head, giving the airport as its new symbol an American bald eagle.

An airlift pilot taking off from Rhein-Main for Tempelhof did not simply aim his aircraft toward Berlin and then relax for the duration of the ninety-minute flight. Carrying out General Tunner's orders following the Black Friday nightmare, Red Forman and his team had drawn up carefully worked-out procedures that governed every move a plane made, beginning with the overall instructions the pilot received from his squadron operations officer. A special kit held maps of his route and details of the navigational aids along the way, and just before takeoff a navigations officer described the specific picture at that moment. Other officers passed along intelligence, such as information on Soviet activities in or near the air corridors, that might affect the flight and gave the latest weather reports.

Aboard their aircraft, which had to be fitted into the three-minute beat of Tunner's airlift rhythm, a crew received instructions from the tower for departure time and flying altitude. Once airborne, the plane became one moving part of a great extended machine, which operated on a precisely determined pattern. The pilot followed his takeoff heading until he reached a 900-foot altitude, then turned south, homing on the Darmstadt beacon, climbing to 4,000 feet as he passed over it, and proceeded on for twenty-two miles to Aschaffenburg, continuing the climb until he reached his assigned altitude (5,000 to 7,000 feet). The pilot then turned northeast to Fulda, a key point because it was the last station before the aircraft reached the Soviet zone. Here each pilot, speaking *en clair,* reported the time as he passed directly over Fulda, thereby informing the pilot behind him whether he was early, late, or on time and thus enabling adjustments in speed to be made.

Now the pilot entered the twenty-mile-wide corridor leading over the Soviet zone to Berlin. Having passed the last beacon, he navigated by dead reckoning—since he could now receive no help from the ground— maintaining airspeed of 170 miles per hour. Forty minutes later the plane came within range of the Tempelhof control station, and when it reached the beacon called the Tempelhof Range, Tempelhof control directed it northwest to the Wedding beacon, with speed reduced to 140 miles per hour and altitude now at 2,000 feet. Control now instructed the pilot to turn right and descend to 1,500 feet, and then turn right again for the final approach. (For an easterly landing at Tempelhof, the turns would be left instead of right.) At this point the radar station turned the aircraft over to Tempelhof tower to handle the landing.

At the best of times the approach to Tempelhof had its problems. "The Berlin climate," said a French diplomat, "is appreciated more by the natives than by visitors. It is customary in Berlin to mention the weather only when it is a clear day." The cloudiness and fogginess made weather conditions a continuingly acute concern. The Americans and the British set up a system of minimum altitudes for landings—200 feet for Gatow and 400 feet for Tempelhof, with its surrounding ring of tall buildings. (Besides the apartments, pilots had to be wary of an unusual hazard, the tall brick tower of a brewery, whose notably stubborn owner had beaten off even Hermann Göring's attempts to get rid of it when the Luftwaffe used Tempelhof as a base, and who now had no intention of yielding to Allied pressure.) "We come down to the level of 400 feet for Tempelhof," General Tunner said. "If you can see the field, you land. If you can't, shove forward your throttles and turn on the course for home." The general publicly declared that he would reduce to copilot status "any pilot who failed to land with ceiling and visibility *greater* than four hundred feet and a mile" and would "court-martial any pilot who did land with ceiling and visibility *less* than four hundred feet and one mile." He said this purely for rhetorical effect, he admitted, but it got his message across.

All the procedures for each stage of the flight received close attention from Tunner's experts, with speeds of climb and descent being determined by careful research; a pilot in a fighter plane specially equipped with calibrated instruments flew alongside each transport to check its airspeed indicator. Flight altitudes, at first ranging at 500-foot intervals from 5,000 feet to 7,000 feet, were finally cut to two heights. Thus, if the airlift had in its first days possessed a measure of old-time, seat-of-the-pants flying heroics, that quality had quickly given way to organization and professionalism. But, if it lacked theatricality, this kind of professionalism demanded and got stamina, skill, and courage almost on an assembly-line basis.

The Berlin Air Safety Center, established by the Allied Control Council at the beginning of the occupation and quartered in a large, dilapidated gray stone building, monitored all the flights. There the Soviet representative, one Captain Zorchenko, continued to appear every day just as he had done before the East-West disruptions in June, but while the American and British airmen in the center worked furiously to keep tabs on the dense stream of airlift traffic, Zorchenko, with little to do (since the Soviets made available almost no information about their own operations), sat reading Russian books and magazines and even American comics, for which he seemed to have developed a fondness. But more seriously, he often posted a blanket warning above his almost-empty section of the racks that held flight details: AS OF THIS DAY SOVIET AIRCRAFT OF ALL TYPES WILL OPERATE AT VARIOUS TIMES IN THE VICINITY OF THE AMERICAN AND BRITISH CORRIDORS, FROM TREETOP LEVEL TO 30,000 FEET.

Harassment by the Russians, who maintained a proprietary attitude toward these corridors as well as toward the ground below, took various forms. In accordance with Zorchenko's warning, Soviet pilots would sometimes buzz the heavily loaded airlift planes. "It's a helpless feeling," said General Tunner, "when, as you're grinding along in a cargo plane, a MIG suddenly screams down out of nowhere to miss you by a few feet"—though finally pilots became so used to these attempts at intimidation that they could laugh them off. At other times the Russians would put on antiaircraft practice, with guns shooting upward at a target towed by a plane and shells sometimes bursting in the corridor. Typical was this newspaper report in the airlift's early months that "an American pilot reported Russian antiaircraft shells exploded in sight of his plane last night in the American air corridor over the Soviet zone. American officials said the Russians were holding target practice and that this was the fifth incident of the kind in recent months." Sometimes flares would streak up from the ground toward planes in flight; ground fire of one kind or another struck airlift planes on fifty-five recorded occasions.

Leaving Berlin one day, "cleaning up" the plane as he gained altitude, a U.S. pilot saw a Soviet fighter headed straight for him, as if challenging him to a truly deadly game of chicken. With a loaded C-54 and not much speed to call on, the American chose simply to keep on course, straight toward the Russian, who finally veered away. Another flier described a different kind of problem: "We'd be flying our route to and from Berlin, using homing beacons, and we'd get a call from radar saying to steer left because we were getting out of the corridor. But according to our instruments we were right on the money. What the Russians were doing was setting up false beacons, to lead us out of the corridor, which would give them a chance to register a protest or, even worse, send up a Yak fighter to shoot us down." Essentially, said this pilot, the Russians "wanted to let us know that they were in business and that if we got out of the corridor bad things might happen to us."

To the profound exasperation of U.S. authorities, some later incidents that involved straying out of the corridors were created by the pilots themselves. The secretary to the U.S. commander at Tempelhof recalled how fliers who were finishing their tours would sometimes "get smart" and fly out of a corridor to see what the Russians would do—which involved scrambling Yak fighters that would force down (though not shoot down) the plane, leading to wearying negotiations to recover plane and crew.

One GI, Sergeant Bill Palahunich, a communications specialist from Pittsburgh, frequently sought assignment to the Air Safety Center. Of Ukrainian background, Palahunich wanted to take advantage of the arrangement whereby, like the system that had prevailed with the generals on the Allied Control Council, each of the four occupying powers provided the meals from its national cuisine on a monthly rotating basis. "I was just nineteen," Palahunich said, "and I could put those stuffed cabbage rolls away. So I tried to work it when the Russians were doing it." One day in the canteen, when the attendant asked whether he would like one more, he politely told her that she might as well save herself some needless running back and forth by bringing him two more.

That same day, Palahunich heard three young Soviet soldiers at a nearby table chatting in Ukrainian. After eavesdropping for a few minutes, the sergeant hailed them in their language, adding, "I like to eat stuffed cabbage rolls just like you do." The soldiers were puzzled. How was it that this American could speak Ukrainian? Why was he working in the center? After he explained that he was merely a soldier assigned to the job, they began firing questions about the United States. Could you travel here and there, could you get rid of the president if you wanted to? Did you have to check in with the authorities when you wanted to go from one village to another? They listened carefully but heard his answers with obvious skepticism.

Palahunich's duty when assigned to the center was to keep track of the number of Soviet planes flying in the U.S. corridor from Frankfurt. Once, when he realized that the interpreter had merely gone through the motions of making a phone call to supply a figure and had produced a made-up answer—one understating the level of harassment of the airlift flights—the sergeant called him on it, in Ukrainian. Immediately the interpreter went off, returning with a superior officer—the "little general," Palahunich called him—who began saying, "Spy! You spy! Nobody in the United States speaks anything but English."

No, Palahunich said, he wasn't a spy, he was merely a soldier. He just happened to be one who had a great fondness for stuffed cabbage rolls.

Following the Western ambassadors' meeting with Stalin and Molotov, while the diplomats toiled over drafts of an agreement to submit to the Soviet foreign minister at their work session, Army Secretary Royall and other officials discussed with their men in Berlin, Clay and Murphy, the implications of the generalissimo's proposal for settling the Berlin crisis. Immediately Clay pointed to the most specific of the issues, the question of the currency. If Bedell Smith had agreed to withdraw the Western mark without an arrangement for four-power control over currency and credit, the move "could be disastrous to our position in Berlin"; specific conditions should be arranged by the military governors. Further, the Allies could hardly refuse to agree to a meeting of the Council of Foreign Ministers, but they should not allow the prospect of such a meeting to interfere with their determination to proceed with a government in western Germany, which was urgently needed. "It is our surest way to [a] strong position when we meet [the] Soviets," Clay said, and, besides, "if we fail now we may never have as favorable an opportunity."

Overall, Clay said the next day, "assuming a reasonably satisfactory solution is obtainable for the Berlin currency issue, there is obviously no other course of action left open to us except to accept in principle the Soviet proposal." A few days later he made a strong point of a Berlin political leader's fright at the rumor that the Soviet mark would become the only acceptable currency in Berlin, a situation that would leave the western sectors at the mercy of the Soviet government and its manipulation of credit. If the negotiators in Moscow tended to see the currency issue as a relatively minor technical matter that could readily be resolved, as Clay seemed to suspect, he must insist on Washington's remembering that without a say in fiscal matters, the West would have no position at all in Berlin. If it suspended the developments in western Germany—developments that had caused great controversy among the Germans themselves—it would very likely sacrifice the local political leaders who had taken the risk of supporting the London program.

Five o'clock in the afternoon on August 6 saw the Western ambassadors, document in hand, back in Molotov's office. The draft agreement they brought called for the immediate lifting of the Soviet blockade and of the West's counterblockade; the convening of meetings concerning Berlin and Germany; and the establishment of the Ostmark, under four-power control, as the single currency for Berlin, with a "freedom of banking" proviso for all sectors of the city. The Western representatives anticipated a few objections, but nothing major; they had, they felt, both satisfied their own governments and met Stalin's requirements.

When the meeting began, the ambassadors quickly saw, if they had needed reminding, that dealing with Molotov apart from Stalin had its own distinctive tone; this session resembled the August 2 meeting only in its lack of acrimony. Molotov pounced on the issue of postponing the scheduled September 1 convocation of the German constitutional assembly and would not let go. Repeatedly he waved aside Smith's and Roberts's objections that such a meeting was not equivalent to the establishment of a government and that, in any case, Stalin had agreed that negotiations could proceed without the West's being required to suspend activities in western Germany. When (as recorded in Molotov's diary) the foreign minister spoke of Frankfurt as the "capital of West Germany," Smith chided him for "looking far into the future"; Molotov retorted that he was looking no further than was necessary within the framework of the questions being discussed. But, said Smith, the Western governments did not think that Berlin had ceased to be the capital. Nonsense, Molotov said in effect: "It is impossible to close one's eyes to that which exists. Even if the fact that Berlin has ceased to be the capital of Germany is not talked about, everyone nevertheless sees it." In any case, Generalissimo Stalin had "precisely and in detail" set forth the position of the Soviet government, and that was that. If the Western powers had stuck to what they had agreed to in the meeting with Stalin, then the first step forward would have been taken. Unfortunately, however, they had not; thus the negotiators had to deal with a new position.

This kind of tough slogging, focused on details about the general issue of Germany and leading to nothing directly concerning Berlin, could hardly produce results. The ambassadors sought to limit the discussion to Berlin, though they showed themselves willing to discuss the monetary question. From start to finish, said Smith, "the meeting was the exemplification of [the] typical Soviet tactic of trying to sell the same horse twice."

It also demonstrated another tactic, the good cop–bad cop routine (a concept not yet widely established in the popular culture of the era and thus perhaps not familiar to the ambassadors). Did it produce the desired result? So it appears to have done. "I have the impression," Smith told the State Department concerning Molotov, that "he is completely skeptical of producing agreement on Germany by conference at any level, while Stalin seems still to lean toward the idea that eventually some agreement may result." Smith did not know that apart from whatever discussion Stalin allowed within the confines of a conference room before a point of view became a policy, he permitted no public dissension thereafter. Of course, the ambassadors did not comprehend the unlimited scope of the generalissimo's power. A comment by James Forrestal on these Moscow negotiations illustrates the extent to which U.S. authorities were working in the dark. They estimated, said the secretary of defense, that when Stalin and Molotov "reported the results of their negotiations with the Western powers to the Politburo they were informed that they 'had lost their shirts' "— hence, as they saw it, the stiffening of Molotov. Not only did this conclusion display ignorance of the real locus of power in the Soviet Union, it showed no awareness of the "good cop–bad cop" approach as a deliberate, almost-scripted routine. Speaking of the persistent Western belief in the Politburo's habit of intervening to veto Stalin's or Molotov's initial generosity in a negotiation, Walter Millis observed, "It is curious how hard this notion died." Churchill, Stettinius, and other Western representatives all encountered this frustration and employed the same explanation for it. "Only slowly," Millis commented, "did it seem to dawn on the West that the Russians might be using a standardized technique."

This technique preserved Stalin's useful "Uncle Joe" image while making highly effective use of Molotov's gifts, in particular the relentless stubbornness that had won him the nickname "Stone Ass" from Franklin Roosevelt. For his part, Molotov held no lofty view of the Western officials with whom he dealt. When, years later, an interviewer commented to him that he and Stalin had ordered people shot because of their opinions, whereas "in a bourgeois democracy senators are never placed before a firing squad," Molotov immediately replied: "That's because in bourgeois democracies they don't do what needs to be done."

The ambassadors had no special reason to pay particular attention to Molotov's aide, who sat quietly listening in on this August 6 meeting— Andrei Smirnov, the deputy foreign minister specializing in German affairs who had written the secret March 12 memorandum outlining strategy for a blockade of Berlin. Nor could the ambassadors and their political chiefs have known any of the details about Stalin's meeting on March 26 with Wilhelm Pieck and his delegation of Soviet zone Communists, in which the generalissimo had proposed to kick the West out of the city.

In the August 6 meeting and others that followed, Molotov acted as Stalin's faithful agent, haggling over rights, definitions, and dates in the drafts the two sides exchanged. The foreign minister had a frustrating, one-sided way of seeming to presume that issues on the table had already been settled, as when he declared that, since the Allies had agreed to the use of

Soviet zone currency in all of Berlin, "it was natural and proper that it should be introduced under Soviet authority"; Marshall had told Smith that he must not yield in any way with respect to control of the currency used in Berlin. Molotov also made a great point of the ambassadors' failure to make explicit mention of four-power control of the currency when they talked with Stalin; Smith riposted that four-power control in Berlin clearly meant four-power control of the issuance of currency. Molotov's general insistence in these talks on settling the question of four-power control of Germany before taking up the reestablishing of four-power control in Berlin reminded Frank Roberts of the Leninist thesis that the general question must be decided first, before single aspects of it can be discussed.

Responding to Western stipulations about lifting the transport restrictions, Molotov wanted to raise only those imposed after June 18, not those that had come in March, on the grounds that the real problem had arisen only after the June currency reform. From afar, Marshall told Smith that the State Department saw "a certain danger in becoming involved in protracted negotiations with Molotov on the currency or other questions of substance in view of our declared determination not to negotiate under pressure of the blockade." The August 6 meeting had one consequence that, when looked at closely, could have been found greatly enlightening by President Truman, Secretary Forrestal, and other Western Kremlin watchers who spent time speculating about the distribution of Soviet power between the Politburo and Joseph Stalin. On the next day, a proposed draft four-power communiqué won the formal endorsement of the Politburo—but until then, this reputedly potent body had played no recorded part in the entire Berlin crisis. Possibly Stalin wanted its stamp recorded because the document contained the stipulation that the Western powers would suspend "the realization of the decisions of the London Conference on formation of a government of West Germany" pending a conference of foreign ministers or other representatives of the four powers.

But the East-West wrangling continued in ambassadorial sessions with the foreign minister on August 9, 12, and 16. During one meeting an unanticipated light moment occurred when Smith, either from politeness or from a wish to hear from somebody besides Molotov, asked Andrei Smirnov whether he had any comments to make. This was not in the script. Smirnov looked startled—though an able official, he sat at Molotov's side only to listen, not to talk. Molotov, just as surprised, did a sort of cinematic double-take and then said that if Smirnov had anything to say, he should certainly say it. Smirnov managed to turn down the opportunity.

The August 16 session lasted almost four hours, "all very hard going," as Smith put it. It was, in essence, a grueling editing session, though it concerned a document barely more than a page long; the ambassadors had produced a new proposed communiqué, the result of a reconciliation of Western and Soviet drafts, which they handed to Molotov. The document set August 25 as the date for removing all limitations on transport between Berlin and the Western zones and between the latter and the Soviet zone; also on August 25 the B-mark would be withdrawn and the Ostmark would become the only currency for Berlin—contingent, however, on the reaching of an agreement by the commanders in Berlin on four-power control over the issuance of the Ostmark for Berlin.

After looking the document over, Molotov declared that it lacked the point that had been proposed from the very beginning of the transactions— there was no "synchronicity" (simultaneity) in implementing the lifting of the restrictions and the withdrawal of the B-mark, because the West was attaching conditions to this withdrawal, a point that made the August 25 date meaningless. Smith explained that the ministers had "tried to guarantee the simultaneity and the maintenance of a firm date and, at the same time, to guarantee the organized release and regulation of the circulation of the new currency in Berlin." Roberts declared that it was not a question, as Molotov implied, of letting the Germans profit from the currency situation and "win out over the Allies."

Molotov, who desired no currency regulation, then returned to the idea of using June 18, not March 1, as the defining date for the imposition of the transport restrictions, because, as he had previously maintained, it was the announcement on that date of the currency reform in the Allied zones that had "complicated the situation in Berlin." No more than previously could the ambassadors accept such a date or such a definition. The foreign minister then wrote out in longhand his own version of the communiqué, which spoke of "detailed arrangements" concerning the currency for Berlin but included no requirement for four-power control. The negotiators were making rapid progress to nowhere.

"There was no hope at any time during tonight's conversation of getting an agreement to our draft," Smith said in his report to Washington on this exhausting session. The essential problem was that the West insisted on four-power regulation of the "flow and use" of Berlin currency and the Soviets wanted no such control. The ambassadors would now make a final try with Stalin.

These dealings in Moscow found Yves Chataigneau in an embarrassing position, as the French political crisis continued, with Marie existing as premier only on a kind of sufferance, since he could not win the support of the Socialists; the saving grace for France was the presence of Robert Schuman at the Quai d'Orsay. These same days saw an even uglier than usual situation developing in Berlin. Clay reported to Bradley and Draper that Soviet propaganda in newspapers and over the radio had become "more personal in character and vicious and scurrilous in tone." Communist police had been brought in from the Soviet zone to foment disorder, and every day saw fresh incidents. Clay expected the Russians to provoke local disturbances for the purpose of involving U.S. personnel. He wished to avoid retaliatory measures, however, in order not to disturb the negotiations in Moscow, but the changed Soviet attitude, as he called it, seemed to be significant.

The ambassadors returned to the generalissimo's office on August 23, again at nine o'clock in the evening. Stalin, still jovial, sprang a surprise by saying, "Well, I have a new draft." Smith commented that the generalissimo fully deserved his reputation as a strategist (he outflanked "all of our careful rehearsals," Smith said in his report to Washington) and, that being the case, the two sides could compare drafts, since the ambassadors had brought their own. Pleased that the two documents had many points of agreement, Smith proceeded to ask two questions to see whether Stalin would abide by his earlier statements or would endorse Molotov's later departures from them. Would Stalin lift the blockade completely or only remove the restrictions imposed after June 18? How would the four powers control the money to be used in Berlin? Overruling Molotov, or seeming to do so, Stalin said, somewhat vaguely, that the "restrictions lately imposed" would be lifted. For Berlin, he suggested that a financial commission under arrangements to be made by the four commanders could handle currency affairs.

Before adjourning to try, once again, to thrash out details and arrangements with Molotov, the ambassadors had to deal with Stalin's insistence on the central Soviet point. The agreement, the generalissimo said, should include a statement to this effect: "The question of the London decisions and of the formation of a West German Government was also discussed in an atmosphere of mutual understanding. The adoption of any decision on this subject was, however, deferred until the next meeting of the Council of Foreign Ministers." As the ambassadors immediately realized, these bland words concealed a very sharp hook. This kind of "mutual understanding" would leave the western Germans hanging, with its implication that, with no say in the matter, they had been included in a horse trade in the Kremlin—blockade concessions in exchange for suspension of the western German government. Smith went through the motions of agreeing to submit the statement to Washington but frankly declared that it would hardly be found acceptable. For Stalin, however, this effort represented the last chance to maneuver the postponement of a possibly pivotal event—the convening, on September 1, of the Parliamentary Council, which had the mission of drafting a constitution for the new German republic.

Yet at this point, it seemed, the ambassadors had managed to achieve a possible agreement on Berlin without yielding any ground on the overall German question. Now, at eleven o'clock in the evening, they trooped off to Molotov's office to begin work on a directive to the commanders in Berlin. Once again, men representing two sides, four countries, various languages, and discordant purposes attempted to produce and edit, line by line, a document that could possess great meaning for the world. Anyone who had ever participated even in monolingual group editing on a school or club newsletter could sympathize with these negotiators as they struggled to turn two drafts into one. Did, for example, the Soviet mention of "the existing procedure for interzonal commerce" mean that the Western powers would be "attached to the Soviet organ"? Molotov replied that he could not say precisely, but he thought there would not be such an "attachment"; mention of the export-import organ was therefore eliminated. But they still had to deal with the existing procedure for interzonal commerce—whatever it might be. Finally Smith suggested replacing the words "in accordance with the existing procedure" with the words "taking into account the existing procedure" and making the words "existing procedure" plural. Smith also suggested splitting the phrase into two parts. Molotov argued for leaving it singular, and Smith yielded. Molotov declared that this was a very important point. Smith agreed but commented that he was not an expert in the field of commerce and could not fully figure out all of these problems. Molotov declared that he was no expert either, but he nevertheless knew it was an important question.

In this and the following hairsplitting sessions, the foreign minister's displeasure with the Western refusal to yield on the western German question showed itself in truculence and readiness to wrangle over "each word and every sentence." But by August 27 this contentious group had managed to produce the needed document, which was sent off to the four military governors in Berlin. Even at this point Molotov withdrew his assent, as the Western representatives saw it, to a communiqué concerning the meetings and the directive, unless he could insert a paragraph about the London decisions.

When the Defense Department sent General Clay the text of the agreement, he immediately objected to its failure to make plain the status of Berlin as a city under four-power control, with the supervisory Kommandatura. It meant, he said, "a politically separate Berlin under Soviet currency." Nevertheless the military governors would do their best, he said: the document gave them the assignment of devising the basis on which the Ostmark should be accepted as the sole currency for the city. Quite remarkably, the directive allowed the military governors only a week's time to deal with a problem that had previously resisted all efforts to find a solution. Clay objected to the vague word "recently"—Stalin's word—defining the restrictions that would be lifted. And without an explicit statement of Berlin's quadripartite status, said the general, the Germans themselves would not think that the agreement had restored the four-power equality that had been broken by the blockade. Clay's superior, Secretary Royall, and even General Marshall and his advisers did not consistently seem to realize that unless agreement with the Soviets made its points in completely and unambiguously explicit language, with absolutely no room left for inference, the Kremlin would interpret it in any manner it desired or would simply disregard it altogether. Smith needed this reminder, too, or so the secretary seemed to feel when he cabled his concern about the document's lack of "any confirmation of the principle of quadripartite administration of Berlin." But as U.S. officials could not know at the time, Stalin for five months had maintained no thought of bringing back four-power rule.

On August 26, the day before the ambassadors in Moscow finished their work on the directive for the commanders in Berlin, General Clay seemed surprisingly optimistic about the possible results of the negotiations—more so than about President Truman's chances in the coming election. In a letter to General Bradley concerning the almost-perpetual topic of his departure from Germany (the question had come up in one form or another since the middle of 1946), Clay observed that with his old foe John Foster Dulles looking very much like the next secretary of state, a new commander in Germany would soon be called for. "If there is agreement in Moscow which leads to the lifting of the Berlin embargo," Clay wrote, that would be the time to announce his request for retirement, rather than immediately after the change in administrations; the latter might make his retirement into a controversial issue, a prospect he found abhorrent. Bradley agreed that the announcement of Clay's retirement should come "sometime between some kind of an agreement with the Russians about Berlin and election day." But Clay's optimism—surprising, in any case—proved short-lived. If the airlift should continue, he wrote Bradley two weeks later, "I must stay it out unless the army decides otherwise."

CHAPTER 19

"No Frenzy, No Flap"

JOSEPH STALIN HAD gone into the negotiations with the West with two aims; only one of them now remained. He and his faithful Molotov had not won even a moment's postponement in the execution of the London decisions, as everybody called the western German program, but they still could anticipate "kicking them out" of Berlin—soon the coming of autumn fogs would settle the matter of the airlift. Before the working group had even completed the directive for the commanders, Frank Roberts, on orders from Bevin, had complained to Molotov about the rising disorder in Berlin—the tide of turbulence described by Clay to General Bradley on August 21. Many of these incidents were raids from the Soviet sector into one of the Western areas, reminiscent of scenes along the trenches in World War I; city officials and even policemen sometimes found themselves dragged away in the crudest kind of kidnapping. When Roberts suggested to Molotov that with four-power negotiations due to start immediately, Marshal Sokolovsky be instructed to make every effort to keep Berlin calm, Molotov retorted that the marshal already had all the orders he needed.

On Thursday, August 26, a crowd of several thousand people—men, women, and children—organized by the SED, waving banners and carrying signs, besieged the Berlin city hall, which was in the Soviet sector. Warned of the likelihood of a demonstration, the local authorities had postponed the meeting of the city assembly scheduled for that afternoon, but the next day the menace of a mob looking even more serious than Thursday's forced the adjournment of that morning's session; in effect, unhampered by the Soviet-controlled police under Paul Markgraf, the mob drove out the members of the city assembly.

Dr. Otto Suhr, the head of the Magistrat—the city administration—and his colleagues decided to make one more attempt to hold an assembly session, even if they would have no protection from the police. Though telling Suhr that the city government, not the military government, should make the decision, Colonel Howley, the American commandant, supported the idea, saying that "if the Russians can frighten the city government out of office, that will please them more than anything else." Agreeing, Suhr, who believed that the assembly owed it to its citizens to convene regularly, arranged for a meeting at noon on September 6. "It was the last meeting that body ever held there," Howley said, "because of a series of nightmare happenings that would be written off as incredible—any place in the world except Berlin." The members had to make their way into the building through the familiar "goon squads," which then smashed the doors and occupied the building.

Finding themselves dislodged again, the assembly members, seeking shelter, made their way to the British sector. But others present were not so fortunate. General Clay (who, despite Robertson's view of him as hotheaded, tended to view matters with notable calmness) told Draper in a teleconference mostly concerned with other matters that "the deputy mayor [Ferdinand Friedensburg, substituting for the ailing Louise Schröder] foolishly and without our knowledge took forty odd plain clothes men from western sectors over to keep order. Uniformed police of Soviet sector under direct orders of Soviet officer started to arrest them. They rushed into offices of three western liaison representatives where some are still at siege. However, Soviet sector police broke into our office and led about twenty of the poor devils off to death or worse." Despite his strong wish, Clay said, he made no move to send U.S. MPs into the Soviet sector to help the Americans who were "being pushed around." He summed up his feelings to Draper: "Pride is a cheap commodity, thank God, or I could never hold my head up."

As Howley explained, when Markgraf got wind of Friedensburg's request for the police from the Western sectors, he sent in "Markgraf police," as the Germans called them, to find and seize the "Strum police" (named for the former deputy chief who had fled the Soviet sector). If Clay's teleconference had taken place a few hours later, he could have told Draper that after dragging away the sobbing twenty policemen at tommygun point, the Russians kept the remaining twenty-six men under siege until General Ganeval negotiated free passage for them, promised by Sokolovsky and agreed to by Kotikov on his "word of honor." But after the policemen emerged from the building and were loaded into French trucks, Soviet-sector police hijacked the trucks at gunpoint and carried their captives away to imprisonment in the Soviet sector. Moscow had certainly not ordered its proconsuls to work for harmony during the period of four-power negotiations.

On Clay's orders, Howley sought out Kotikov to protest the Soviet failure to prevent a mob from invading the city hall and disrupting the government. He was met by a set-piece speech in which the Soviet commandant, speaking for public consumption in the presence of "the usual group of attendants," declared that there had been no mob but merely a group of peaceable workers who wanted to petition their city government. The trouble had been caused by the Western powers, who wanted to keep these citizens from delivering their legitimate petition, an effort they were trying to make with the help of Western nationals in civilian clothes (Kotikov's version of a goon squad). American reporters had been on hand to produce stories putting the Soviet command in an unfavorable light. Beyond that, Western liaison officers had added to the disturbance through their own drunkenness and disorderly conduct. At the end of this harangue, which consumed an hour and a half, Howley indicated that if the Russians refused to provide security for Americans in the Soviet sector, the Americans might then be forced to reexamine their own policies in relation to Soviet activities and facilities in the U.S. sector. He was not making a threat, Howley said when questioned by Kotikov; he was merely acknowledging that the apparent change in Soviet policy would call for a fresh look by the Americans at their own procedures. Kotikov then agreed to provide the requested security, a pledge, Clay noted with a touch of perverse and limited optimism, that would probably hold for a few days.

On September 9, seeking a way to fight back against the attack on the city government and at the Russians generally, a vast crowd of Berliners—estimated at 300,000—gathered in the square before the old Reichstag. Ernst Reuter—the "Lord Mayor without office," as Howley called him—Dr. Suhr, and others denounced the Communists' drive to control all of Berlin, and the crowd shouted back *"Freiheit!"* Reuter entreated the Western Allies not to trade Berlin away in a deal with the Russians. Later, as the crowd was breaking up, several young men climbed the Brandenburg Gate, tore down the red flag flying from the top, and, scrambling back down, set it on fire. Soviet guards from a nearby war memorial rushed up, seized the flag, and fired into the crowd. A roar, with a sound of riot, rose up from the people. A squad of British MPs arrived just in time to save the Russians from possible dismemberment, though other Russians delivered a second and final volley into the crowd. Remarkably, as it seemed to Howley, the Russians were "rebuilding a terrific hate balance in the German ledger."

Bedell Smith had felt no surprise when reports from turbulent Berlin indicated that the four military governors were making no progress in creating a document implementing the agreements reached in Moscow. He wanted to tell Molotov, he cabled Marshall, that "we are not such fools as to believe for one minute that this aggression could have begun or could continue without active support and prompting" of the Soviet authorities. But the secretary rejected the suggestion, preferring to leave the situation in

When Major General William H. Tunner arrived in Germany at the end of July, the airlift had found the organizer it needed. As commander of the fabled World War II "over the Hump" airlift from India to China, Tunner had become the chief American expert on the transport of cargo by air. "When it comes to airlifts," he said, "I want rhythm," and he put the Berlin operation (below) on a beat "as constant as jungle drums."

General Tunner immediately saw the need for more room to handle
more planes; work crews assembled new runways from plates of pierced
steel (top). To build the new airport at Tegel, U.S. authorities hired
thousands of German civilians to haul rubble from bombed-out
buildings to the site of the runway. *Trümmerfrauen*—"rubble women"—
made up 40 percent of the work force (bottom).

The airlift battled German fogs with a new system, ground control approach (GCA) radar, that guided planes onto the runways. In a trailer with a radar unit that used 700 vacuum tubes (right), GCA operators talked pilots into a spiral out of the sky. Following General Tunner's strict airlift rhythm, planes came in every three minutes around the clock (below).

The constant roar of transport planes too reassured Berliners that the West would not abandon them. As winter weather made flying more difficult, Soviet-sponsored newspapers reported that the airlift would falter. The pilots continued to fly. Their operation's own newspaper, *The Task Force Times*, turned to gallows humor, as in this cartoon poking fun at the forecasters (below).

Lieutenant Gail Halvorsen endeared himself to Berlin by parachuting candy bars to the children who waited for him at the Tempelhof Airport runway (dust jacket) and visiting hospitals (right).

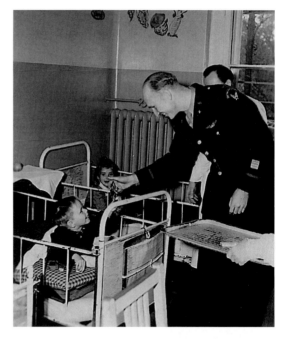

As another treat for Berlin's children, the Americans sent Christmas presents specially delivered by the 86th Fighter Wing's football mascot, Clarence. (But was that really Clarence?)

In November, President Truman won reelection in one of the greatest upsets in American political history. When the people knew the facts, Truman wrote Winston Churchill, "they went along with me"; important among those facts had been Truman's refusal to back down in Berlin. Dean Acheson (right), who succeeded General Marshall as secretary of state at the beginning of 1949, called Truman "the captain with a mighty heart." Only a few days after he took office, Acheson had the opportunity to respond to a major development—a hint from Stalin that it might be the Russians who were ready to back down.

To feel out the Soviets, Acheson chose wry law professor Philip Jessup, deputy chief of the U.S. mission to the United Nations (above). Though negotiations would drag on for three months, it had become clear that the West had won the battle of wills over Berlin. Also clear was the continuing cost of the airlift—as shown below by this crash in June 1949.

In late afternoon, September 30, 1949, a dramatic chapter in air history came to its end when the last airlift flight left Rhein-Main air base. For more than a year, the airlift had kept the Western sectors of Berlin supplied with food and fuel, at a cost of sixty-five lives. With this new kind of fighting, the West had won the first major battle of the cold war.

Berlin for a separate discussion. At one point in the quadripartite meetings, the patient Clay reported to Washington that "the going is tough" but added that he was not yet ready to predict the outcome. Not only was Sokolovsky ignoring the understanding the Western ambassadors believed themselves to have reached with Stalin, he even insisted on controlling air traffic into Berlin and announced that on September 6 the Soviet air force would begin maneuvers that would require the use of the Allied air corridors. In an aide-mémoire of September 18, Molotov backed up Sokolovsky's demand, alleging that it fell under the Control Council's decision on air traffic taken "as far back as 1945." The ambassadors rejected the claim.

For his part, Stalin failed to keep a meeting with the ambassadors that supposedly had been arranged. It appeared that he had gone to a spa to take the waters, and Molotov said firmly, "his treatment would not permit of interruption." In the summary of overnight telegrams prepared for the president, the White House naval aide reported that the ambassadors were "pessimistic as to the outcome of the discussions." They were right—the negotiations were dead. At this point, the Allies found themselves divided on strategy; as Bevin's biographer put it, "arguments broke out . . . between the Americans and Bevin about what to do next."

One afternoon in September a visiting journalist strode along Wiesbaden's cobbled old Taunusstrasse and, turning into the drab building that housed the headquarters of the Berlin Airlift Task Force, climbed the three steep flights of stairs to General Tunner's office. Beyond the general's window the slate shingles of the steep roof of the neighboring building bore a large disfiguring stain. As the reporter sat talking with Tunner just after lunch, a hinged flap swung open on the slate roof, a dishpan appeared in the opening, and a cascade of greasy water poured down the slope and began dripping from the eaves. Tunner watched as a red hand pulled the pan back inside and then grasped the flap, yanking it back into place and letting it fall with a thud.

A moment later the phone rang; the caller had interesting news. For the third straight day the U.S. airlift had set a new tonnage record: in the past twenty-four hours, ending at noon, 472 flights had carried 3,572.2 tons to Berlin. This total, combined with 1,450 tons brought in by the British, meant that, for the first time, the Allies had delivered more than 5,000 tons of supplies in a single day. Immediately Tunner called General LeMay to pass along the good news. He also readily shared the figures with the reporter. Well aware that the achievements of the airlift were making matchless propaganda, Tunner had fought to lift security restrictions on total tonnage figures. He also knew that the facts would inspire the Vittles fliers themselves.

The Soviets had chosen this same day, September 10, as one of those to make good on Captain Zorchenko's frequent threat concerning air operations near the Allied corridors. After informing the Air Safety Center that Soviet planes of all types, singly and in groups, would be operating over the entire Soviet zone, the Russians demanded that the Allies supply full details (including not only the purpose of a flight but even the pilot's name) of all American and British flights "not later than an hour before the take-off."

The warrant for this request appeared to be the claim that the air corridors had been established by the Soviet military command rather than by any four-power agreement; the Russians were thus trying to decide unilaterally one of the questions being battled over in the quadripartite meetings. In rejecting the request, U.S. officials declared that they would continue supplying standard flight information but would not accede to the demand for excessive details. As their next action—it was hardly a response, since the Western rejection could not have surprised them—the Soviets sent up Yak fighters and Ilyushin medium bombers which sped over Berlin at high altitudes; some of the fighters dropped below 10,000 feet to stunt over the U.S. sector. Some observers considered these maneuvers an overture to a large Communist rally planned for the following Sunday in memory of "victims of fascism." Despite this intermittent harassment, the airlift continued that day on its methodical way toward its record-breaking performance.

Two weeks later, paying Tunner a return call after surveying the scene in Berlin, the reporter noticed that, although the after-lunch slop water on the neighboring slates had evaporated, the greasy stain had grown considerably larger since his first visit; a potato peeling, caught between shingles, waved like a tiny flag in the light wind. After staring at the scene for a long moment, Tunner turned to the visitor and, as if he had been looking not at the grubby nearby roof but at a far-off horizon, began to preach his personal air-transport gospel. Since his experience in the Hump operation, he said, he had always thought of China, and almost all of the other Eastern countries, as a "lean, hungry man climbing up a trail with a heavy pack on his back"; that picture really fitted all of the world except for parts of North America and Western Europe, which moved on wheels. Air transport, Tunner had believed, could lift people out of the "back-toting" stage, and now the success of the airlift had proved it. "We now know, as we never knew it in the Air Force before," he declared, "that we can fly anything, anywhere, any time. Climate, mountains, oceans—those can't stop us." It was natural for Tunner, with his background and his current accomplishments, to profess such an enthusiastic belief. But he had other reasons for his expansiveness. Although the bleakness of his official surroundings did not reflect his rise in status, his accomplishments in just a few weeks had won him General Clay's strong support.

The airlift could keep the Allies in Berlin, Clay had now decided. But it must have greater capacity. The general pressed Washington for sixty-nine C-54s, to be delivered immediately, and forty-seven more by December 1, "if lift is still continuing at that time." (He finally won full approval on October 21; Washington felt as nervous as ever about assigning all of its eggs to the Berlin basket.) The fogs of November, Berlin's worst flying time, lay ahead, and after them would come the whole panoply of winter weather hazards. Whatever Tunner might believe about the triumphs of the airlift in these September days, his political masters and their diplomats carried a heavy load of doubt. No one could question, however, that the general and his staff of transport specialists had with impressive speed refined Operation Vittles into an operation that conformed remarkably to his credo, as he later expressed it: "The actual operation of a successful airlift is about as glamorous as drops of water on stone. There's no frenzy, no flap, just the inexorable process of getting the job done. In a successful airlift you don't see planes parked all over the place; they're either in the air, on loading or unloading ramps, or being worked on. You don't see personnel milling around; flying crews are either flying, or resting up so that they can fly again tomorrow. Ground crews are either working on their assigned planes, or resting up so that they can work on them tomorrow. Everyone else is also on the job, going about his work quietly and efficiently. The real excitement from running a successful airlift comes from seeing a dozen lines climbing steadily on a dozen charts—tonnage delivered, utilization of aircraft, and so on—and the lines representing accidents and injuries going sharply down. That's where the glamour lies in air transport." It was simply a fact, Tunner said, that "airlift experts run airlifts better than combat experts." But many of these combat experts, though professing no great personal ambition in the realm of transport, nevertheless seemed to find Tunner's "fact" a hard one to swallow. For all his success in his first six weeks on the job, the airlift chief's troubles with higher commanders had not ended.

To keep in close touch with his men and their problems, Tunner spent much of his time on the go—flying, inspecting, talking. Soon after he imposed his system on the airlift, he called a meeting to discover what the pilots thought of it and what suggestions they had for improvement. Seeking frankness from the men who did the actual flying, he bypassed their commanding officers and made the meeting an informal session, complete with a keg of beer. The pilots did not hold back but offered criticisms and suggestions concerning, in particular, the need for more beacons, for rigid enforcement of climbing speeds, and for greater emphasis on safety procedures. The men also talked about living conditions, making the point that the barracks into which they were jammed were so noisy that sleep was often hard to come by, even when they were exhausted. Food came in for its share of criticism as well. Listening carefully, Tunner and his staff noted the points, and the general did his best to respond to them. Even so, many of the crews had to live in tents for several months. Morale also suffered from the crews' uncertain status, as the air force continually extended their TDY (temporary duty) status. "They were always crying about going home," Tunner said. "Always wanted to go home. My staff wanted to go home, too." The men had "kissed their wives and said, 'I'll see you in ninety days.' " That problem, Tunner said, he never solved.

As the days passed, Tunner made constant rounds of the airlift stations. Sometimes, he said, after his jacket became so grimy with coal dust that he could pass as just another GI, "I learned a lot about my command from pilots who thought they were talking to just another airplane driver." One day he carried this anonymity to a remarkable level in an encounter at Wiesbaden with a lieutenant busily engaged in a preflight inspection of his Skymaster. Giving this visitor in the nondescript jacket an affable greeting, the pilot returned to his task.

"Is this your first mission?" asked Tunner. The pilot said that it was. "Would you mind if we took this ship to Berlin?"

"You're damn right I'd mind," he declared. "I want to fly it myself."

Accepting the pilot's refusal to turn over the controls of his plane to somebody else, Tunner walked away without saying a word.

As the organization's little newspaper, the *Task Force Times,* put it, "the lieutenant who said no to a general and got away with it, went on to Berlin." But the general showed no displeasure with the lieutenant's spirit.

Tunner stayed on the go day and night. Startled tower operators might see him standing beside them at three o'clock in the morning, checking up. "He was all business," Bill Palahunich recalled. "He expected you to do your job—no foolishness—but he would listen to you if you had a good point to make." The general approached his task like an executive and also like a teacher, combining these qualities in a way that made him more than anything else a coach—exhibiting the combination of strong leadership, attention to detail, and love of competition that characterizes the Knute Rocknes and Adolph Rupps who train others to win at football and basketball. Hence he established rivalries between the various outfits taking part in the airlift. The *Task Force Times* had the assignment of keeping track of the competition: Did a unit make its daily quota or did it fail to meet it? Soon, Tunner noted, "the chief topic of conversation on every base was the daily tonnage records." Indeed, the world soon learned more about tonnage and its relation to individual aircraft than it had ever known before.

The *Task Force Times,* edited by Lieutenant Bill Thompson, played another role, particularly through the cartoons of Tech Sergeant John Schuffert, whose drawings, like those of Bill Mauldin in World War II, did not sugar-coat the realities of the situation they dealt with. They were "raw and bitter and played up everything disagreeable on the Airlift," Tunner said with approval, "but they brought a smile to their readers' faces." Tunner came to the airlift as that most American of phenomena, an efficiency expert, but he proved to be an expert with a human face.

In a characteristic adaptation to reality, the people of Berlin, accustomed just a few years earlier to hearing the rumble of Allied B-17s, B-24s, and Lancasters arriving with bombloads of TNT to drop on the city, brought the concept up to date by dubbing the benign planes and crews of the airlift "raisin bombers." As the Berliners came to seem less and less like enemies and more and more like friends and even heroes, one American pilot gave his own inventive twist to the airlift's nutritional nomenclature. Having had no chance to see anything of Berlin outside the landing field, Gail Halvorsen, a lean-faced, prematurely balding twenty-seven-year-old lieutenant from Garland, Utah, became curious enough about the city to hitch a ride from Frankfurt to Tempelhof on July 19, a day off for him. Outside the airport he stopped to break out his movie camera and shoot some film of Vittles planes as they came in to land. Within a few minutes he had attracted a crowd of perhaps thirty boys and girls, most of them eight to ten years old.

As a transport pilot, Halvorsen had spent time in Italy, Africa, and South America. A man who loved children and talked about having a houseful of his own some day, he took note of a striking difference between the Berlin youngsters and those he had seen in other cities. These children did not ask, "Any gum, chum?" They did not beg. "None of them jerked at my pants or threatened to knock my block off," Halvorsen said. "They wanted to try out their English on me." It wasn't that the children didn't want candy—"they just lacked the brass other kids have."

Sympathizing with these wide-eyed youngsters, the lieutenant fumbled in his pockets and came up with a few sticks of chewing gum, which he handed out. Then, from somewhere, he got a brand-new idea. He told the children that if they would wait tomorrow at the end of the airport runway, he would drop candy to them from his airplane. They did not forget the promise, and neither did the pilot. That evening he spent some time tying up candy and gum in handkerchiefs, and the next day, as his C-54 glided toward the runway, three tiny parachutes came floating down from the flare chute in the bottom of the aircraft. The children rushed for the bounty brought them by the *"Schokoladenflieger,"* as Halvorsen quickly became known. The lieutenant had started something indeed: the chocolate bombing became a daily feature of the airlift. Halvorsen quickly ran out of handkerchiefs and old T-shirts and shorts, as he produced twenty parachute loads a day. The chocolate at first came from Halvorsen's own ration, but with the demand greatly outrunning this supply, other pilots began contributing, and soon crew chiefs and other personnel joined them. The number of parachute loads delivered in "Little Vittles," as Halvorsen called the operation, continued to climb.

Albert Eisenhuth, then a boy of eight, recalled Halvorsen's dropping candy—Hershey bars. Although he managed to get some of them, Eisenhuth said, it was hard, because there were so many youngsters wanting them and mobbing the airport. Successful children wrote letters to Halvorsen, calling him "Uncle Sam" or "Captain American."

Needing more help, Halvorsen turned to the men at his old station, Brookley Air Force Base at Mobile, Alabama—Operation Little Vittles could use more candy and more handkerchiefs, the lieutenant explained. The post commander responded by issuing an order declaring that any officer or enlisted man seen with a handkerchief would be required to turn it in for Little Vittles, and the city of Mobile mounted a handkerchief-and-candy drive. When the story appeared in newspapers across the country, the operation quickly acquired not only stacks of candy bars but fifty pounds of handkerchiefs, which Halvorsen himself ferried to Germany in a C-54 that had received its 1,000-hour overhaul in the United States. By the next January, Halvorsen and other airlift crews that had joined in Operation Little Vittles had dropped more than 250,000 candy parachutes at the end of the Tempelhof runway. When Halvorsen was rotated back to the States, the management of Little Vittles was taken over by Captain Laurence Caskey, who, in turn, was succeeded by Captain Eugene T. Williams.

Albert Eisenhuth and other youngsters would spend all day at Tempelhof watching the planes land, seemingly almost every second; they came for the spectacle, not just for the chocolate bars. Using American toy airplanes, which were sold in Western sector shops, Berlin children even created their own airlift game, *Luftbrücke* (air bridge); the young pilots would set their toy planes down on sand runways, to be met by toy trucks and wagons, which drove up to the doors of the planes and picked up whatever bits of tiny cargo were inside; this cargo was then carried off to playhouses, like freight being delivered. Gunter Kostka, a Berlin native who was seven at the time, later called the sight of the Vittles planes "the beginning of a love affair with the Americans." It was not a minor point that the rising generation figured in this affair from the very beginning.

One of Halvorsen's young fellow officers, Lieutenant Donald Butterfield, also played a central part in an activity involving German children. When his unit, the 86th Fighter Wing, returned to its base at Neubiberg from Tripoli, where it had gone to take gunnery practice, the lieutenant brought along a camel named Clarence, bought (for twenty-four dollars) to serve as mascot for the outfit's football team. But in the days leading up to Thanksgiving and Christmas 1948, a greater destiny for Clarence loomed up. The airmen decided to sponsor the collection of food for needy youngsters in Berlin; they would fly it to Tempelhof in a C-47, bringing Clarence along as escort. No mere observer, the camel would be equipped with saddlebags and would help distribute the bounty. After that appearance, the camel would be flown all over the American zone of Germany to inspire donations for Operation Vittles.

Clarence's arrival at Tempelhof disappointed nobody. Shepherded by harried teachers and airport MPs, more than five thousand schoolchildren gave Clarence a boisterous welcome, even though he agreed to step down from the plane only after some serious coaxing by Lieutenant Butterfield. The camel had done an outstanding job as a stimulator of donations, however; the C-47 carried 7,000 pounds of food and gifts of various kinds, which were distributed at Christmas. The only negative comment anyone heard came from a frazzled teacher who exclaimed, *"Nur ein Kamel für so viele Menschen*—only one camel for so many people!" But this would by no means be Clarence's only visit to the children of Berlin. After visiting Nuremberg, Stuttgart, and Heidelberg, he would return to Berlin from time to time with more Christmas cheer.

As Clarence became established as a prominent figure in the airlift, perceptive observers might have noted that "Clarissa" would have been a far more appropriate name. In fact, the Clarence that was winning increasing fame was an impostor. Unfortunately, when Butterfield had brought the original Clarence to Germany, he had also brought along a donkey. Before Clarence had even made his first public appearance, the donkey had broken his leg with a vicious kick; the camel had to be destroyed. Mounting a top-secret operation, Lieutenant Butterfield had sent to Africa for "Clarissa," which was flown in as the first camel's replacement.

Not all Berlin children, however, succumbed to the blandishments of candy and camels. One day the Tempelhof base commander received a letter of complaint from a seven-year-old girl who lived near the field—inconveniently near, it appeared. She had four chickens, the girl said, and the noise of the planes kept them so upset, they were failing to produce their normal number of eggs. She wanted compensation—and at that time, said

Bill Palahunich in flight control, "an egg was an egg!" Admiring the little girl's "brass," Palahunich and his associates called on the mess sergeant, who not only produced two dozen eggs but threw in five pounds of flour. Others contributed Hershey bars and chewing gum, and most valuable of all, Palahunich himself contributed a pack of cigarettes. Even after the elaborate currency reform, cigarettes were still as good as cash.

On September 13 President Truman received a letter from Norman Thomas, the widely respected if chronically unsuccessful Socialist Party aspirant to the presidency (he appeared on the presidential ballot six times, including 1948). Commending the president for the "patience and firmness" the Western powers had displayed in negotiations about Berlin, Thomas, who had always opposed dictatorships whether of the right or the left, proposed that the U.S. government take the Berlin question to the United Nations. "I believe," Thomas wrote, "the Kremlin's actions fall within the provisions of paragraph 2 of Article II concerning the functions of the General Assembly." Thomas also proposed that the State Department confer with all the presidential candidates about going to the UN, thus, as far as possible, taking relations with the Soviet Union out of the realm of campaign politics. This move, Thomas said with considerable relish, "would put Henry Wallace on the spot." If the Progressive Party candidate did not go along with the proposal, he would lose influence, and if he did join in, it would "make things more difficult for Stalin." In a related speech that same weekend, Thomas said that "this great appeal for a peace resting on some exercise of elementary decency" should have the support of all candidates, whatever their party.

President Truman, however, did not need any encouragement to present the Berlin case to the UN. That move had already begun.

CHAPTER 20

"A la Dynamite!"

In its effort to bring the Berlin situation before the United Nations, the State Department had found itself frustrated by British and French opposition. These allies did not see the UN as the arena in which to settle the question because they looked on the General Assembly as a talking shop that could produce no action and would be unlikely in any case to condemn Soviet conduct; many of the small countries would probably abstain from any vote. In the Security Council, of course, the Soviets could veto any resolution for action. The Americans wished to use the UN to establish the West's juridical rights in Berlin, but for Bevin, clarifying this "fundamental" question would solve nothing in itself—how could the UN raise the blockade? It was "a question of power, not of juridical right." But even though in the long run power would of course determine what happened, legalistic points often had considerable significance. Had Bevin forgotten, for example, that the existence of "a mere scrap of paper" gave Britain a juridical basis for declaring war on Germany in 1914?

With the collapse of negotiations in both Moscow and Berlin, Western diplomacy moved into the third phase of its effort to deal with the blockade. On September 20, the day before the opening of the third session of the General Assembly in Paris, Marshall, Bevin, and Schuman met in Schuman's office at the Quai d'Orsay to decide on a plan of action, so that they would no longer "improvise, as in the past." The French foreign minister declared that the Allies ought to move quickly, in order "not to lose not only time but more authority and prestige." Over the next two days, as the General Assembly began its session in the Palais de Chaillot, in an auditorium with a huge stage, the three foreign ministers decided to have the London Committee of ambassadors draw up a note for Moscow specifying their demands concerning Berlin; this note was delivered on September 22. If the Kremlin should return no satisfactory answer, the Western powers would indeed call on the UN. Meanwhile, Andrei Vyshinsky turned a speech to the assembled delegates into a violent indictment of the American "policy of expansion." The Soviet reply to the Allied note, which came on September 25, added nothing fresh to the continuing dispute; all the West had to do if it really wanted a settlement, it maintained, was to live up to the Moscow agreement. The Western Allies answered by declaring, on September 27, that they were bringing the Berlin question to the attention of the Security Council.

On this same day, the Berlin city assembly called for the UN to demand the lifting of the blockade. After a measure of procedural wrangling, the Security Council voted 9–2 to take up the question; Vyshinsky then declared that the Soviet Union would not involve itself in such proceedings, but he could not veto a procedural motion. As it turned out, neither he nor his Ukrainian fellow dissenter even boycotted the discussion. They stayed in their places but denied themselves the chance to affect the flow of events.

On October 5 Marshall, in Paris, received a piece of startling news. A teletype message from President Truman informed the secretary that Chief Justice Fred Vinson would shortly be flying to Moscow to explain to Stalin the depth of America's desire for peace and mutual understanding. Aghast, Marshall decided he must rush home for a direct talk with the president. But the new project had already encountered forceful opposition in Washington. As soon as Undersecretary Lovett saw a copy of the message Truman intended to send to Stalin, he had rushed from his office and, in an official car with red light flashing and siren shrieking, dashed to the White House to explain to the president that he must cancel the mission. Aside from its intrinsic inappropriateness following the efforts of the three Western ambassadors in Moscow, the three foreign ministers had just agreed to engage in no more negotiations with the Kremlin; instead, they had turned to the United Nations. Lovett told the president that Marshall (who had neither resigned nor sulked earlier in the year, when Truman had embarrassed the U.S. representatives at the UN by his abrupt recognition of Israel) would certainly be forced to leave this time; the Vinson mission— which the chief justice himself had attempted to decline—would bypass both the United Nations and America's allies, and it would have been arranged without consultation with Marshall. Besides, Stalin could hardly fail to see it as anything but American waffling on Berlin. As for Ernest Bevin, the foreign secretary had been ruffled enough by the spring fiasco in Moscow; he would hardly sit still for this new behind-the-scenes outflanking operation, even if, in reality, it called for no substantial discussion but merely the expression of high sentiments.

Truman, like the other national leaders, certainly wished to head off any drift toward catastrophe: on September 13 a high-level briefing on "bases, bombs, Moscow, Leningrad" had left him saying grimly: "I have a terrible feeling afterward that we are very close to war." Despite such dangers the public stood behind the president. In the spring, cold war tensions had begun to raise his approval rating from its very low 30 percent. In July the public, less informed but more determined than the administration and its military advisers, had favored staying in Berlin "even if it means war" by a lopsided 80 percent to 11 percent. Clark Clifford had accurately seen that, for all its general inconvenience, the blockade of Berlin could become a political blessing. "In times of crisis," Clifford noted, "the American citizen tends to back up his president."

No one could question, however, the American public's preference for peace over war. Behind the proposed new diplomatic move toward Moscow lay not only Truman's fears but the calendar: the presidential election was coming in less than a month. With the polls predicting a certain defeat—on September 9 one leading pollster had even declared that Dewey's huge lead in the race made further polling pointless—Truman had succumbed to the blandishments of two new speechwriters, one of whom, an advertising-agency veteran, thought a bold move like the Vinson mission would brighten the president's image, perhaps even close the gap with Dewey. "The Mission to Moscow matter caused enormous tensions within the staff," recalled Truman's aide George Elsey; even Clark Clifford, probably the most relentlessly political member of the staff, had seen it, as Elsey saw it, as a piece of "transparent gimmickry." Truman had even reserved time on the radio networks before he ran into the decisive opposition of Lovett and Marshall.

Unfortunately for candidate Truman aboard his whistle-stop train, however, details of the proposed mission fell into the hands of his bitterest newspaper opponent, the *Chicago Tribune,* which published the story on October 8. The next day, attacked not only by the *Tribune* but by normally milder critics for "playing politics with the nation's foreign policy," Truman left off campaigning to return to Washington for a meeting with Marshall, who had flown in on Truman's own plane, the *Independence* (a modified DC-6 commercial airliner), from which he emerged looking gray and weary. After this conversation, the president gave the only public explanation of the Vinson mission available to him: he had acted out of his "continuing great desire to see peace firmly established in the world." A French chronicler described the move simply as "an electoral operation." Domestically, at least, Truman may have had the last laugh: vacuous as the idea seemed to many observers, White House mail concerning it ran four to one in its favor. The American public, it seemed, maintained its faith in the mysterious magic of face-to-face talk by the men at the top.

Officials at lower levels, however, continued to find talk unprofitable. Somewhat confusingly, though Security Council meetings and actions were separate from those of the General Assembly, these proceedings ran concurrently. Council sessions attracted the greatest attention. "When we met as the Council," said Philip Jessup, the U.S. deputy representative to the United Nations, "we sat on the stage as if in a play. During the debate on the Berlin blockade we had what the theatre world would call 'a good house.'" Jessup, who had been put in charge of the Security Council operation for the United States, had been assured of Marshall's support for "any action he took provided it was not appeasement."

Neutral members of the Security Council now went to work to find a solution for Berlin. Their effort contained familiar elements: raising of the blockade and of the counterblockade the Allies had imposed on the movement of goods from western Germany to the east; agreement by the Allied commanders on the mechanism for making the Eastern mark the official currency for Berlin; and a meeting of the Council of Foreign Ministers. These elements held little appeal for the Western powers, who had just stepped off that same endlessly spinning merry-go-round. The Americans, in particular, still wanted to be vindicated by receiving the juridical support of the UN. The West, after all, had met coercion not with force but with peaceable resourcefulness and ingenuity; mediation, with both sides held to be at fault, did not seem much of a reward for this laudable restraint. Bohlen reminded Jessup, however, that the United States sought condemnation of Soviet actions not for its sake alone but in the hope of producing a changed Soviet position. Still, the Americans, on October 25, approved the draft resolution, since the neutral group "had tried to meet our essential requirements and the British and French were ready to accept it."

But Vyshinsky, in a richly metaphorical mood, had already declared it "useless to think that the USSR delegation will bite at this bait. It is naive to believe that the USSR delegation will stick to the glue which has been spread over the piece of paper which is now called the Berlin question." The Soviets saw no reason to agree to any lifting of the blockade, and when the time came to vote, Vyshinsky vetoed the resolution. The Soviet delegate compounded the problem—at least, linguistically—by denying the existence of any blockade of Berlin; since it did not exist, no resolution could properly speak of it. Vyshinsky insisted that the Council of Foreign Ministers, not the UN, was the proper forum for discussion of the Berlin question, and he also told the president of the Security Council that before the blockade could be lifted, Soviet zone currency must be introduced in the western sectors of Berlin.

Andrei Vyshinsky's declaration that no blockade existed in Berlin echoed the Soviet line. Had he chosen to speak of a blockade with many unusual features, however, he would have been closer to the mark. The Soviet-controlled Radio Berlin filled the air around the clock with anti-Western propaganda, for instance, but the electric power that kept the station going came from Allied Berlin, since the tower stood in the French sector. In compensation, the Russians furnished the electricity for Gatow airport, on the edge of the Soviet sector; the same current illuminated the powerful searchlights with which the Russians tried to blind pilots taking off from Gatow. The British likewise supplied power for a Russian fighter field. At any time it chose, either side could have pulled the plug in any of these and other situations, but both found the trade-offs acceptable.

In contrast, no trade-offs characterized the blockade on the ground. Here the Soviets made every effort to establish and maintain a complete cordon around western Berlin. By the time Vyshinsky was speaking in Paris, the Soviet-sector police were operating ninety-two checkpoints and five "collecting centers" on the seventy-seven-mile periphery of the Western sectors; these control points commanded every street connecting the Western sectors with the Russian sector and zone. Every car or truck entering a Western sector had to obtain clearance documents from a collecting center. If the vehicle held "contraband goods"—a category including food and coal—police seized the car and impounded its load. Pedestrians did not get off lightly, either. Police were particularly likely to search them if they were carrying Western newspapers. Even worse was possession of Western marks. Not only would the person carrying them lose the money, he or she would be arrested for committing a criminal offense.

The Soviets maintained that these controls existed to curb black-market activity—one of the many arguments put forth originally to justify the overall blockade—though they clearly were intended to frighten the people out of doing anything to make the blockade easier for the people of Allied Berlin to bear. Yet people did not always resist the temptation to carry coal in handbags or in other likely containers across sector boundaries. Coal was gold, and acquiring an extra measure of it often seemed worth the risk.

In mid-October, as the UN representatives wrangled in Paris and the daily oppressiveness of the blockade continued, the American occupation authorities conducted an opinion survey in the three Western zones of Berlin. Teams of German interviewers asked residents several questions, including how they expected the conflict to be resolved. When the results were collated and analyzed, the Americans could see that the Berliners felt little optimism. Only 17 percent anticipated a four-power agreement, while 46 percent foresaw continuing conflict; 27 percent expected the city to be divided into East Berlin and West Berlin.

How would the people "like to see the Berlin situation solved"? The largest group, 39 percent, wanted a peaceful agreement, with a return to four-power administration; another 25 percent believed that the Russians should leave Berlin, with a further 24 percent saying that all four powers should depart. Women (30 percent) were twice as likely as men (16 percent) to say that they wanted the Russians to leave, while more men (30 percent) than women (20 percent) expressed a rather unrealistic desire for all four powers to get out. But the poll revealed no men-women differences in what people thought would actually happen.

Another set of questions produced markedly emphatic answers. Asked "if you had to decide what the Western Powers should do in respect to Berlin, what would you personally suggest?" *58 percent* favored breaking the blockade by force; only 13 percent opted for trying to bring about agreement with the Russians by peaceful means. Almost half of the respondents (46 percent) favored firm steps to solve the situation, *even if such steps would lead to war.*

Although many Western-sector Berliners clearly wanted the West to take more vigorous action, they almost unanimously endorsed what the Allies had done. Nobody wanted them to leave, and only 1 percent thought that they would. As the Information Services Division stated in its report, "this is one point on which there is no discrepancy between desires and expectations."

At the Security Council, despite American acceptance and Soviet rejection of the neutral group's draft resolution, Philip Jessup found it striking "how often one person after another stressed the point that we must convince others that we really wanted a settlement." The fieriest example of this attitude was offered by Herbert Evatt, the famously hot-tempered Australian minister of external affairs, who was serving as president of the General Assembly. (Once, on a wartime visit to Washington, Evatt had conceived the remarkable notion of administering a dressing-down to General Marshall—a project that died rapidly. "I've heard how you conducted yourself in other offices," Marshall told his visitor. "Now you are not going to conduct yourself like that here!") In a reprise of Ernest Bevin's comment to Chip Bohlen in July, Evatt now "snarled" to Jessup: "So you want to start another war, do you? Well, we're not going to let you do it!" On November 13, in a cable urging Truman to make fresh efforts to settle the Berlin crisis, Evatt helpfully pointed out the importance of "personal contact, personal trust and personal confidence and comradeship between the leaders of the great powers." In turning to the UN, as Evatt did not seem to realize, the

United States and its partners had attempted to take a new step toward solving the crisis after other efforts had failed.

One question, at least, had been settled some days earlier, on Tuesday, November 2. In what could justly be called the greatest political upset in American history, President Truman had confounded the pollsters and astounded even his own supporters by defeating Governor Dewey in the presidential election, winning by some two million votes; neither Henry Wallace's Progressives nor Strom Thurmond's Dixiecrats had kept him from attaining a clear-cut victory. "The astonishingly favorable result was accomplished by Harry Truman with his own efforts, by his complete conviction of the righteousness of his cause, and without assistance from any other person," Admiral Leahy noted in his diary. *Time* magazine, whose guiding spirit, Henry R. Luce, normally professed scant admiration for Truman, shared this opinion: "The President had fought a singlehanded fight without parallel in history. He did it all himself." Suddenly, after one long night of watchful uncertainty—on the part of everybody except Truman himself—the president's political situation had been transformed. No longer the vice-presidential inheritor considered primarily as a transitional figure to the next administration, President Truman now had the authority that comes to a winner. When his train arrived back in Washington from Missouri, said Leahy, a very old Washington hand, Truman was met by "the greatest reception that I have seen in Washington"—a crowd estimated to number 750,000.

Though many factors contributed to the president's upset victory, no one could doubt that a retreat from Berlin, and the likely consequent collapse of the U.S. position in Germany, would have brought a Truman as well as an American defeat. The blockade also cut support for Henry Wallace by strengthening the conviction, as one scholar later wrote, that "Wallace's call for cooperation with the Soviets was hopelessly fanciful"; further, the Western stand in Berlin won Truman the votes of many German-Americans. The success the airlift had achieved during the summer and early autumn had saved the president's political career. A few weeks later, *Newsweek* made its own wry comment on the press and the election by sending, as Christmas gifts, bottles of Old Crow bourbon to the fifty leading Washington correspondents who had unanimously predicted a Dewey victory.

Though the Vinson mission had foundered before it could bring President Truman and his secretary of state into public collision, Marshall told his associates during the Paris meetings of the United Nations that he would shortly return to the United States for an operation (he would have a kidney removed) and he therefore intended to resign his office. When the members of the delegation reacted vehemently, telling him what an irreplaceable asset to the United States he was, the general responded wholly in character. In a private conversation next day, he told Jessup that he regarded the protests as flattery and he didn't like that kind of thing. Marshall would have been pleased to have Jessup take his place as head of the U.S. delegation in Paris, but he advised the president to appoint instead the widely experienced and influential John Foster Dulles, who at the moment would have been secretary of state–designate if Thomas E. Dewey had won the election. Dulles solemnly promised Marshall that he would act in completely nonpartisan fashion.

The UN secretary-general, Trygve Lie, then made his own attempt to advance matters, with a proposal for the UN itself to devise a solution to the Berlin currency problem and submit it to both sides. This effort, in which Herbert Evatt also played a part, dragged on from mid-November until February 11, 1949, when the experts who made up the committee reported that they had not found it possible to develop a plan that all four powers would accept. In reality, the only practical result that phase three of the West's diplomatic campaign had produced was the freezing of the currency situation in Berlin month after month. Could the United States at least make the West mark the sole legal tender in the U.S. sector, even though the British and the French objected to any such Western action without the agreement of the Soviets? In January the American representative in the currency talks proposed such an action, but General Clay did not endorse it. "We are losing ground daily through our failure to make the west mark legal tender," he conceded, but unilateral U.S. action would cause serious financial and political problems with the other Western Allies. The three powers would have to act together.

In presenting the Berlin case to the United Nations, said Jessup, the United States, despite its obvious influence in the organization, had risked having to accept an unsatisfactory solution; but the result, no great surprise, was no solution at all. Until the airlift faced the test of winter, would the Soviets really consider lifting the blockade?

"Airplanes require constant maintenance," General Tunner said; this general truth applied with particular force to the planes carrying out the airlift. Besides the strains caused by around-the-clock flying with little relief, the C-54s suffered from stresses resulting from their use, as Tunner commented, for purposes directly opposed to those for which they had been designed. Created to carry people on long flights, they found themselves in the airlift hauling heavy cargo on short runs. Engines fought to lift the greater-than-anticipated loads to flying altitude, and the high proportion of takeoffs and landings wore out some components—landing gear, tires, and brakes—at a fast rate. Not only did the C-54s carry heavy loads, but two-thirds or more of their burden was coal, which, as Jack Bennett had immediately realized during his June 23 telephone conversation at Wiesbaden, could defeat any kind of packaging and sift into nooks and corners of the planes, scarring cables and corroding electrical contacts.

Tunner worked to meet the maintenance problem in a variety of ways. Most impressively, he moved the key 200-hour inspections from the outdoor facility at Oberpfaffenhoffen, near Munich, to Burtonwood. Apart from other problems at Oberhuffin'puffin', as the airmen called it, planes washed on winter days would have quickly been encased in ice, whereas Burtonwood, besides being easier to pronounce, despite all its difficulties became one of the most valuable parts of the entire airlift operation. During his conversation with the reporter who called on him in September, General Tunner made the point that if the visitor had come a little later, he could have gone to England to visit Burtonwood, lying about halfway between Manchester and Liverpool, which was just beginning its reactivation. "We're putting about twenty-five hundred men in there," Tunner said, "not only for this operation but for all of USAFE. Our maintenance is looking up now and it will get better as we go along."

One of these twenty-five hundred men opening up the newly reactivated World War II base was a young mechanic named Robert Mix. A farm boy from Minnesota, Mix had become captivated by flying as a youngster and had soloed in a "little old" Piper Cub before he was even old enough to acquire a student license. Shortly afterward, Mix's father, suffering from poor health, moved the family off the farm and all the way to Los Angeles, where Mix graduated from high school. Not caring much for the big city and "kind of at a dead end," Mix enlisted in the air force in January 1948, under a program that gave him his choice of specialized schooling. After completing basic training in Texas, he went off to Biloxi, Mississippi, to aircraft engine mechanics school.

By the time Mix had completed his course, the airlift had started and USAFE had arranged for the reopening of Burtonwood, which had served the U.S. and British air forces during the war as a major maintenance center. Some 30,000 people had worked on the whole base, but this great facility had been allowed to run down during the three years leading up to the airlift. The Operation Vittles planes needed such a center because, as Tunner explained, aircraft require several levels of maintenance besides constant attention at the squadron level. "They require periodic maintenance at every twenty-five hours of flight up to two hundred hours, when they undergo a major inspection. At one thousand hours, a comprehensive overhaul must be performed." To take care of all these needs, the work of airlift maintenance must be spread around, relieving the pressure on the mechanics of the individual groups and squadrons. For the 1,000-hour inspections, the planes could be flown back to the United States; Burtonwood would provide the 200-hour checks.

The U.S. advance party of twenty-five airmen appeared at Burtonwood on August 10. The newly reopened base would soon need mechanics by the hundreds, and Robert Mix, "a brand-new GI with one stripe," became one of the first to arrive. "We climbed off a TWA Constellation into mud," Mix said, "and we more or less had to fend for ourselves." The base was enormous, with a perimeter of more than seventy miles, marked by clumps of Nissen huts intermingled with farm fields. The new arrivals had to scrounge up cots and mattresses—"biscuits," the locals called the thin, hard pads—wherever they could find them in the huts. These biscuits were not only hard but damp through and through, and Mix, who had managed to find a fairly intact hut with a potbellied stove, awoke the next day to the sight of steam rising from his mattress.

Reflecting Tunner's mass-production approach to every aspect of the airlift, Burtonwood would perform what was called production-line maintenance (PLM), a method pioneered in the Hump operation by Tunner's maintenance officer, Lieutenant Colonel Robert White. In contrast to the procedure in the standard "bucket shop" maintenance system, in which a crew of mechanics swarmed over a plane carrying out the entire inspection, under PLM the plane moved from station to station, like a car on an assembly line, with specialists performing their particular functions at each stage. When Mix and his fellow mechanics arrived at Burtonwood, crews of workmen were putting together large maintenance stands, built of heavy rough-cut boards that had to be imported from Germany because of the timber shortage in England. Each of the three hangars had three of these stations.

When a C-54 arrived from Germany for its inspection, it presented an appalling sight—wings coated with oil and grease, the inside often black with coal dust. A tractor first towed the new arrival over into what were called the wash racks. At that location "they would shovel the coal dust out as best they could," usually getting almost a pickup load of it; then the crew would spray the plane, often inside as well as out—though the cleaners had to use care here, since hosing the insides while very much coal or flour dust remained could produce an intractable sludge more difficult to deal with than the dry dust. When washing was complete (it could take as much as 125 man-hours), a tractor towed the plane across the field and into a hangar. Hinged doors in the work stand would drop down to make room for the propellers so that the plane could move right up to the stand, where the mechanics would immediately go to work on it, walking around on the platform as they performed their checks.

At the first station, Mix explained, the mechanics removed cowlings and inspection plates. In the middle dock, to which Mix was assigned, mechanics would inspect the engines, each one having its particular crew waiting for it. Rigidity characterized these assignments—a mechanic would exclusively work on number-two engines, for instance, rather than moving around from one to another. ("This wasn't written in stone, of course," Mix commented. "If you got your engine finished and others needed a hand, you would help out.") Mainly, Mix said, they would "find minor oil leaks in bush-rod housings and rocker-box covers—that sort of thing. A flight control crew would thoroughly inspect cables and other electrical components." Then the mechanics would perform as much maintenance as possible on the spot. Problems they could not handle during the eight-hour shift then received the attention of the crew at the third dock. The plane thus received diagnosis first, then had its immediate needs attended to, with the men at the third dock offering longer-term care; each of the hangars operated under this specialized arrangement. A plane could normally go through the entire procedure during an eight-hour shift.

"It was a little bit awkward at first," Mix said, "because it was a new experience for the air force as well as for us, but, surprisingly, it began to work very well. We were cranking out aircraft really smoothly by the end of the airlift. Of course, that R-2000—Pratt & Whitney—engine was very reliable. In my thousand-plus hours of flying as a crew member on a C-54, I can only recall one engine that had a severe mechanical failure. A cylinder head popped, but we didn't have to shut the engine down. We didn't even know it was broken till after we landed. The C-54 in my opinion was an extremely honest, reliable airplane."

Alongside the official organization and procedures, unofficial arrangements promoted the assembly-line efficiency of Burtonwood. Mix, as the chief of the "microcosm" crew working on his engines, followed the practice of "any crew chief worth his salt. He would have a locker over at one side of the hangar with at least one generator in it, possibly a carburetor, a whole bunch of little actuator motors, nuts and bolts of all descriptions, rocker-box covers—things you knew you were normally going to need."

The crew chief, of course, would have these items unofficially. One particular feat pulled off by the mechanics far outshone the squirreling away of a few parts in lockers. Though Burtonwood officially frowned on the word *cannibalization,* mechanics nevertheless drew on a mix of new and used parts in rebuilding C-54 engines. Taking advantage of the sprawling nature of the base, enterprising mechanics "shuffled paperwork around" to the point of being able, like magicians, to make a C-54 disappear by moving it into a hangar in a remote part of the base and also deadlining it on the official records. "Late at night," Mix said, "you could sneak into the hangar and get the part you needed—provided it was still there."

Burtonwood operated three shifts: "twenty-four hours a day those aircraft were going through there. The only thing that would hold them up was adverse weather—too foggy, when it was impossible to bring the aircraft in. If there was a day or two when they couldn't get them in, then when they could, there would be scheduled landings every few minutes, and we'd have to work like crazy to try to get them back out." Although the mechanics devoted themselves to their work, the base commander employed a unique method of ensuring the quick turnaround of C-54s. "There was a little guy in the next hangar that just *looked* important," Mix said, "and they got him a trench coat with colonel's eagles on it. If a flight crew was balking at accepting an aircraft, that little guy would walk out there and sell it to them."

Weather constituted a problem not only for pilots coming into Burtonwood but for the men on the ground. It was "the poorest—rain, sleet, smog—of anywhere in Britain," Tunner said. Burtonwood itself was "dingy, dirty, and depressing-looking. Living quarters, containing only those tiny English coal stoves, were cold and dank." In addition, "the chow was greasy and tasteless." Conditions progressively improved, however, Mix said; notably, civilian carpenters enclosed the Nissen huts, making them more livable.

The establishment of Burtonwood represented a vital step for Tunner and the airlift. Another of the general's steps involving maintenance played an important part, both symbolic and pragmatic, in the transition of Berliners from foes to allies and friends. With the shortage of manpower his most acute problem, the general asked himself a question: Surely the great German Luftwaffe had commanded an ample supply of mechanics? Of course it had. Well, then, find them and put them to work. The solution seemed logical enough, but even if plenty of mechanics were available, Tunner did not have the power to use them; in fact, occupation regulations forbade him to contemplate any such action. As a defeated people, Germans could work for the Allies only in menial jobs, such as hauling rocks for airport runway construction—work, like social life, represented the possibility of fraternization, which remained officially forbidden—and permission to breach the regulations could come only from the military governor, General Clay.

But here Tunner found himself the victim of another prohibition—a purely internecine ban on fraternization between certain Americans. The terms of Tunner's writ in Germany, handed down in a letter from General LeMay, did not allow him any official contact with Clay; he must keep dutifully to the channel going up through USAFE—and hence LeMay—making no upward diagonal approaches to the military governor.

Tunner, however, did not feel himself required to turn down an opportunity if one should present itself. One day, while making one of his frequent trips to Tempelhof to check on operations, he saw Clay arriving at the airport for a flight to the U.S. zone. Although he described the subsequent encounter as occurring purely by chance, it is unlikely that Tunner made great efforts to avoid being noticed by the military governor.

"Any problems, Tunner?" General Clay asked, playing his hoped-for part to perfection.

Yes, there was indeed a problem, Tunner replied—a shortage of mechanics. But he knew how to solve the difficulty, he said, if the military governor would give him permission to hire Germans for the jobs.

Ever the quick decision-maker, Clay said, "Go ahead and do it. Tell Curt I said it's O.K."

That was that—no one in LeMay's headquarters would question such a green light. Tunner ordered his staff to get busy recruiting. In taking this step, the general, an intensely practical man, was acting for purely practical reasons; he had dealt with the same problem in the Hump operation by employing native mechanics, and despite the different political circumstances in the two situations, he sought to reap the same advantages in Germany. But seeking out Germans had its obvious symbolic importance, and fortunately for Tunner, he had timing on his side. No commander, and no army, wants two enemies at once, and with the Russians oppressing the Berliners, it was increasingly absurd for the Western Allies to be defending the Germans and at the same time treating them as foes. Actions like hiring German mechanics dramatized the point.

To serve as the focal point for the recruiting, "I got a German general," Tunner later said. This officer, Hans von Rohden, was a maintenance specialist who had served in air transport during the war. He also knew something about airlifts, including what not to do, since he had been at Stalingrad when the Luftwaffe had tried and failed to keep the besieged German Sixth Army supplied by air. The memory of this failure had possibly helped persuade the Russians to regard airlifts as desperate measures with little chance of success. (For some reason, Tunner, though only one generation removed from Germany himself, had the idea that the name Rohden meant "rat," a point, fortunately, that he did not hold against the general.) Rohden "was a very fine maintenance type," Tunner said, "so I put him in my engineering section." Since the local mechanics could not read English and of course had no familiarity with the C-54, Rohden rounded up translators who produced German versions of the manuals and tech orders.

He also "put out the word through some sort of underground he had, and we had a very fine flow of German airplane mechanics from the ex-Luftwaffe." Eventually these mechanics actually outnumbered the Americans in the operation.

Tunner stressed the importance of learning from experience, such as his use of native mechanics in India. Officers at USAFE headquarters, he recalled, expressed strong skepticism on hearing about his plan. With no way of screening the mechanics, he had to depend for their reliability on Rohden's judgment. He would regret taking on the Germans, he was told, "because they'll throw things into your machinery, and they'll sabotage you." There was even a rumor that people were putting bombs in the coal. Tunner found such ideas absurd. The mechanics were "just as interested as I am," he retorted, "in getting those people in Berlin fed." Further, "when a man has got a wife and children, and he is living in your community, [and] he is depending on the pay you give," would he be likely to be a saboteur? Only a veteran underground Communist might fit that picture, and none of those appeared. As Tunner summed it up: "We had no trouble."

During World War II an American civilian army employee named H. P. Lacomb had spent much of his time building airfields in the Brazilian jungle. While he was engaged in this isolated kind of work, he developed a unique special skill, but after the war was over, he disappeared into the general working population, keeping up no particular contacts with the army. By the time the Berlin airlift had been in operation for just two weeks, it became obvious to air force engineers that somebody like Lacomb would have to be discovered or, if a search revealed no such person, one would have to be invented.

Tempelhof presented the first case. It boasted an elegant terminal building that had opened in 1935, with seven underground stories that during the war had housed German fighter pilots and staffs and contained not only a complete hospital but an assembly plant for Messerschmitt aircraft. But the lone runway, made of sod, belonged to a different era. Early in the occupation the Americans had updated it with steel mats laid on a rubber base, but the continuing impact from the stream of heavily loaded and even overloaded airlift planes quickly began pounding the mats to pieces and plowing holes in the underlying surface.

When General Tunner arrived, he took note of the "ingenious but wild" method the engineers had developed to try to keep the runway functional. Work crews made up of U.S. engineers, Berliners, and displaced persons who still had no homes would line up, rush onto the strip after a plane had gone by, lift the steel planking, and pour a mixture of asphalt from buckets and sand from wheelbarrows into the holes in the surface, straighten the planks, and reweld them together. While this frantic activity took place, a lookout kept a sharp eye on the approach of the next incoming plane. Lieutenant Colonel Kenneth Swallwell, one of Tunner's Hump veterans who specialized in installations, told the general that this situation could not continue; Tempelhof must have two additional runways, one to handle traffic and another for backup when either of the others needed repairs.

This judgment came as no surprise to anybody; even before Tunner's arrival, U.S. authorities had begun efforts to deal with the problem. But one fact loomed over all others. In 1945, when the Russians had stripped the western sectors of Berlin of every kind of machine and device down to wall fixtures and bedpans, they had not overlooked bulldozers, shovels, and other pieces of construction equipment. In the spring of 1948 the Russians could hence look on with some complacency as the Allies tried to base a huge airlift on two small airports that were never intended to handle such heavy, relentless traffic. To all doubters, east and west, this situation simply offered one more reason the airlift had little chance of even coming close to accomplishing its purpose. Even if the Americans had stockpiled heavy equipment in western Germany, they could not move it along the railroad or the autobahn, through the blockade, and into Berlin. Nor could graders, bulldozers, and other such massive machinery be loaded into C-47s or C-54s and flown into Tempelhof.

But the Russians and other skeptics had not taken into account the remarkable talents of H. P. Lacomb, whose wartime work in Brazil had made him into a surgeon in steel, a master whose dexterity with an oxy-acetylene torch, combined with his knowledge of the nerves and muscles under the surface of heavy machines, enabled him to slice these monsters into pieces that could be lifted into airplanes, hauled to their destinations, and then welded back into working condition.

Responding to the call for help from Germany, the Pentagon scoured the country, found this extraordinary specialist working in a routine job at a civilian airport, and added him to the stream of varied experts being dispatched across the Atlantic to buttress the airlift. On arrival at Frankfurt, Lacomb set up his workbench at the Rhein-Main air base. When heavy machines arrived from the United States, he proceeded to dissect them with his torch, carefully pack the pieces, and send them off to Berlin. He would then fly to meet them and patiently perform his restorative surgery, putting these priceless steel Humpty Dumpties back together again. Lacomb's work, together with the labor of work gangs, made possible the fast construction of the second runway, also a pierced-steel strip, which went into service on September 8. On August 23 workers also started building the third runway, this one of asphalt.

Despite the energy and ingenuity that went into all these efforts to build up Tempelhof, the Allies soon realized that this airport and Gatow could not handle the amount of traffic the airlift required. Neither field had any room in which to grow. If the mission came to require more facilities, the airlift commanders would have to design and create a brand-new airport, a possibility that hardly seemed likely to be realized. All the land outside the American and British sectors was forbidden territory, and a great city surely would not have within its borders a large enough tract of suitable and available land. But a search quickly turned up an ideal site near the Tegel lake in the borough of Wedding in the French sector, a great rolling field some 8,000 feet long and 4,000 feet wide; symbolically enough, perhaps, the field had served Hermann Göring's Luftwaffe as a training ground for antiaircraft divisions. As a bonus, no tall buildings stood around the field—the approach would present no problems.

Fortunately, the French seemed to have stopped their the foot-dragging. General Ganeval immediately agreed to the American proposal to build the field and control the traffic; the French would manage the unloading and would maintain the facilities after they were built; they would also thereby gain an airport in Berlin for their own use. Colonel Swallwell supervised the design of an up-to-date airport with emphasis on facilities for quick turnaround; the runway would measure 5,500 feet by 150, with a taxiway connecting it directly to the unloading docks.

Construction of the new airfield proceeded at the speed that characterized all airlift activities that summer. On August 7 a telephone call from Frankfurt ordered Major Frank McGuire, post engineer at the army's Würzburg ordnance depot, to "go immediately to Berlin." As he flew into Tempelhof for the first time, McGuire immediately saw why the airlift needed another airport: "It was like going through a door. You look in apartment-house windows on one side and you look in apartment-house windows on the other side. With the job they had to do, it was obvious that they weren't going to be able to do it with Tempelhof." When McGuire arrived at the great field that was going to become the new airport, he learned that he would be in charge of construction. Asked whom he reported to, he gave a shrug: "We didn't have time to report to anybody."

A native of Baltimore and a 1928 ROTC graduate of Johns Hopkins (a university, he enduringly felt, that looked down on undergraduates), McGuire had served in a variety of engineering posts since the early days of World War II. As an indication that his superiors had not called him to Tegel by accident, his record showed that he had been involved in building a number of projects requiring speed and improvisation, notably including an enormous ordnance plant in St. Louis that had to sit on a forty-degree slope, as well as various airfields. Arriving at the Tegel site, "way out in the sticks," McGuire was struck by the sight of enormous earth berms, perhaps fifty feet high, flanking the field. Nobody seemed to know what the Germans had intended to use them for, but McGuire thought they might have had something to do with canals. In any case, since their millions of cubic feet of earth would have to be moved, they posed a major challenge to the builders of the new field.

To assemble a labor force for Tegel, U.S. authorities broadcast a call for volunteers; a worker would receive 1.20 marks an hour (the reformed mark had a stated value of 30 cents), together with a hot meal. This incentive, with patriotism not necessarily playing a secondary role to hunger, brought out hordes of Berliners, from peasants in wooden shoes to once well-off ladies in silk dresses; professors and scientists turned up along with common laborers. Forty percent of the laborers were women, who became renowned as *Trümmerfrauen* (rubble women). During the hot days of early September, many of them came to the job in bathing suits while the men wore shorts or trunks. At the peak of the effort, some 17,000 Berliners worked in the three daily shifts (later two), digging, loading and unloading brick and rock, hauling sand and asphalt. "We had more women than men that did all the earth moving," said a U.S. officer. "These people would work for one ladle of potato soup and a big chunk of black bread. And they moved the earth by hand."

Lacking trucks, the Americans found a few wrecks, as McGuire called them, that the Russians had left behind when they took away from the Western sectors all devices that seemed useful, and patched them up to help in the moving. "We made one truck run and then we would pull three others behind it"; the Germans called these four-car trains *Anhänger* (literally, trailers). McGuire also succeeded in having thousands of shovels flown in from the American zone, so that in a sort of dirt brigade, workers could move earth along from pile to pile.

When it came to actual construction of the field, McGuire faced the challenge of finding enough cement to lay a concrete foundation two feet thick. Diligent searching of Berlin failed to produce it; nor could the airlift planes sacrifice part of their daily cargo to fly in a few tons per plane. Thoroughly aware that their assignment called for imagination and innovation, the engineers accepted the suggestion that they use the material the Allied air forces had created a few years earlier—the endless tons of rubble from bombed-out buildings. "Berlin was nothing but rubble," McGuire said, "so we had gangs of people out in the city cleaning it up. We loaded it on the trucks in the *Anhänger*s that we were fixing up and dragged the stuff in there and dumped it in the runway." The operation could not always proceed with precision: "We had graded the runway as best we could, and in some cases it was deep enough for the runway base and in other places it was three times as deep as it needed to be," but "you couldn't watch everything."

At this point McGuire needed heavier equipment—tractors to pulverize the layers of bricks, steamrollers to flatten them into more compact layers. This material would be topped off with a layer of stone bound with asphalt. For the stone, McGuire said, "we literally took up the ballast right off the S-bahn"—the municipal railway system. Carrying out this plan called for an array of tractors, graders, rock crushers, and other machines, none of them to be found in Berlin, except for a few venerable pre–World War I steamrollers. Without Lacomb and his skills, the task would have been impossible, but not only was the master on hand, he could impart his knowledge to disciples who then shared the work.

Construction began on September 5, with New Year's Day the target for completion. Actually, McGuire observed, "if it wasn't done then, it wouldn't have gotten done" but would have had to wait until the next year, because the fog came down to the ground and "you couldn't even see what you were doing." The foundations of the runway consumed enormous quantities of the crushed brick—some one million cubic feet. Working along with the German civilians, 150 Americans operated the bulldozers, graders, and other big machines. Overall, the airlift brought eighty-one pieces of heavy equipment into Berlin, some of it simply disassembled, much of it dissected in the Lacomb manner, then reconstituted.

As the work on Tegel progressed, with the Berliners making their massive contribution, McGuire declared that the army engineers could move the target completion date up to December 15, but they did even better than that. On November 5, just two months after the great task began, the runway received its first flight, and on the afternoon of Wednesday, December 8, an elaborate ceremony marked the official completion of the job. Flags of the Allies lined the access roads and the unloading apron, but fittingly enough, they were sometimes hard to discern through the cold gray fog that covered the area. In just four months from Major McGuire's arrival, the engineers and the great labor force through a miracle of production had transformed a very large vacant lot into a new link in the airlift miracle of transport.

One special detail remained to be settled. Here General Ganeval made a dramatic contribution. The not-quite-twin towers of the Soviet *Berliner Rundfunk* (Radio Berlin) stood in the French sector; at 240 and 360 feet high, with no lights, they represented a hazard for aircraft approaching Tegel. On December 12 Robert Murphy pressed the French to deal with the problem, pointing out in addition to the technical reasons the desirability of "getting rid of a station used by the Russians for their propaganda." Raising the question with his Soviet counterpart, General Kotikov, Ganeval declared that if the Russians failed to remove the towers by a certain date, or at least to light them, he would act on his own, and, he told Colonel Howley, he assured Kotikov that he always kept his word. The Americans added that they would pay full compensation for the dismantling of the towers, but Kotikov refused to discuss the question.

Ganeval did not take long to act. Having invited the Americans at Tegel to a morning meeting in his office on December 16, he offered attractive refreshments and engaged the group in agreeable if seemingly purposeless conversation. At ten-forty a loud explosion interrupted the chitchat; the windows rattled and the room rocked. Rushing to the windows, the *convives* saw the two radio towers buckling and collapsing. Only then did they realize the special nature of Ganeval's party. An eyewitness described the work of Ganeval's *sapeurs* as "a very neat bit of demolition. The tower rose about fifty feet in the air, then laid over and broke in two on landing."

"We held our breaths," said Howley. "The Russians blustered but backed down." Berliners who telephoned Soviet headquarters to ask why the station had gone off the air were given talk about "technical difficulties." Kotikov himself came to Ganeval's office to demand "how he could have done it."

Savoring the moment, the French general replied: "*A la dynamite, et par la base*—with dynamite and from the base!"

CHAPTER 21

"We Flew When Birds Walked"

NOVEMBER: THE FIRST and in some ways the worst of the months that would give the airlift its ultimate test—not the coldest, not the snowiest, but the messiest with heavy fogs and freezing rain. To cut down on interruptions in traffic at Tempelhof, the U.S. authorities decided to install a series of high-intensity approach lights that could penetrate at least some of the murk. The existence of the nearby rows of apartment buildings meant that the best area in which to install the lights was the Thomas cemetery in Neukölln, just east of the airport. There the beacons could be placed on towers of graduated heights, starting with ground level; these towers would be made of the kind of steel mesh normally used for landing strips. A possible problem loomed when it became evident that carrying out the installation would require the relocation of several graves.

THE COLD WAR DOESN'T EVEN SPARE THE DEAD, declared a headline in the illustrated supplement of a Communist newspaper, but the local western Berlin authorities, enthusiastic supporters of the airlift, urged the Americans to move ahead quickly. Karin Hueckstaedt remembered that when the Americans began digging, none of the local people protested. "They had to put the approach lights into the graves," she said, "and nobody said anything. We were grateful that they did it." Charlotte Beelitz saw the changes when she went to the cemetery to visit the graves of her parents. "The planes came very close over the houses and right down onto the runway. A plane would be so close that just for a couple of seconds you had the feeling you could reach out and touch it. It was so close, but we were happy because the more that came, the better our life was."

The stiffening of Tempelhof and the remarkable creation of Tegel changed the airlift odds substantially. Yet nothing the Allies could do could affect Berlin's daunting weather. The cartoonist for the *Task Force Times* caught this reality by showing two pilots, headed for their briefing, pausing at the door of the weather office when they saw the body of the weather officer hanging from a rope while fog swirled around the room. "Weather must really be bad to-day," observed one of the fliers. Hans-Karl Behrend recalled a Communist newspaper's own cartoon comment on the weather: a drawing labeled "Winter in West Berlin" showed a plane with a pilot dropping a single lump of coal suspended from a tiny parachute. "It was clear that the meaning of it," Behrend said, "was that maybe in summer the Allies could do something, but in winter it would all be over."

Uwe von Tschammer remembered one night when he missed "the humming and all the engines." The next morning he heard on the radio that the airlift had been interrupted owing to bad weather, fog, and low ceiling. The newspapers assured the people that the Allies would keep the airlift going as long as necessary, but "the ordinary individual didn't trust the papers any more because during the war they had said so much that didn't come true. So we said, let's wait and see."

"The 'battle for Berlin,' " wrote a correspondent, summing up the picture in early autumn, "has been, from the United States point of view, a magnificent achievement and yet a discouraging ordeal." It had certainly surprised the Russians, yet it had also had a substantial debit column: "the coal transported is insufficient for lighting and communications, much less for industrial uses; unemployment caused by the closing of industrial enterprises is increasing. The chaotic nature of the city's financial structure and the collapse, under Russian assault, of the painfully erected quadripartite control system and the elected government, have advanced the social and economic disintegration of Berlin." The costs of the airlift ran high as well. "Its efficacy during the winter months—if the West should be forced to continue it—is a matter of some dispute"; "if the West should be forced to continue it" meant if direct negotiations in Moscow and United Nations intervention in New York both proved fruitless, as all discussions had done up to that point.

Although the ground forces felt that "despite the airlift Berlin's situation is deteriorating steadily"—a view the correspondent seemed to share—the success of the airlift thus far had turned the original air force pessimism into confidence and even cockiness. Some of the airmen at Frankfurt took a jaunty view indeed. After flying a billion pounds of supplies into Berlin on more than 67,000 flights—as of October 30—they felt that the operation should no longer be called Vittles but should be renamed "Frankensteinovitch's Monster." By imposing the blockade, they felt, the Russians had managed to create a powerful weapon to be used against themselves not only now but in the future.

A negotiated settlement might be the policymakers' desire, but with diplomacy unlikely to settle the issue until the Vittles fliers had been tested by winter, the airlift would go on. General Tunner credited the Russian pilots with ability and skill, but observed that unlike Western fliers they always stayed underneath the cloud cover, never piercing it to take advantage of the brilliant blue above. This characteristic convinced the general that "the Russian unfamiliarity with instrument flying led them to take our airlift too lightly. . . . They did not think we could do it." Thus, like everyone else, the Russians waited to see whether Operation Vittles could meet the test of winter.

At the beginning of November, Bill Martin, the MATS pilot from Houston, had just graduated from squadron commanders' school at Panama City, Florida, and flown off to California on his way to Japan when rush orders turned him in a different direction. A veteran of seven years' service in transport flying, with many hours as a test pilot in all types of military aircraft, Martin now found himself assigned to Great Falls, Montana, where the air force trained replacement pilots for Operation Vittles. The pilots already stationed in Germany who had welcomed the challenge when the airlift began now needed relief from the operation's relentless around-the-clock demands. Others, rushed across the Atlantic—sometimes with only two or three hours' notice—had been given no time to make any personal arrangements for themselves or their families and then had seen this "temporary duty" stretch on for week after week. Recognizing the urgent need for a rotation system to produce fresh aircrews for Berlin, General Kuter ordered the creation at Great Falls of a three-week school for instructing C-54 pilots in the intricacies of airlift flying; the course shared the nickname Little Vittles with Lieutenant Gail Halvorsen's more colorful operation at Tempelhof. Unlike most of his classmates, Martin had experience in C-54s and was on active duty at the time of his assignment to Great Falls; but the bulk of the pilots there came from the reserve and had not flown since their days on World War II bombers. They had much to pick up in just three weeks, and at Great Falls as surely as in Berlin, a mistake could mean death.

The Little Vittles instructors sought to train the men to respond to all the actual conditions they would encounter in Germany. Great Falls proved an inspired choice for this mission, since its fog, ice, and other wintry features matched the worst qualities of Berlin. The pilots used the same compass course as that governing the flight from Rhein-Main to the Tempelhof corridor; they called their training path the Little Berlin Corridor. Letdown and landing procedures copied those at Tempelhof, with all approaches being made by GCA (ground control approach), at that time a new and remarkable development.

In GCA, radio led the pilots to the immediate vicinity of the field, and then ground control approach radar took over. At Tempelhof, operators working in a curtained room in a trailer with an NPR-11 mobile radar unit established an electronic aerial funnel (which, in the days before transistors and microchips, drew on seven hundred vacuum tubes, enough for more than a hundred radios) into which the planes flew, keeping a pilot continuously informed of his altitude; the precision operator broadcast corrections to keep the plane lined up on its approach down the center line of the runway. The precision operator then literally talked the pilot in a spiral down to the bottom of the funnel. "The pilot," a reporter said, "must have complete faith in the GCA man's ability to keep him from flying into the ground." Without GCA the Allies would be forced to yield control of Tempelhof, Gatow, and Tegel to the "thick, shrouding vapor that stitches off the sky from the land, that paralyzes all air transport." Of all the instruction at Great Falls, Martin believed, the instruction in instrument flying was much the most important.

The planes at Great Falls carried ample cargo—enough sand-filled drums to give them an overall weight of thirty-two tons, comparable to that of the planes flying into Berlin; the pilots even had to make three landings at thirty-five tons' gross weight. Because of Tempelhof's short runways, the pilots had to get used to putting their planes down in the first part of the runway at Great Falls; this instruction had particular importance because the barrier of buildings around Tempelhof gave pilots an almost instinctive tendency to land high, or to wish to do it. ("It was a steep landing," Bill Palahunich said. "It took full flaps, and pilots didn't like it.") Pilots received instruction in navigation and radar, and they, as well as engineers, had to learn the workings of the C-54 engines and electrical system.

While Martin and his classmates were spending their intensive three weeks at Great Falls, the airlift itself began encountering the anticipated winter challenges. November, said one pilot, "is when the fog rolls in as soon as the sun goes down. You seldom had much wind, and the nights were very quiet—ideal for the formation of fog. When the dew point and the temperature got very close together, you knew what you were in for. If you were coming back home to Rhein-Main and you heard the temperature was fifty-three and the dew point was fifty-three, you knew darn well what was going to happen."

One day when Bill Palahunich was working in Tempelhof flight control, he had a little fun with Gail Halvorsen by giving him an unexpected instruction to put his windshield wipers on—the radar showed rain showers that the pilot had not yet reached. Halvorsen went along with what seemed to be a harmless joke, only to express his thanks almost immediately—in about two minutes, he said, it took everything he had to keep the plane level and flying in the right direction—and then to raise another question when he received what seemed a premature instruction to shut the wipers off again.

On November 1, arriving right on schedule, fog shut down traffic at Tempelhof; at Gatow flights were spaced out to five-minute intervals. (On the same day the U.S. Air Force announced the standardization move of grounding the last C-47s in the airlift; within days all the loads would be carried only by C-54s or their navy equivalents, R-5Ds, two squadrons of which had been assigned to the task force at the beginning of the month.) The next night the low visibility took a heavy toll when a C-47 still on the job, trying to land at Wiesbaden, overshot the field and, on a second pass, plowed into the ground before reaching the runway; five men died and five suffered serious injuries. That night of impenetrable fogs halted operations at Tempelhof and Gatow for ten hours; Allied pilots were getting "cold feet," claimed a writer in *Tägliche Rundschau*, because of the weather and inferior planes, but in late morning the two airports began receiving traffic again. "We flew," pilots liked to say, "when birds walked."

On November 10 the Soviet Military Administration inserted itself into this particular situation by warning that Soviet fighters would force down any transports that strayed from the air corridors, a declaration that drew angry replies, partly because the Russian statement implied that the Allies were using planes without identification markings. Fog struck again on November 12, limiting operations at Rhein-Main and Wiesbaden for the next two days. It then moved on to Tempelhof and Gatow, which on November 14 lay for eighteen hours under a densely impenetrable blanket; by eleven o'clock that night, however, aircraft were managing to land at Gatow at five-minute intervals. But next day a U.S. Navy R-5D carrying five tons of coal came down short of the Tempelhof runway, slid into an embankment, and caught fire; every member of the crew suffered either injuries or burns, but nobody was killed. That same day, besides the fog over Berlin, the airlift suffered from intermittent fog and rain squalls over Rhein-Main and Wiesbaden; a reporter cheerfully noted that "Berliners predict this sort of weather will predominate until early December." Then on November 17 a British Dakota went down in the Soviet zone. Three days later dense fog halted traffic for six hours at Tempelhof and Gatow; Tegel, whose finishing touches were being administered, did not come into use that day at all. The Berlin fog saw the month of November out with its strongest effort—on the thirtieth, General Tunner reported, the city was smothered by a pea-souper so dense that "you couldn't drive a car." That day only one plane landed.

Earlier, despite the anticipated grimness of the November catalogue, General Clay had expressed optimism. On October 21 he had reported to Washington, as Admiral Leahy noted, that he could continue to feed the population in the U.S. sector by airlift indefinitely, "unless the Soviets use force, which he does not expect." The president also said, that same day, that he intended to remain in Berlin unless the Americans were driven out by superior force. Early in November, well aware of the weather ahead, Clay nevertheless predicted that the airlift would maintain an average of four thousand tons a day "without difficulty."

On November 16, after the four-day spell of severe fog, the airlift authorities deemed the airlift to have passed its first test, and on November 26 USAFE headquarters announced that during the "worst weather month" of the year, the airlift had delivered an average of 4,051 tons a day, just a bit above Clay's forecast. The fliers had achieved this level only because they had taken advantage of clear days to bring in as much as 6,000 tons to offset days when few planes could get through. On November 28 Clay celebrated this remarkable Allied achievement by ordering a coal bonus of 28,000 tons delivered to Berlin families; with a total tonnage of 113,588, the airlift had beaten the worst month for flying. But to be sure, there was plenty of fog and ice to come.

A special bright spot marked this November. Almost a century and a half earlier, after Napoleon's conquest of Prussia, scholars had come together in an act of intellectual rebuilding to create the University of Berlin. Now, with American help, Berliners played a reprise of that moment. More than two thousand professors and students left what had become the oppressive atmosphere of the university to create in the American zone the Free University of Berlin.

On December 5, a month after President Truman's celebrated electoral triumph, Berliners went to the polls to choose members of the city assembly. Across the Atlantic the central question for U.S. voters had been the identity of the winner; Berliners, in contrast, had to wonder whether they would have the chance to vote at all. This election had become necessary because the two-year terms of assembly members had expired. The voting was late, however, because city officials, fearing the possible repercussions in the volatile political situation, had delayed submitting the required election notice to the occupation authorities until October 2, although by law this procedure should have been set in motion in early September. Scheduled for November 14, the election encountered sabotage on the part of the Soviets, who took over the city printing plant, temporarily blocking the preparation of voter lists. After the authorities rescheduled the election for December 5, the Russians attempted to have some of the Allied-sector parties banned from participation as fascists and militarists, while seeking full play for Communist-run groups in those same sectors. What all this meant was that the election would take place in those sectors but not in the

East. With the Soviets forbidding the people in their sector to take part, the city government limited the election to the three Western sectors; the Eastern-sector representatives would, if they chose, continue in office. As General Clay explained to Washington, the Berlin government did not wish to be responsible for splitting the city.

During the summer and autumn, the Soviets had also been building up their authority in their zone by creating an indigenous armed force; units of this Alert Police force (*Bereitschaften*) lived in barracks and trained like soldiers. The Alert Police would serve as an auxiliary force to Soviet army units in Germany; former Wehrmacht generals had the task of instilling military discipline. On October 21 Admiral Leahy noted a report from General Clay that the Soviets were developing "an armed police force in the Soviet Zone that can control the German population." Robert Murphy had suggested that the Americans consider establishing a similar force in the U.S. zone, but, Leahy noted, the French objected to the idea and it therefore might not prove practicable. Clay's assessment, though accurate, was something of an understatement. The project, on which Walter Ulbricht had been working for the past year, actually aimed at creating an armed force that could take the place of Russian troops after the signing of a peace treaty. After all the occupying forces pulled out, the Communists would thus have the only army in Germany.

At the moment Marshal Sokolovsky and General Kotikov had no shortage of forces, foreign or domestic. During the election campaign Kotikov threw in his Berlin goon squads to break up meetings, but the Western parties fought back. The SED also mounted a fear campaign, trying to convince Berliners that the Allied forces would soon be pulling out of the city, thus delivering the subliminal message that the people should be friendly to the Soviet occupiers, who would remain. Most suspensefully, these and other Communist moves led to the widely held belief—much stronger than a rumor—that the Soviets planned a coup, in which they would simply seize control of the city government.

On November 29 Marshal Sokolovsky prepared the way by charging the Allies with supporting "dangerous activities taking place in the Western sectors of Berlin, seeking to disorganize and split the uniform municipal administration." The Allies, he said, wished to create a separate government so that "the Western Military Governments can work uncontrolled" and could "further the activities of the anti-democratic and known reactionary forces in their sectors." The next day, in response to the wishes of their leaders, delegates to a meeting of various Communist and Communist-supported organizations (the Extraordinary Assembly of City and District Deputies) dutifully voted the existing Magistrat out of office and installed a successor group. Fritz Ebert, son of Friedrich Ebert, the first president of the Weimar Republic, became mayor *(Oberbürgermeister)* of this dictated new municipal government. With the coup having taken place, General Kotikov offered his formal blessing, declaring that he would give "the provisional democratic Magistrat" all the help it needed. Commenting to Washington on this development, Clay observed that it rendered pointless all the diplomatic activity in Paris.

On December 1 Ferdinand Friedensburg, in Western eyes still the acting mayor, found himself barred from city hall by Soviet-sector police. He and other officials moved westward and continued with the electoral campaign; the transparent illegitimacy of the November 30 coup guaranteed a good turnout of voters on December 5. Almost two-thirds of those voting supported the Social Democrats, and finally, a year and a half after his original election, Ernst Reuter became mayor; he could no longer be ruled out by a Soviet veto, though he would preside only over the Western sectors.

By recognizing the new Communist Berlin government, so the CIA informed President Truman on December 10, the Soviet Union had given evidence of a new estimate "concerning its capabilities in the Berlin dispute." Originally, said Admiral Hillenkoetter, director of central intelligence, the Soviets had clamped on the blockade in order to win concessions in relation to western Germany, with expulsion of the West from Berlin as a secondary aim. Now the Kremlin had apparently concluded that its Western Germany aims were beyond its reach and was concentrating, instead, on forcing the West out of Berlin either immediately or in the long run. (The admiral presumably did not know about Stalin's "let's kick them out" remark in March to Wilhelm Pieck; even if he had known, however, he would not have had to conclude that his ranking of Stalin's priorities was wrong.) As the new first step, Admiral Hillenkoetter felt, the Russians would probably tighten the blockade. With its bargaining position thus enhanced, the USSR would then call on the UN neutral nations to agree that, in any settlement, the new Soviet-controlled eastern Berlin government must be merged into the overall government of the city. Acceptance of this claim would allow the Soviets to acquire control over key positions and ultimately to assume complete administrative power in the city. Thus the Kremlin, though having failed to win its great German objective, would receive a very handsome consolation prize. This cheerful analysis rendered bleak, indeed, the prospects for any useful diplomatic discussions.

As a supplement to the election, the Western Allies announced on December 21 the resumption of Kommandatura meetings, so that actions of Mayor Reuter's new city government could receive the proper approval from the occupying powers. The Soviets were welcome to return to the

Kommandatura, they said, but they did not seem to expect that to happen. Indeed, there were now two cities, East Berlin and West Berlin—names that would become standard in the following years, though the halves would not be separated physically for another thirteen years—and two muncipal governments. But public services—transit, water, gas, sewerage—continued across sector boundaries; though divorced, East Berlin and West Berlin remained locked in interdependence.

CHAPTER 22

"Here Comes a Yankee . . ."

AFTER COMPLETING THE airlift training course at Great Falls, Bill Martin and his classmates moved on to Westover Air Force Base in western Massachusetts, the American end of the MATS highway over the North Atlantic. Through this gateway passed all of the aircrews, aircraft, equipment, and supplies destined for Germany and the airlift; it was a place of transition, and the fliers did not linger there. Arriving in Germany on December 23, Martin and the other new arrivals received cordial welcomes from earlier Vittles crews who were eager to start for home. On Christmas Day, which happened to be Martin's wedding anniversary as well, he made his airlift inauguration with three round trips to Berlin.

Though the Great Falls graduates came to Germany well trained to carry out their unique assignment, at least one newcomer proved that it is impossible to teach everything to everybody. Shortly after arriving, this pilot sought out the briefing officer to ask: "Is it permissible to ride an airlift plane to Berlin when I have a pass or a leave?" No, said the officer, that was contrary to task force regulations. "Well, then," said the new man, "could you give me a copy of the train schedule to Berlin?"

Martin, and now many other pilots, flew not out of the Frankfurt-area airports, Rhein-Main and Wiesbaden, but from Fassberg in the British zone. When the airlift began in June, the British had operated their C-47 Dakotas; high-winged, triple-tailed Avro Yorks (transport versions of the famous Lancaster bombers); and other land planes out of Wunstorf, a base sitting right in the mouth of the westbound corridor from Berlin. But when airlift traffic quickly overloaded this base and its facilities, the RAF transferred its Dakotas to the former Luftwaffe base at Fassberg, sixty miles northeast of Wunstorf. Located in an attractive forest area, this airfield, which during the war had served the Germans as a base for interceptors, had been built as an elegant facility for Hermann Göring's favored young men, with such niceties as porcelain vomit basins mounted on day room walls for the convenience of *Flieger* who had poured down too much beer. Used by the RAF as a maintenance base, Fassberg needed additional buildings and facilities for its role as home to the Dakotas. By the end of July, it was ready to receive its new tenants.

From the day of his first flight to Berlin, General Tunner had kept in mind the strong points of the RAF bases. The northern corridor, from the border of the British zone to Berlin, was only about 110 miles long, just two-thirds the length of the southern corridor. Fassberg itself lay only 145 miles from Berlin, or fifty-five minutes' flying time, compared with 280 miles for Rhein-Main. Hence two planes based at Fassberg could do the work of three based at Rhein-Main. Planes from Fassberg could make five round trips a day, compared with three and a half from Rhein-Main, and thereby save 100 gallons of gasoline for each plane. Besides, as Tunner had seen on that first trip, the northern routes passed over low country "as flat as a football field," with no hazards like the Taunus Mountains and their influence on the weather. Still another factor entered Tunner's thoughts: study of German weather over the past fifty years indicated more benign patterns in the north—although, as a French diplomat and climatic commentator observed, "Continuously affected by the maritime climate of the West and the Baltic, on the on hand, and on the other by the land mass of the East, the weather in Berlin is rarely at rest."

In August, after negotiations with the RAF, Tunner won agreement to base U.S. planes at Fassberg. The first group of C-54s, some forty transports, arrived on August 22; the British Dakotas moved on to still another former Luftwaffe base, this one at Lübeck. On the whole, the Anglo-American cooperative arrangement at Fassberg worked well, though Tunner had not made any allowance for the likelihood of severe culture shock when the U.S. fliers were given their first breakfast kippers. (Bill Martin encountered his first kipper at Hamburg; in discussing the memory, he could barely bring himself to describe it. Fortunately, he said, at Fassberg the Americans, unlike the British, had an ample supply of real eggs.)

Though Tunner did not say in so many words that one of his purposes in basing Skymasters at Fassberg was to move toward a unified command, he had been convinced since shortly after his arrival in the theater that efficiency and effectiveness demanded combining the American and British operations. With C-54s now flying out of Fassberg, obviously the two air forces had to develop close coordination. With "all of us going into more or less the same bases, and escaping collisions only by miracles," the solution lay in forming a single organization under a single command, and Tunner knew exactly how this necessary goal should be attained. His relations with LeMay had by now turned so mellow that when he proposed the creation of a combined task force under his own command, LeMay immediately agreed.

The two Americans flew to Bückeberg, the headquarters of Air Marshal Sir Arthur Sanders, commander of the British Air Forces of Occupation. While accepting the need for a high level of integration of the U.S. and British efforts, Sanders argued for a coordinating committee (a favorite device of the British even when no foreigners are involved) instead of a unified command. The air marshal saw and disliked the fact that with the Americans contributing 80 percent of the airlift effort, the commander of any combined task force would unavoidably be American. His discomfort was understandable but would not be allowed to determine the outcome of the discussions, which lasted through several sessions. LeMay, who was preparing to return to the United States to take over the Strategic Air Command, remained adamant: "Sanders might as well have been talking to his cigar."

On October 14, with LeMay's departure for the United States scheduled for the next day, he and Sanders signed the agreement creating the Combined Airlift Task Force; Tunner would command, and Air Commodore J. W. F. Merer would serve as his deputy. The agreement mandated the merger of the U.S. and British airlift forces "in order that the resources of each participating service may be utilized in the most advantageous manner"; the primary mission was simply to deliver "the maximum tonnage possible." This latter clause said more than might be obvious. Previous airlift efforts had focused on achieving the delivery of a *minimum* amount of supplies to Berlin; now that the emphasis had shifted to *maximum,* larger planes took precedence over smaller ones: the Skymaster outranked the Dakota. The British now had the only DC-3s in the airlift, since Tunner, working toward his dream and goal of a smooth, rhythmic beat, had withdrawn the C-47s; all U.S. planes would now carry the same amount of cargo and fly at the same speed, performing like identical elements on an assembly line. In addition, as Russ Reynolds, one of the U.S. pilots, pointed out, you could concentrate spare parts, and the hydraulics people, the electricians, and other specialists would all be dealing with the same type of engine, propeller, and other components.

During this time RAF engineers, working to an American design, began turning still another of the apparently limitless number of old Luftwaffe bases into another field for C-54s. This field was at Celle, between Fassberg and Wunstorf, and like Fassberg it would increase the efficiency in the use of U.S. aircraft. But the transfer of C-54s to bases in the British zone had its limits. Despite the great advantage conferred by the shorter run to Berlin, and the generally more favorable northern weather pattern, the shifts in weather patterns meant that operations had the best chance of avoiding complete interruption if airlift planes were spread between the two zones. Celle began operations as a U.S. base on December 15, with new-comers from Great Falls assigned to it as well as to Fassberg or the bases around Frankfurt.

Assignments, once made, were fixed. Martin and the other Americans posted to Fassberg always flew from there, and all planes from bases in the British zone went into Gatow and, from early December, into Tegel. Oc-casionally, however, if weather demanded it, a pilot for Tegel might be diverted to Tempelhof. Actually, Martin's training at Great Falls had been for Tempelhof; he and his fellow pilots at Fassberg picked up details concerning Tegel by flying as copilots. Martin first confronted the reality of the Tempelhof challenge on a foggy evening when, after being switched from Tegel, he made his approach through a ceiling he judged to have been about 300 feet. "When I broke out," he said, "it seemed like I was in a crab"—a yawing motion—"and I was looking into somebody's window. There were lights on in there, and I could see these people sitting around a table, eating their dinner. I had heard about how narrow that corridor was going into that place, but that was my first experience. To eyeball it that close—these people eating dinner while I'm flying an airplane right by them!" Martin realized later that the yaw had been no accident; ground controllers had turned him in that direction in order to fit him into the slot between the rows of buildings.

"That was the kind of instrument flying we were doing," Martin said. "We were flying around the clock. They had each squadron flying twenty-four hours a day; they had to break up the crews into four sections, to give some time off, so every twelve days we got three days off. The day was divided into blocks, from four in the morning to noon, noon to eight o'clock at night, and eight to four. From Fassberg it was about an hour and fifteen minutes going in and about an hour coming out, because we were moving faster. If you took one of the first planes out in your eight-hour-block that you were on, you were likely to make a third trip. The way the schedule was worked out, if you took one of the later planes, then you would make your two flights, and the next section would take over. But a lot of times, if you took off early, then you had another three hours, and it made for about an eleven-hour day that you'd been on. So one of the main things we had to do was get enough sleep." Another pilot, diverted from one base to another, ended up flying four consecutive missions over the span of a day and a half, finally returning to Wiesbaden with the confession that at one point he had waked up to realize that all the other crew members had been asleep too, leaving the automatic pilot to handle the plane on its own.

In one of the various "peculiarities" of the schedule, as Martin put it, the crews would receive their preflight briefing on the weather before their shift officially began. This meant that, if they were in the lead in the early block, they had to get up by two-thirty in order to have breakfast and then get transportation down to the flight line to go to the operations office for the briefing. But since "we knew we were going to be flying, regardless," as Martin put it, the crews finally decided that if they could see the light on top of the flagpole, which was not much more than fifty feet high, they would be going out, and hence they could skip the briefing. November may have been the worst flying month, but months of foggy weather remained on the calendar; only rarely, however, would limited visibility cause the cancellation of flights.

Nor did equipment problems exert much effect on the schedule. The aircraft, heavily overworked like the men who flew them, operated under stresses far beyond normal. "These airplanes had been flying since they were brought over to Germany from all parts of the world," Martin said—"flying around the clock, as much as possible, with, you might say, minimum maintenance. It got so that, as long as your engines were working all right— that is, the magnetos, the props, and other basic things—if your cylinder-head temperature gauge was out, as long as your oil-temperature gauge was working, you took the airplane. Or vice versa. If the RPM gauge for an engine was out, then you used the synchronizer—you could even your engines up with it. A lot of times the heaters weren't working, either—that's when it really got bad; you'd get icing on the windshield. Sometimes we would take this heavy-duty spotlight we had in the cabin and hold it up against the windshield. If we left it there long enough, it would put out enough heat to melt the ice. It would give you about an eight-inch hole to look through for your landing." But, Martin added with admirable phlegm, "with instrument flying that didn't make much difference." A general principle had evolved: "As long as you have one instrument that indicates something about what you need to know, go ahead and take the plane, and if we ever get any parts for this we'll fix it."

Very early one morning, preparing to fly back from Tegel to Fassberg, Martin discovered that the starter for his number-two engine refused to work. With no replacements available, he waited till daylight and then took off on three engines. The "ruthless priorities of the airlift," commented the writer Richard Collier, "decreed that many men lay their lives on the line." He offered the particular example of an incident at Rhein-Main, when a sergeant named Emery Hedges red-lined a plane because of a cracked landing gear, only to have the operations officer erase the entry. "We want this plane to fly," the officer said coldly.

In the overall realm of maintenance, General Tunner had to endure continuing frustrations. Though he had advocated reopening Burtonwood and had seen it adopt production-line maintenance, the base did not operate as part of the airlift organization but functioned as a direct arm of USAFE. Nor could Tunner deal directly with the Air Materiel Command, headquartered at Wright-Patterson Air Force Base in Ohio, which had charge of air force procurement, supply, and maintenance. As it happened, Burtonwood went into operation just when General LeMay left Germany to return to the United States. LeMay's departure did not represent a happy development for Tunner. The two officers had a cordial farewell at Wiesbaden, when LeMay assured Tunner that he was doing a good job; for the verbally parsimonious LeMay, this simple declaration of fact amounted almost to burbling. Thus parted two very different men who yet were more alike than either seemed to realize, with their identical standards of professionalism and performance.

In Lieutenant General John K. Cannon, LeMay's successor as U.S. Air Force commander in Europe, Tunner confronted a newcomer to the world of the airlift. A well-known officer who had built up an outstanding combat record as a high commander in World War II, Cannon did not arrive in Germany as a professed admirer of transport airmen. While the whole world marveled at the airlift, with its double defiance of the Soviets and the German weather, Cannon like many other combat fliers seemed, in contrast, to look on the operation as a perhaps rather demanding but not essentially remarkable parcel-post service—just put the packages on those planes and get them off again. The proper business of a military pilot was to destroy the enemy, not to deliver groceries! Cannon proceeded as if Operation Vittles amounted only to a subsidiary concern for USAFE; under his regime, spare parts and tools craved by the mechanics at Burtonwood would remain on the shelves at the Erding Air Force Depot in Bavaria, in case they should be needed by any USAFE units in Germany. Though mechanics like Bob Mix back at Burtonwood had no knowledge of high-level clashes of viewpoints and policies, they quickly devised their own creative solutions to shortages of tools and other maintenance items.

Aside from the problems caused by Cannon's belief in the important distinction between combat fliers and freight haulers, Tunner's first meeting with him began explosively. Cannon opened it by protesting the establishment of the CALTF—not so much the concept itself as the fact that the agreement had been reached before his arrival. Small, almost wizened, Cannon in his youth had suffered severe facial burns in an airplane crash; he had emerged from plastic surgery with a face that wore an almost perpetual smile, "regardless," as Tunner noted, "of his inner feelings." At the moment, however, Tunner had little difficulty in divining his new chief's emotions. Whatever Cannon thought of transport fliers, he apparently had expected to include command of the "now famous" airlift among his many duties, only to find himself one of the two bosses (along with a British air marshal) of the real commander. He also may not have been altogether pleased that, in news reports, Tunner's appointment as head of the CALTF upstaged his own assumption of command of USAFE.

Tunner later conceded his own partial fault in the conversation: "I may have been a little impatient with him. I was then forty-two, cocky and confident. . . . I did not feel that I needed any advice from an aging combat man of fifty-six years." All he really wanted, Tunner said, was to be left alone: "I knew best how the job should be done." Despite the unquestionable truth of that point, Cannon may well not have felt like expressing his agreement with it. On the other hand, curiously, neither General Vandenberg, the air force chief, nor his successive viceroys in Europe displayed any awareness of the incalculable contribution the airlift was making to the image of the air force, an image of particular importance at a time when this brand-new independent service was fighting the navy for U.S. strategic supremacy.

In the following weeks, Cannon kept close watch on the CALTF commander. Daily and sometimes hourly, Tunner noted, his "American master" wanted information and explanations: "Why did I do this, why did I not do that?" In contrast, Air Marshal T. M. Williams, Sanders's successor—a big, florid-faced, easygoing South African—never interfered with Tunner as long as the supplies kept flowing into Berlin. "I could do as I pleased," Tunner said.

Only once did he get out of his depth and find himself neatly overruled. During the winter he took a two-day pass to visit Charles J. V. Murphy, a *Fortune* writer who had done a story on the airlift during the summer and was now wintering on the Riviera while ghostwriting the duke of Windsor's autobiography. As the commander of the famous airlift, Tunner received an invitation to dine with the duke and duchess at their nearby house. During the evening, a bit carried away by his hosts' interest in the operation, Tunner found himself inviting them to pay a visit to his fliers, who were slugging it out day and night in the cold and darkness and would enjoy the chance to see and even chat with the eminent couple. The official invitation, Tunner explained, would have to come from his masters, General Cannon and Air Marshal Williams; this was especially true, he reminded himself, since he could hardly entertain distinguished guests in his third-floor walkup at the Schwarzerbock Hotel, with its entrance through the bathroom.

Back in Germany, Cannon, after some discussion, accepted the idea and agreed to entertain the Windsors at the mansion he had inherited from General LeMay. But Tunner must also get Williams's approval, which Cannon thought would probably require conferring with London. Though the air marshal occupied an office fully equipped with couches, chairs, and coffee tables, he had the unusual habit of spending most of his time standing at a drafting board, with his papers arranged on a small table at his side. When Tunner came into his office, Williams waved him to an easy chair and then took up his familiar stand by the board. After complimenting his visitor on the functioning of the airlift and engaging in a few other pleasantries, the air marshal listened as Tunner described his delightful evening with the Windsors and discussed the benefits he thought a visit from the duke and duchess could bring to his fliers during these weeks of winter doldrums.

For the first time ever with Tunner, Williams moved from behind his drawing board; then he lit his pipe, standing wordless for perhaps two minutes. After that, he sat down in a chair facing Tunner and, with a twinkle in his eye, said, "Bill, who is the duke of Windsor?"

Tunner knew better than to offer any further justification of his idea. In the gentlest way possible, he had learned that the British government wanted nothing to do with the former king and his wife.

Nobody would have dreamed that one of the world's most popular comedians would play a part in transforming General Tunner's maintenance situation. As it happened, Bill Martin and his classmates flew in to Fassberg just when a traveling troupe of American politicians and entertainers arrived in Germany, the leading luminaries being newly elected Vice President Alben W. Barkley, for the politicians, and Bob Hope, for the entertainers. Martin recalled that Hope came to Fassberg and, joining the operators in the tower, sang over the microphone for the flight crews.

As soon as the visit from Hope, the actress-model-tennis player Jinx Falkenburg, and the songwriter Irving Berlin was announced, it aroused great anticipation among the airlift crews. But the men at Fassberg did not know that their visit from the "Christmas Caravan" took place only because General Tunner himself threatened a rebellion. On December 23 Tunner had learned to his disgust that, although the airlift had provided the stimulus for the trip, none of the shows were scheduled for airlift bases. "There was no reason," he said, "for any entertainer, least of all one of Hope's stature, to put on a show for the occupation troops"; it was the hardworking men of the airlift who deserved the treat. Defying his current bête noire, General Cannon, the task force commander demanded that the Hope show appear where his men could attend it; otherwise, he said, no mention of the airlift should appear in any of the publicity. "Think of what the press back home would make of that," Tunner noted with some satisfaction. Cannon saw the point, too; Hope, completely unaware of the backstage battle, suddenly found his itinerary rearranged, with three new performances added; thus the Christmas Caravan came to Fassberg.

On the Skymaster bringing Hope's troupe across the Atlantic to Wiesbaden, Tex McCrary, a veteran air force publicist (and Jinx Falkenburg's husband), had briefed Irving Berlin on the remarkable job being done by the airlift crews, in particular making the point (and thereby unknowingly summing up the Cannon-Tunner conflict of perspectives) that many of the pilots had been converted from their glamorous role as wartime fighters into haulers of freight. After wondering what kind of Christmas present he might bring the Vittles fliers, Berlin surprised nobody when he hit on the idea of giving them a new song. When a group of some three hundred men heard "We're growing fonder of 'the wild blue yonder' making a buck flying a truck" and "We'll be there earning stripes and bars in our old freight cars, until the airlift gets the air," they shouted their approval. This response led the *Task Force Times* to print the lyrics in one of its issues, so that those attending the shows could bring copies along and join in a community sing. The only negative note came from the announcement, in the same issue, that owing to her "last-minute movie commitments," the Christmas Caravan would not include Jane Russell, the famously mammiferous star of Howard Hughes's then-scandalous movie *The Outlaw.*

During his performances, Hope delighted his audiences with comments about breaks in the drudgery of airlift flying coming "when a Russian fighter will swoop up and buzz an American plane, take a look, see the food and drool to the ground." The weather was so bad, he said, that "you need instruments just to walk along the street." When flying in, he "remarked to the crew chief that the weather was a little soupy and he said, 'Soup I'd settle for—this stuff has noodles in it.'" More seriously, Hope declared, in an inversion of Robert Burns's famous line, that every plane was "loaded with food, fuel and faith in man's humanity to man."

Significantly, Hope's entourage included, on the political side, not only Barkley but Stuart Symington, who had been secretary of the air force since its establishment fifteen months earlier. Whether by oversight or simple insouciance, General Cannon left the secretary in Tunner's hands for Christmas Eve. By the end of the evening, the powerful visitor had acquired a thorough understanding of Tunner's point of view, not only about shortages but about the bleak conditions—"none too good in summer, terrible in winter"—in which many of the airlift crews lived. Another participant in the conversation was the famous General Jimmy Doolittle, whom, as it happened, General Vandenberg had recruited as an adviser on matters that included materiel and supply.

Next day Symington and Tunner met Cannon for a tour of the Rhein-

Main operation. Stopping in the maintenance section, the secretary got a golden earful from a mechanic who declared that he needed better tools. When the secretary asked why that was, the man declared that he had been forced to buy his own screwdriver, wrench, and pliers—"and they ain't worth a good god-damn." Silence descended on the group as Cannon turned red.

When Symington and Doolittle stopped at Burtonwood, they also found ample room for improvement; the secretary was actually shocked at what he saw. The crowding, the bedbugs, and the mud were bad enough, but the men added other details. "One boy had no teeth and said he had tried for months to get them, without results. He could not digest his food, and he hated to go downtown because he did not smile and [people] thought he was homesick." The men showed their powerful visitors "showers which were bad. They said there was little warm water." Symington saw "latrines unspeakably filthy—worse than any I have ever seen on any base housing American soldiers and even worse than any of my experience in World War I."

With the help of an exhaustive memorandum from Tunner, Symington took vigorous and effective remedial action. After months of feeling that the needs and problems of the airlift never came to the attention of persons who could help solve them, Tunner basked in this new high-level attention: "None of us could have asked for a more wonderful Christmas present."

Looking forward from October, before the worst fogs and ice and snow had moved in, an American newsmagazine had commented that victory in Berlin would not come cheap: the pilots "expect more wrecks, more loss of life, when winter comes. Dollar cost is mounting." But, the magazine declared, "if Western Berlin can scrape through the winter and keep production up, this will be a major setback for Russia." As it appeared from Washington, the Russians might "choose to put an end to the drama of the air lift by interfering with the air corridors or seizing Berlin by force at the risk of war. Otherwise, if Russia sits tight, there is a good chance that the air lift will win the battle of Berlin for the Western powers." When Vice President Barkley and Secretary Symington returned to Washington, they took with them the clear knowledge that, for all its daily problems, the airlift was winning—indeed, had won—the battle.

Strangely, the much-reviled weather made its own contribution to the success of the airlift. The persistent fogs posed their great challenge to the fliers, but the very existence of such weather meant that temperatures had not fallen to normal winter levels—nor did they do so in the ensuing weeks.

The airlift crews coped with the fogs, and they might well have found ways to cope with the hazards to equipment and runways created by chilling winter winds, but the morale and the militancy of the people of Berlin depended on the warmth, limited as it was, brought them by airlifted coal. Low temperatures—even normal low temperatures—could have created needs the airlift could not meet: a bad winter could have given the Russians the victory they could not otherwise win.

Even though fate chose to give them a mild winter, the Berliners did not enjoy an easy life. Electricity and power came on just twice a day on a rotating schedule, for two hours each time, so that housewives sometimes had to get out of bed in the wee hours to cook meals. "Every household received a certain number of kilowatt hours," said Hans-Karl Behrend, "and on top of that, every person also received something. At home I was in charge of inspecting the kilowatts. Every day, and sometimes twice a day, I watched the meter, because going over your amount of kilowatts meant not only a fine but having your electricity cut off for a week or two."

Even in the face of such a penalty, Berliners, no more devoted to austerity than people anywhere else, found ways of evading the restrictions. While visiting friends one evening, Behrend expressed astonishment at seeing lights on and homemade electric heaters glowing. As, by now, an experienced meter reader, he took a professional look at the dial, which turned out to have only three digits. "It was probably installed during World War I," he said, "and so what the people did was to burn as much as they could, and when the dial got up to 999 it went back to zero and started again." Other families, as Behrend said, applied what they learned in high school science, putting a heavy magnet on the frame of the meter to stop the dial from turning. Still others drilled a very fine hole through the meter and blocked the dial mechanically.

"When I came home after work and there was no electricity," said Alice Sawadda, "I had to use candles. But they were very expensive and rare, so you used one candle as you moved through the house. Since you could not listen to the radio without electricity and it was cold in the rooms, we went to bed and I would put my crystal radio on my pillow to listen. We got American stations and German stations. Housewives would get up in the middle of the night if that was when the electricity was on to do their ironing or other things that required electricity." For Karin Hueckstaedt, the availability of electricity, even at two A.M., meant that it was time to go to the movies. "I would go over to my girl friend's house and throw stones at the window." Families with gas stoves also had restrictions, because the gas (made from coal) went off at nine o'clock every night.

Pursuing more sources of energy, the occupation authorities ordered Berliners to cut the trees in the parks to obtain 350,000 cubic meters of wood. Here the Allies met with rebellion. The Berliners, loving their trees and parks, indicated that they would rather shiver than cut more than 120,000 cubic meters. That was a matter for them to decide, Colonel Howley said, adding, "Personally, I thought it wiser to cut the trees and keep warm. Trees can always be grown again." The airlift would do what it could, but it worked under strong limits.

Karin remembered the airlift as the time of her life when she had the least to eat, even less than during the war or just after it. Particularly strong in her memory were the dried potatoes, not only the conventional white variety but sweet potatoes, which the Berliners had never seen and mistook for carrots. Yet at any time Karin and her mother could simply have registered for rations in eastern instead of western Berlin. The Soviets had an open offer to feed all Berliners, which families could accept without having to move or change jobs. But neither Karin's mother nor very many other people accepted the offer; they saw it for the pyschological ploy it was and chose to stick with the West.

In spite of the emphasis the Allies placed on coal shipments over food, by the end of the year Berlin coal reserves had slumped to the dangerous level of just 65,000 tons. But "when conditions seemed blackest, the weather miraculously improved, and thenceforth air deliveries increased rapidly," said Colonel Howley. "More planes began to arrive daily, our new radar equipment reduced the weather hazard, we perfected loading and handling techniques, and very soon reached eight thousand tons a day." Not only did the coal warm the population, it was now in ample enough supply that the authorities could permit the limited revival of manufacturing—Berlin, through exports to western Germany, could begin to help support itself. "Defiantly," said Howley, all boxes and shipping crates were stamped MADE IN BLOCKADED BERLIN. Coal also acquired its own special bit of verse, which quickly became famous in the world of the airlift. One day a pilot heading in from Fassberg, queried about his cargo, offered in reply:

> *Here comes a Yankee with a blackened soul,*
> *Headin' for Gatow with a load of coal.*

At the Wiesbaden airfield, a December visitor to Germany, the *New York Herald Tribune*'s eminent political columnist, Joseph Alsop, watched with great interest as workers loaded a C-54 with ten tons of canned applesauce, dried apricots, cement, and roofing paper for Berlin. After making its trip and landing at Tempelhof, the plane joined a line of Skymasters waiting to be unloaded. Then a truck pulled up and fifteen "shivering" Germans piled out, flinging themselves on the cases of cargo, as though "their lives depended on speed, which indeed [they] did." In an insightful subsequent column, Alsop caught the essence of the airlift for his readers. Though it originally was "a brave, dramatic and dangerous last-minute expedient, there is no more flavor of emergency about the present air-lift operation than there is about the operations of the New York Central Railroad. What is stirring about the air lift, rather, is simply the showing of an often vaunted, but not always conspicuous, national trait—American efficiency." In organizing air transport to "a sort of peak of completeness," the commanders had tossed "all romance of the 'wild blue yonder' variety" out of the window, because the "essence of the whole business, as in the business of an industrial assembly line, is to reduce every individual, whether pilot, engineer or ground transport officer, to the status of a cog in a vast machine." Alsop gave full credit to General Tunner for applying to air transport the principles preached early in the century by the famous pioneer of scientific management, Frederick Winslow Taylor, who gave the world the dictum: "In the past the man has been first; in the future the system must be first."

Whether Tunner employed Taylor's somewhat debatable concepts consciously or intuitively is an open question, but the results definitely fitted the basic prescription—a prescription made truly potent and less abstract by Tunner's top-to-bottom involvement with procedures and people. The pilots, Alsop noted, "must be precisely trained to operate with the mechanical precision on which their lives and the fate of their planes depend. The endless, carefully-directed streams of airplanes must be woven under, over and around each in the congested Berlin area, so that a visual picture of the traffic pattern looks like a madman's game of cat's cradle." But most important of all was the "unquestionable success" of the airlift; doubts and questions that appeared in discussions back in the United States Alsop dismissed as "nonsense."

Another December visitor to Berlin, Army Secretary Kenneth Royall, asked Colonel Howley what new steps the Russians might take to injure the West further. There were not many, the colonel replied. "If the Russians had thought there was anything more they could do to us, they would have done it already." On the last day of the year, in a piece of admirable symmetry, a C-54 from Fassberg, piloted by Captain Gene M. Patton, landed at Tegel to complete the one hundred thousandth flight of the airlift. By midwinter, as Howley put it, "everybody knew that the airlift was a success and that the blockade had failed."

On a Sunday in January, the Berliners, who during the airlift had repeatedly shown their gratitude to the Allies, found an impressive new way to honor their heroes. Without letting the Americans know about it, they decided to celebrate the two hundredth day of the airlift by "paying their respects to the flyers who brought them their daily bread," as one reporter put it. Early in the morning the streets in the Tempelhof district began to fill with people dressed in the best clothes they had. "They brought modest gifts for the flyers—small hand-carved toys, old silver or china salvaged from the ruins of the city." They came all day, thousands and thousands of them, breaking through police lines to rush onto the field and present their gifts personally to the aircrews, who in those two hundred days had performed what had seemed impossible: feeding and warming them and thus keeping a great city alive through the air.

CHAPTER 23

Parading for Easter

ALL THROUGH THE afternoon, the night, and the next morning, they kept coming, roaring into Tempelhof, Gatow, and Tegel, averaging a landing every minute. The radio towers crackled constantly, keeping in touch with the two hundred aircraft always in flight under the cloudless skies stretching in sunshine and moonlight from Berlin to the Rhine. On many an occasion, Bill Tunner as a practitioner of scientific management had shown himself to be a hard man to satisfy. But now, in April 1949, he exceeded his past performances.

Since the completion of 100,000 Vittles-Plainfare flights at the turn of the year, the figures had marched upward in an impressive parade. On January 13 the airlift in 755 flights delivered 6,678.9 tons to Berlin, a total second only to that of the special, all-out performance on Air Force Day, the previous September 18—well before the onset of wintry weather. By the end of January, the airlift crews had hauled 171,960 tons, setting a new record for a single month. On February 23, in a great burst of effort, the fliers smashed the old Air Force Day record by more than 900 tons with a 7,897 total, and just three days later they crossed the 8,000–ton barrier with twenty-five tons to spare. March saw the previous one-month record demolished with a total of 196,160.7 tons. On April 11 the airlift carried 8,246.1 tons in 922 flights. These astounding figures far surpassed anything hoped for, or even dreamed of, in the early days.

In December personnel of the 317th Troop Carrier Wing had begun arriving at Celle, the second British base taken over by U.S. Vittles elements. At this former Luftwaffe field, tucked away in a scenic forest area and little used since the end of the war, workers had built a large ramp with flood-lights for around-the-clock operations, a refueling center, and other facili-ties required to develop a loading base that could supplement Fassberg. By February the new field was playing its full part as one more funnel for vital Berlin-bound cargo—in Celle's case, mostly coal, although flour had heavy representation, too. The Tegel airport had rapidly gone onto General Tunner's three-minute rhythmic schedule, especially serving as a receiving point for coal and for diesel fuel and gasoline carried by British air tankers.

A new Fassberg commander, Colonel Jack Coulter, had arrived in January. Bill Martin credited him with bringing entertainers to the base, because of the show-business connections of his lively and popular wife, the movie star Constance Bennett. In a number of important ways, Coulter would win praise for his successful efforts to make Fassberg a tolerable station. Prior to his taking command, the Americans looked on Fassberg as a hardship post, not only because of the kippers-and-Brussels-sprouts cuisine but also because of such deficiencies as the rarity of hot water in the grim barracks; another kind of irritation came from the enforcement of a class system in seating at the base movie theater. Altogether, after a night on one of the slablike mattresses, an American pilot seemed undecided whether to consider Fassberg hell or merely a concentration camp; in essence, at Fassberg the "luxury-loving GI," as John Toland once called the American serviceman, met the realities of British postwar austerity. When Colonel Coulter came, he succeeded in changing food and furniture and hence morale. Speaking of his choice of Coulter for the job, Tunner commented that he had sent one of his best officers to Fassberg; he neglected to say that three previous appointees had run into serious problems in sharing command of a British base.

Thus in early April General Tunner could justly feel that things were going well: "We even had all the planes we needed: 154 assorted British types, 225 C-54s, with an extra 75 in the maintenance pipeline and at the Great Falls school, and 200 of the 225 in daily service in the corridors." The organization had by now acquired such polish that its commander had fifty up-to-the-minute charts always ready to tell him whatever he needed to know; he could be perfectly informed without leaving the air room at his headquarters. This array of facts, gratifying in itself, nevertheless disturbed Tunner. Thing were going *too* well—that was it! Remarkably, complacency now threatened an operation in which few people had professed much faith just months earlier. And the clear response to complacency was competition. The general had exploited the idea of competition during his command of the Hump operation, where the threat came not from complacency but from isolation. But even if the fliers at the various bases in India never saw any Japanese, they could battle each other to make the daily quota, and the resulting spirit of rivalry had led to the "Christmas present" flights Tunner's men had given him. Now, in Germany, the situation called for something truly special.

Getting his staff together, Tunner explained his idea. Looking back to the Hump Christmas and to the thundering success of Air Force Day, the general declared that, with Easter Sunday just a few days away, the airlift would stage "an Easter parade of airplanes, an Easter Sunday present for the people of Berlin." They would set no public goal, in order to give the Russians no opening for chortling if the effort fell short, but Tunner aimed at a target of 10,000 tons. For the sake of simplicity and efficiency, action would focus on one kind of cargo—coal—of which a 10,000-ton stockpile sat ready to be loaded onto planes and flown into Berlin. When General Cannon's deputy warned that trouble would ensue if a big day were to be followed by a large decrease the next day, Tunner made a key point. After a supreme effort, the total would certainly decrease, but it would decrease "to a higher plateau than had formerly obtained."

This point had earlier eluded General Robertson, who had always tended to believe that the Americans exaggerated the figures of deliveries. Though he supported the airlift originally, he had continued to think of it as only a short-term measure with shaky prospects—sometimes to the annoyance of Ernest Bevin. Speaking of Air Force Day, Robertson had told London that "this special effort was only made possible by taking extraordinary measures which resulted in a falling off in figures for subsequent days." Robertson also did not seem to see, beyond the figures themselves, the morale-building and propaganda value of a great public triumph. However, as commander of CALTF since the previous October, Tunner was the man who set the agenda.

The operation began at noon on Friday, April 15, with notices of quotas appearing on the "howgozit" boards at all the loading bases. Tunner later noted slyly that since the total was divided among all the squadrons, the press did not immediately catch on. The crews, however, saw the significance of the special higher quotas and greeted them with enthusiasm, fueled partly by the knowledge that big results would produce big prizes in cigarettes. Everybody, said Tunner, "was rarin' to go," and soon all were caught up in the spirit of the great effort. Planes landed and took off more frequently than normal, trucks rolled in and out a bit faster, and the unloading crews sweated more heavily. As the *Task Force Times* observed, however, "despite the driving determination of all personnel concerned to expedite landings and takeoffs and to reduce loading and unloading time," the general scene did not display frenzied rushing about: "The men know their jobs and do them with systematic efficiency." Supervisors, checkers, and crew chiefs worked with great care to coordinate the efforts of loaders and unloaders—Berliners, Poles, and displaced persons from the Baltic countries—truck drivers, and maintenance personnel. Transport officers and operations officers worked together to ensure split-second timing in the support phase of the operation. For their part, administrative officers made sure that the necessary rail and road equipment was on hand to take care of the incoming commodities. Night and day, under floodlights and the warm early-spring sun, workers emptied the record bounty—mostly coal, together with flour and some other supplies—into the trucks drawn up to the cargo doors of the planes.

Tunner shuttled between Berlin and the various loading bases like a fighting Shakespearean king, "applying a needle here, a pat on the back there." Some time after midnight he arrived at Fassberg, where he saw Constance Bennett and other wives down on the flight line, passing around coffee and doughnuts. Colonel Coulter proudly declared that the base was running 10 percent ahead of its quota. Well and good, Tunner replied, but not up to the performance at Celle, where they were "really on the ball." This was no fabrication, although the Celle figure Tunner had been given was 12 percent, not hugely different from Fassberg's. Coulter, as desired, immediately turned on his heel and rushed off to stiffen his troops.

During his shuttling, Tunner received a comeuppance of his own. When he tried to hitch a ride from Tempelhof back to Wiesbaden, the pilot glanced at his regulation flying jacket, which showed no general's stars, and shouted: "You'll have to shake your tail and get aboard. We're in a hurry." Not displeased, the general hustled to follow orders.

Like the other units involved, Bill Martin's 313th Air Transport Group resolved to make "as many trips into Berlin as we could." They adopted the goal of matching the number of flights to their outfit's designation—a symmetrical ideal that exerted strong appeal on the commanding officer. Carrying its customary powdered coal made into pellets and packed in canvas bags, the group exceeded its previous tonnage record by a wide margin. Whether by accident or a little deliberate planning, the fliers also exceeded the goal of 313 flights—by one. They enjoyed both their success and the joke, but that symmetry-disrupting three hundred and fourteenth flight "tore the colonel up."

Even before midmorning, Tunner had received the news that his fliers had passed the 10,000–ton mark, with several hours still to go. As news of the great project spread, reporters began appearing at headquarters, their numbers quickly swelling. At about two o'clock in the afternoon, American officials gathered at Tempelhof to greet the crew of the final plane in the operation, which touched down at 2:14, its fuselage adorned with hastily painted large red letters and numbers: 12,941 tons, 1,398 flights. The pilot, Lieutenant Blaine Herren, of Redding, Iowa, received a special welcome from Major General James Hodges. "I didn't even know I was on a record run," Herren said. "All I knew was that everybody seemed to be going all-out." This all-out record, awed reporters noted, had shattered the old (April 11) record by 4,694 tons and 476 flights; in percentage terms, by an actually unbelievable 64 percent. During the operation the electronic network spread continuous instructions, making 39,640 radio contacts.

A backhanded tribute to the scope of the Easter Parade came from a Soviet officer at the Air Safety Center. When Western representatives protested his notices of stepped-up Russian activities in the air corridors—air-to-air firing, bombing, and parachute jumping—he said, "I cannot accept the protest. Your traffic pattern is changing so rapidly it is impossible to keep charts." Yet in a remarkable instance of self-destructive timing, the Soviet-sponsored newspaper *Tribune* chose this particular weekend to deride Vittles and Plainfare. Despite the favorable weather on Friday, the article said, the fliers had managed to deliver only 4,000 tons of cargo; the airlift, it declared, had failed.

Giving a technical dimension to his "gigantic Easter present to the populace of Berlin," General Tunner observed that the operation had been designed to "determine the problems incurred in air-cargo handling and air traffic control when operating the maximum number of trips to Berlin." Other officers said simply that the Americans and the British had set out to learn just how many planes could be landed in Berlin in a twenty-four-hour period. The radio control system was pushed to the "absolute saturation point," one officer said. "There were no mishaps. It was a perfect performance." General Bourne, the British commandant in Berlin, said of the Easter Parade: "It was a wonderful effort by all concerned."

General Clay, declaring the parade "a magnificent job," made some telling specific points. Even on normal days during the coming summer, he said, the airlift could easily deliver more than 8,000 tons—an amount considered by Berlin city officials enough not only to feed the Berliners in the Western sectors and to support essential industry but also to make possible the revival of industry shut down by the blockade, thereby earning cash and reducing unemployment. With the additional aircraft he had requested, "we can supply Berlin by air as well as it was supplied by rail and highway before the blockade was imposed." Before the blockade, Clay said, the Western zones had sent sixteen trains daily into Berlin, four of them carrying passengers and military traffic, the other twelve bringing food, coal, construction material, and other supplies of all kinds. Each of these twelve carried, on the average, a load of somewhat more than 800 tons, with the total daily figure thus amounting to about 10,000 tons. Looking back five years to the war, Clay compared the achievement of the Easter lift, with its almost 13,000 tons, with the situation at Cherbourg when he had taken over temporary direction of the port. There, he said, supply officers had aimed at receiving and sending out 12,000 tons a day to maintain the U.S. First and Third armies in the fighting in France. Thus the West had now shown that with its air organization and technical skill, it could not only keep a city alive, it could, as air force officers immediately pointed out, keep combat divisions in the field. Tunner had proved everything he wanted to prove about air transport, demonstrating the truth of the claims he had made in his Air Commerce Day speech in New York a year earlier. Later Tunner expressed his gratitude—he did not say whether to Joseph Stalin or simply to fate—for "the opportunity to prove once again that we could carry anything anywhere anytime."

The Easter season produced a revealing and amusing example of Russian attention to details of all kinds. In its review of a new German movie *Der Ruf (The Call),* the periodical *Soviet Art* criticized the performance of the film's dark-haired, beautiful twenty-three-year-old star, Rosemary Murphy—through no fault of her own, the daughter of the man who had until recently been the most prominent American diplomatic figure in Germany and one of the strongest anti-Communists, Ambassador Robert Murphy. Though he had been called to Washington to become chief of the new German-Austrian division of the State Department, Murphy was well remembered on all sides in Berlin.

The ambassador had departed with many admiring thoughts about American achievements during his four-year partnership with General Clay. He left from Tempelhof on a snowy February night, admiring the airlift at "its spectacular peak," with powerful searchlights turning night into day and huge snow shovels keeping the runway clear. "As my plane started down the runway," he said, "I looked out at my friends who were standing in the snow waving good-bye, and at the unloading crews who did not even glance at them. Those German-American teams never wasted a moment."

For all his appreciation of the airlift in action, however, Murphy still held to his belief that, as he and Clay had recommended, the United States should have directly challenged the blockade at its outset by sending an armed convoy onto the autobahn at Helmstedt. The blockade, Murphy said some years later, was "the one occasion in my long career where I feel I should have resigned in public protest against Washington's policy." Even though he did not imagine that his resignation would have changed the course of events, he wrote, "I still deeply regret that I was associated with an action which caused Soviet leaders to downgrade United States determination and capability." From this point of view, the success of the airlift was irrelevant. The operation might represent an organizational and technical triumph, but it also represented a failure of political will.

Dean Acheson, who on January 21 had returned to the State Department after a year and a half's absence, strongly disagreed with this view. In regarding the decision to use the airlift as "a surrender of our hard-won rights in Berlin," said the new secretary of state, Murphy was being "silly." The airlift, Acheson believed, had proved the best way of affirming Western rights in Berlin while putting the burden of any initiation of hostilities on the Russians.

By their remarkable feats during the Easter weekend, wrote the magisterial Drew Middleton of the *New York Times,* the airlift fliers had won a signal victory for the West in the "cold war" (a concept still new enough for the *Times* copy editors to insist on the quotation marks). But, beyond the spirit and the technical virtuosity that the Easter Parade displayed, and beyond its affirmation of the effectiveness of the airlift, what did it mean at that moment in the struggle between the West and the Soviet Union? To Middleton, the achievement came at a perhaps decisive time in the crisis over Berlin. Demonstrating the murkiness through which leading journalists as well as politicians viewed the Kremlin, Middleton observed that U.S. officials had for some time believed that Russian political strategists, "in opposition to the military leaders," had been pondering ending the blockade. The thunderous success of the Easter Parade would give the political advisers a strong argument in this supposed debate, because an augmented airlift during the summer could build up stockpiles that could easily see Berlin through the next winter: the West would thus have nothing to worry about.

For some time, indeed, rumors about the Soviet desire to end the blockade had swirled through Western capitals. Behind them lay the plain fact that it had backfired in every respect—surely the Russians must realize it. Instead of frightening the Western powers, the blockade had brought them together—they had succeeded both in maintaining their German policy and in remaining in Berlin. It had given the West an arena in which to develop in air transport a new and potent weapon for future conflicts. It had presented the West with a great opportunity to create favorable propaganda—an opportunity that had been put to highly effective use. It had brought about the creation of the counterblockade, which had denied the Soviet zone raw materials that therefore had to come from the Soviet Union itself. Beyond these points, the blockade appeared to have guaranteed that everybody in the Western sectors of Berlin would nourish an undying hatred of the Russians, while it transformed the relationship between the Berliners and the Allies: "a love affair with the Americans" had surely been the last thing on the mind of anybody in the Kremlin. Altogether, the Russians had thoroughly demonstrated the truth of the Chinese insight that represents "crisis" by an ideogram combining the characters for "danger" and "opportunity," with the West having seized the day.

But the calculus of decision might hold another factor: Did Allied leaders, behind the scenes, really want the Russians to raise the blockade? Up to this point Joseph Stalin and his colleagues had shown no sign that they had ever read the Aesop fable in which the wind and the sun compete to remove a man's cloak; the wind with its bluster only causes the man to clutch the cloak more tightly about him, but the sun manages to win the contest by using nothing more violent than a warm smile. The wind blowing from the depths of Russia had contributed heavily not only to the fogs that physically challenged the airlift but to the readiness of the western Germans to form a state. Might not the relaxation of the blockade, some writers asked, weaken this drive for the unity of western Germany? By switching from bluster to smile, the Kremlin might even win from the Germans the kind of paradoxical gratitude that comes to a person who seizes a hostage and then generously allows his prisoner to have a sip of water or a piece of bread, or perhaps even a short walk. An American official said that the Easter Parade triumph, with its proof of the airlift's permanent viability, offered the Russian political leaders the final evidence they needed to abandon the blockade.

To be sure, everyone believed, some sort of face-saving formula would have to be found before the Soviets could actually make a move. (Certainly they could hardly claim that they had needed ten months to repair a few miles of railroad track and patch up a faulty bridge or two—the "technical difficulties" they had presented as their original excuse for the blockade.) This reasoning grew out of a belief in the existence of competing points of view in the Kremlin, in the idea that the Soviet leaders had a conventional concern for their own image, and in the further idea that these leaders would calculate the advantages and costs of continuing the airlift in the same way as Western observers calculated them. In reality, these observers still had no way of breaching the Kremlin walls. They still did not know how power was held inside them or how much its wielders concerned themselves about such matters as saving face or even how they would define it.

But the U.S. State Department did possess a thorough assessment of the blockade and the airlift and their context. George Kennan's Policy Planning Staff had produced a study in October as part of its response to an order by the National Security Council to outline a U.S. position on Berlin following the breakdown of the August talks with Stalin and Molotov. Because the Allied stand in Berlin had inspired confidence in the population of the city and taken on great symbolic importance in the struggle between East and West, said this secret document, the West could not leave Berlin under circumstances that would render West Berliners subject to Communist "oppression and revenge"; such a withdrawal would shake the confidence of Europeans generally in the Western determination to stand up to Russia. But it was also true that Berlin could not be left indefinitely dependent on the airlift for its sustenance. Though the airlift had proved to be a great technical achievement, the West had to look at psychological and political considerations as well: "We must recognize that the population of a great city, particularly one which is in dire need of reconstruction on a grand scale, cannot get along indefinitely with just the absolute minimum of food and fuel." Sooner or later, sacrifice and uncertainty would lead to unrest and resentment, even against the Americans. Calculations about the efficacy of the airlift should therefore not be overrated—the operation gave the West time to find a solution to the problem but it did not in itself constitute a solution.

On the other hand, noted Kennan's report, the Berlin deadlock had also created a serious problem for the Russians. What they stood to gain in Berlin, where the West had only a weak position, they were already losing in the rest of Germany. Because of the Berlin conflict, the Allies could go much further now in "risking the establishment of a German authority" than would have been the case early in the year: "If the continuation of the present deadlock threatens us with the loss of Berlin, it threatens them with the loss of Germany itself." Thus the Russians found themselves under great strain, just as the Allies were. Even so, the State Department planners could not bring themselves to believe in the possibility of any settlement that would leave the Western Allies with their "rightful status" in Berlin without involving an overall agreement on Germany. The Russians might express acceptance of some such arrangement, said the planners, but regardless of what they might say (and here the reader can clearly see the hand of Kennan), "the objective possibilities for sabotage and evasion in practice, combined with the formidable native talents of the Russians in this direction," made clear the impossibility of any genuine solution along these lines. In October, at the time of this report, Kennan and his group could see an answer, if any, coming only in the form of an entirely new kind of development, such as mutual East-West withdrawal from Berlin, leading to a general end to military government in Germany overall. It was their warrant, of course, to suggest lines of overall policy and to regard the airlift as an instrument, not as a policy.

Did the situation look any different after the airlift winter, in the spring of 1949? The mysteries shrouding the Kremlin certainly did not deter those who searched everywhere for clues to the designs of its inscrutable denizens.

Figaro, the Paris newspaper, reported that a tall, mysterious man who was neither a diplomat nor a Russian had made a trip to Washington to extend feelers for a settlement. Some observers made much of the alleged fact that Andrei Gromyko had smiled during the opening session of the UN General Assembly. Soviet officers were said to have emerged from months of isolation to attend a U.S. Army cocktail party in Berlin, at which they behaved reasonably well. (Though social contacts between Allied and Soviet officers had indeed been sparse during the blockade, occasional meetings of one kind or another took place. Compelled one day to invite General Kotikov to a lunch conference, Colonel Howley found himself not thrilled when the Soviet commander complained that the chicken was tough. "It ought to be," Howley fired back. "It had to fly all the way from Frankfurt." Kotikov glared but stopped himself from replying.) A more substantial clue came from Dean Acheson, who declared that the U.S. government had never closed or had any thought of closing any avenue of communication with the Soviet Union. Smiling as he spoke, Acheson said that all avenues were open, as they always had been.

CHAPTER 24

Lake Success to Park Avenue

THOUGH MYSTERIOUS TRAVELERS and supposed smiles had little to do with East-West developments, the rumors about a possible end to the airlift held solid truth. The starting point on this trail—the very quiet, almost unnoticed starting point—was Stalin's office in the Kremlin, on Sunday, January 30, 1949. As has often been the case in such matters, a journalist served as the catalyst. In those days, foreign reporters in quest of a story would file various questions by telegraph with the Soviet Foreign Ministry in the hope that Stalin would deign to provide answers, as he did often enough to encourage the practice. On January 27, in accordance with this custom, Kingsbury Smith, European head of the International News Service (the wire agency then operated by the Hearst newspapers), addressed a series of questions to the generalissimo. The third of these asked whether the Soviet Union would be prepared to remove the restrictions on access to Berlin if the Western powers would agree to postpone the establishment of the West German government, pending a meeting of the Council of Foreign Ministers "to consider the German problem as a whole."

This question evoked what sounded like a specific answer from Stalin: "Provided the United States of America, Great Britain and France observe the conditions set forth in the third question, the Soviet Government sees no obstacles to lifting the transport restrictions on the understanding, however, that transport and trade restrictions introduced by the three powers should be lifted simultaneously." Kingsbury Smith's resulting news beat, appearing immediately in Hearst newspapers, created a stir not only in Washington but across the country and in Europe.

Secretary of State Acheson was spending his usual quiet Sunday on his little farm in Montgomery County, Maryland, just north of Washington, when he got word of Smith's story. He immediately sat down to make notes for a response to a diplomatic proposal that had not officially been made, and next morning he took his draft to the Oval Office for a talk with the president. Like the secretary of state, Truman knew nothing more than what he had read in the papers. Missing the real point, however, the press called attention not to Stalin's comments about Berlin but to his "peace offer": in answer to Smith's other questions, the generalissimo said that he would consider cooperating with the United States in the issuance of a "peace declaration," that the Soviet Union "naturally" would cooperate in disarmament under such a pact, and that he would have no objection to meeting with President Truman to discuss the concluding of the pact.

Excited reporters, questioning the White House press secretary about the possibility of such a meeting, were told that the president had on numerous occasions said that he would be pleased to have Premier Stalin visit him in Washington. (Truman had indeed invited Stalin to the United States during their talks at Potsdam, and again following Winston Churchill's Iron Curtain speech.) Smith, playing it straight and pushing his story to an even higher level, immediately cabled Moscow again: Would Stalin accept Truman's "invitation"? The generalissimo answered promptly, declaring that he had always wanted to visit Washington, but he fell back, as always, on the refusal of his vigilant doctors to allow him to travel by air or sea. Perhaps the president could come to Yalta (a possibility about as likely at that time as a British prime minister's agreeing to attend a conference in Munich) or, failing that, somewhere in Poland or Czechoslovakia.

Not wishing to give his comments any air of special significance, Acheson held off discussing Smith's long-range interview until his regularly scheduled press conference on the following Wednesday. The secretary, who had not anticipated so major a development during his first few days in office, systematically disposed of all but Smith's third question, making it clear that the administration saw nothing new in Stalin's answers nor any suggestion that the Soviet premier was contemplating a change in Soviet behavior, and that it would certainly not engage in any negotiations in which its allies did not take part. Acheson also commented on Stalin's reply to Smith's follow-up question about the possible site of a Truman-Stalin conference. Observing that Stalin seemed to be "effectively grounded," Acheson spurned any idea that "the President of the United States for the fourth time should travel half way around the world to meet Premier Stalin and on this occasion to do so for the purpose of talking with him on a matter so tenuous that it defies specific statement."

Then, coming to the point of real interest to U.S. policymakers, the secretary of state briefly traced the history of negotiations over the "illegal blockade of Berlin," including the changing reasons the Soviets had offered for their imposition of the "restrictions": they had talked first about technical transportation problems and then they had invoked the currency reform. Saying that the developments in western Germany did not rule out a four-power agreement on Germany as a whole, the secretary observed that if the Soviets really wanted to discuss the issues, the normal diplomatic channels were open. But Acheson did not mention one particular point in Stalin's reply to Kingsbury Smith's third question. When Bohlen had read the text of Stalin's answers, he noted immediately that the generalissimo had made no mention of the currency problem, the issue that had been fought over in countless hours of East-West meetings. After Bohlen pointed out this omission to Acheson, the secretary and his colleagues agreed that the Kremlin had sent a "cautious signal" of its readiness to end the blockade and that this signal would need a cautious and quiet reply, one giving the Soviets no opening to use divisive tactics or to raise its price. ("I was on the lookout for such a signal from the Soviets," Bohlen said, "because the counterblockade was hurting the Communists a great deal.")

Fending off questions from reporters probing for any story behind the story, Acheson confined himself in the press conference to bland answers, pointedly observing that the Soviets could best show seriousness of purpose in "some other channel than the channel of a press interview." In his opening statement Acheson had said that he wished to talk about Smith's questions and Stalin's answers "quite candidly but quite realistically." He set this remark in a context in which he spoke of the interest of Americans in peace as sacred and fundamental, adding that "the hopes of hundreds of millions of people throughout the world are pinned on the preservation of peace. No man of conscience would tamper with those hopes or use the raising or the lowering of them" as a pawn in any international political maneuver.

The secretary would immediately find out what strong feelings many Americans had about even the faintest glimmer of a move toward understanding with the Soviet Union. When the United Press reported from London that Western Europeans were relaxing after Acheson's assurances that President Truman would be making no private deals with Premier Stalin, the *Courier-Journal* of Louisville declared that no doubt the French, British, and other foreign offices felt relief, but, the newspaper asked, "What about the plain people of Europe and the world?" These people would not know the nuances of the situation, would not follow the fine thread of Acheson's reasoning, and would see only that Stalin had suggested the smoking of a peace pipe and that Truman had turned him down; the Russians, the paper said, had human psychology on their side. In an echo of the famous *Chicago Tribune* wishful-thinking DEWEY DEFEATS TRUMAN headline in its early editions of the previous November 3, the editorial bore the title: "Stalin Defeats Truman in Millions of Minds."

Expressions of faith in the magic of face-to-face conversation came from many sides. The belief—an old one for Americans—seemed widespread that peace could be detached from an existing situation and treated as an independent entity: if national leaders could just sit down and talk, they could readily reach agreement, whatever their differences. From Independence, Missouri, President Truman's home town, a citizen named James Stobaugh cabled the Kremlin offering his family's one-and-a-half-story frame house as a good meeting place for president and premier. "Away from the glitter and pomp where the only armed force in evidence is the traffic patrol on the highway," said Stobaugh, "I believe any and all differences may be solved." Though firmly endorsing everything Acheson had said, Truman himself unbent enough to say, in answer to a reporter's question, that yes, if Stalin would come to Washington, he would have Mrs. Truman get the guest room ready.

In the front line of Berlin, however, the Western Allies announced a step-up in the counterblockade: the Bizone would now be closed to all truck freight shipments intended for the Soviet zone, as it long had been to rail freight. (Quite remarkably, this move had not been made months earlier.) For its part, the Soviet-sponsored German Communist People's Council called during this week for mass demonstrations against the occupation policies of the Western Allies.

Perhaps the shrewdest reading of Stalin's words came from the columnist Stewart Alsop, who declared that the answers to the first, second, and fourth questions had "about as much significance as if he had come out flatly in favor of an early spring and a late fall." But the third answer was different, because Stalin had made the postponement of the West German government his price for lifting the blockade without mentioning the currency issue. It was now clear, said Alsop, that the blockade had thus far been a disastrous failure as an instrument of Soviet policy. It had wrecked the Communist parties throughout Germany and brought on the counterblockade, which had made the Soviet zone a great economic and political liability to the Russians. Hence one could reasonably suppose that the Kremlin was beginning to doubt whether the game was worth the candle.

Acting with President Truman's blessing, the State Department did not sit back and wait to see what happened with the game and the candle. Shortly after Acheson's press conference, Philip Jessup, still deputy chief of the U.S. mission to the United Nations, came down from New York to discuss the new situation with Acheson, Bohlen, and other department officials. Thus began the fourth phase of the overall Allied diplomatic effort to solve the Berlin crisis, which had begun with the notes to Moscow the previous July. Convinced that the American approach should continue in the cautious, casual vein, with only a handful of people involved—the

United States must take great care not to appear eager or to display weakness—Acheson took Bohlen's suggestion to avoid foreign ministries and embassies and use Jessup as the American messenger, with Soviet UN Ambassador Yakov Malik as the recipient and informal private conversation as the method of delivery. "All of us naturally thought of the United Nations," Jessup said, "because the case of the Berlin blockade had been swirling or floating through the channels of that organization for what seemed an interminable period. We were at home in the formal debates of the Security Council"—but, more important here—"equally adept in the use of the diplomacy of the *couloirs*." As his first task, Jessup was to find out whether Stalin's failure to mention the currency problem was purposeful or not. At the appropriate moment—whether it came when he and Malik were sipping orange juice in the delegates' lounge or were standing side by side in the men's room—Jessup would ask his casual question.

In the fifty-two-year-old Jessup, the Americans had as their representative an unusual figure, not a professional diplomat but one of the world's chief authorities on international law who had been a leading candidate for the presidency of Columbia University until the trustees chose General Eisenhower. Tweed-suited and wool-tied (though he often wore a statesman's homburg), Jessup had brought no professorial pedantry to UN debates but had quickly shown himself a nimble-witted speaker with a gift for calming tensions. He also, for what it was worth, had developed a friendly cut-and-thrust relationship with Malik, who seemed to enjoy repartee. One day when the Russian chided him about the spectacular failure of the American pollsters to produce accurate forecasts concerning the presidential election, Jessup replied, "Dr. Gallup should transfer his activities to your country. It would be much easier for him to predict the results of elections there."

Jessup's scholarly achievements gave him special value to American diplomacy. "They know his reputation and they have read his books," said a former U.S. solicitor general. "It is like arguing before a judge for whom you have great respect. There is no question of personal feelings being involved. It is simply the law." Jessup took considerable offense at a later comment by Robert Murphy on his friendly relations with Malik. He had been unable to convince the "Columbia professor," said Murphy, speaking as a career diplomat, that "Soviet negotiators cannot be influenced by personal friendships." Jessup countered that he had never labored under any such illusion but that he found friendly relations a help when carrying on diplomatic negotiations. That was, indeed, a fact of life at the United Nations, "to which not all career diplomats have been exposed." (In this same vein, Murphy seems never to have persuaded his close colleague of four years, General Clay, that friendly relations with Marshal Sokolovsky could have no real significance.) Bohlen, who worked closely with Jessup, praised him as "an excellent diplomat, who could always be counted on to carry out with intelligence and precision the instructions he received from his government."

With his "humorously etched" face and his anecdotal approach to discussion, Jessup fitted well his new role as casual conversationalist. At the time, before it took up residence in Turtle Bay on the East Side of Manhattan, the United Nations met in a remodeled factory in the cheerfully named town of Lake Success, near Mineola, Long Island. On Tuesday, February 15, in advance of a debate at which all representatives, certainly including Malik, would be present, Jessup chose his moment. When, as usual, the Soviet ambassador dropped into the lounge before the meeting began, Jessup, loitering near the door, greeted him with a "nice day" comment. (The weather was a subject, Jessup said, "on which we could usually agree.") The two men chatted for a moment before Jessup made his move. By the way, he said, in Stalin's recent statement about the situation in Berlin, he had noted no reference to the currency question, and he wondered whether the omission was accidental. In response, Malik said coldly that he had no information on the subject. Well, Jessup said, if Malik should get any information, perhaps he would pass it on. The two men then shook hands and went into the Security Council meeting room.

Jessup then ran into a bit of a buzzsaw. Having made a memorandum of the conversation, he classified it "secret" and marked it for distribution to eight persons—the American ambassador to the UN, Warren Austin, together with four members of his staff, and three State Department officials in Washington, including Chip Bohlen. "I was promptly and properly scolded by Bohlen for my indiscretion," Jessup said; "the memorandum was reclassified 'Top Secret' and all copies distributed to the mission in New York were called in." Orders heavily restricted any further distribution. Nobody knew how far this démarche would get, but a leak to the press would certainly kill it where it stood.

A month went by with no response from the Soviets—a month during which the airlift continued to flourish, carrying more than 8,000 tons a day for the first time, and in which Stalin could also give his "peace offensive" a chance to produce maximum embarrassment for the West in the way described by the *Courier-Journal*. Stalin chose this same month to demote his faithful servant Molotov to deputy foreign minister and replace him with Andrei Vyshinsky. The last such change, when Molotov had replaced Maxim Litvinov as foreign commissar in 1939, had signaled Stalin's move toward rapprochement with Hitler. Did this new move indicate some kind of comparable fresh trouble from the Soviet Union? No diplomats who dealt with the Russians would miss Molotov's unflagging obstinacy and pettifoggery, but Vyshinsky brought to his new position his renown as the venomous chief prosecutor in the Great Purge trials ten years earlier; the change would not necessarily represent an improvement. Jessup had also acquired a new job, moving up to become United States ambassador at large; this position called for him to be based in Washington, though he would still have a hand in UN matters. Then, on March 14, the U.S. mission received a telephone message conveying the news that Malik would like to see Jessup the next time he came to New York. A meeting was arranged for the following day.

The two men talked in Malik's office on the second floor of the Soviet mission, a stone mansion at the corner of Park Avenue and Sixty-eighth Street. The occasion did not find the ambassadors in the best of shape: Jessup wore a bandage over a burn he had acquired while putting out a fire on the kitchen stove, and Malik, a burly man who looked like a retired fullback, was recovering from a siege of lumbago. After due exchanges of sympathy, Malik explained that he had come down with the lumbago in Tokyo and had been treated by an American nurse whose vigor in the use of hypodermic needles had made him yell; it was the first time, he said, that he had been in the hands of an American woman. Well, said Jessup, would it be the last time? Malik chose to laugh that one off.

After these pleasantries—a typical exchange between these two men—they sat down on opposite sides of a small table, while Malik read aloud a prepared statement that said in essence that Stalin's omission of any reference to the currency question was "not accidental." Moscow had told him, Malik said, that the currency problem could be discussed in relation to the overall German problem at the proposed meeting of the foreign ministers. (Whatever the relative emphases Stalin may originally have intended to give the peace offensive and the omission of the currency question, he had now presented a line of policy.) Jessup observed that the Soviets did not have to urge postponing the establishment of a West German government as a condition for holding the meeting of the Council of Foreign Ministers, since such a government did not yet exist. In further discussion, the two agreed that a "mutual and simultaneous" lifting of blockade measures would be necessary. Would the blockade continue during the meeting of the foreign ministers? Malik said he did not know. As the meeting wound up, Jessup told Malik that he would always be glad to talk if any further information became available.

This discussion represented, as Jessup said, "opportunities to be exploited and dangers to be avoided." Leaks posed the greatest of the possible dangers—the more people who knew about the discussion, the greater the threat to security. Should the State Department tell the British and French? What if Moscow decided to make this and any other private discussions public, exaggerating them as proof of surrender by the West? Allies and others would see the United States negotiating on its own a settlement of the Berlin question. Though Jessup made no mention of it in his description of the talks, the Truman administration, after its problems with the British and other allies during the previous year over Bedell Smith's peace discussion with Molotov and the abrupt reversal of position on trusteeship for Palestine, could hardly afford to engage in anything else that smacked of double-dealing. Even Truman's train-platform soliloquy about "old Joe" Stalin could make nervous allies question the American decision-making process.

Jessup brought British and French UN representatives into the secret when he came to New York on March 21, Monday of the following week, for a second talk with Malik. In this conversation the Soviet ambassador reported that the Soviet Union would agree to a reciprocal lifting of the blockade if the two sides agreed on a date for a meeting of the Council of Foreign Ministers. Pressing Malik, Jessup was told that the date for lifting the blockade could be earlier than the date of the meeting. When Malik quoted Jessup as saying in their earlier meeting that the West would "call off" the formation of a West German government if a CFM meeting was scheduled, Jessup made a quick correction; he had said, he reminded Malik, that if the CFM met soon, it would do so in the absence of a West German government, simply because such a government did not yet exist. Malik conceded the point. This gambit by Malik represented almost the last Soviet effort to find a formal way to stave off the creation of West Germany.

With a special session of the General Assembly opening on April 5, Jessup, still a member of the U.S. delegation, returned to New York. By this time Bevin, Schuman, and their ambassadors in Washington had all joined the act. (When Bevin suggested that the group tell General Assembly President Herbert Evatt to keep his hands off Berlin, Acheson responded that such a warning would produce the opposite effect.) It was agreed that Jessup would continue meeting with Malik; in a session with the Soviet representative on April 5, Jessup read aloud a just-drafted Allied statement summarizing understandings that had been reached. It declared emphatically that "the question of the establishment of a Western German government does not arise in the consideration of arranging a meeting of the Council of Foreign Ministers in the reasonably near future"—the West was emphatically making no promises about any postponement with respect to West Germany. The CFM meeting, Jessup thought, might well take place in five or six weeks; well, then, Malik asked, did that mean that the West would suspend preparations for a West German government for five or six weeks? Experienced in dealing with the Russians and thus with the obsessive Russian negotiating style, Jessup explained again that such preparations could not in any case be completed in five or six weeks, but that the West made no promises at all about that date and was agreeing to no interruptions or suspensions.

In Soviet minds the idea of delaying the establishment of the West German government still refused to die. On the next Sunday afternoon, April 10, Jessup went uptown to the Soviet mission in response to a telephone call from Malik. The Soviet ambassador read him a statement in which Vyshinsky accepted the conditions that had been discussed (the Russians spoke of the new foreign minister as if he were the decision-maker), on the understanding that no West German government would be established during the meeting of the CFM. Jessup had to remind Malik of the previous statements about this issue. "I had the impression," he said, "that Malik knew perfectly well what our position was but that Vyshinsky still hoped, without breaking off the dialogue, to rephrase the 'understanding' in such a way as to delay the establishment of the West German government."

But delay was not in the cards. Two days earlier Acheson, Bevin, and Schuman had issued a communiqué in which they declared that they had reached complete agreement on the new statute governing the occupation of Germany, on constitutional questions, and on a range of other subjects. Wisely, Acheson did suggest that a number of specific chores would have to be performed before the new government could come into being; thus the East-West negotiations would have ample time to produce results. Essentially, the Allied agreement called for giving the new German government freedom of action in most administrative and legislative areas; a civilian High Commission would replace military government, and the three Western zones would be completely fused.

On April 12, recognizing that the Jessup-Malik talks had now become an established diplomatic exchange and were giving rise to rumors in the press, Secretary Acheson suggested that President Truman enlarge the circle of those in the know to include the secretary of defense and Generals Bradley and Clay. During these days Clay was fighting a personal battle of his own. Having made his plans to step down as military governor on May 15, he expressed concern—almost dismay—at General Bradley's wish to put off a decision on the date for his relief until negotiations with the German Parliamentary Council were concluded. "I thought I had the right to retire," Clay told Washington a bit crustily, pointing out that he lacked the financial means to be able to change plans easily. He also declared his total lack of interest in exchanging his military governor's cap for the hat of the first U.S. high commissioner: "I came as an Army officer to do a job for the Army and I wish to leave as an Army officer." Bradley yielded on both points.

As director of the Office of German and Austrian Affairs, Robert Murphy came to Germany in April to serve as a mediator between Clay and the State Department and to help (and to some extent guide) Clay in the negotiations concerning the creation of a West German constitution. Since Murphy had not been allowed to tell Clay about the Jessup-Malik meetings, the general spoke with genuine candor when he told a press conference in Berlin that he knew of no talks concerning the lifting of the blockade. The imminence of his retirement did not lessen his chagrin, as he put it, at learning about the negotiations, before Washington got official word to him, from the newspapers and from General Robertson. He was, said Jessup, "understandably annoyed."

The arc of actual negotiations and the arc of rumors were now intersecting. After further talks between the diplomats, complete with haggling, Tass published on April 26 a statement, described by Jessup as "reasonably factual," declaring that the Soviet government was prepared to lift the blockade and to hold a meeting of the CFM. Arriving at Sixty-eighth and Park to see Malik in order to establish precisely what the two sides were agreeing to, Jessup had to push his way through a mass of reporters and photographers that threatened to block the intersection. Inside, the two negotiators replowed some familiar East-West ground: When had the blockade begun? March 1, 1948, said the statement Jessup read; March 30, countered Malik—the later the date, the more restrictions the Soviets could try to keep; the key point, Jessup said, was that *all* restrictions must be removed. The U.S. statement also called for ending the CFM meeting in the second week of June (because other matters would then require Acheson's presence back in Washington). But, Malik said, was it understood that the CFM could take up all questions concerning Germany, including the currency issue? Yes, said Jessup, presumably sighing, it was understood.

To Jessup, "the process seemed endless." In a meeting on April 29, Malik told Jessup that the Soviets wanted to have the CFM meeting in Paris, beginning on June 10; they would lift the blockade a week earlier. On behalf of the Western Allies, Jessup proposed May 23 for the meeting, with May 9 as the date for lifting the restrictions. In discussing a draft communiqué offered by Malik, the two engaged in another fencing match about the date the blockade began. In a further exchange of memoranda, Malik and his chiefs accepted Western dates for the beginning of the blockade and the CFM meeting but proposed May 12 for ending the blockade. Finally, on May 4, the long and winding negotiating trail, with all its switchbacks, reached its end when the representatives of the four powers, meeting in Jessup's office at 2 Park Avenue, produced a simple, three-paragraph communiqué which the governments next day released to the press:

1. All the restrictions imposed since March 1, 1948, by the Government of the Union of Soviet Socialist Republics on communications, transportation, and trade between Berlin and the Western zones of Germany and between the Eastern zone and the Western zones will be removed on May 12, 1949.
2. All the restrictions imposed since March 1, 1948, by the Governments of France, the United Kingdom, and the United States, or any one of them, on communications, transportation, and trade between Berlin and the Eastern zone and between the Western and Eastern zones of Germany will also be removed on May 12, 1949.
3. Eleven days subsequent to the removal of the restrictions referred to in paragraphs one and two, namely, on May 23, 1949, a meeting of the Council of Foreign Ministers will be convened in Paris to consider questions relating to Germany and problems arising out of the situation in Berlin, including also the question of currency in Berlin.

The communiqué did not call for any delay in the establishment of the West German government—the Western Allies had never wavered on this point—and on May 8, four years to the day after Field Marshal Wilhelm Keitel had surrendered the German armed forces to Marshal Georgi Zhukov and Air Chief Marshal Sir Arthur Tedder in Berlin, Parliamentary Council delegates meeting in Bonn adopted the Basic Law *(Grundgesetz),* as the Germans carefully called the establishing document to distinguish it from a true constitution, which would embrace all of the country, West and East.

On this same day Dr. Konrad Adenauer, a veteran anti-Nazi political figure who served as president of the council and would soon become the first chancellor of West Germany, wrote General Clay that "undoubtedly it is due to your prudent and purposeful attitude that Western Germany, after the chaos of the catastrophe, is now back on the road to the reconstruction of a sound economic and political life." Clay's work in the service of his government, said Adenauer, had been accomplished to the profit of Germany and the advantage of Europe.

CHAPTER 25

The Gates Go Up

ON THE GREAT Grafenwöhr parade ground, once a drill field for Hitler's troops, 11,000 U.S. soldiers wheeled through a ninety-minute review. A 105-millimeter battery fired a seventeen-gun salute, and overhead in a bright blue sky, as the general watched with a suggestion of tears in his eyes, squadrons of P-47s spelled out a gigantic word: C-L-A-Y. Then the Thunderbolts, joined by twenty F-80s, the first U.S.-production jet fighters, swept low over the grandstand in a final salute.

"My heart is filled with pride and joy," the slightly built, graying, homeward-bound U.S. commander told reporters. On the day before, May 3, President Truman had announced Clay's retirement (to be effective, as he had wished, on May 15), saying that the general deserved the thanks of the American people "for his execution of one of the toughest tasks and accomplishments of American history." During the four years he had given to this task, Clay had attracted criticism from all sides—from the French, for his determination to get the German economy up and running; from the British, who liked at times to picture him as erratic and impulsive and were displeased at his rejection of General Robertson's "military socialism" and his playing the role of "the one Saint who can save the Germans"; from Germans (Social Democrats, in particular) who thought him too unyielding; from the U.S. State Department, which sometimes found itself deeply upset at his asserting the right to make policy: he had little hesitation in making it plain that he "did not welcome interference from Washington intruders," as John Kenneth Galbraith put it, and on many occasions had protested confused or contradictory instructions from the Pentagon or Foggy Bottom by asking to be relieved.

But from the whole unprecedented four-year tangle, Clay had emerged as the West's chief symbol in Germany of determination and democracy. His concern for Germany's interests, wrote two British historians, "endeared him to its people and won him the trust which his colleagues had never inspired." John J. McCloy, Clay's successor as American proconsul in Germany, said that "it was General Clay's wisdom, persistence, courage, drive, devotion to duty, and knowledge of governmental practices that marked him as the one above all others who could meet the exacting needs of his mission." Charlotte Beelitz, speaking years later, said simply, "Everybody who was of that generation knows his name. It is engraved with an iron pencil in everybody's skin."

McCloy, a leading Manhattan lawyer-banker, president of the World Bank and former assistant secretary of war, would succeed Clay in the new era in which high commissioners would replace military governors. General Koenig would join Clay in retirement, and the distinguished veteran diplomat André François-Poncet would come back to Germany, where he had been ambassador in the 1930s, as French high commissioner. As the lone member of the Western trio to stay on, Robertson, who had once said of Clay, after a tough bargaining session, that "he looks like a Roman emperor—and acts like one," would now be in a position to exert specially strong influence on events; ready for the challenge, he had already appeared at public events in morning coat instead of his army uniform.

A week later in Berlin, the evening of Wednesday, May 11, began with something of a surprise. As darkness fell, lights came on all over the city, as if an air-raid blackout had ended; for the first time in eleven months, the Russians were supplying electricity to the Western sectors. At one minute after midnight, two U.S. soldiers, their helmets shining silver in the moonlight, raised a black-and-white-striped steel barrier, and Private Horace Scites of Logan, West Virginia, gunned the engine of the first jeep to leave Berlin and sped westward on the autobahn. With him rode Lieutenant William R. Frost of Louisville. The two men drove off to the cheers of a crowd of about five hundred men and women, some of them in evening dress, who had gathered for this special occasion.

A few minutes later the jeep, followed by private cars, approached a Russian checkpoint, a battered white shack surrounded by Soviet officers and enlisted men, many of them anxiously studying their watches to make sure the timing was correct. When the jeep roared up to the checkpoint, the soldiers quickly waved it through. The cars followed without fuss; nobody asked the passengers to produce documents.

A crowd also gathered in Helmstedt, at the British-Soviet zonal boundary, near the entrance to the Berlin autobahn, to watch a similar scene. The boundary installations, both British and Russian, gleamed with fresh paint; workmen had cut weeds along the sides of the long-unused highway and repainted border signs. Traffic choked the streets of the town; all hotel rooms were taken. A few seconds after midnight, the gate swung open and cars and trucks moved onto the highway. An hour and three-quarters later, for the first time in almost a year, cars from Helmstedt arrived in Berlin.

Draped in flags and bedecked with boughs, locomotives rumbled up to the Soviet Marienborn checkpoint. The first train, primarily for military passengers and reporters, left Helmstedt at 1:23; it arrived in the newly open city at 5:08. A few minutes after the passenger trains departed, a freight train with coal from the Ruhr passed through Marienborn, bound for Berlin. The first American train left Helmstedt at 5:05, carrying eight soldiers and five civilians as passengers and a carload of milk. The isolation of Berlin had ended, and with it had gone the Allied counterblockade.

Overhead during the day, however, the drone of airlift planes continued unchanged. Although West Berliners could once again enjoy such treats as oranges and fresh fish and real, not dehydrated, potatoes, nobody, Allies or Berliners, felt ready yet to depend solely on ground transportation and supply. General Cannon, who appeared by now to have developed a measure of appreciation for the accomplishments of the transport fliers, declared: "The lift will continue as at present until an adequate stockpile is available and we are certain that surface transportation can meet all the requirements of Berlin."

The general had good reason for his caution. Already, in the first flush of traffic freedom, the Russians wished to show that they still controlled the roads and rails running through their zone. Soldiers at Soviet checkpoints were turning back German trucks trying to leave Berlin, telling drivers they needed licenses from the East German administration or the SMA. The Russians also declared that they would decide the number of Western trains a day—six passenger, sixteen freight—and that all of them must have Soviet zone crews and engines. The Western Allies responded with an angry letter—the blockade seemed to be ending not with a bang but a snarl, which would never completely go away.

Speaking at his regular news conference, not quite a hundred days after the press session that had launched the fourth and finally productive diplomatic search for a solution in Berlin, Secretary Acheson credited the lifting of the blockade to "the superb performance of the pilots and their supporting crews, ground crews and so forth who have been for ten months conducting this airlift." But, he added, for all its achievement, the airlift had not solved the German problem: "The lifting of the blockade puts us in the situation in which we were before the blockade was imposed." The history of the Berlin blockade, Acheson later wrote, offered a typical demonstration of Soviet political values and diplomatic method, showing "the extreme sensitivity of Soviet authorities to developments in Germany and an almost equal lack of judgment in reacting to them." As for the kind of negotiations that ended the blockade, Sir William Hayter later observed that they required no particular skill, because "the Russians are not to be persuaded by eloquence or convinced by reasoned arguments. They rely on what Stalin used to call the proper basis of international policy, the calculation of forces." You could only change their minds, Hayter said, if you demonstrated that what they wanted to do was not possible.

The city assembly had declared May 12 a holiday in Berlin. Though leery of allowing themselves to believe wholly in the coming of good fortune, Berliners filled the streets, cheering arriving convoys and welcoming relatives who had been away from home when the barriers went up and thus had spent the past eleven months in the Western zones. Alice Sawadda and her boyfriend celebrated at a café, where they ordered cups of chocolate and two pieces of cake. "But we could not eat so much," she said, "because our bodies were not used to it. For a very long time, I even dreamed at night that I would go to a café and order these cakes and other foods."

At a special city assembly meeting in the Rathaus Schöneberg (town hall), the members heard speeches from Dr. Suhr, Mayor Reuter, and Konrad Adenauer. After Franz Neumann read the names of the men known at that time to have been killed in the airlift, members adopted a resolution renaming the square at Tempelhof as Platz der Luftbrücke (Airbridge Square). The assembly members also honored the departing General Clay, giving him a spontaneous standing ovation when he came into the chamber; "his popularity," noted a British writer, "was undoubted." Reuter declared that "the memory of General Clay will never fade in Berlin. . . . We will never forget what he has done for us."

Berliners could also honor themselves. The old *Berliner Unwille* proved deeper and finer than simply the pretentiousness and brashness for which other Germans had always criticized them. Whatever the Allies might have done, the airlift could not have succeeded without the ability of the Berliners to bear up under these strange and difficult conditions. The citizen of Berlin still represented what Goethe saw two hundred years earlier: *"ein verwegener Menschenschlag"*—an audacious type of human being. But at the same time the airlift drew on another human strength. As Alice Sawadda experienced it, its greatest force came from the way "we all helped each other. The world helped us, and we were not forgotten."

Mayor Reuter described his pleasure at the fact that the Russians had climbed down, but he knew the struggle for the city would continue in one form or another. When the Communists in East Berlin called for meetings to end the split in the city government, Reuter declared: "Work with those people? Never!"

Despite the official lifting of the blockade, "those people" showed few signs of wanting to work with the West Berliners or the Western Allies. Niggling kinds of harassment, similar to the vexing interference that had marked the run-up to the blockade a year earlier, obstructed the flow of road, rail, and barge traffic. Perhaps, in accordance with what one specialist in Russian culture called "old market dickering," the Soviets were setting the table for the Council of Foreign Ministers meeting; traditionally, they favored a threat of force, a bullying start, after which they could give way to the point everybody else regarded as the proper place to begin; thus, again like the hostage taker, they could win credit for relaxing their position. West Berlin's *Tagesspiegel* declared that the lives of the men who died supplying Berlin "weigh heavily in the scales of freedom, and when in a few days the foreign ministers meet in Paris, they will not be permitted to forget these men who made the supreme sacrifice in the battle for democratic rights."

In Bonn, on May 23—as it happened, the opening day of the CFM meeting in Paris—Konrad Adenauer, as president of the Parliamentary Council, proclaimed the Federal Republic of Germany. That door now seemed closed and locked to the Russians. In Paris, surprising the other foreign ministers, Vyshinsky opened the first session by ignoring Europe altogether and proposing to discuss arrangements for a peace treaty with Japan. This nightmarish distraction threatened to stall the meeting before it had got under way, since the West could hardly agree and Soviet negotiators tended to attach "importance amounting almost to mystique" to the agenda, always objecting to moving on to a new item until agreement had been reached on the first—a rigidity akin to the Leninist principle of refusing to discuss any particulars until the general question was settled. But as if finally remembering that the Soviets, not the West, had sought the meeting, Vyshinsky proceeded, next day, to present the Soviet proposals for Germany; these called for what the foreign minister termed a return to Potsdam, with four-power control of the country and unanimity again the dominating principle. What advantage would this move hold for the western Germans? Acheson likened it to "asking a victim of paralysis who was three-quarters recovered to return to total paralysis."

The conference took place in the Palais Rose, a pink marble mansion of Edwardian elegance built by a Frenchman for his American bride. "Its *fin de siècle* design and decor," said Acheson, "gave our wholly unreal meetings an incorrigible musical comedy setting and atmosphere." The ministers sat at the usual large round table, but these sessions in the grand salon afforded the secretary of state an unusual diversion. As the discussions droned on, with everything undergoing translation not once but twice, Acheson could amuse himself by studying the frescoed ceiling, which featured satyrs in hot pursuit of nymphs through clouds.

After days of talk and ceiling gazing, the West presented its counter-proposal, under which the just-born West German constitution would extend its umbrella over the Soviet zone. But the Soviets could not afford to accept this program, just as the West could not accept Vyshinsky's package. The latter would give the Soviets a veto over everything that happened in Germany, the first would leave them with no position at all. Hence they would settle for the Eastern zone and the status quo. The West tried but failed to secure its own secure corridor from Helmstedt to Berlin.

Having fulfilled the agreement signed in Philip Jessup's office on May 4—that is, that a meeting would be held—the foreign ministers, with the "mousy issue of [their] mountainous labor" evident, finally ended their deliberations at six o'clock in the evening of June 20. But then came a surprising twist, a small incident providing a striking glimpse into the functioning of the Soviet hierarchy and the relationship between the government and the Communist Party. At eight o'clock Vyshinsky telephoned Robert Schuman to demand that the council reconvene; he wanted an amendment in the details of agreements looking toward a treaty for Austria—the one area in which the conference had made measurable progress. Vyshinsky could not explain why he needed the new provision he wanted, but his fellow ministers already knew. In their routine tapping of the Soviet embassy telephones, French intelligence officers had listened in on a call—for some reason, *en clair*—from Vyshinsky's deputy in Moscow, Andrei Gromyko. Though a subordinate and almost thirty years younger than the foreign minister, Gromyko had torn into Vyshinsky for agreeing to the terms in question—he must get them changed; the deputy could engage in such brutal talk to a nominal superior, it seemed, because he stood higher in the Communist Party. But Bevin waved off the request, and Acheson and Schuman agreed. Midnight saw the secretary of state aboard the *Independence,* on his way home.

A group of U.S. Army engineers gave the airlift a final distinct twist of their own. Early in March, about three months after the Tegel airport had gone into operation, heavy-equipment operators and maintenance specialists at the 7742nd Engineer Base Depot at Hanau, near Frankfurt, had received orders detaching them for service in Berlin. After being held up by the heaviest snow of the winter, the engineers became airlift passengers, arriving in Berlin on March 20. Billeted in Wedding near Tegel and renamed the 503d Engineer Company with the somewhat paradoxical added identification "Light Equipment," they immediately set to work building a second runway and new taxiways for the field.

Though Berliners worked on this project as they had done on the first runway, their numbers were strikingly different—about 300 as opposed to the 17,000 of the preceding summer and autumn. What made the difference was the availability of equipment left on-site from the earlier construction together with the large number of additional pieces that had been flown in using, as a unit chronicler wrote, "the now well known Lacomb method of disassembly and reassembly." Flights continued as the engineers worked on the taxiways connecting the terminal, the original runway, and the new second runway. Equipment operators reported that "the arriving and departing aircraft would nearly brush the overhead frames of the bulldozers with their landing gear as they passed over the taxiway intersections." Looking to the future, the planners had not only called for a larger runway than the first one (6,500 feet long, 200 feet wide) but had included grading to make possible future operations by aircraft that required 8,000 feet of runway.

The official lifting of the blockade on May 12 did not stop airlift operations, nor did it affect the work of the 503d. When the company finished its task on July 24, after four months of around-the-clock effort without a break, the commanders decided to celebrate the achievement with a joint parade by U.S. and French units. This fraternal event gave rise to a bizarre aftermath. During the striking of the colors, the American flag dropped to the ground, where, by some mischance, a French officer trampled on it. After the troops had been dismissed, the U.S. commander asked the French to turn the flag over to the Americans so that they could dispose of it in the official way, by burning it. Curiously, however, the French refused this request. This development did not sit well with the men of the 503d, who decided that evening—perhaps after a round or two of commemorative drinks—to capture a French flag and give it the treatment the American flag had received. "The result," the unit chronicler noted with a measure of restraint, "was a riot of relatively significant magnitude." An entire company of MPs turned out to put down the fighting, which smoldered throughout the night, sometimes erupting into fresh confrontations.

Trying to look beneath the surface, the chronicler theorized that some of the American behavior might have stemmed from resentment of the French for contributing no planes to the airlift and doing very little to help develop Tegel. On the other hand, after the strenuous four months the American engineers had put in, they "might have been entitled to celebrate the completion of their work." In any case, the next morning, escorted by MPs, the men of the 503d dutifully boarded the train that would take them back to their home base at Hanau.

The airlift continued through the summer of 1949, stocking West Berlin's warehouses and larders. Not surprisingly, final figures on flights and tonnages vary, though not a great deal. General Tunner, an eminently qualified authority, gives them, as of September 1, 1949, as 276,926 flights, which hauled 2,323,067 tons of supplies into Berlin—just about a ton apiece for the people of the Western sectors. The official estimate of cost was $300 million, which Tunner thought too high (he naturally wanted to make air transport look as cheap and efficient as possible); he argued that the approximately $150-a-ton figure should be lowered, especially taking into account the airlift's reliance on cheap labor, mostly GIs and displaced persons. An RAF historian put the tonnage at 2,325,809: 1,586,530 tons of coal, 538,016 tons of food, 92,282 tons of petroleum products. The U.S. Air Force carried 76.7 percent, the RAF 17.0 percent, and civil aircraft 6.3 percent.

The airlift was a success story of two neglected sides of fighting forces: the air transport service and the engineers. Though the British played a large part, it was essentially an American kind of performance, organizing people and equipment on a large scale to cope with an emergency without worrying about precedents. It had about it something of the quality of the reply General Pershing once gave a French officer who expressed skepticism concerning the military prowess of the Americans newly arrived in France in 1917. When told it would take thirty years to form a competent general staff, Pershing retorted: "It never took Americans thirty years to do anything."

For Bill Martin, "Those were the good days. Action—the most exciting part of your life." Russ Reynolds, another American pilot, summed up his feelings: "It gives you a sense of pride. It's like a rescue service. In the military the main goal is to break things and kill people. In this, you're in the business of saving lives." In the end it was the fliers themselves, many of them hastily flung into the operation, many of them with little training for flying of that kind, whose steady performance of their duty kept the West in Berlin and kept Berlin in the West.

The Luftbrücke Memorial carries a list of sixty-five persons who lost their lives in the airlift: 31 American and 18 British service crew members, 11 civilian fliers, 5 Germans. When the first airlift fatalities occurred, in the early days of this remarkable endeavor, the *Tagesspiegel* declared: "An airman who crashes in the course of supplying Berlin is for us more than a transport pilot who has died in an accident; he is a man who has given his life for a free world."

"The Stakes Could Hardly Have Been Greater"

AT A FEW minutes past three o'clock in the afternoon of April 4, 1949, Dean Acheson, standing at the lectern in the State Department auditorium, welcomed a group of distinguished guests to Washington. These visitors, the Western European foreign ministers, had come to sign the North Atlantic Treaty, a document finally ready to appear in public after much negotiation not only among the various countries but between the U.S. administration and the Senate. In spite of fears on Capitol Hill, for the first time in its history the United States was joining an alliance in peacetime.

The foundation for the treaty had been laid a year earlier by Ernest Bevin's efforts toward a Western union in Europe and, in the United States, by the Senate's 64-4 passage, in June 1948, of the Vandenberg Resolution, which encouraged American participation in "regional and other collective arrangements for individual and collective self-defense." The Atlantic, formerly considered a barrier dividing the New World from the Old, would now look increasingly like a highway tying together the members of an oceanic community. For the moment, however, the people in the auditorium could not have been blamed for harboring doubts about the entire enterprise; as everyone waited for the ceremony to begin, the Marine Band offered its own keynote, playing "I've Got Plenty of Nothin'," followed by "It Ain't Necessarily So."

The discussions and negotiations leading to the creation of the North Atlantic Treaty had proceeded on their own track, parallel to the mounting and execution of the Berlin airlift—as the treaty was being signed in Washington, Philip Jessup was still engaged in his talks in New York with Yakov Malik aimed at bringing about the lifting of the Soviet blockade. On a third track during the same period the West Germans completed preparations for the establishment of the German Federal Republic. What relation did the airlift—both the effort and the success—bear to the creation of the treaty and of the new republic? As one historian observed, the Western commitment to the establishment of West Germany antedated the imposition of the blockade, as did moves toward the North Atlantic Treaty. (Bevin made his first Western union proposal on January 22, 1948.) Despite the crisis in Berlin, both sets of negotiations proceeded slowly, probably no more rapidly than would have been the case without a blockade.

But the pace of these events did not relate to the magnitude of the influence of the blockade and the airlift on events to come in Europe. "In retrospect," said Avi Shlaim, the student of crisis decision-making, "it is clear beyond any shadow of doubt that this was the most critical crisis of the cold war." Indeed, "the stakes could hardly have been greater. . . . [T]he future of Germany, the future of Western Europe and the future of the precarious postwar international order all hung in the balance." The blockade represented the climax of the struggle for power over Germany and, consequently, over Europe.

The airlift presented a variety of ironies and paradoxes:

> Though the blockade cast a long shadow before it, the Western Allies had devised no plan to meet it.
>
> When the airlift began, political and military leaders had little faith in it, looking on it, at best, as only a temporary measure while negotiations took place.
>
> U.S. Air Force leaders saw it as a threat to the worldwide deployment of their aircraft and did not grasp the publicity advantages it could and would bring.
>
> Everybody thought anybody could handle it. Only after General Wedemeyer pressed General Tunner on General Vandenberg did everybody see the vital importance of having the right organizer and director.
>
> If the Russians had begun imposing their transportation and communications restrictions in July instead of in March, General Clay would not have been present in Berlin to become the symbol of resistance.
>
> Beyond that, if the Russians had waited until autumn for the actual blockade, the weather would probably have prevented the Allies from establishing the airlift.
>
> Since in Stalin's view the airlift was not supposed to succeed, Soviet intelligence was reluctant to report its effectiveness; the generalissimo therefore chose to wait for winter in the belief that the

operation would fail. In its own deliberations, Soviet intelligence displayed more faith in the airlift than Western leaders had.

Of fundamental importance, Joseph Stalin, widely regarded in the West as formidably shrewd and resourceful, misjudged the situation at every turn. His attempt to kick the Western powers out of Berlin not only failed but produced a political realignment that shaped the future course of the cold war. In that charged year the people regarded at the beginning as enemies of the Allies turned into friends and even heroes. The West made its misjudgments, too, but its mistakes were fewer and nothing as significant as those of Stalin and his colleagues.

Ernest Bevin told Ambassador Lewis Douglas that he would rather "hang on to the bitter end and be driven out if necessary rather than voluntarily give way." But neither of these alternatives presented itself. Instead, despite the shakiness of the position into which they had put themselves, the Allies defended their besieged Berlin. The airlift proved a technical, political, and psychological triumph, building confidence in the United States among the people of Western Europe. When the editors of the *Economist* had published their urgent call for "hard thought and high courage," they could not even faintly have imagined the mighty effort and the remarkable results these qualities would produce in the following months. The airlift had enabled the development of the German Federal Republic to continue; the fact of this development, not the timetable it followed, constituted the central reality.

The same truth applied to the creation of the North Atlantic Treaty. The treaty went into effect in August, following its ratification by France, and in September the member foreign ministers agreed to establish military committees; though no real military organization existed until 1951, after some months of the Korean War, the structure had been put in place and the alliance guaranteed that the United States would not abandon Europe, as it had not abandoned Berlin.

"On the whole," said Shlaim, "the American policymakers stood up to stress well and coped fairly effectively and even creatively with the acute dilemmas posed by the Soviet ground blockade. Unquestionably, there were instances of impaired cognitive performance, especially manifestations of greater rigidity, which could be traced directly to the intense stress they were experiencing, but these were not sufficiently pervasive to disrupt what was in essence a rational and calculated process of decision-making." Given the failure of the political leaders, the intelligence experts, and the military authorities to make plans for dealing with the blockade until the situation had thrust itself upon them, that verdict is a tribute to adaptability if not to foresight.

The overall story from 1945 through 1949 was a chronicle of negotiations on all levels between two sides ill equipped to understand each other even on such points as the fixing of an agenda—from meetings in the Kremlin to debates in the Allied Control Council to brusque confrontations in the Berlin Kommandatura. And when negotiations failed, another kind of factor came into play—the can-do spirit that, directed by General Tunner, drew on American innovation and drive at its most effective. Negotiation and innovation thus shaped the first phase of the developing cold war, a back-and-forth dance of action and reaction that ended with the lifting of the blockade, the signing of the North Atlantic Treaty, and the establishment of separate republics in East and West Germany. The airlift proved to be the hinge on which the entire era turned.

Although it received heavy criticism from Walter Lippmann and other influential observers, containment became official American policy in Europe—in practice, if not always in name—after the Berlin blockade and the airlift. The Russians implicitly acknowledged that the positions of the two sides had now become fixed, and "the foreign ministers who had held a series of increasingly fruitless conferences in 1948 and 1949 no longer met. Any further discussion seemed pointless; they were to assemble again only the year after Stalin's death." After the airlift defeated the blockade, the cold war in Europe, as Howard K. Smith put it, "settled down to years of glowering and menacing."

Despite the many misjudgments and mistakes made by the West, "to establish a symmetry between East and West is to misread the origins and the character of the cold war," said the historian Walter Laqueur. "The claim that a more rational Western policy could have averted it can be made only if one leaves out of sight some essential factors: the intransigence of communist ideology in the postwar period, the dynamics of Stalinism and totalitarian societies in general, and Stalin's paranoia. Soviet policy was a mixture of realpolitik and persecution mania, of rational and irrational factors." Hence, "the basic difference between the West and the Soviet Union could not have been resolved by gestures and declarations, however forthcoming, on the part of the West. The cold war could have been avoided only if the Soviet Union had not been possessed by the idea of the infallibility of its own doctrine." As Maxim Litvinov had put it in 1946, the underlying cause of the trouble between the West and the Soviet Union was the Soviet conviction that conflict between Communist and capitalist worlds was inevitable. "These convictions," said Arthur Schlesinger, "transformed an impasse between national states into a religious war, a tragedy of possibility into one of necessity."

The development of this religious war, as Schlesinger called it, saw the West—including, emphatically, many Americans—create a sort of retaliatory corollary of the Soviet worldview. John Foster Dulles, secretary of state from 1953 to 1959, summed up this Manichaean absolutism in his famous declaration that since Communism is wicked, "neutralism is immoral." Americans with this view tended to look with distrust on non-aligned countries and to treat various repressive rulers and regimes around the world as true democratic communicants, as long as they professed the anti-Communist faith.

With specific reference to the division of Berlin and the problems that followed, V. M. Molotov expressed his point of view in his usual succinct way: "The thing is, if it hadn't been Berlin there would have been another snag somewhere else. We had different goals and positions, and the snag came up in Berlin." With equal compression and clarity, the old foreign minister explained that he had considered it his chief duty as foreign minister "to extend the frontier of our Fatherland to the maximum."

In October 1950 General Clay returned to Berlin to take part in a unique ceremony, the installation in the tower of the Schöneberg town hall of the Freedom Bell (Freiheitsglocke), a replica of the Liberty Bell donated to West Berlin by the people of the United States. A crowd of half a million Berliners greeted the general, and Mayor Reuter announced a new name for Kron-prinzenallee, the street in front of U.S. headquarters: Clayallee. When the general died, thirty years after the airlift, a Berliner who had lived through those days offered a simple characterization: "He was the best of them all."

Summing up the character of Ernest Bevin, Dean Acheson said that the foreign secretary understood power: "He knew that choices had to be made, often choices between unpleasant alternatives, and never was misled, as so many well-meaning people are, into believing that the necessity for choice can be transcended by a flight of eloquence"; even in the frequent times of disagreement, Bevin proved a sturdy and dynamic ally.

The record of General Clay's ultimate chief, President Truman, who had not only ridden out the storm in Berlin but performed his own political miracle, received a wonderfully terse summary from a tourist who visited his birthplace at Lamar, Missouri, in 1994. "He was as good as the rest," she said, "and a lot better than some." In the Berlin crisis he proved to be even better than that.

To some observers, only one detail seemed to be lacking in the Berlin that followed the airlift. In all the sprawling city, could not some road or street—perhaps one named for a long-forgotten Hohenzollern—be re-christened Tunnerallee?

From the end of the airlift until the end of the cold war, Berlin would remain two cities, with two governments, reflecting the division of the country of which it had once been the sole capital. Though the city did not in itself possess conventional strategic importance, the Western Allies through their heroic effort to maintain their position had guaranteed that it would continue to be a sensitive spot; in 1961 Premier Nikita Khrushchev would describe it as the "testicles of the West," which he could squeeze whenever he felt like it.

Later in that year this division would find brutal symbolization in the building of the Berlin Wall, essentially a fence closing off West Berlin from East Germany. Another twenty-eight years would elapse before television screens around the world showed Berliners hacking chunks of concrete from the wall and dancing on top of it, offering symbolic and physical proof that the cold war had finally come to its end. West Berlin and East Berlin had once again become simply Berlin.

SOURCES AND BIBLIOGRAPHY

Key to Sources of Papers and Other
Archival Materials Cited in the Notes

George C. Marshall Library (GCML); U.S. Army Military History Institute and the Bowman Special Berlin Collection (MHI); Air Force Historical Research Agency (AFHRA); Library of Congress (LC); Office of History, Office of the Chief of Engineers (OCE); Seeley G. Mudd Library, Princeton University (SGML); William Rigdon Papers, Georgia Southern College (WRP); Russian Foreign Ministry Archives (RFMA); Public Record Office, London (PRO).

It is perhaps useful to remind the reader that nowadays, thanks to photocopying, a given document may well be found in any of several repositories. I note, in particular, the current availability at the Military History Institute of a great range of documents from the National Archives. A citation in these notes therefore indicates the collection in which I encountered the particular document; other researchers may find that same document in another library more convenient for their purposes. (At least some of the time, of course, one ought to experience the special kind of excitement that comes from handling original documents rather than copies.)

Interviews appear as citations in the Notes with the name of the person interviewed.

In addition to journals dealing with history and political science, extensive use has been made of *Collier's,* the *Courier-Journal, The Economist, Life,* the *Nation,* the *New Republic, Newsweek,* the *New Yorker,* the *New York Times,* the *Saturday Evening Post, Time, U.S. News & World Report,* and the newspaper wire services. With their ability to catch living moments, electronic media sources also made contributions, particularly documentaries presented on the Public Broadcasting System, the Arts and Entertainment Network, and the History Channel.

Official Publications and Documents

Air Ministry and Central Office of Information. *The Berlin Airlift.* Text by Dudley Barker. London: His Majesty's Stationery Office, 1949.

Carlyle, Margaret, ed. *Documents on International Affairs, 1949–1950.* Royal Institute of International Affairs. London: Oxford University Press, 1953.

Control Commission of Germany (British Element). *Notes on the Blockade of Berlin 1948—from a British Viewpoint in Berlin.* HQ, British Troops Berlin; RAF Gatow; HQ Airlift BTB; Military Government BTB. 1949.

Heidelmeyer, Wolfgang, and Guenter Hindrichs. *Documents on Berlin, 1943–1963.* Munich: R. Oldenbourg, 1963.

May, Ernest R., ed. *Anxiety and Affluence: 1945–1965.* Vol. 8 of *A Documentary History of American Life.* New York: McGraw-Hill, 1966.

Merrill, Dennis, gen. ed. *Documentary History of the Truman Presidency.* University Publications of America.

Vol. 8, *The Truman Doctrine and the Beginning of the Cold War, 1947–1949.* 1996.

Vol. 16, *Cold War Confrontation: Truman, Stalin, and the Berlin Airlift.* 1997.

U.S. Department of State. *Germany 1947–1949: The Story in Documents.* 1950.

———. *Foreign Relations of the United States* [FRUS], 1945. *The Conference of Berlin (the Potsdam Conference).* 2 vols. 1960.

———. *Foreign Relations of the United States, 1947.* Vol. 2, *Council of Foreign Ministers; Germany and Austria.* 1972.

———. *Foreign Relations of the United States, 1948.*

Vol. 2, *Germany and Austria.* 1973.

Vol. 4, *Eastern Europe; the Soviet Union.* 1974.

———. *Emergence of the Intelligence Establishment. Foreign Relations of the United States, 1945–1950.* C. Thomas Thorne, Jr., and David S. Patterson, eds. Glenn W. LaFantasie, gen. ed. Washington: U.S. Government Printing Office, 1996.

———. *Department of State Bulletin,* 1948–1949.

Manuscripts

Bailey, Thomas E. "Born in Berlin: The Story of the 503d Engineer Company." (MHI)

Clay, Lucius D. Papers. (GCML)

Condit, Kenneth W. "The History of the Joint Chiefs of Staff." Vol. 2, 1947–1949. (MHI)

Donnelly, Charles H. Papers. (MHI)

Howley, Frank Papers. (MHI)

Leahy, William D. Diary. (Manuscript Division, LC)

Maginnis, John J. Papers. (MHI)

Molotov, V. M. Diary. From archives of the Soviet Foreign Ministry; translated for this project by Igor Sopronenko and Cynthia Ruder.

Conference Papers

"The Soviet Union, Germany, and the Cold War, 1945–1962: New Evidence from Eastern Archives." Papers from the June 28–30, 1994, conference, Kultur-wissenschaftliches Institut, University of Essen.

   Creuzberger, Stefan. "Opportunism or Tactics? Ernst Lemmer, the Soviet Occupation Authority, and the Treatment of New 'Key Documents.'"

   Gobarev, Victor. "Soviet Military Plans and Activities in the Berlin Crisis, 1948–1949."

   Laufer, Jochen. "The Soviet Union and the Division of Germany into Zones."

   Loth, Wilfried. "Stalin's Plans for Postwar Germany."

   Narinsky, Mikhail. "Soviet Policy and the Berlin Blockade, 1948."

   Pennachio, Chuck. "Origins of the 1948–49 Berlin Airlift Crisis: New Evidence from East German Communist Party Archives."

   Wettig, Gerhard. "All-German Unity and East German Separation in Soviet Policy, 1947–1949."

Books and Articles

Abramson, Rudy. *Spanning the Century: The Life of W. Averell Harriman, 1891–1986.* New York: Morrow, 1992.

Acheson, Dean. *Sketches from Life.* New York: Harper, 1961; Popular Library ed., 1962.

———. *Present at the Creation: My Years in the State Department.* New York: Norton, 1969.

Adams, Henry H. *Witness to Power: The Life of Fleet Admiral William D. Leahy.* Annapolis: Naval Institute Press, 1985.

"Airlift to Berlin." *National Geographic,* May 1949.

Ambrose, Stephen. *Eisenhower: Soldier, General of the Army, President-Elect, 1890–1952.* New York: Simon and Schuster, 1983.

———. *Rise to Globalism.* 5th rev. ed. New York: Penguin Books, 1988.

Anderhub, Andreas, and Jack O. Bennett. *Blockade, Airlift and Airlift Gratitude Foundation.* Berliner Forum, n.d.

Anderson, Terry H. *The United States, Great Britain, and the Cold War, 1944–47.* Columbia: University of Missouri Press, 1981.

Andrew, Christopher, and Oleg Gordievsky. *KGB: The Inside Story.* New York: HarperCollins, 1990.

Ardagh, John. *Germany and the Germans.* 3rd ed. New York: Penguin Books, 1995.

Backer, John H. *The Decision to Divide Germany.* Durham, N.C.: Duke University Press, 1978.

———. *Winds of History: The German Years of Lucius DuBignon Clay.* New York: Van Nostrand Reinhold, 1983.

Baedeker, Karl. *Northern Germany.* Leipzig: Karl Baedeker, 1897.

Balfour, Michael. *Germany: The Tides of Power.* London: Routledge, 1992.

Barghoorn, Frederick C. "The Soviet Union Between War and Cold War." *Annals of the American Academy of Political and Social Science* 263 (May 1949).

Bark, Dennis L., and David R. Gress. *A History of West Germany*. Vol. 1: *From Shadow to Substance, 1945–1963*. London: Basil Blackwell, 1989.

Barnett, Correlli. *Britain and Her Army, 1509–1970*. New York: William Morrow, 1970.

Bennett, Jack. "The German Currency Reform." *Annals of the American Academy of Political and Social Science* 267 (January 1950).

Bering, Henrik. *Outpost Berlin: The History of the American Military Forces in Berlin, 1945–1994*. Chicago: edition q., inc., 1995.

Bess, Demaree. "Will We Be Pushed Out of Berlin?" *Saturday Evening Post,* July 31, 1948.

———. "What Did the Airlift Really Prove?" *Saturday Evening Post,* June 25, 1949.

Black, C. E. "Soviet Policy in Eastern Europe." *Annals of the American Academy of Political and Social Science* 263 (May 1949).

Bland, Larry I., ed. *George C. Marshall Interviews and Reminiscences for Forrest C. Pogue*. Lexington, Va.: George C. Marshall Research Foundation, 1991.

Blum, John Morton. *Roosevelt and Morgenthau*. Boston: Houghton Mifflin, 1970.

Bohlen, Charles E. *Witness to History*. New York: Norton, 1973.

Bolten, Seymour R. "Military Government and the German Political Parties." *Annals of the American Academy of Political and Social Science* 267 (January 1950).

Borowski, Harry R. "A Narrow Victory: The Berlin Blockade and the American Military Response." *Air University Review* 32, no. 5 (1981).

Bradley, Omar N. *A Soldier's Story*. New York: Holt, Rinehart and Winston, 1951; Popular Library ed., n.d.

Bradley, Omar N., and Clay Blair. *A General's Life*. New York: Simon and Schuster, 1983.

Brandon, Henry. *Special Relationships*. New York: Atheneum, 1988.

Brecht, Arnold. "Re-establishing German Government." *Annals of the American Academy of Political and Science* 267 (January 1950).

Browder, Robert Paul, and Thomas G. Smith. *Independent: A Biography of Lewis W. Douglas*. New York: Knopf, 1986.

Buffet, Cyril. *Mourir pour Berlin: La France et l'Allemagne, 1945–1949*. Paris: Armand Colin, 1991.

Bullock, Alan. *Ernest Bevin: Foreign Secretary, 1945–1951*. New York: Norton, 1983.

Byrnes, James F. *Speaking Frankly*. New York: Harper & Brothers, 1947.

———. *All in One Lifetime*. New York: Harper, 1958.

Calder, Angus. *The People's War*. New York: Pantheon, 1969; Ace Books ed., 1972.

Calvocoressi, Peter. *Survey of International Affairs, 1947–1948*. Royal Institute of International Affairs. London: Oxford University Press, 1952.

Carter, Marshall S. "Unforgettable George C. Marshall." *Reader's Digest,* July 1972.

Charles, Max. *Berlin Blockade.* London: Allan Wingate, 1959.

Charlton, Michael. *The Eagle and the Small Birds.* Chicago: University of Chicago Press, 1984.

————. *The Price of Victory.* London: British Broadcasting Corporation, 1983.

Childs, David. *The GDR: Moscow's German Ally.* London: George Allen and Unwin, 1983.

Childs, J. Rives. *American Foreign Service.* New York: Henry Holt, 1948.

Chuev, Felix. *Molotov Remembers.* Edited by Albert Resis. Chicago: Ivan R. Dee, 1993.

Churchill, Winston S. *Triumph and Tragedy. The Second World War.* Vol. 6. Boston: Houghton Mifflin, 1953.

Clare, George. *Before the Wall: Berlin Days, 1946–1948.* New York: Dutton, 1989.

Clay, Lucius D. *Decision in Germany.* Garden City, N.Y.: Doubleday, 1950.

Clifford, Clark. *Counsel to the President.* New York: Random House, 1991.

Collier, Richard. *Bridge Across the Sky.* New York: McGraw-Hill, 1978.

Colville, John. *The Fringes of Power: 10 Downing Street Diaries, 1939– 1955.* New York: Norton, 1985.

Conquest, Robert. *Stalin: Breaker of Nations.* New York: Viking Penguin, 1991; Penguin Books ed., 1992.

Craig, Gordon A. *The Germans.* Rev. ed. New York: Putnam, 1991.

Crankshaw, Edward. "The Man Who Holds the Key to War." *New York Times Magazine,* October 13, 1948.

Daniels, Jonathan. *The Man of Independence.* Philadelphia: Lippincott, 1950.

Daniels, Robert V., ed. *A Documentary History of Communism in Russia.* Hanover, N.H.: University of Vermont/University Press of New England, 1993.

Davidson, Bill. "The Mayor the Soviets Hate." *Saturday Evening Post,* February 5, 1949.

————. "The Surprising Mr. Jessup." *Collier's,* July 30, 1949.

Davies, Andrew. *Where Did the Forties Go?* London: Pluto Press, 1984.

Davis, Arthur N. *The Kaiser as I Know Him.* New York: Harper, 1918.

Davison, W. Phillips. *The Berlin Blockade.* Princeton: Princeton University Press, 1958.

Deighton, Anne. *The Impossible Peace.* New York: Oxford University Press, 1990; Clarendon paperback ed., 1993.

DeSantis, Hugh. *The Diplomacy of Silence.* Chicago: University of Chicago Press, 1979; paperback ed., 1983.

Detzer, Karl. "Riding the Berlin Airlift." *Forum,* March 1949.

Diesel, Eugen. *Germany and the Germans.* New York: Macmillan, 1931.

Djilas, Milovan. *Conversations with Stalin.* Translated by Michael B. Petrovich. New York: Harcourt, Brace and World, 1962.

Donovan, Frank. *Bridge in the Sky.* New York: David McKay, 1968.

Donovan, Robert J. *Conflict and Crisis: The Presidency of Harry S. Truman, 1945–1948.* New York: Norton, 1977.

Druène, Bernard. *Français à Berlin.* Berlin, 1949.

Edmonds, Robin. *Setting the Mould: The United States and Britain, 1945–1950.* New York: Oxford University Press, 1986.

———. *The Big Three.* New York: Norton, 1991.

Eisenhower, David. *Eisenhower: At War, 1943–1945.* New York: Random House, 1986.

Eisenhower, Dwight D. *Crusade in Europe.* Garden City, N.Y.: Doubleday, 1948.

Engler, Robert. "The Individual Soldier and the Occupation." *Annals of the American Academy of Political and Social Science* 267 (January 1950).

Feis, Herbert. *Churchill—Roosevelt—Stalin: The War They Waged and the Peace They Sought.* Princeton, N.J.: Princeton University Press, 1957; paperback ed., 1966.

Ferrell, Robert H. *George C. Marshall.* New York: Cooper Square, 1966.

———. *Harry S. Truman: A Life.* Columbia: University of Missouri Press, 1994.

———. ed. *Off the Record: The Private Papers of Harry S. Truman.* New York: Harper and Row, 1980.

———. ed. *Truman in the White House: The Diary of Eben A. Ayers.* Columbia: University of Missouri Press, 1991.

Fisher, Paul. *The Berlin Airlift.* Scott Air Force Base, 1959; reprinted from *Bee-Hive* (United Aircraft Corp.), Fall 1948.

Fontaine, André. *Histoire de la guerre froide.* Vol 1: *De la révolution d'Octobre à la guerre de Corée, 1917–1950.* Paris: Fayard, 1965.

Fossedal, Gregory A. *Our Finest Hour: Will Clayton, the Marshall Plan, and the Triumph of Democracy.* Stanford, Calif.: Hoover Institution Press, 1993.

Friedrich, Carl J. "Military Government and Dictatorship." *Annals of the American Academy of Political and Social Science* 267 (January 1950).

Gablentz, O. M. von der. *The Berlin Question in its Relations to World Politics, 1944–1963.* Vol. 19, Documents and Reports. Forschungsinstitut der deutschen Gesellschaft für auswärtige Politik e.v. Munich: R. Oldenbourg, 1964.

Gaddis, John Lewis. *Strategies of Containment.* New York: Oxford University Press, 1982.

———. *The Long Peace.* New York: Oxford University Press, 1987.

Gardner, Lloyd C. *Spheres of Influence.* Chicago: Ivan R. Dee, 1993.

Gardner, Lloyd C., Arthur Schlesinger, Jr., and Hans J. Morgenthau. *The Origins of the Cold War.* Waltham, Mass.: Ginn, 1970.

Gardner, Richard N. *Sterling-Dollar Diplomacy.* Exp. ed. New York: McGraw-Hill, 1969.

Gatzke, Hans W. *Germany and the United States.* Cambridge, Mass.: Harvard University Press, 1980.

Gelber, Lionel. *America in Britain's Place.* New York: Frederick A. Praeger, 1961.

Gilbert, Martin. *Never Despair. Winston S. Churchill.* Vol. 8. Boston: Houghton Mifflin, 1988.

Gimbel, John. *The American Occupation of Germany.* Stanford, Calif.: Stanford University Press, 1968.

Glines, Carroll V. "Before the Colors Fade: Berlin Airlift Commander." *American Heritage* 20, no. 6 (1969).

Gooch, G. P. *Studies in German History.* London: Longmans, Green, 1948.

Grathwol, Robert P., and Donita M. Moorhus. *American Forces in Berlin: Cold War Outpost, 1945–1994.* Washington, D.C.: Legacy Resource Management Program, Cold War Project, Department of Defense, 1994.

Griffith, William E. "Denazification in the United States Zone of Germany." *Annals of the American Academy of Political and Social Science* 267 (January 1950).

Gromyko, Andrei. *Memories.* New York: Doubleday, 1989.

Gunther, John. *Behind the Curtain.* New York: Harper, 1949.

H.R.H. Viktoria Luise. *The Kaiser's Daughter.* Translated and edited by Robert Vacha. Englewood Cliffs, N.J.: Prentice-Hall,1977.

Harbutt, Fraser J. *The Iron Curtain.* New York: Oxford University Press, 1986; paperback ed., 1988.

Hargrove, Erwin C. *Presidential Leadership.* New York: Macmillan, 1966.

Harriman, W. Averell, and Elie Abel, *Special Envoy to Churchill and Stalin, 1941– 46.* New York: Random House, 1975.

Harrington, Daniel F. "American Policy in the Berlin Crisis of 1948–1949." Ph.D. diss., Indiana University, 1979.

Harris, Seymour E. *The European Recovery Program.* Cambridge, Mass.: Harvard University Press, 1948.

Hartmann, Frederick H. *Germany Between East and West.* Englewood Cliffs, N.J.: Prentice-Hall, 1965.

Hastings, Max. *Bomber Command.* New York: Dial Press/James Wade, 1979; Touchstone ed., 1989.

Hathaway, Robert M. *Ambiguous Partnership: Britain and America, 1944– 1947.* New York: Columbia University Press, 1981.

———. *Great Britain and the United States: Special Relations Since World War II.* Boston: Twayne, 1990.

Haxthausen, Charles W., and Heidrun Suhr, eds. *Berlin: Culture and Metropolis.* Minneapolis: University of Minnesota Press, 1990.

Hayter, William. *A Double Life.* London: Hamish Hamilton, 1974.

Hechler, Ken. *Working With Truman.* New York: Putnam, 1982.

Henderson, Nicholas. *Inside the Private Office.* Chicago: Academy Chicago, 1987.

Hersey, John. *Aspects of the Presidency.* New Haven and New York: Ticknor and Fields, 1980.

Higgins, Marguerite. *News Is a Singular Thing.* Garden City, N.Y.: Doubleday, 1955.

Hilldring, John H. "What Is Our Purpose in Germany?" *Annals of the American Academy of Political and Social Science* 255 (January 1948).

Hirsch, Felix. "Lessons of the Berlin Crisis." *Forum,* October 1948.

Hirschfeld, Hans E., and Hans J. Reichhardt. *Ernst Reuter aus Reden und Schriften.* Berlin: Colloquium Verlag, n.d. [1963?].

Hixson, Walter L. *George F. Kennan: Cold War Iconoclast.* New York: Columbia University Press, 1989.

Holloway, David. *Stalin and the Bomb.* New Haven: Yale University Press, 1994.

Holmsten, Georg. *Potsdam.* Berlin: Haude & Spenersche Verlagsbuchhandlung, 1971.

Horne, Alistair. *Harold Macmillan.* Vol. 1, *1894–1956.* New York: Viking, 1989.

Howard, Michael. "Governor-General of Germany." Review of *The Papers of General Lucius D. Clay,* Jean Edward Smith, ed. *Times Literary Supplement,* August 29, 1975.

———. "Checks and Mates." Review of *The Balance of Power,* by Michael Sheehan. *Times Literary Supplement,* August 16, 1996.

Howley, Frank. *Berlin Command.* New York: Putnam, 1950.

———. "I've Talked 1600 Hours with the Russians." *Reader's Digest,* May 1949.

Hubatsch, Walther, et al., eds. *The German Question.* Translated by Salvator Attanasio. New York: Herder Book Center, 1967.

Hull, Cordell. *The Memoirs of Cordell Hull.* Vol. 2. New York: Macmillan, 1948.

Humes, James C. *The Wit and Wisdom of Winston Churchill.* New York: Harper-Collins, 1994; HarperPerennial ed., 1995.

Hürlimann, Martin. *Die Residenzstadt Potsdam.* Berlin: Atlantis, 1933.

Innes, Hammond. "The Art of Airlifting." *Military Review,* July 1953; digested from *The Sphere,* Nov. 1, 1952.

Isaacson, Walter, and Evan Thomas. *The Wise Men.* New York: Simon and Schuster, 1986.

Jackson, Robert. *The Berlin Airlift.* Wellingborough, Northants: Patrick Stephens, 1988.

Jaworskyj, Michael, ed. *Soviet Political Thought.* Baltimore: Johns Hopkins University Press, 1967.

Jenkins, Roy. *Truman.* New York: Harper and Row, 1986.

Jensen, Kenneth M., ed. *Origins of the Cold War.* Rev. ed. Washington, D.C.: United States Institute of Peace Press, 1993.

Jessup, Philip C. "The Berlin Blockade and the Use of the United Nations." *Foreign Affairs* 50, No. 1 (October 1971).

———. "Park Avenue Diplomacy—Ending the Berlin Blockade." *Political Science Quarterly* 87, no. 3 (September 1972).

Johnsen, Julia E., comp. *The Dilemma of Postwar Germany.* New York: H. W. Wilson Co., 1948.

Jonas, Klaus W. *The Life of Crown Prince William.* Translated by Charles W. Bangert. London: Routledge and Kegan Paul, 1961.

Jonas, Manfred. *The United States and Germany.* Ithaca, N.Y.: Cornell University Press, 1984.

Jones, Joseph M. *The Fifteen Weeks.* New York: Harcourt, Brace & World, 1955.

Kahn, E. J., Jr. "Die Luftbrücke." *New Yorker,* May 14, 1949.

———. "Soldier in Mufti." *New Yorker,* January 13, 1951.

Kalijarvi, Thorsten V. "The Persistence of Power Politics." *Annals of the American Academy of Political and Social Science* 257 (May 1948).

Keesing's Research Report. *Germany and Eastern Europe Since 1945.* New York: Scribner, 1973.

Keiderling, Gerhard. *Die Berliner Krise 1948/49.* Berlin: Akademie Verlag, 1982.

Kennan, George F. "The Sources of Soviet Conduct." *Foreign Affairs* (July 1947).

———. *American Diplomacy, 1900–1950.* Chicago: University of Chicago Press, 1951.

———. *Realities of American Foreign Policy.* Princeton, N.J.: Princeton University Press, 1954.

———. *Russia and the West Under Lenin and Stalin.* Boston: Atlantic–Little Brown, 1961.

———. *Memoirs 1925–1950.* Boston, Little, Brown, 1967.

Kessler, Harry. *In the Twenties: The Diaries of Harry Kessler.* Translated by Charles Kessler. New York: Holt, Rinehart and Winston, 1971.

Klurfeld, Herman. *The World of Drew Pearson.* Englewood Cliffs, N.J.: Prentice-Hall, 1968.

Kohn, Hans. *The Mind of Germany.* New York: Charles Scribner's Sons, 1960; Harper Torchbooks ed., 1965.

Krieger, Wolfgang. "Was General Clay a Revisionist? Strategic Aspects of the United States Occupation of Germany." *Journal of Contemporary History* 18, no. 2 (1983).

———. "Making Germany Safe for Europe: General Lucius D. Clay and American Policy on Germany, 1945–1949." *Valley Forge Journal* 3, no. 3 (1987).

Krock, Arthur. *Memoirs: Sixty Years on the Firing Line.* New York: Funk and Wagnalls, 1968.

Kunetka, James W. *City of Fire.* Englewood Cliffs, N.J.: Prentice-Hall, 1978.

LaFeber, Walter. *America, Russia, and the Cold War, 1945–1975.* 3rd ed. New York: John Wiley, 1976.

Laloy, Jean. *Yalta.* Translated by William R. Tyler. New York: Harper and Row, 1988.

Landy, Pierre. *Berlin et son statut.* Paris: Presses universitaires de France, 1983.

Laqueur, Walter. *Europe Since Hitler.* New York: Holt, Rinehart and Winston, 1970: Pelican Books ed., 1972.

Larson, Deborah W. *Origins of Containment: A Psychological Explanation.* Princeton, N.J.: Princeton University Press, 1985.

Launius, Roger D. "The Berlin Airlift: Constructive Air Power." *Air Power History* 36, no. 1 (1989).

Launius, Roger D., and Coy F. Cross II. *MAC and the Legacy of the Berlin Airlift.* Scott Air Force Base, Ill.: Military Airlift Command, 1989.

Leahy, William D. *I Was There.* New York: Whittlesey House, 1950.

Leffler, Melvyn P. *A Preponderance of Power.* Stanford, Calif.: Stanford University Press, 1992.

Leffler, Melvin P., and David S. Painter. *Origins of the Cold War.* London and New York: Routledge, 1994.

LeMay, Curtis E., with MacKinlay Kantor. *Mission with LeMay: My Story.* Garden City, N.Y.: Doubleday, 1965.

Leonhard, Wolfgang. *Child of the Revolution.* Translated by C. M. Woodhouse. London: Ink Links Ltd., 1979; original ed., 1957.

Lewin, Moshe. *Russia/USSR/Russia.* New York: The New Press, 1995.

Lundestad, Geir. *East, West, North, South: Major Developments in International Politics, 1945–1990.* Translated by Gail Adams Kvam. Rev. ed. Oslo: Norwegian University Press, 1991.

McClain, Linda. "The Role of Admiral W. D. Leahy in U.S. Foreign Policy." Ph.D. diss., University of Virginia, 1984.

McCoy, Donald R. *The Presidency of Harry S. Truman.* American Presidency Series. Lawrence: University Press of Kansas, 1984.

McCullough, David. *Truman.* New York: Simon and Schuster, 1992.

McFarland, Stephen C. "The Air Force in the Cold War." *Airpower Journal.* Fall 1996.

McInnis, Edgar, Richard Hiscocks, and Robert Spencer. *The Shaping of Postwar Germany.* London: J. M. Dent, 1960.

McLellan, David S., and David C. Acheson, eds. *Among Friends: Personal Letters of Dean Acheson.* New York: Dodd, Mead, 1980.

Macmillan, Harold. *Tides of Fortune, 1945–1955.* New York: Harper and Row, 1969.

Maddox, Robert James. *From War to Cold War.* Boulder, Colo.: Westview Press, 1988.

Maginnis, John J. *Military Government Journal.* Amherst: University of Massachusetts Press, 1971.

Maier, Charles S., ed. *The Cold War in Europe.* New York: Markus Wiener, 1991.

Maihafer, Harry J. *Brave Decisions.* Washington, D.C.: Brassey's Inc., 1995.

Malia, Martin. *The Soviet Tragedy: A History of Socialism in Russia, 1917–1991.* New York: The Free Press, 1994.

Masur, Gerhard. *Imperial Berlin.* New York: Basic Books, 1976.

Mason, John Brown. "Lessons of Wartime Military Government Training." *Annals of the American Academy of Political and Social Science* 267 (January 1950).

Massie, Robert K. *Nicholas and Alexandra.* New York: Atheneum, 1967; Dell ed., 1969.

Mastny, Vojtech. *Russia's Road to the Cold War.* New York: Columbia University Press, 1979.

———. *The Cold War and Soviet Insecurity: The Stalin Years.* New York: Oxford University Press, 1996.

Mayers, David. *George Kennan and the Dilemmas of U.S. Foreign Policy.* New York: Oxford University Press, 1988.

———. *The Ambassadors and America's Soviet Policy.* New York: Oxford University Press, 1995.

Merry, Robert W. *Taking on the World.* New York: Viking, 1996.

Messer, Robert L. *The End of an Alliance.* Chapel Hill: University of North Carolina Press, 1982.

Millis, Walter, ed. *The Forrestal Diaries.* New York: Viking Press, 1951.

Misse, Fred B. "Truman, Berlin and the 1948 Election." *Missouri Historical Review* 76, no. 2 (1982).

Mitchell, Broadus. "How to Save the 'Third World.' " Review of *The Dollar Crisis,* by Thomas Balogh. *New York Times Book Review,* April 2, 1950.

Moll, Kenneth L. "The Berlin Airlift—How Airpower Came of Age in the Cold War." *Air Force and Space Digest,* July 1968.

Montgomery, Field Marshal the Viscount of Alamein. *The Path to Leadership.* New York: Putnam, 1961.

Moran, Lord [Charles Wilson]. *Churchill: The Struggle for Survival, 1940–1965.* Boston: Houghton Mifflin, 1966.

Morgenthau, Hans J. *Politics Among Nations.* 5th ed. New York: Knopf, 1973.

Morgenthau, Hans J., and Kenneth W. Thompson, eds. *Principles and Problems of International Politics.* New York: Knopf, 1950.

Morris, Eric. *Blockade: Berlin and the Cold War.* New York: Stein and Day, 1973.

Mosely, Philip. "The U.S. Occupation of Germany." *Foreign Affairs* 28, no. 4 (July 1950).

Moskin, J. Robert. *Mr. Truman's War.* New York: Random House, 1996.

Mount, Ferdinand, ed. *Communism.* Chicago: University of Chicago Press, 1993.

Mueller, John. "Quiet Cataclysm: Some Afterthoughts About World War III." *Diplomatic History* 16, no. 1 (1992).

Murphy, Charles J. V. "The Berlin Airlift." *Fortune,* November 1948.

Murphy, David E., Sergei A. Kondrashev, and George Bailey. *Battleground Berlin: CIA vs. KGB in the Cold War.* New Haven, Conn.: Yale University Press, 1997.

Murphy, Robert. *Diplomat Among Warriors.* Garden City, N.Y.: Doubleday, 1964.

Naimark, Norman M. " 'To Know Everything and to Report Everything Worth Knowing': Building the East German Police State, 1945–1949." Working Paper No. 10, Cold War International History Project, Woodrow Wilson International Center for Scholars, August 1994.

———. *The Russians in Germany.* Cambridge, Mass.: Harvard University Press, 1995.

Nelson, Daniel J. *Wartime Origins of the Berlin Dilemma.* University: University of Alabama Press, 1978.

Neumann, Franz L. "Soviet Policy in Germany." *Annals of the American Academy of Political and Social Science* 263 (May 1949).

New Yorker Book of War Pieces. New York: Shocken Books, [n.d.]; original ed.: New York: Reynal and Hitchcock, 1947.

Nicholas, H. G. *The United States and Britain.* Chicago: University of Chicago Press, 1975.

Nicholls, A. J. "The Parties That Were Kept Out." Review of *Politics After Hitler,* by Daniel E. Rogers. *Times Literary Supplement,* August 3, 1996.

Ninkovich, Frank. *Germany and the United States.* New York: Twayne, 1995.

O'Donnell, J. P. "The Mayor Russia Hates." *Saturday Evening Post,* February 5, 1949.

Park, Bert E. *Ailing, Aging, Addicted: Studies of Compromised Leadership.* Lexington: University Press of Kentucky, 1993.

Parrish, Scott D., and Mikhail M. Narinsky. "New Evidence on the Soviet Rejection of the Marshall Plan: Two Reports." Working Paper No. 9, Cold War International History Project, Woodrow Wilson International Center for Scholars, March 1994.

Parrish, Thomas. *Roosevelt and Marshall: Partners in Politics and War.* New York: William Morrow, 1989.

———. *The Cold War Encyclopedia.* New York: Henry Holt, 1996.

———, ed. *The Simon and Schuster Encyclopedia of World War II.* New York: Simon and Schuster, 1978.

Pearcy, Arthur, Jr. "The Berlin Airlift." *American Aviation Historical Society Journal* 34, no. 3 (Fall 1989).

Pechatnov, Vladimir O. "The Big Three After World War II." Working Paper No. 13, Cold War International History Project, Woodrow Wilson International Center for Scholars, July 1995.

Peel, Roy V. "The 1948 Preconvention Campaign." *Annals of the American Academy of Political and Social Science* 259 (September 1948).

Peterson, Edward N. *The American Occupation of Germany: Retreat to Victory.* Detroit: Wayne State University Press, 1977.

Pirus, Douglas I. "The Berlin Airlift." *American Aviation Historical Society Journal* 23, no. 3 (1978).

Pogue, Forrest C. *The Supreme Command.* Washington, D.C.: Office of the Chief of Military History, 1954.

———. *George C. Marshall.* Vol. 4, *Statesman.* New York: Viking, 1987.

Polenberg, Richard. *War and Society: The United States 1941–1945.* New York: Lippincott, 1972.

Pommern, Reiner, ed. *The American Impact on Postwar Germany.* Providence and Oxford: Berghahn Books, 1995.

Potter, F. H. "The Berlin Airlift As I Remember It." *Friends Journal* 20, no. 2 (Summer 1997).

Raack, R. C. *Stalin's Drive to the West.* Stanford, Calif.: Stanford University Press, 1995.

Reichelt, Paul. *Deutsche Chronik, 1945 bis 1970.* Freudenstadt: Eurobuch-Verlag, 1970.

Renwick, Sir Robin. *Fighting With Allies.* New York: Times Books, 1996.

Reporting World War II. Part 2. New York: Library of America, 1995.

Reston, James. *Deadline: A Memoir.* New York: Random House, 1991.

Reuss, Martin. "In Memoriam: The First Berlin Crisis." *Military Review* 59, no. 5 (1979).

Reynolds, David, ed. *The Origins of the Cold War in Europe.* New Haven: Yale University Press, 1994.

Richler, Mordecai, ed. *Writers on World War II.* New York: Knopf, 1991.

Riha, Thomas, ed. *Readings in Russian Civilization.* Vol. 3, *Soviet Russia, 1917–1963.* Chicago: University of Chicago Press, 1964.

Robinson, Donald. "They Fight the Cold War Under Cover." *Saturday Evening Post,* November 20, 1948.

Robson, Charles B., trans. and ed. *Berlin—Pivot of German Destiny.* Chapel Hill: University of North Carolina Press, 1960.

Rossiter, Clinton. *The American Presidency.* 2nd ed. New York: Harcourt Brace Jovanovich, 1960; New American Library ed., 1962.

Rostow, W. W. *The Division of Europe After World War II: 1946.* Austin: University of Texas Press, 1981.

Rubinstein, Alvin Z., ed. *The Foreign Policy of the Soviet Union.* 3rd ed. New York: Random House, 1972.

Ruddy, T. Michael. "A Cautious Approach to the Militarization of Containment." *Historian,* May 1986.

———. *The Cautious Diplomat: Charles E. Bohlen and the Soviet Union, 1929–1969.* Kent, Ohio: Kent State University Press, 1986.

Sakwa, Richard. *Gorbachev and His Reforms 1985–1990.* New York: Prentice-Hall, 1991.

Schapiro, Leonard. *Russian Studies.* Edited by Ellen Dahrendorf. New York: Viking Penguin, 1987. Penguin Books ed., 1988.

Schlauch, Wolfgang. "Zur amerikanischen Deutschland- und Besatzungspolitik." *Archiv für Sozialgeschichte* 20, 566–71.

Schlesinger, Arthur, Jr. "Some Lessons from the Cold War." *Diplomatic History* 16, no. 1 (1992).

Schmitt, Hans A., ed. *U.S. Occupation in Europe After World War II.* Lawrence: Regents Press of Kansas, 1978.

Schuman, Frederick L. *The Cold War: Retrospect and Prospect.* 2nd ed. Baton Rouge: Louisiana State University Press, 1967.

Schwartz, Thomas Alan. "Lucius D. Clay: Reluctant Cold Warrior?" Review of *Lucius D. Clay: An American Life,* by Jean Edward Smith. *Diplomatic History* 16, no. 4 (1992).

Shecter, Jerrold L., trans. and ed., with Vyacheslav V. Luchkov. *Khrushchev Remembers: The Glasnost Tapes.* Boston: Little, Brown, 1990.

Sheehan, Michael. *The Balance of Power: History and Theory.* London and New York: Routledge, 1996.

Sherwood, Robert E. *Roosevelt and Hopkins.* New York: Harper, 1948.

Shirer, William. *The Rise and Fall of the Third Reich.* New York: Simon and Schuster, 1960.

Shlaim, Avi. *The United States and the Berlin Blockade, 1948–1949: A Study in Crisis Decision-Making.* Berkeley: University of California Press, 1983.

———. "Britain, the Berlin Blockade and the Cold War." *International Affairs,* Winter 1984.

Sissons, Michael, and Philip French, eds. *Age of Austerity 1945–51.* London: Hodder and Stoughton, 1963; Penguin Books ed., 1964.

Slusser, Robert M., and Jan F. Triska. *A Calendar of Soviet Treaties, 1917–1957.* Stanford, Calif.: Stanford University Press, 1959.

Small, Melvin. *Democracy and Diplomacy.* Baltimore: Johns Hopkins University Press, 1996.

Smith, Gaddis. *Dean Acheson.* New York: Cooper Square, 1972.

Smith, Howard K. *Events Leading Up to My Death.* New York: St. Martin's Press, 1996.

Smith, Jean Edward. *The Defense of Berlin.* Baltimore: Johns Hopkins University Press, 1963.

———. *Lucius D. Clay: An American Life.* New York: Henry Holt, 1990.

———. ed. *The Papers of General Lucius D. Clay.* 2 vols. Bloomington: Indiana University Press, 1974.

Smith, Richard Norton. *Thomas E. Dewey and His Times.* New York: Simon and Schuster, 1982.

Smith, Walter Bedell. *My Three Years in Moscow.* Philadelphia: Lippincott, 1949.

Snell, John L., ed. *The Meaning of Yalta.* Baton Rouge: Louisiana State University Press, 1956; paperback ed., 1966.

Sokolovskii (Sokolovsky), V. D., ed. *Soviet Military Strategy.* Translated, etc., by Herbert S. Dinerstein, Leon Gouré, and Thomas W. Wolfe. A Rand Corporation Research Study. Englewood Cliffs, N.J.: Prentice-Hall, 1963.

Spanier, John. *American Foreign Policy Since World War II.* New York: Praeger Publishers. Various editions, 1960–1993.

Special Study of Operation "Vittles." *Aviation Operations* 11, no. 5 (April 1949).

Speer, Albert. *Inside the Third Reich.* New York: Macmillan, 1970.

Spencer, Otha C. *Flying the Hump.* College Station: Texas A&M University Press, 1992.

Stalin, J. V. *Stalin's Letters to Molotov.* Edited by Lars T. Lih and Oleg Naumov. New Haven: Yale University Press, 1995.

Strang, Lord. *The Foreign Office.* London: George Allen & Unwin, 1955.

———. *Britain in World Affairs.* New York: Praeger, 1961.

Swinton, Lord. *Sixty Years of Power.* New York: James H. Heinemann, 1966.

Taylor, A. J. P. *The Course of German History.* New York: Capricorn Books, 1962.

Taylor, Graham D. "The Rise and Fall of Antitrust in Occupied Germany, 1945–48." *Prologue,* Spring 1979.

Tedder, Lord Arthur. *With Prejudice.* Boston, Little, Brown, 1966.

Terry, Sarah Meiklejohn, ed. *Soviet Policy in Eastern Europe.* New Haven: Yale University Press, 1984.

Thompson, Kenneth W. *Cold War Theories: World Polarization, 1943–1953.* Baton Rouge: Louisiana State University Press, 1981.

Trevor-Roper, H. R. "Is Russia Falling Between Two Plans?" *New York Times Magazine,* July 18, 1948.

Truman, Harry S. *Memoirs.* Vol. 1, *Year of Decisions.* Garden City, N.Y.: Doubleday, 1955; Signet ed., 1965.

———. *Memoirs.* Vol. 2, *Years of Trial and Hope.* Garden City, N.Y.: Doubleday, 1956.

Truman, Margaret. *Harry S. Truman.* New York: Morrow, 1972.

Tuchman, Barbara W. *The Proud Tower.* New York: Macmillan, 1966; Bantam ed., 1967.

Tunner, William H. *Over the Hump.* Washington, D.C.: Office of Air Force History, 1985; original ed.: New York: Duell, Sloan, and Pearce, 1964.

———. "A Case of Identity: VIPs and the Berlin Airlift." *Aerospace Historian* 16, no. 2 (1969).

Turner, Henry Ashby, Jr. *Germany From Partition to Reunification.* New Haven: Yale University Press, 1992.

Tusa, Ann. *The Last Division.* Reading, Mass.: Addison-Wesley, 1997.

Tusa, Ann, and John Tusa. *The Berlin Airlift.* New York: Atheneum, 1988.

Vandenberg, Arthur H., Jr., ed. *The Private Papers of Senator Vandenberg.* Boston: Houghton Mifflin, 1952.

Vizetelly, Henry. *Berlin Under the New Empire.* 2 vols. New York: Greenwood Press, 1968; reprint of 1879 edition.

Volkogonov, Dmitri. *Stalin: Triumph and Tragedy.* New York: Grove Weidenfeld, 1991.

Walker, Martin. *The Cold War.* New York: Henry Holt, 1993.

Walker, Richard L., and George Curry. *Edward R. Stettinius, Jr.—James F. Byrnes.* New York: Cooper Square, 1965.

Ward, Patricia Dawson. *The Threat of Peace: James F. Byrnes and the Council of Foreign Ministers, 1945–46.* Kent, Ohio: Kent State University Press, 1979.

Watson, George M., Jr. *The Office of the Secretary of the Air Force, 1947–1965.* Washington, D.C., Center for Air Force History, 1993.

Weigley, Russell F. *History of the United States Army.* Enlarged ed. Bloomington: Indiana University Press, 1984.

Wile, Frederic W. *Men Around the Kaiser.* Indianapolis: Bobbs-Merrill, 1914.

Wilentz, Sean. "Speedy Fred's Revolution." *New York Review of Books,* November 20, 1997.

Willets, Gilson. *Rulers of the World at Home.* New York: Christian Herald–Louis Klopsch, 1899.

Williamson, David. *A Most Diplomatic General: The Life of General Lord Robertson of Oakridge.* London: Brassey's, 1996.

Wilson, Lawrence. *The Imperial Kaiser.* New York: Dorset Press, 1991.

Windsor, Philip. *City on Leave: A History of Berlin, 1945–1962.* London: Chatto and Windus, 1963.

Wood, Larry. "A Visit to Truman's Birthplace." *Ozarks Mountaineer,* October/November 1994.

Woods, Randall B., and Howard Jones. *Dawning of the Cold War.* Athens: University of Georgia Press, 1991.

Wragg, David. *Airlift: A History of Military Air Transport.* Novato, Calif.: Presidio Press, 1987.

Wylie, Philip. *Generation of Vipers.* New York: Rinehart, 1942.

Zayas, Alfred M. de. *Nemesis at Potsdam.* Rev. ed. London: Routledge and Kegan Paul, 1979.

Zhukov, G. K. *The Memoirs of Marshal Zhukov.* New York: Delacorte Press, 1971.

Ziemke, Earl. *The U.S. Army in the Occupation of Germany, 1944–1946.* Washington, D.C.: Center of Military History, 1975.

Zink, Harold. *American Military Government in Germany.* New York: Macmillan, 1947.

———. *The United States in Germany, 1944–1955.* New York: Van Nostrand, 1957.

Zubok, Vladislav, and Constantine Pleshakov. *Inside the Kremlin's Cold War.* Cambridge, Mass.: Harvard University Press, 1996.

NOTES

Introduction: War by Other Means

2 an antagonist "conventionally": Balfour, 165.
2–3 American reporter: The correspondent was Karl Detzer.
2 Even dehydrated beets: Hans-Karl Behrend interview.
3 "The Russians no longer scoff": Detzer.

Chapter 1   The Prize

7 Eisenhower's concern is discussed in Ambrose, *Rise to Globalism,* 408.
8 "who fear the Russians": Virginia Irwin in *Reporting World War II,* 711.
8 "Each stone": *Newsweek,* May 7, 1945.
8 "ruins, craters": *Time/Capsule,* 1945, 98.
8 "a weird impression": Tedder, 684.
8–9 "There are tens of thousands": Martha Gellhorn in *Reporting World War II,* 677.
9 "In Germany": Martha Gellhorn in Richler, *Writers on World War II,* 647.
9 Bodies described in Bradley, *A Soldier's Story,* 526.
9 Murrow describes his visit in *Reporting World War II,* 681–84.
10 "behind the barbed wire": Gellhorn in *Reporting World War II,* 724.
10 Zhukov call from Stalin: Zhukov, 627–28.
10 Tedder's aide: Interview with Wing Commander Leslie Scarman by Forrest Pogue for *Supreme Command,* February 25, 1947 (MHI).
11 "deeply suspicious nature" and following quotation: Tedder, 685.
11 "We have three flags": Interview with Tedder by Forrest Pogue for *Supreme Command,* February 13, 1947 (MHI).
11 "the Russians nearly": Tedder interview.
11–12 "Much was said": Zhukov, 631.
12 Tedder's toast and Vyshinsky's speech: Tedder interview.
12 "the Soviet generals": Zhukov, 631.
13 "would seem a prelude": Masur, 15.
13 "had not grown up": Haus in Robson, 7. This essay discusses the background of Berlin as the capital of Germany.
14 Goethe on the Berliner: Masur, 22.
14 "mere village": Haus in Robson, 9.
14 Population figure from Haus in Robson, 14.
14 Mann quotation, *Yale Review,* December 1945, 238.
14–15 Quotations about the parade from Wilson, 17.
15 The smells of sewers are described in Vizetelly, vol. 1, 14–15.
15 Building boom described in Vizetelly, vol. 1, 19.

15 "Immense suction pump": Vizetelly, vol. 1, 29.

15 Haus makes this and the following observations in Robson, 24.

16 Baedeker quote: *Northern Germany* (1897).

16 "All I can do": Quoted in Tuchman, 354.

16 "Wondrous and eloquent" and "the world at large": Wile, preface.

16 "The streets of Berlin": H.R.H. Viktoria Luise, 75.

17 Mommsen quoted in Tuchman, 360.

17 Berliners in World War I: Haus in Robson, 26.

17 "especially in aesthetics": Haus in Robson, 36.

17–18 "skeptical, rather than enthusiastic": Haus in Robson, 35.

18 "the dictatorship": quoted, Kessler, 455.

18 "fundamentally averse": Haus in Robson, 43.

18 "behaved like a schoolboy": H.R.H. Viktoria Luise, 185.

19 "magnificent sport-field": Shirer, 65.

19 "steel skeleton": Speer, 80.

19 "nothing but": quoted, Speer, 75.

19 "a huge meeting hall": Speer, 74.

19 the meteorological problem: analyzed in O'Donnell, 389.

19 Göring quote: Shirer, 517 (note).

19–20 RAF raid: Thomas Parrish, *Encyclopedia of World War II,* 58.

20 "future enemy moral collapse": Hastings, 47.

20 "there is no power": quoted, Hastings, 43.

20 "Hitler and his Nazi gang": quoted, Humes, 128.

20 "we can wreck Berlin": quoted, Hastings, 257.

21 "I thought my last hour": H.R.H. Viktoria Luise, 219.

Chapter 2   *"Frau . . . komm!"*

23 "Declarations—that's like algebra": quoted, Laufer (Conference Papers), 1.

23 "under any circumstances": From Harry Hopkins's notes of the meeting; Sherwood, 711.

23 "present close collaboration": Heidelmeyer and Hindrichs, *Documents on Berlin,* 1.

24 "German central administration": Heidelmeyer and Hindrichs, *Documents on Berlin,* 4.

25–26 For discussion of FDR, Eisenhower, and the zones of occupation, see Pogue, *Supreme Command,* 348–51.

26 "supreme authority": Heidelmeyer and Hindrichs, *Documents on Berlin,* 7.

26 "made it plain": Truman, *Year of Decisions,* 335.

27 Ike with Harry Hopkins: Sherwood, 914.

27 "as small inside": Stephen Ambrose, National Press Club, April 1997.

27 "the zenith": David Eisenhower, 819.

27 "let down after the excitement": John S. D. Eisenhower, quoted, Ambrose, *Eisenhower,* 415.

28 Marshall took explicit note: Jean Smith, *Lucius D. Clay,* 267.

28 "the necessity of protecting these roads": Notes of June 29 meeting by Major General Floyd C. Parks in Jean Smith, *Papers of General Lucius D. Clay,* 32.

28 "might be interpreted" and following quotations: Clay, 26.

29 "If they see anybody" and all other material relating to Uwe von Tschammer from interview.

29 "Three of my closer friends" and all the following Ingeborg Dedering quotations from *Courier-Journal* (Louisville), April 17, 1948.

30 "We were half-starved" and all other material relating to Karin Hueckstaedt from interview.

30 "The Russians were always very keen" and all other material relating to Alice Sawadda from interview.

31 "One went to the right" and all other material relating to Charlotte Beelitz from interview.

31 "It was fortunate" and all other material relating to Hans-Karl Behrend from interview.

33 On the idea of Soviet revenge for German misdeeds, see Naimark, *Russians in Germany,* 71–72.

33 Czarina Alexandra: Massie, 329.

33 "Woe to the land": Naimark, *Russians in Germany,* 72.

33 Women who were "willing": Zink, *United States in Germany,* 137.

34 "the reports of women" and following quotations: Naimark, *Russians in Germany,* 71–73.

34 "The taking of Berlin": Naimark, *Russians in Germany,* 79–80.

34 "The resulting combination": Naimark, *Russians in Germany,* 115.

35 Scene at the Ehenmal: Joel Sayre in *New Yorker,* July 28, 1945.

35 "Remain solitary on a Berlin street": Joel Sayre, *New Yorker,* July 28, 1945.

35 "Since it was": Maginnis (Manuscripts), 313 (MHI).

Chapter 3   To the Fantasy House

36 Descriptions of the crown prince and crown princess: Davis, 179–82. Dr. Davis, an American, had quite a cordial relationship with the Kaiser. Two decades after the Potsdam Conference, the German-born actor Werner Klemperer, preparing for his role as Colonel Klink in the television comedy series *Hogan's Heroes,* would model his character on Crown Prince Wilhelm, "a notorious, pompous, not terribly bright, stuffy, womanizing pain in the ass." Robert Graysmith, *The Murder of Bob Crane* (Berkley ed., 1994), 128.

36 a handshake: Klaus Jonas, 157.

36 called it Scottish: Klaus Jonas, 159.

37 "mock-Elizabethan windows": Charles L. Mee, *New York Times,* August 5, 1973.

37 "saved the Reich": *New York Times,* March 10, 1933.

37 "a demagogue": H.R.H. Viktoria Luise, 178.

37 "prominent government officials": Zhukov, 667

38 "grave discussions": Churchill, *Triumph and Tragedy,* 571.

38 Churchill telegram: May 12, 1945. Churchill, *Triumph and Tragedy,* 572–73.

39 "the vast manifestations": Churchill, *Triumph and Tragedy,* 570.

39 "an *iron curtain*": Churchill, *Triumph and Tragedy,* 573.

39 Departure for Europe: Log of President's Trip to the Berlin Conference, Rigdon Papers (WRP).

39–40 Diary excerpts, Ferrell, *Off the Record,* 49.

40 "If you fellows": Jenkins, 67.

40 Legs trembling: Robert Bogue interview.
40 "cocky little guy": Peggy Fuller interview.
40 "spending hours": McClain, 268.
41 "You tell him": Margaret Truman, 177.
41 "Under such circumstances": Bohlen, 256.
41 Truman and the house: Ferrell, *Off the Record,* 50.
41 "Ten weeks": Ferrell, *Off the Record,* 51, n. 1.
42 Churchill reaction to Truman: Churchill, *Triumph and Tragedy,* 630.
42 Hayter reaction: Hayter, 29.
42 Truman quote on Churchill: Ferrell, *Off the Record,* 51.
42–43 "the most vigilant bodyguard": quoted, Hersey, 39.
43 "I am only sorry": *New York Times,* July 17, 1945.
43 "the deluded Hitlerian populace": Ferrell, *Off the Record,* 52.
43 Churchill comments to Mary: quoted, Gilbert, 61.
43 "This is what would have happened" and following quotation: *New York Times,* July 17, 1945.
44–45 Donnelly descriptions from Donnelly MS (MHI).
45 Stalin's lateness: Volkogonov, 499.
45 Beria's arrangements for Stalin: Volkogonov, 498–99.
45 "Nothing much": Gromyko, 97.
46 "You could if you wanted to": Truman, *Year of Decisions,* 378.
46 "I told Stalin" and following quotation: Ferrell, *Off the Record,* 53.

Chapter 4 Veils of Understanding

47 "the Emperor of Austria": Hayter, 28.
48 "understood each other": Gromyko, 97.
48 Ideological discussion and quotation from Vishniak: Thomas Parrish, *Roosevelt and Marshall,* 473–74.
49 "greatest expression": quoted from Vyshinsky, *The Law of the Soviet State,* in Daniels, 219.
49 Conrad quotation from Hayter, 129–30.
50 Trainin discussion from Jaworskyj, 342.
50 "on a broader democratic basis": Yalta declaration, quoted, Thomas Parrish, *Encyclopedia of World War II,* 695.
50 "policy should be based" and following quotations: Hayter, 28.
51 "the law of war": Central Archives, Soviet Ministry of Defense; quoted, Volkogonov, 49.
51 "This war": Djilas, 114.
51 "the time to grab": Thomas Parrish, *Cold War Encyclopedia,* 295.
51 "a strong, independent": Churchill, *Triumph and Tragedy,* 636.
51 "an extremely important": Zhukov, 638.
52 "It must look good": quoted, Laloy, 96.
52 "even in Berlin" and following quotation: from Raymond Daniell, *New York Times,* July 8, 1945.
53 Admiral Leahy and his JCS colleagues: McClain, 212.
53–54 Potsdam agenda: U.S. Department of State, *Conference of Berlin,* vol. 1, 57.
54 Discussion of date for recognition of Polish regime: Maddox, 71.

54 "to give Russia her share": State Department, *Conference of Berlin,* vol. 1, 59.

55 "what has become of her": State Department, *Conference of Berlin,* vol. 1, 96.

55 Reparations committee discussion: State Department, *Conference of Berlin,* vol. 1, 183–84.

55 Maisky to Stalin and Molotov: Pechatnov, 19.

56 Byrnes on Maisky: Byrnes, *All in One Lifetime,* 302.

56 "horse-trade": McClain, 307.

56 Churchill declaring and Stalin's reply: State Department, *Conference of Berlin,* vol. 1, 207.

57 "bringing their mouths": quoted, Maddox, 76.

57 "no single German": State Department, *Conference of Berlin,* vol. 1, 211.

Chapter 5 "Unmitigated Skepticism and Despair"

58–59 Material from Donnelly (Manuscripts) (MHI).

60 "Diagnosis not yet complete": Kunetka, 172.

60 Stimson and Churchill: Churchill, *Triumph and Tragedy,* 637.

61 Truman would inform Stalin: Ferrell, *Off the Record,* 54.

61 "all this nightmare picture": Churchill, *Triumph and Tragedy,* 638.

61 "Believe Japs will fold up": Ferrell, *Off the Record,* 54.

61 Anticipated date: McClain, 310.

61 "How did it go?" Churchill, *Triumph and Tragedy,* 670.

62 Gromyko's thoughts: Gromyko, 109.

62 Kurchatov and the bomb: Chuev, 56.

62 "the Americans have been doing all this work": Gromyko, 109.

62 Molotov and the bomb: Chuev, 56.

62–63 Djilas on Stalin: Djilas, 96–97.

63 "Stalin often said": Chuev, 53.

63 "they could not have played": Chuev, 56.

63 Truman on Stalin: Ferrell, *Off the Record,* 55.

64 "straightforward, hard-hitting trader": quoted, McClain, 295.

64 "a Wesleyan minister": Moran, 300.

64 Truman's concerns about Stalin: Ferrell, *Off the Record,* 58.

64 "You build a post office": quoted, Maddox, 65.

64 Truman comments on Stalin: Daniels, 278–79.

65 Molotov on Poland: Chuev, 54.

65 "Washington's attempts": Gromyko, 108.

65 "certainly displayed": Halifax to Churchill, *Triumph and Tragedy,* 481.

65 Truman's private account (unsent letter to Dean Acheson, March 15, 1957): Ferrell, *Off the Record,* 348–49.

66 George VI comment: Anthony Howard in Sissons and French, 16.

66 "about as much as it is possible" and "so aggressive": Byrnes, *Speaking Frankly,* 78.

67 Bevin "commanded the confidence": Macmillan, 55.

67 "It's not Devon": Charlton, 47.

67 "we may do better with Bevin": quoted, Deighton, 11.

67 "You don't keep a good dog": quoted, Thomas Parrish, *Cold War Encyclopedia,* 15.

67 "her terrible war losses": Gromyko, 88.

67 "quiet as a mouse": Gromyko, 114.

67 "a Churchill man": Chuev, 50.

67 "was like a Communist": David Watt in Sissons and French, 126.

68 "the final delimitation": Heidelmeyer and Hindrichs (Official Publications and Documents), *Documents on Berlin,* 16.

68–69 Kennan quotations: Kennan, *Memoirs,* 258–59.

69 "striped pants boys": quoted, McClain, 290.

69 "After the defeat of Hitler": Shecter, 144.

69 "Czar Alexander": Molotov, 73

69 "Stalin even started": Shecter, 144.

69 Kennan on concessions to Stalin: interview, *News Hour,* PBS, April 18, 1996.

Chapter 6 The Sinews and the Curtain

70 "the genial sunshine": quoted, Gilbert, 159.

70 Comments to Lord Moran: Moran, 328.

70–71 "Dear Winnie": Ferrell, *Harry S. Truman,* 234.

71 "ganging up": Byrnes, *Speaking Frankly,* 349.

71 "one hell of a people": *Life,* quoted, Polenberg, 40.

71 Ruark quotation: *Time,* March 4, 1946.

71–72 "Don't get up": *Newsweek,* March 18, 1946.

72 Truman on Churchill speech: Gilbert, 197.

72 "as familiar in Missouri": Anne O'Hare McCormick, *New York Times,* March 6, 1946.

72–73 Quotations from Churchill speech: *New York Times,* March 6, 1946.

74 Clay on his brothers: Jean Smith, *Lucius D. Clay,* 29.

74 "had to go to school": Jean Smith, *Lucius D. Clay,* 30.

74 "After I had been battling": Kahn, "Soldier in Mufti."

75 Clay quotations from Clay, 6–7.

76 "Long before the war": Blum, 518.

76 "an agreement glued together": Peterson, 42.

76 "before the main tasks of the occupation": Loth (Conference Papers).

77 "if we had then realized": Clay, 16.

77 Douglas quotation from Robert Murphy, 251.

77 "you had a tremendous amount": Jean Smith, *Lucius D. Clay,* 231.

77 Clay self-defense: Jean Smith, *Papers,* 8.

77–78 "just remember that": Jean Smith, *Lucius D. Clay,* 234.

78 "too vindictive": Jean Smith, *Lucius D. Clay,* 233.

78 Military Government Law No. 8: Ziemke, 34.

78 "there might as well have been laws": Howard K. Smith, 180.

78 "the days of waiting": Maginnis (Manuscripts), 555 (MHI).

78 "no non-GI vehicles": Howley (Manuscripts), 107–108 (MHI).

79 "to make matters worse" and following quotation: Maginnis (Manuscripts), 555–56 (MHI).

79 "HITLERS COME AND GO": Maginnis (Manuscripts), 552 (MHI).

79 Maginnis wondered: Maginnis, *Military Government Journal,* 259.

80 The scene in Berlin: Clay, 31–32.

80 "humanitarian touch": Clay, 16.

80 During this ten-day "dawn period": Howley personal diary, July 1945 (MHI).

80 "too much of our planning": Jean Smith, *Papers,* 6.

80–81 "if there ever had been": Clay interview, 1973 (MHI).

81 "Washington must revise" and following quotations: Jean Smith, *Papers,* 8.

81 "our directives can be flexible": Jean Smith, *Papers,* 12.

81 "bubble up" and "personally responsible": quoted, Peterson, 60–61.

81 "General Clay's exceedingly high abilities": quoted, Peterson, 97–98.

Chapter 7 General and Chargé

82 Origin of *Kommandatura:* Landy, 2.

82 The development of the situation in Berlin is well described by Davison; see, e.g., p. 30.

82 Control Council meeting place: Druène, 182–83.

83 Population figures: "The Government of Berlin under Inter-Allied Control," report by Dr. W. Friedmann, Econ. Div. CC (British) (MHI).

83 Clay confirmed as the high-ranking officer in communication from Kennan to the author, June 20, 1996.

83 "truly excellent relations": Druène, 185.

84 Clay and Sokolovsky: Peterson, 102 (notes).

84 Relationships of delegation members: Druène, 185.

84 Clay forbade Germans: Peterson, 102 (notes).

84 "We are going to": quoted, Jean Smith, *Lucius D. Clay,* 253.

84 Clay with interviewer: November 8, 1972. Clay papers (GCML).

84 "engineering habit": Zink, *American Military Government,* 27.

85 On the French view see Gimbel, especially note to p. 18.

86 Clay believed it "essential": Peterson, 67.

86 Control Council sessions: Druène, 185.

87 "gradual strangulation" of the opposition: Ben Fowkes, quoted in Pennachio (Conference Papers).

87 "I don't wonder": Howley to Maginnis, April 7, 1946; Howley Papers (MHI).

87–88 "there wasn't much to steal": Behrend interview.

88 "One thing I had been discovering": Maginnis (Manuscripts), 553A (MHI).

88 "We took reparations": Chuev, 60.

89 "dismantle any further plants": Jean Smith, *Papers,* 218.

89 "Economic integration": Jean Smith, *Lucius D. Clay,* 352.

89 Galbraith on Clay: *Fortune,* January 1947.

90–91 Kennan describes the writing of the Long Telegram in *Memoirs,* 292–94. The bulk of the message itself appears on pp. 547–59.

91 "there is a fundamental divergence": quoted, Deighton, 51–52.

91 "very lack of moderation": quoted, Jensen, 38–39.

92 Zhdanov: quoted, Thomas Parrish, *Cold War Encyclopedia,* 350.

92 "sometimes almost unbearable": quoted, Deighton, 42.

92 "hot" analysis: Margaret Truman, 347.

92–93 "the realities which it described": Kennan, *Memoirs,* 295.

93 Truman and Byrnes at Potsdam: McClain, 308.

93 Washington "was still rocking": Acheson, *Sketches,* 57.

94 "pulled back into his shell": *Time,* March 25, 1946.

94 "we propose to stand": quoted, *Time,* March 25, 1946.

94 "ruling circles of the United States": Novikov to Molotov, September 12, 1946; quoted, Jensen, 12.

94 Molotov on Litvinov: Chuev, 69.

94 Views of Litvinov, Maisky, and Gromyko: Pechatnov, 16–18.

95 "Poland—a big deal!": Pechatnov, 23.

95 "worst diplomatic storm": *Newsweek,* March 25, 1946.

95 "would cut the throat": *New York Times,* March 7, 1946.

95 "hard core of indisputable": quoted, *Time,* March 18, 1946.

96 "Winnie, Winnie": *Newsweek,* March 25, 1946.

96 Stalin on Churchill: in *Pravda,* March 14, 1946, quoted, Gilbert, 212.

96–97 Molotov comments: Chuev, 59.

97 "knowing how far": *New Yorker,* May 20, 1996.

Chapter 8 Power in the Balance

98 "avoiding the spotlight": Byrnes, *All in One Lifetime,* 368.

98 Quotations from Byrnes's speech: Byrnes, *Speaking Frankly,* 190.

99 an internal document written two months earlier: For background, see Clay, 73–78, and Jean Smith, *Lucius D. Clay,* 379–82.

99 "a poor counselor": quoted, Rubinstein, 198.

99 "the unofficial funeral": Barrington Moore, quoted, Rubinstein, 188.

99 "most effective speech": Byrnes, *All in One Lifetime,* 368.

99 "The people of the United States": Byrnes, *Speaking Frankly,* 193.

99–100 "Since the surrender of Germany": Acheson, *Present,* 212.

100 "perhaps the last means": FRUS, 1947, vol. 2, 849.

100 "Berlin is apt": FRUS, 1947, vol. 2, 851.

100 "U.S. and British monopolists": FRUS, 1947, vol. 2, 855.

100 "had not had the pleasure of meeting": FRUS, 1947, vol. 2, 855.

102 Meanings of "balance," etc.: The historian, cited by Sheehan (p. 15), was A. F. Pollard. See also Michael Howard, *Times Literary Supplement,* August 16, 1996.

102 "a fluid stream": quoted, Spanier (6th ed.), 37.

103 "It was our first experience" and "another revelation": Bohlen, 245–46.

103 "the pessimism" and following comment: *Newsweek,* October 1, 1945.

103 "sporadic acts": quoted, Spanier, 37.

103 "If you tell Congress": quoted, Millis, 444.

103 "Nations must rely" and following quotations: Morgenthau, 143–44.

104 Byrnes reporting to the president: Bohlen, 250.

104 "American generals": Ferrell, *Harry S. Truman,* 253.

105 S. L. A. Marshall reaction: conversation with the author.

105 "no military glamour": Acheson, *Sketches,* 123.

105 "because when he takes": quoted, Thomas Parrish, *Roosevelt and Marshall,* 137.

105 "a class of stoopnagels" and "where you desperately": Wylie, 235–36.

106 Hopkins observation from Sherwood, 774.

106 "we are at the point of decision": Pogue, *Statesman,* 164–65.

106 "this island would be": quoted, Thomas Parrish, *Cold War Encyclopedia,* 86.

106 "These congressmen had no conception": Acheson, *Present,* 219.

107 "with the support": Acheson, *Present,* 221.

107 Leahy observations from diary, March 7, 1947 (LC).

107 Leahy observations from diary, March 10 and March 11, 1947 (LC).

108 "with utmost vigor": *Acheson,* Present, 220.

109 "flamboyant anti-Communism": quoted, Ruddy, *Cautious Diplomat,* 72.

109 Quotations from Clay: Jean Smith, *Papers,* 308. See also Clay, 145–46.
110 "Clay is a fine fellow": Backer, *Winds of History,* 136.

Chapter 9 "Irrevocably Divided . . .
Two Hostile Camps"

112 "under the Russian skin": Bedell Smith, 15.
112 "break through the crust": Bedell Smith, 26.
112 "the first essential": Bedell Smith, 31.
112 "everything from fur coats": Bedell Smith, 34.
112 "The main issue": Bedell Smith, 211.
112 "had been speculating": Bedell Smith, 215–16.
113 "quiet and firm": Bullock, 375.
113 Smith's hair color: Bohlen, 262.
113 "I want you to do this": Pogue, *Statesman,* 172.
113 Marshall and Davis: Acheson, *Sketches,* 127.
113 Opening of the conference: Bedell Smith, 216.
113 "Where are we?": Bedell Smith, 217.
114 "We can discuss": Jean Smith, *Papers,* 327.
114 "the resources of the Ruhr": Clay interview (SGML).
114 Dulles was "very active": Bohlen interview (SGML).
114 Marshall "tempted to accept": Clay interview, Clay Papers (GCML).
114 Stalin's view: Loth (Conference Papers).
114–15 Bohlen's view: Bohlen interview (SGML).
115 "to get General Smith": Clay interview (MHI).
115 Quotations from Truman speech: Truman, *Years of Trial and Hope,* 106.
115–16 "willingness to cooperate": Bedell Smith, 220.
116 Interview with Stalin: Bedell Smith, 220–222.
116 Smith's summing-up: Bedell Smith, 229.
116 Bevin to Attlee: Bullock, 388.
116 "to ensure": Byrnes, *Speaking Frankly,* 311.
117 *New Times:* Scott Parrish, 11. Molotov's involvement described to Parrish by Valentin Berezhkov.
117 Stalin possibly looking for cooperation: see Scott Parrish, 9.
117 Marshall delivered his radio address on April 28. See discussion in Pogue, *Statesman,* 197–200. Bullock, taking note of the essence of the speech, quotes key lines (388).
117–18 Leahy and Lindbergh: Leahy diary, March 31, 1947 (LC).
118 Leahy on Wallace: Diary, April 15, 1947 (LC).
118 "It appears to me": Diary, April 18, 1947 (LC).
119 Leahy's reaction to Marshall's speech: Diary, April 29, 1947 (LC).
119 Leahy's reaction to congressman's attack: Diary, May 8, 1947 (LC).
119–120 Bevin and Strang: Acheson, *Sketches,* 10.
120 "the program must be evolved": see Thomas Parrish, *Cold War Encyclopedia,* 208–209. For the work of the Policy Planning Staff in the development of the plan, see Kennan, *Memoirs,* chapter 14.
120 "invisible damages": Bohlen interview (SGML).
120–21 Text of Marshall's Harvard speech in *New York Times,* June 6, 1947.
121 "he was concerned" and Bevin "caught this": Bohlen interview (SGML).

121 Leahy diary entry July 1, 1947 (LC).

121 Novikov to Molotov: see Scott Parrish and Narinsky (Conference Papers).

122 Soviet spy reference from Narinsky, "New Evidence on the Soviet Rejection," 45–46.

122 On Soviet ideas and rhetoric, see, e.g., Schlesinger; Mueller.

122 "the ideological conception": quoted, Mueller.

122 "You Americans": Litvinov quoted by Molotov, Chuev, 68.

123 In his vivid as well as extremely rare close-up view of Stalin, Djilas produced one of the most insightful and widely quoted works of the cold war period. Djilas, *Conversations with Stalin.*

123 New Soviet line: Riha, 678. See also Barghoorn.

124 "if we are going to do secret": U.S. Department of State, *Emergence of the Intelligence Establishment,* 175.

124 Truman's letter of instruction: State Department, *Emergence,* 13.

124 Souers memorandum: State Department, *Emergence,* 346–47.

124 Byrnes wanted State to control interpretation: State Department, *Emergence,* 319.

124 "inherited a going concern": State Department, *Emergence,* 365.

124 "independent, entirely self-sufficient": Ludwell Lee Montague, quoted in State Department, *Emergence,* 366.

125 "if I didn't fill the slots": Thomas Parrish, *Cold War Encyclopedia,* 327.

125 "decidedly inadequate": State Department, *Emergence,* 805.

125 Marshall would stay: Pogue, *Statesman,* 277.

125–26 "practical steps taken": Narinsky (Conference Papers).

126 "genuinely democratic": Condit (Manuscripts), 118.

126 "one or other piece": quoted, Bullock, 494.

126 "most intelligent Europeans": State Department, FRUS, vol. 2, 1947, 725.

126 "must have courage": Jean Smith, *Papers,* 476 (November 3, 1947).

126–27 Chaos convinced the secretary: Clay interview (MHI).

127 "By making use of the sharp": Narinsky (Conference Papers).

127 "the resentment of the Germans": Jean Smith, *Papers,* 476.

Chapter 10   ". . . With Dramatic Suddenness"

128 The Circassian visitor: Leahy diary, January 9, 1948 (LC).

130 Masaryk and journalist: Brandon, 41.

130 "permanent minister": Aristide Briand, quoted, *Time,* September 13, 1948.

130 "My greatest mistake": Charlton, *Eagles,* 75.

130 Czechoslovakia "would always speak": Charlton, *Eagles,* 71.

130 The background of Bevin's speech is given in detail in Bullock, 513–21.

131 Clifford on naming the Marshall Plan: *New York Times,* June 5, 1987.

131 "Problems of fundamental": Harris, 75.

132 "a more Machiavellian approach": quoted, Pogue, *Statesman,* 242.

132 "worldwide relief program": *Time,* June 14, 1948.

132 "tobacco people": Bland, 556.

132 Bevin's argument: Bullock, 520.

132 "We can act": Bland, 556.

132 "the critical period": Bullock, 526.

133 "Fairy tales": *Time,* June 28, 1948.

133 Steinhardt thoughts from FRUS, 1948, vol. 4, 743.

133 Marshall press conference: Ferrell, *George C. Marshall,* 131.

133–34 Clay message: Excerpts here are quoted from Leahy diary, April 1, which gives the message in full. Clay's text does not appear in Jean Smith, *Papers,* which was prepared before this telegram was declassified. *Papers* does, however, give the text of Dratvin's message, as part of a teleconference between Clay and Pentagon officials (600–4).

135 "I propose": quoted, Leahy diary, April 1 (LC).

135 "It is important": Clay teleconference (his third of the day) with the Pentagon; Jean Smith, *Papers,* 606.

135 "I think their decision" and following quotations from March 31 teleconferences, Jean Smith, *Papers,* 601–6.

136 "it remained for a few days": Clay, 359.

136 "Had I enough hair": Bradley and Blair, 477–78.

136 "FOR MANY MONTHS": Clay to Lieutenant General Stephen J. Chamberlin for the chief of staff; Jean Smith, *Papers,* 568–69. The excerpt here is about half of the message.

137 "a new attitude": Clay, 354.

137 "a dangerous course": Jean Smith, *Lucius D. Clay,* 464.

137 "did not consider": Clay, 354.

137 Clay intended the warning only for tactical use: Jean Smith, *Lucius D. Clay,* 467.

137 Clay's special assistant for intelligence: Robert H. Ferrell, review of *Harry S. Truman and the War Scare of 1948* (New York: St. Martin's, 1993), in *Journal of American History,* December 1994.

137 "Moscow's attempt": Kennan, *Memoirs,* 401.

137 "Further military advances": Kennan, *Memoirs,* 546.

137–38 Bohlen quotations: Bohlen, 222.

138 Armed forces figures from Bradley and Blair, 473; on the state of the armed forces, see also Weigley, 485–504.

138 "serving as policemen": Bradley and Blair, 474.

138 "We are playing with fire": quoted, Millis, 373; see also Bradley and Blair, 475.

139 French pessimism: see Bullock, 536–37.

139 On calibration, see Thomas Parrish, *Cold War Encyclopedia,* 51.

139 "probably operable" and no bombs ready for immediate use: McFarland. For estimate of fifty in 1948, see Mastny, 58.

140 The supercarrier died in the budgeting process: Though the navy lost this round of the struggle, it ultimately entered the strategic game with the Polaris missile, which could be fired from a submerged submarine.

140 CIA forecast: Millis, 395. Delay in producing the estimate discussed in State Department, *Emergence of the Intelligence Establishment,* 973.

Chapter 11   A Salami for the Slicing

141–42 March 20 meeting described in Clay, 356, and in Murphy to secretary of state, FRUS, 1948, vol. 2, 883–84.

142 Moscow meetings and Smirnov memorandum: see Narinsky (Conference Papers); also see Mastny, 43.

143 "great confusion": Naimark, *Russians in Germany,* 307.

143 "Let's make a joint effort": Zubok, 52.

143 Ivanov interview: Gobarev (Conference Papers).

143 "military-political blackmail": Gobarev (Conference Papers).

144 "There is a change in spirit": Letter, March 29, 1948 (unsigned), in Maginnis Papers (Manuscripts), MHI.

144–45 Murphy report to the secretary of state April 1, 1948; FRUS, 1948, vol. 2, 885–86.

145 "yoking him with a senior official": Howard, "Governor-General of Germany."

145 "Above all, young man": Robert Murphy, *Diplomat,* 453.

146 "By the exercise": *Current Biography,* 1943, 545.

146 "bungled a delicate and difficult": *Current Biography,* 1943, 545.

146 "the idea of cooperating": *Current Biography,* 1943, 546.

146 "Lawrence of North Africa": *Current Biography,* 1943, 542.

147 Clay had admired Murphy: Clay, 2.

147 For discussion of salami tactics, see Thomas Parrish, *Cold War Encyclopedia,* 279.

147 Sokolovsky's orders: see Narinsky (Conference Papers).

148 "I want to skin this bear": *Time,* June 28, 1948.

148 "almost unthinkable" and "unbecoming to an American": Clay, 360.

148 "Despite the imaginative reporting": Murphy to secretary of state, FRUS, 1948, vol. 2, 889.

148 "our women and children": Jean Smith, *Papers,* 614–15.

148 "immediate evacuation": Jean Smith, *Papers,* 611.

148 "offering resistance to our pressure": Narinsky (Conference Papers).

148–49 Aircraft crash and subsequent discussion are described by Clay in Jean Smith, *Papers,* 618–19.

149 April 10 teleconference with Bradley and Clay as the only participants is in Jean Smith, *Papers,* 621–25; see also Clay, 361.

150 Soviet report to Moscow: Narinsky (Conference Papers).

150 "new and impossible": Clay, 362.

150 "The situation here" and following scenario of the developing drama in Berlin: Charles [Morgan?] to Maginnis, Maginnis Papers (Manuscripts) (MHI).

151 "We felt very scared": Sawadda interview.

151 "there were a lot of threats": Huckstaedt interview.

151 "a few people who otherwise": May 5, 1948, Maginnis Papers (Manuscripts) (MHI).

151 "strength of determination": Murphy to secretary of state, FRUS, 1948, vol. 2, 893 (April 13).

151 "most of the French": Murphy to secretary of state, FRUS, 1948, vol. 2, 894 (April 15).

152 "It was clear": Druène, 187 (MHI).

152 "create a situation": Chase to secretary of state, FRUS, 1948, vol. 2, 901 (April 29).

152 "It would take a wheelbarrow" and following exchanges: Druène, 187 (MHI).

152 "completely farcical character" and following quotations: Chase to secretary of state, FRUS, 1948, vol. 2, 902 (April 29).

152–53 Kommandatura meeting at the end of May: Murphy to secretary of state, FRUS, 1948, vol. 2, 905 (May 29).

153 "to force furnishing": Jean Smith, *Papers,* 676.

153 Clay in press conference: *New York Times,* June 13, 1948.

153 "Final break" meeting is described by Druène (187) and Murphy to secretary of state, FRUS, 1948, vol. 2, 908 (June 17).

153 "the cars are defective" and "the stations are congested": *Time,* June 28, 1948.

154 The track ties were rotten: Behrend interview.

154 Howley quotations: interview for July 28, 1948. Howley Papers (MHI).

154 "for urgent repairs": *Time,* June 28, 1948.

154 "The barges couldn't continue": Behrend interview.

154 "It was really scary": Hueckstaedt interview.

154 "There are evil forces": quoted, *Time,* July 5, 1948.

154 "Give your baby a bath": Howley, Papers, 203.

155 "real crisis": Jean Smith, *Papers, 623.*

Chapter 12   A Matter of Money

156–57 Currency discussion based chiefly on Bennett, "The German Currency Reform," and Zink, *United States in Germany,* chapters 16–17.

157 On GI currency manipulation, see Harrington, 61.

157 "no doubt feared": Bennett. The discussion is based on Bennett and on Zink, *United States in Germany,* chapters 16–17.

157 "impose control over the amount": A. Zverev, January 21, 1947; quoted, Narinsky (Conference Papers).

157 "Judging by past experiences": Howley interview, July 28, 1948; Howley Papers (Manuscripts) (MHI).

158 "critical" session: Jean Smith, *Papers,* 539.

158 "based on the absence of economic unity": Jean Smith, *Papers,* 554.

158 "new printed money": Murphy to secretary of state, FRUS, 1948, vol. 2, 873 (February 1).

158 The West had to accept the proposal: Jean Smith, *Papers,* 561.

159 "steadily deteriorated" and following comments: Murphy to secretary of state, FRUS, 1948, vol. 2, 878–79 (March 3).

159 Analysis by prominent economist: Harris, 267.

159–60 Clay views in early 1948: Clay, 204.

160 For London conference, see FRUS, 1948, vol. 2, part I; Calvocoressi, 261–63; Bullock, chapter 13. Many other sources, of course, also discuss this important conference.

160 June 1947 meeting: Grathwol and Moorhus, 26.

160 "took the rapid-fire treatment": FRUS, 1948, vol. 2, 20 (January 9).

160–61 Caffery and Bidault: FRUS, 1948, vol. 2, 20–21 (January 10).

161 "In point of fact": Jean Smith, *Papers,* 534.

161 "proceed as rapidly as possible": quoted, secretary of state to the British ambassador, FRUS, 1948, vol. 2, 24 (note 1) (January 13). The following quotations from Marshall are from the same document, 25.

161 "express alarm": Murphy to secretary of state, FRUS, 1948, vol. 2, 11 (January 8).

161–62 NSC memorandum: State Department, *Emergence,* 640–41.

162 May 4, 1948, memorandum: State Department, *Emergence,* 668.

162 Operations "would be contrary": Alfred McCormack, quoted in *Emergence,* 197.

162 "psychological warfare": Marshall, *Emergence,* 616.

162 "Lenin so synthesized": *Emergence,* 669. "Contest" is substituted for obviously incorrect "context" following "sporting," and brackets are omitted in the last sentence as not having to do with its meaning.

163 "organized public support": Kennan, *Emergence,* 670.

163 Letter to Forrestal: *Emergence,* 724–25.

163 "Billions of these": Bennett.

164 GI conversation: *Time,* June 28, 1948.

165 "The possibility was suggested": Bennett.

165 Russians "apparently were caught off guard" and following quotations: Howley Papers, July 28, 1948 (Manuscripts) (MHI).

166 Streetcar collector: *New York Times,* June 26, 1948.

166 "separate monetary camps": Bennett.

166 "It is impossible": Howley Papers, July 28, 1948 (MHI).

166–67 The June 23 meeting and its aftermath are described in many books and articles and by Howley, Howley Papers, June 28 (Manuscripts) (MHI).

167 "Anyone who leaves Berlin": *Time,* June 28, 1948.

167 The boy with the rock: Howley Papers, July 28 (Manuscripts) (MHI).

167 "They are mad" and "This is not Prague": *Time,* July 5, 1948.

Chapter 13   A Few Days' Grace

168 "as those we now know": *Newsweek* and *Time,* July 5, 1948.

168 Douglas report: Douglas to undersecretary of state, FRUS, 1948, vol. 2 (April 17).

171 "Doublecrossers all": Ferrell, *Off the Record,* 140.

171 Eleanor Roosevelt's letter quoted, Hechler, 64.

171 Truman and James Roosevelt: Robert J. Donovan, 401.

171 "I want to say to you": quoted, Hechler, 67.

172 "convince the people" and Truman's dismissal of Johnson and Wilson: Hechler, 69.

172 "blackguarding Congress": Robert J. Donovan, 399.

172 "full of bounce" and following quotations: *Time,* June 28, 1948.

172 Gromyko observation: *Time,* June 28, 1948.

173 Murphy report: Murphy to secretary of state, FRUS, 1945, vol. 2, 910 (June 19).

173 "utilize all media" and following quotation: secretary of state to U.S. embassy in London, FRUS, 1948, vol. 2, 911 (June 21).

173 Clay to Draper: Jean Smith, *Papers,* 696–97.

173–74 Clay to Royall: Jean Smith, *Papers,* 697–99.

174 "we cannot be run over": Clay to Royall and Collins, Jean Smith, *Papers,* 700.

174 "overlooked": *Current Biography,* 1947, 556.

174 "hysteria to get the boys": *Current Biography,* 1947, 555.

174 "the potential warlike strength": *Current Biography,* 1947, 556.

175 CLAY DECLARES and following quotations: *New York Times,* June 25, 1948.

175 "The Americans": Jean Smith, *Papers,* 701.

175 "a good question": Jean Smith, *Papers,* 702.

175 "Neither he nor I": Jean Smith, *Papers,* 704.

175 "I am still convinced": Clay to the Department of the Army, FRUS, 1948, vol. 2, 918.

176 Bradley's fear: Bradley and Blair, 480–81.

176 "in his wilder moments": quoted, Williamson, 127.

176 "holy Soviet borders": Gobarev (Conference Papers).

176 the Russians could put up tank barriers: Bohlen, 276.

176 "that the Soviet leadership": Gobarev (Conference Papers).

177 "Soviet passive interference": Sidney W. Souers to National Security Council, "U.S. Military Courses of Action with Respect to the Situation in Berlin," July 28, 1948 (MHI).

177 Clay and Sokolovsky: Jean Smith, *Papers,* 709–10, and Clay, 372–73.

177 "But I know Sokolovsky": Howley, *Berlin Command,* 12.

178 June 25 cabinet meeting: Harrington, 84.

179 Forrestal as Knox's automatic successor: Millis, xxii.

179 "The suggestion of a tough fistfighter": Millis, xx.

179 "you can't make a hero" and following quotation: see Forrestal sketch in *Current Biography,* 1948, 223.

179 "trigger-happy Russian pilot": quoted, Harrington, 85.

179 "there has been some difference": Memorandum for the chief of staff from deputy director, plans and operations, June 28, 1948 (MHI).

Chapter 14   Anatomy of a Response

181 "The Western countries": *Economist,* July 24, 1948.

181 Bradley quotations: Bradley and Blair, 479.

181 Truman comments on Stalin: *New York Times,* June 12, 1948. These remarks appear with minor differences in Robert J. Donovan, 400.

182 "the gang who run Russia": Millis, 395.

182 "the men around Stalin": Hirsch.

182 The meeting in Royall's office is described in Millis, 453.

183 "The Berlin crisis": Millis, 454.

183 "We were going to stay period." This much-quoted observation was noted by Forrestal and comes from Millis, 454. The following comments are on p. 455.

183 "only future developments": Memorandum for the chief of staff from deputy director, plans and operations, June 28, 1948 (MHI).

183 "major Soviet effort": Royall to Clay, FRUS, 1948, vol. 2, 929 (June 28).

183–84 Leahy's observations are from diary, June 28, 1948 (LC).

184 Truman reflections: Ferrell, *Off the Record,* 140.

185 "any further act of aggression": FRUS, 1948, vol. 4, 834.

185 "as far as the United States is concerned": FRUS, 1948, vol. 4, 850 (May 8). For all the telegrams involved in this démarche, see 834–38, 840–41, and 847–64. See also Bedell Smith, 157–66, and Bullock, 558–59.

185 "Whether the episode was taken": Bullock, 559.

185–86 The Truman-Bevin disagreements over Palestine and the related complexities are well presented by Robert J. Donovan, 312–31, and 369–87. See also Jenkins, 115–23, Bullock, 559–65, and Renwick, 142–45.

186 "a righteous God-damned Baptist tone": quoted, Daniels, 319.

186 For Marshall remarks, see Pogue, *Statesman,* 371, and Clifford, 13–14.

187 "to keep our UN delegation": Ferrell, *Harry S. Truman,* 311.

187 "probably was the factor": Jenkins, 115.

187 Eleanor Roosevelt wrote: Jenkins, 122.

187–88 Hargrove comments: Hargrove, 147–48.

188 "At times he had the look of greatness": Rossiter, 147.

188–89 Yugoslav party Central Committee statement: *New York Times,* July 1, 1948.

189 "move his finger": quoted, Shecter, 600.

189 Definition of a crisis: Shlaim, *United States and the Berlin Blockade,* 5.

189–90 Murphy's June 26 message to secretary of state: FRUS, 1948, vol. 2, 919–21.

190 "Russian reaction": Truman, *Years of Trial and Hope,* 124.

190 "constitute a political defeat": quoted, Shlaim, *United States and Berlin Blockade,* 12.

191 "showing great calmness" and following quotation: *New York Times,* June 26, 1948.

191 As reported by Douglas to Washington: Douglas to secretary of state, FRUS, 1948, vol. 2, 921 (June 26).
191–92 "The statement that we intend to stay": *New York Times,* June 26, 1948.
192 "continue to maintain": secretary of state to Douglas, FRUS, 1948, vol. 2, 926–28.

Chapter 15   "The Air Force Can Carry Anything"

193 Tunner speech: *New York Times,* May 24, 1948.
193 "an enterprise running": Charles J. V. Murphy.
194 "Curt, have you got any planes": LeMay, 415; Robert Murphy, 355. This conversation appears in other sources, with slight variations in wording.
194 "a pretty modest start": LeMay, 415.
195 "sufficient airlift": Clay to Wedemeyer, April 2, 1948; Jean Smith, *Papers,* 611.
195 "I never dreamed": LeMay, 415.
195 Soviet intelligence did not foresee airlift: David Murphy, et al., 51.
195 "would consider leaving": *New York Times,* June 26, 1948.
195–96 Stocks of supplies: Wragg, 76.
196–97 LeMay background from LeMay and various magazine accounts; "youthful, burly": see LeMay sketch in *Current Biography,* 1944.
197 "shuddered at the trance-like conditions" and following quotations in this paragraph: LeMay, 401–5.
197 "political aspects": *U.S. News,* July 30, 1948.
197 "I was breaking other nations' laws": LeMay, 412.
198–99 Captain Jack O. Bennett interview; Anderhub and Bennett, 53–54.
199 "buckle down," "never realized" and "We'll have to get some help": LeMay, 415.
199 "substantially increase the morale" and "seriously disturb": Clay to Draper, June 27, 1948; Jean Smith, *Papers,* 707–8.
200 "that long-legged major": Thomas Parrish, *Roosevelt and Marshall,* 260.
200 "There is no question": Charles J. V. Murphy.
200 Robertson believed that he had given the idea to Clay: Williamson, 127; Bullock, 576.
200 "made a very favourable impression": Bullock, 576–77.
201 "like crows": Charles J. V. Murphy.
201 "coming down clumsily": Howley, *Berlin Command,* 205.
201 Aircrews on Guam: Jim Harrison interview.
201–02 "it would take more than five times": Charles J. V. Murphy.
202 Flying boats on the Havel: Control Commission (Official Publications and Documents), 78–79.
202–03 "Hell's fire": Tunner, *Over the Hump,* 159.
203 "Secretaries of Army and Defense": Leahy diary, June 30, 1948 (LC).
203–04 Bevin and Macmillan statements: *New York Times,* July 1, 1948.
203 "a good general": Bess, "Will We Be Pushed Out of Berlin?"
204 "I could never hope": Bess, "Will We Be Pushed."
204 "We are in Berlin": *New York Times,* July 1, 1948.

Chapter 16   "Gigantic Tonnages in a Max Effort"

207–08 Quotations on Rhein-Main from *New York Times,* July 3, 1948.
208 Sokolovsky's reply and city assembly action: *New York Times,* June 30, 1948.

208 Reuter's request to General Ganeval and Bidault's response: Buffet, 185.

209 Murphy's response to Sokolovsky: FRUS, 1948, vol. 2, 932.

209 Koenig "unavailable": Buffet, 184.

209 "politely but coldly" and following quotations: Clay, 367.

209 Quotations from Tarbe de Saint-Hardouin and Noiret in Buffet, 185.

209–10 Massigli's point: Buffet, 187.

210 "from the total defeat": secretary of state to Ambassador Panyushkin, FRUS, 1948, vol. 2, 951.

210 "Sokolovsky's illogical approach": Harrington, 100.

210 Plaque and flowers: Tunner, *Over the Hump,* 217.

210 Quotations from Soviet note: Panyushkin to secretary of state, FRUS, 1948, vol. 2, 963–64.

211 Leahy quotations from diary, July 14, 1948 (LC).

211 Truman to Bohlen: quoted, Harrington, 102.

211 "Senator Barkley and I": Truman, *Years of Trial and Hope,* 207.

211 "My, how the opposition screams": Ferrell, *Off the Record,* 144.

212 Stalin's belief in Wallace's probable victory: See Truman to Eleanor Roosevelt, in Ferrell, *Off the Record,* 125.

212 Tunner with Kuter: Tunner, *Over the Hump,* 159.

212 One thoroughly prejudiced advocate of air transport: this student did not speak for attribution.

212 "I still remember each flight": Tunner, *Over the Hump,* 6.

213 "some of the features": Tunner, *Over the Hump,* 160.

213 "That's not the way": Tunner, *Over the Hump,* 159–160.

213 Tunner to Vandenberg: Tunner interview (AFHRA).

213 "he could live": Tunner interview (AFHRA).

214 "some hot-shot": Tunner, *Over the Hump,* 162.

214 "any of his best officers": Wedemeyer quoted, Tunner interview (AFHRA).

214 "O.K., Bill": Tunner, *Over the Hump,* 162.

214 LeMay comments: LeMay, 416.

215 the council deemed it wise to go ahead: Millis, 457.

215 The July 19 meeting is summarized by Forrestal in Millis, 459.

215 "We'll stay in Berlin" and "I have to listen to a rehash": Ferrell, *Off the Record,* 145.

215 "the hottest damn place": Ferrell, *Off the Record,* 145.

215 Clay talk with Forrestal: Millis, 460.

216 The July 22 meeting is described in Truman, *Years of Trial and Hope,* 124–26, and Clay, 368 (he mistakenly gives the date as July 20). Forrestal gives an account of his July 21 talk with Clay (in Millis, 459–60).

217 "We are unable": State Department, *Emergence of the Intelligence Establishment,* 349.

218 "to contribute its share": Truman, *Years of Trial and Hope,* 126.

218 "inspired by the understanding": Clay, 368.

Chapter 17   "We Stand Here on the Soil"

219 Tunner meeting with LeMay: Tunner interview (AFHRA) and *Over the Hump,* 166.

219 "It was pretty obvious": Tunner, *Over the Hump,* 166.

219 "You can occupy": Tunner interview (AFHRA).

220 "to be sucked up": Charles J. V. Murphy.

220 Tunner in India: Spencer, 138–45. See also Tunner, *Over the Hump,* chapter 3.

220 "I took twenty people" and "Don't denude the outfit": Tunner interview (AFHRA).

221 "most proficient and intelligent": Tunner, *Over the Hump,* 13.

221 "we were even writing": Tunner, *Over the Hump,* 166.

221 Tunner and staff on first day: Tunner, *Over the Hump,* 166–67.

221 "a real cowboy operation" and "confusion everywhere": Tunner, *Over the Hump,* 167.

222 "Thanks to their genius": Charles J. V. Murphy. Following quotations from Tunner interview (AFHRA).

222 "just a pretty green foothill" and following quotations: Tunner, *Over the Hump,* 168.

223 "For a mass air operation": Charles J. V. Murphy.

223 "full of observations": Tunner, *Over the Hump,* 168.

223 "airplanes require constant maintenance": Tunner, *Over the Hump,* 171.

223 "two planes based at Fassberg": Tunner, *Over the Hump,* 170.

224 "highly experienced communicators" and following quotations: Tunner interview (AFHRA).

224 "some of the most beautiful girls": Tunner, *Over the Hump,* 171.

224 "get the entire procedure": quoted, Charles J. V. Murphy.

224 "Our apartment": Hueckstaedt interview.

225 "There was noise": Sawadda interview.

225 "Nobody heard anything": Tschammer interview.

225 "We don't have": Beelitz interview.

226 Tunner describes the flight in *Over the Hump,* 152–55.

226 "This is a hell of a way": Tunner, *Over the Hump,* 153.

227 "air-traffic control": quoted, Charles J. V. Murphy.

227 "was flying around in circles": Tunner, *Over the Hump,* 154.

227–28 Letter from anonymous Berliner: Catharine Cleveland scrapbook.

228 Bedell Smith letter to Clay: Clay Papers (GCML).

228 "in view of the many changes": Jean Smith, *Papers,* 597.

228 Bradley to Clay (May 4, 1948): Clay Papers (GCML).

229 "without precipitating": Clay to Bradley, May 22, 1948, Clay Papers (GCML).

229 "further crises": Bradley to Clay, Clay Papers (GCML).

229 "Like presidents before and since": Harrington, 133.

229 "the Politburo" and following quotations: FRUS, 1948, vol. 2, 971 (July 20, 1948).

229 "I know all of you Americans": Bohlen, 279.

230 "redolent with appeasement": secretary of state to Ambassador Douglas, FRUS, 1948, vol. 2, 975 (July 21, 1948).

230 "Americans were generally wrong": Sir William Strang, quoted, Williamson, 132.

230 "a definite weakening": teletype conference between State Department and embassy in London, FRUS, 1948, vol. 2, 1948, 978 (July 22, 1948).

230 Bevin had to beat off attacks: see, e.g., Macmillan, 57.

230 Robertson's views: Williamson, 127–30.

230 "The United States had no expectation": Jessup, "Berlin Blockade and the Use of the United Nations."

231 For a memorable characterization of Schuman, see Acheson, *Sketches,* 33–55.

231 "I pointed out": Bedell Smith, 239.

232 "to discuss the situation": Bedell Smith, 240.

232 Smith's July 31 meeting with Molotov: Bedell Smith, 241.

Chapter 18   On Kremlin Evenings

233 "confronted us with the flat alternative": Bedell Smith, 242.

233 "unquestionable and absolute": FRUS, 1948, vol. 2, 991 (July 26).

234–35 Smith's report of the meeting with Stalin appears in his dispatch to Marshall, dated August 3 (FRUS, 999–1006). Smith also describes the meeting in *My Three Years in Moscow,* 242–45. Buffet (202–3) gives an interesting account from the French point of view, including mention of the French government's leeriness of "unforeseeable changes of course by the American government."

235 Smith's second message to Washington: FRUS, 1006–7 (August 3). Chataigneau expresses pleasure as well; his superiors—and Roberts's—are pleased but not without reservations (Buffet, 203–4).

235 Bohlen's view: Millis, 469.

235 Bevin and Molotov: Bohlen, 255.

235–36 Bohlen advises caution: FRUS, 1013–14 (August 4).

236 Foreign Office and Massigli: Buffet, 204.

236 Smith's euphoria: FRUS, 1006.

236–37 Flight procedures from *Special Study of Operation Vittles* and interviews with pilots.

237 "The Berlin climate": Landy, 10.

237 "We come down to the level": Tunner interview (AFHRI). Following comments, Tunner, *Over the Hump,* 173–74.

238 "AS OF THIS DAY": Charles J. V. Murphy.

238 "It's a helpless feeling": Tunner, *Over the Hump,* 185.

238 antiaircraft practice: *New York Times,* October 14, 1948.

238 "an American pilot": unidentified newspaper, Catharine Cleveland scrapbook; article datelined Berlin, August 11.

238–39 game of chicken: Martin interview.

239 "We'd be flying": Reynolds interview.

239 fliers would sometimes "get smart": Cleveland interview.

239–40 Palahunich material from interview.

240 "could be disastrous" and "It is our surest way": Jean Smith, *Papers,* 749.

240 "assuming a reasonably satisfactory solution": Jean Smith, *Papers,* 752.

240 local political leaders: Jean Smith, *Papers,* 760.

240–41 The August 6 meeting with Molotov is described in Smith to secretary of state, FRUS, 1018–21; the department's reply follows (1021–23). Molotov's diary (Manuscripts) (RFMA) presents a third-person-style stenographic transcript of this meeting and subsequent meetings. See also Buffet, 204–5.

241 Exchange between Molotov and Smith: Molotov diary (Manuscripts), Fond 0129, Opis 32, Papka 205, Delo 7, List 14 (RFMA).

241 "the meeting was": Smith to secretary of state, FRUS, 1018.

241 "I have the impression": Smith to secretary of state, FRUS, 1020.

242 Comments by Forrestal and Millis: Millis, 482 and note.

242 "in a bourgeois democracy": Chuev, 272.

243 Frank Roberts reminded: Shlaim, "Britain, the Berlin Blockade and the Cold War."

243 "a certain danger": secretary of state to Smith, FRUS, 1023 (August 7).

243 Endorsement of the Politburo: Narinsky (Conference Papers).

243–44 Smith's report of the August 16 meeting with Molotov: FRUS, 1948, vol. 4, 1042–47 (August 17).

243 "all very hard going": Smith to secretary of state, FRUS, 1042–47 (August 17).

244 "synchronicity" discussion: Molotov diary (Manuscripts), Fond 0129, Opis 32, Papka 205, Delo 7, List 82–112 (RFMA).

244 "complicated the situation in Berlin": Molotov diary (as above).

244 "there was no hope": Smith to secretary of state, FRUS, 1042–47 (August 17).

244–45 Clay to Bradley and Draper (August 21): Jean Smith, *Papers*, 776.

245 Smith's report of the August 23 meeting with Stalin: FRUS, 1948, vol. 4, 1065–68. See also Bedell Smith, 248–50.

246 The editing session: Molotov Diary (Manuscripts), Fond 0129, Opis 32, Papka 205, Delo 7, List 115–120 (RFMA).

246 "each word and every sentence": Bedell Smith, 251.

246–47 Clay's reaction: August 24 teleconference with Royall and others, Jean Smith, *Papers*, 778–85.

247 "any confirmation of the principle": secretary of state to Smith, FRUS, 1948, vol. 4, 1048.

247 "If there is agreement": Clay to Bradley, August 26, 1948, Clay Papers (GCML).

247 "sometime between some kind": Bradley to Clay, September 2, 1948, Clay Papers (GCML).

247 "I must stay it out": Clay to Bradley, September 12, 1948, Clay Papers (GCML).

Chapter 19   "No Frenzy, No Flap"

249 "If the Russians can": Howley, *Berlin Command*, 214.

249 Clay and Draper: Jean Smith, *Papers*, 832 (September 6).

249 "word of honor": Howley, *Berlin Command*, 216.

249–50 Howley's meeting with Kotikov: Jean Smith, *Papers*, 844–45.

250 The September 9 rally is described in Howley, *Berlin Command*, 217–18, and in numerous other sources, including contemporaneous newspaper and magazine accounts.

250 "we are not such fools": FRUS, 1948, vol. 2, 1150 (September 12).

251 "the going is tough": FRUS, 1112 (September 4).

251 "as far back as 1945": Molotov to Western ambassadors, FRUS, 1163.

251 "his treatment": Smith to secretary of state, FRUS, 1157 (September 14).

251 "pessimistic as to the outcome": White House naval aide files, September 14, 1948, in Merrill (Official Publications and Documents), 160.

251 "arguments broke out": Bullock, 593.

252 Quotations come from Paul Fisher's interviews with Tunner. See Fisher.

253 Clay pressed Washington [Bradley]: Jean Smith, *Papers*, 852 and 878 (September 10 and September 23).

253 "The actual operation": Tunner, *Over the Hump*, xi-xii.

254 "They were always crying": Tunner interview (AFHRA).

254 "I learned a lot": Tunner, *Over the Hump*, 178.

254 "He was all business": Palahunich interview.

254–55 "the chief topic": Tunner, *Over the Hump*, 181.

255 "raw and bitter": Tunner, *Over the Hump,* 180.

255–56 Information about Halvorsen from *New York Times,* September 16, 1948; *National Geographic,* May 1949; Palahunich interview. Quotations from Frank Donovan, 147.

256 Eisenhuth memories from interview.

256–57 "the beginning of a love affair": Kostka interview.

257 Lieutenant Butterfield and Clarence from *Stars and Stripes* (n.d.), Catharine Cleveland scrapbook.

257–58 Girl with chickens: Palahunich interview.

258 Norman Thomas letter, White House Central Files—Official File. See Merrill (Official Publications and Documents), vol. 16, document 62.

Chapter 20   *"A la Dynamite!"*

259 "a question of power": Bullock, 593.

259 Meeting in Schuman's office: Buffet, 222.

260 "policy of expansion": quoted, Buffet, 223.

260 The proposed Vinson mission: see, e.g., Pogue, *Statesman,* 407; Robert J. Donovan, 424–25; Hechler, 98–99; Buffet, 224–25; and Bullock, 620, as well as Truman's own explanation and discussion (*Years of Trial and Hope,* 212–19), in which he traces the idea of such a personal international healing mission back to a 1918 fence-mending visit to the United States by Lord Reading, who, as lord chief justice, had occupied a position analogous to Vinson's.

260 "bases, bombs": Ferrell, *Off the Record,* 148–49.

261 "in times of crisis": quoted, Misse.

261 Elsey and Clifford quoted, Hechler, 98.

261 "continuing great desire": Truman's October 9 statement, White House Central Files—Official File. See Merrill, vol. 16, document 75.

261 "an electoral operation": Buffet, 224.

261 White House mail: Harrington, 190.

262 "When we met as the Council": Jessup, "Berlin Blockade and the Use of the United Nations."

262 "any action he took": Bohlen, 281.

262 Bohlen reminded Jessup: FRUS, 1948, vol. 2, 1223 (October 16).

262 "had tried to meet": Jessup, "Berlin Blockade and the Use of the United Nations."

262 "useless to think": quoted, *Time,* October 20, 1948. For Vyshinsky's language, see also *New York Times,* October 9, 1948.

262 Vishinsky told the president of the Security Council: Naval aide files, October 14, 1948. See Merrill (Official Publications and Documents), vol. 16, document 80.

262–63 For the aspects of the blockade discussed here, see especially Air Ministry (Official Publications and Documents), chapter 9, and Control Commission, 10. Carrying coal across sector lines was also discussed by Karin Hueckstaedt in her interview.

263–64 Survey figures: Report No. 147, Opinion Surveys Branch, Information Services Division, OMGUS; November 17, 1948 (MHI).

264 "how often one person": Jessup, "Berlin Blockade."

264 "I've heard how you conducted yourself": Thomas Parrish, *Roosevelt and Marshall,* 249.

264 "So you want to start another war": quoted, Jessup, "Berlin Blockade."

264 "personal contact": White House Central Files—Official File, November 13, 1948. See Merrill (Official Publications and Documents), vol. 16, document 92.

265 Leahy quotations from diary, November 5, 1948 (LC). *Time* quotation from November 8, 1948 issue.

266 Marshall objects to praise: Jessup, "Berlin Blockade."

266 "we are losing ground daily": Jean Smith, *Papers,* 986–87 (January 15, 1949).

266 "Airplanes require constant maintenance": Tunner, *Over the Hump,* 169.

267 "We're putting": Fisher.

267 Tunner on Burtonwood: Tunner, *Over the Hump,* 193.

267–70 Robert Mix and Burtonwood: Mix interview.

271 "Any problems, Tunner?": Tunner, *Over the Hump,* 183.

271 "I got a German general" and following quotations: Tunner interview (AFHRA).

272–74 H. P. Lacomb: see Charles J. V. Murphy.

272 "ingenious but wild": Tunner, *Over the Hump,* 170.

274 "go immediately to Berlin" and following quotations: McGuire interview (OCE). All material relating to McGuire comes from this interview.

275 "We had more women": Norman Delbridge, quoted, Grathwol and Moorhus, 42.

277 "getting rid of a station": Buffet, 239.

277 Ganeval would act on his own: Howley, "I've Talked 1600 Hours."

277 "a very neat bit": *Berlin Observer,* Catharine Cleveland scrapbook.

277 "We held our breaths": Howley, "I've Talked 1600 Hours."

277 *"A la dynamite"*: Buffet, 239.

Chapter 21 "We Flew When Birds Walked"

278 Headline quoted from *Die Woche im Bild,* November 21, 1948.

278 "They had to put the approach lights": Hueckstaedt interview.

278 "The planes came very close": Beelitz interview.

279 "It was clear": Behrend interview.

279 "the humming and all the engines": Tschammer interview.

279 "The 'battle for Berlin' ": Hanson Baldwin, *New York Times,* September 16, 1948.

280 "the Russian unfamiliarity": Tunner, *Over the Hump,* 184–85.

280 Martin material here and later from interview with Urban "Bill" Martin.

280–81 "Little Berlin Corridor" and following quotations: *Stars and Stripes,* n.d., Catharine Cleveland scrapbook.

281 "It was a steep landing": Palahunich interview.

281 November "is when": Reynolds interview.

282 Pilots were getting "cold feet": quoted, *New York Times,* November 4, 1948.

282 "Berliners predict": *New York Times,* November 16, 1948.

282 "you couldn't even drive a car": Tunner, *Over the Hump,* 194.

282 "unless the Soviets use force": Leahy Diary, October 21, 1948 (LC).

283 "without difficulty": *New York Times,* November 7, 1948.

284 the Berlin government did not wish to be responsible: Clay for Draper, *Papers,* 938 (December 2).

284 Alert Police: see Naimark, "To Know Everything."

284 The French objected: Leahy diary, October 21, 1948 (LC).

284 "dangerous activities taking place": Sokolovsky to Robertson, November 29, 1948; Heidelmeyer and Hindrichs (Official Publications and Documents), document 46.

285 "the provisional democratic Magistrat": Heidelmeyer and Hindrichs (Official Publications and Documents), document 48.

285 Hillenkoetter to Truman (December 10, 1948): President's Secretary's Files. See Merrill (Official Publications and Documents), vol. 16, document 101.

Chapter 22 "Here Comes a Yankee ..."

287 "Is it permissible": *Airlift Times* [article dated January 26, 1949].

288 Tunner's thoughts on Fassberg: Tunner, *Over the Hump,* 170.

288 "as flat as a football field": Tunner, *Over the Hump,* 186.

288 "Continuously affected": Landy, 10.

288 "all of us going": Tunner interview (AFHRA).

289 "Sanders might as well": Tunner, *Over the Hump,* 187. (Tunner gives the name as "Saunders.")

289 Quotations from the agreement: Tunner, *Over the Hump,* 187.

289 concentrate spare parts.: Reynolds interview.

290 "When I broke out" and following quotations: Martin interview.

290 at one point he had waked up: Jackson, 75.

291 "ruthless priorities": Collier, 126.

292 "regardless of his inner feelings" and "now famous": Tunner, "A Case of Identity."

293 Tunner's appointment upstaged Cannon's arrival: see, e.g., *New York Times,* October 16, 1948.

293 "I may have been a little impatient" and following quotations: Tunner, *Over the Hump,* 189.

293 Cannon and Williams contrasted: Tunner, "A Case of Identity."

294 "Bill, who is the duke of Windsor?": Tunner, "A Case of Identity."

294 "There was no reason" and following quotation: Tunner, *Over the Hump,* 195.

295 Irving Berlin song: *Task Force Times,* December 23, 1948.

295 Hope quotations from *Stars and Stripes,* December 27, 1948.

295 "none too good": Tunner, *Over the Hump,* 194.

296 Talk with mechanic: Tunner, *Over the Hump,* 196.

296 Symington and Doolittle at Burtonwood: W. Stuart Symington to chief of staff, USAF, December 30, 1948; quoted, Watson, 81.

296 "None of us could have asked": Tunner, *Over the Hump,* 196.

296 Looking forward from October: quotations from *U.S. News & World Report,* October 1, 1948.

297 "Every household" and following quotation: Behrend interview.

297 "When I came home": Sawadda interview.

297 "I would go over": Hueckstaedt interview.

298 "Personally, I thought it wiser": Howley, *Berlin Command,* 232.

298 "when conditions seemed blackest" and following quotations: Howley, *Berlin Command,* 237.

298–99 Alsop column in *Herald-Tribune,* December 27, 1948; quoted in Merry, 175. Subsequent column also in *Herald-Tribune* (n.d.)

299 "If the Russians had thought": Howley, *Berlin Command,* 236.

299 one hundred thousandth flight: Associated Press, December 31, 1948.

299 "paying their respects": Detzer.

Chapter 23   Parading for Easter

301 Tonnage figures compiled from wire-service and other accounts in Catharine Cleveland scrapbook.

302 Tunner had sent one of his best officers: Tunner, *Over the Hump,* 209.

302 "We even had all the planes": Tunner, *Over the Hump,* 218.

303 "an Easter parade of airplanes" and following quotation: Tunner, *Over the Hump,* 219.

303 Bevin's annoyance: Williamson, 132.

303 "this special effort": Robertson to Foreign Office; Williamson, 134.

303 "was rarin' to go": Tunner, *Over the Hump,* 220.

303 *Task Force Times* article dated April 16, 1949.

304 "applying a needle" and "really on the ball": Tunner, *Over the Hump,* 221.

304 "You'll have to shake your tail": *Newsweek,* March 25, 1949.

304 "as many trips" and "tore the colonel up": Martin interview.

304 "I didn't even know": Associated Press, April 16, 1949.

305 "I cannot accept": *New York Times,* April 17, 1948.

305 "gigantic Easter present": *New York Times,* April 17, 1948.

305 Quotations about the operation: Associated Press, April 16, 1948.

305 Clay's observations from the *New York Times,* April 17, 1948, and the Associated Press, April 16, 1948.

306 "the opportunity to prove": Tunner, *Over the Hump,* 22.

306 "As my plane": Robert Murphy, 320.

306 "the one occasion": Robert Murphy, 317.

307 Acheson's comments: Acheson, *Present,* 263.

307 Middleton's analysis: *New York Times,* April 17, 1948.

308–09 Policy Planning Staff document, "Position of the United States With Respect to Germany Following the Breakdown of Moscow Discussions": FRUS, 1948, vol. 2, 1240–47.

310 "It ought to be": Howley, *Berlin Command,* 241.

310 all avenues were open: *Newsweek,* April 25, 1948.

Chapter 24   Lake Success to Park Avenue

311 Stalin's reply: The Berlin Crisis, President's Secretary's Files; see Merrill (Official Publications and Documents), vol. 16, document 114 (p. 37).

312 Missing the real point: see, e.g., *Time,* February 14, 1949, or the various wire-service stories.

312 Acheson quotations from *State Department Bulletin,* February 6 and February 13, 1949.

313 "cautious signal": Acheson, *Present,* 267.

313 "I was on the lookout": Bohlen, 283.

313 See Acheson's own discussion of the press conference in *Present,* 267–68.

313 "What about the plain people": *Courier-Journal,* February 4, 1949.

314 "Away from the glitter": *Courier-Journal,* February 5, 1949.

314 Stewart Alsop column: *Courier-Journal,* February 4, 1949.

315 "All of us naturally": Jessup, "Park Avenue Diplomacy."

315 "Dr. Gallup should transfer his activities": Davidson, "The Surprising Mr. Jessup."

315 "They know his reputation": quoted, Davidson, "The Surprising Mr. Jessup."

315 The "Columbia professor": Robert Murphy, 320.

315 Jessup rejoinder: "Jessup, Park Avenue Diplomacy."

316 "an excellent diplomat": Bohlen, 281.

316 "humorously etched": *Time,* May 16, 1949.

317 Conversation with Malik and following quotations: Jessup, "Park Avenue Diplomacy."

317 For comments on the "peace offensive," see Harrington, 227.

318–19 This and subsequent Jessup-Malik meetings from Jessup, "Park Avenue Diplomacy," and Merrill (Official Publications and Documents), vol. 16, document 114.

318–19 Malik and the West German government: Merrill, vol. 16, document 114.

318 "the question of the establishment": Merrill, vol. 16, document 114.

319 "I had the impression": Jessup, "Park Avenue Diplomacy."

319 On the new statute, see Clay, 428–29.

319 "I thought I had" and "I came": Jean Smith, *Papers,* 1112–13.

320 Clay's chagrin: Clay, 390.

320 "understandably annoyed" and following quotations: Jessup, "Park Avenue Diplomacy."

321 Text of communiqué from *Department of State Bulletin,* May 15, 1949.

321 "undoubtedly it is due": Adenauer to Clay, May 8, 1949, in Clay Papers (GCML).

Chapter 25   The Gates Go Up

322 "My heart is filled": *Courier-Journal,* May 5, 1949.

322 "for his execution": *Courier-Journal,* May 4, 1949.

322 "military socialism": Williamson, 140.

322 "the one Saint": Sir Ivone Kirkpatrick to Bevin, April 4, 1949; quoted Ann Tusa and John Tusa, p. 349.

322 "did not welcome interference": Thomas Parrish, *Cold War Encyclopedia,* 67. On Clay and resignation, see, e.g., Backer, *Winds of History,* 193–94.

322–23 "endeared him to its people": Ann and John Tusa, 351.

323 "it was General Clay's wisdom": Backer, *Winds,* viii.

323 "Everybody who was of that generation": Beelitz interview.

323 "he looks like a Roman emperor": Thomas Parrish, *Cold War Encyclopedia,* 67.

323–24 Opening of the autobahn: *Courier-Journal,* May 12, 1949.

324 "The lift will continue": *Courier-Journal,* May 12, 1949.

324 Acheson quotations: *Courier-Journal,* May 12, 1949.

325 "the Russians are not": quoted, Acheson, *Present,* 275.

325 "But we could not eat": Sawadda interview.

325 "his popularity": Jackson, 140.

325 "the memory of General Clay": quoted, Davison, 273.

325 "we all helped each other": Sawadda interview.

325 "Work with those people": *Time,* May 16, 1949.

326 "old market dickering": Gerald Janecek interview.

326 "weigh heavily in the scales": quoted, Davison, 273.

326 "importance amounting": Acheson, *Present,* 296.

326 "asking a victim": Acheson, *Present,* 297.

326 "Its *fin de siècle* design": Acheson, *Sketches,* 14.

327 "mousy issue": Acheson, *Sketches,* 17.

327–28 Material on the 503d Engineer Company from Bailey (Manuscripts), "Born in Berlin."

329 "It never took Americans": Maihafer, 108.

329 Martin and Reynolds quotations from interviews.

329 "An airman who crashes": quoted, Davison, 268.

Epilogue: "The Stakes Could Hardly Have Been Greater"

330 "regional and other collective arrangements": quoted, Acheson, *Present,* 265.

331 As one historian observed: see Harrington, 257–60.

331 "In retrospect": Shlaim, "Britain, the Berlin Blockade and the Cold War."

331 Soviet intelligence was reluctant to report to Stalin: David Murphy, et al., *Battleground Berlin,* 77–78.

332 "hang on to the bitter end": Shlaim, "Britain."

332 "On the whole": Shlaim, *United States and the Berlin Blockade,* 422.

333 "the foreign ministers": Laqueur, 126–27.

333 "settled down to years": Howard K. Smith, 212.

333 "to establish a symmetry": Laqueur, 127–28.

333 Litvinov: see Chapter 9 of this book.

333 "These convictions transformed an impasse": Schlesinger in *Foreign Affairs,* October 1967, quoted, Laqueur, 129.

334 "neutralism is immoral": quoted, Thomas Parrish, *Cold War Encyclopedia,* 89.

334 "if it hadn't been Berlin": Chuev, 55.

334 "to extend the frontier of our Fatherland": Thomas Parrish, *Cold War Encyclopedia,* 220.

334 "He was the best": *New York Times,* April 18, 1978.

334 "He knew that choices": Acheson, *Sketches,* 30.

334 "He was as good as the rest": Wood.

335 "testicles of the West": Khrushchev's observation has been widely quoted; see, e.g., Reston, 291.

ACKNOWLEDGMENTS

A BOOK OF ANY length and complexity is the result of a collaborative effort, since it could not have come into being without the involvement of many persons all along the line. Sometimes, in acknowledging the contributions of others, writers adopt a weary and almost martyred tone, as if writing the book had been a dreadful experience, an ordeal we managed to survive only because relatives, friends, correspondents, archivists, and others combined to help us emerge from near-disaster. But even if creating a book is a demanding task, it can also be enjoyable and rewarding, and one of its most pleasant aspects is indeed the discovery (and rediscovery) that a great many persons and institutions stand ready to provide all kinds of help; all one has to do is ask. Hence a note of thanks from the author can serve not so much as an expression of gratitude for sharing an ordeal as a recognition that the helpers have made an absorbing adventure possible.

As I try to thank all those who gave me help with this book, I do so with one concern—that I may overlook somebody who made a contribution. Let me say, therefore, that I leave out nobody intentionally; I am deeply grateful to all who helped.

I wish first to express my profound thanks to Colonel (ret.) Stephen L. Bowman, former deputy commander of the U.S. Berlin Brigade, former director of the U.S. Army Military History Institute at Carlisle Barracks, Pa., and now again resident of Berlin. As a professional historian as well as a professional soldier, Colonel Bowman amassed and preserved an unparalleled collection of documents and other papers relating to Berlin to which he gave me access at Carlisle. He also arranged and conducted a number of the interviews, offered much good advice, and was wonderfully forthcoming with other kinds of help.

I also wish to make special mention of the generosity of Catharine Cleveland, who during the Berlin airlift served as secretary to the commander of Tempelhof Air Force Base. Her remarkable personal scrapbook proved to be of unique value, and I thank her for her willingness to leave this treasure in my custody for many months.

Other persons supplying firsthand information in interviews and correspondence included Charlotte Beelitz, Hans-Karl Behrend, Jack O. Bennett, Robert Bogue, Albert Eisenhuth, Peggy Fuller, Jim Harrison, George

F. Kennan (special thanks to Terrie Bramley, Professor Kennan's efficient and helpful secretary), Gunter and Renate Kostka, Karin Hueckstaedt Little, Urban "Bill" Martin, Robert Mix, William Palahunich, Russ Reynolds, Alice Sawadda, and Uwe von Tschammer.

Others who helped with information of various kinds included Timothy A. Chopp, William H. Gross, Kenneth Herman, Professor George C. Herring, Professor Gerald Janecek, Bob Lowe, Dr. Linda McClain, Bernard C. Nalty, Professor Karen Petrone, Professor Kenneth Slepyan, Dean W. Terlinden, Bob Trisler, Col. (ret.) Richard Uppstrom, and Joseph Werner.

Much of the material in this book comes from official documents, letters, diaries, and other archival sources. I am therefore much indebted to the directors and staffs of a number of libraries and other repositories of unpublished materials. I wish to express my thanks to Dr. Richard J. Sommers, assistant director for archives, U.S. Army Military History Institute, Carlisle Barracks, Pa., for his interest and help and to give a special word of thanks to Pamela Cheney of this invaluable archival center; I give warm thanks also to Louise Arnold of the Army War College library for her help with the Special Bowman Berlin Collection; thanks also to Lt. Col. Martin W. Andresen for suggestions and to Michael Winey and Randy Hackenburg for help with photographs. And it is a pleasure, as always, to express my gratitude to Larry I. Bland, Thomas E. Camden, and the other members of the staff of the George C. Marshall Library, Lexington, Va. My thanks also to the staff of the Seeley G. Mudd Library at Princeton University for help with oral history materials.

As anyone who has ever written a book dealing in any way with modern times and the military knows, a list of acknowledgments must give a prominent place to John E. Taylor, the veteran and untiring wizard of the Modern Military Branch, National Archives, long in Washington, now just outside the city in College Park, Md. I am grateful also for the help of various air force historians: David Chenoweth and Roger Miller at the Air Force History Support Office in Washington and Hugh Ahmann and Mickey Russell at the Air Force Historical Research Agency at Maxwell Air Force Base, Ala.; I especially appreciate the interest shown by Mickey Russell and thank him for the information and materials he supplied. I appreciate also the help given by Dr. John Greenwood, formerly command historian of the Engineer School and now at the Center of Military History, and by the staff at the Air Mobility Command, Scott Air Force Base, Ill.

I must make special mention of the invaluable work of the Cold War International History Project of the Woodrow Wilson Center, Smithsonian Institution, whose staff supplied very important information in addition to the working papers written by scholars associated with the project. I am grateful as well to the staff of the National Security Archive in Washington.

I thank also Paul Courtenay for his work in British archives, and Dr. Vladimir Pozniakov for the great efforts he made on my behalf in Soviet/Russian archives (and for the interesting results he produced). I thank Professor Cynthia Ruder and Igor Sopranenko for translating the documents obtained by Dr. Pozniakov.

I owe a very special debt of gratitude indeed to one of the most outstanding specialists on the era with which this book deals, Professor Robert H. Ferrell, not only for reading the entire manuscript but for the care with which he performed this great favor and the valuable suggestions he offered; my mention of Professor Ferrell's reading of the manuscript does not, of course, imply any responsibility on his part for statements contained in the book.

I thank Dick Gilbreath for preparing the maps, Dick Burdette for providing some useful publicity in the early stages of the book, Karen Flynn and Melissa Gardner for transcribing tapes of interviews, and Judith N. Pugh of the Churchill Memorial and Library at Westminster College, Fulton, Mo., for supplying photographs of Churchill's famous visit to the college in 1946.

No one can admire librarians more than I, and is with pleasure that I express my thanks to the hard-working and highly cooperative staff members of the libraries at Berea College, Eastern Kentucky University, and the University of Kentucky; I also thank the directors of these libraries—Anne Chase, Marcia Myers, and Paul Willis—for the many courtesies they have extended to me.

I also wish to express my admiration for the talents of my editor, John Bell, and my thanks for his insightful contributions to the book. With reference to my agent, Stuart Krichevsky of the Stuart Krichevsky Literary Agency, Inc., I cannot do better than quote what I have previously said about him: he is devoted, imaginative, efficient, and cheerful—an ideal agent.

I thank my good friend and fellow author Charles Bracelen Flood for his continuing advice and encouragement. Finally, I once again acknowledge with special pleasure the help of my dear friend Nancy Coleman Wolsk, who offered sound practical advice, participated in research, and—even though, as I say, writing the book did not qualify as an ordeal—gave some very welcome love and support.

INDEX